Estimating and Costing for Interior Designers

A Step-by-Step Workbook

Fairchild Books
An imprint of Bloomsbury Publishing Inc

1385 Broadway   50 Bedford Square
New York   London
NY 10018   WC1B 3DP
USA   UK

www.fairchildbooks.com

First published 2014

© Bloomsbury Publishing Inc, 2014

Library of Congress Cataloging-in-Publication Data
A catalog record for this book is available from the Library of Congress
2013938691

ISBN: PB: 978-1-60901-519-0

Typeset by Precision Graphics
Cover Design by Alicia Freile, Tango Media
Text Design by Andrea Landau
Printed and bound in the United States of America

Estimating and Costing for Interior Designers

A Step-by-Step Workbook

Diana Allison, Ph.D.

FAIRCHILD BOOKS / NEW YORK

Contents

Preface

Interior design is a profession that is a combination of art and science. This means that both sides of an interior designer's brain, the logical side and the creative and emotional side, are engaged through the course of a project. Hand in hand with the logical side is the math aspect of interior design. Many novice interior designers or beginning students don't realize how math-intensive this profession is. From simple conversions of inches to feet and geometry to complex calculations to determine costs of jobs, math is used every day. Residential and commercial designers need to understand the financial implications of the products specified and, for a number of practitioners, how to calculate the prices of these products. There have been few books dedicated to this aspect of the interior design profession.

This book explains the relationship between product sizes and calculations. Step-by-step processes are outlined for calculating materials for the projects we design and create. Examples, scenarios, worksheets, and answers allow the student to understand and then apply the process to real-world situations.

Organization of the Text

This book has been organized in sections, first covering products that are attached to the interior building shell and then covering items that are movable. Sections 1 and 2 discuss wall and ceiling treatments and flooring. Section 3 discusses countertops. Sections 4 and 5 cover window treatments and other soft fabrications such as bedding, pillows, and table coverings. Section 6 explains upholstery. The book begins with a chapter on the overall business of interior design and ends with a chapter that discusses what happens when the client places the order.

Interior design departments in colleges and universities focus on various aspects of the interior design profession. Even though this book has been organized in a certain way, each section can stand alone so that the instructor can determine which sections work best for his or her department's focus. This book can be used by students and practitioners to make sure they are considering all aspects of a project.

Chapter 1

The business of interior design is explained to help the student understand the different professions and supportive teams involved in the interior design field and the interior designer's role with them. The question of why interior designers should know how to calculate prices for materials is examined, and basic terminology in the field is reviewed.

Section 1—Wall and Ceiling Treatments

Section 1 consists of four chapters that cover, respectively, paint, wallcoverings, other wall materials such as wall tile and paneling, and suspended ceilings. In addition to brief explanations of the products, descriptions of sizes and packaging are included. Six worksheets are also included for various products.

Section 2—Flooring

Section 2 consists of three chapters covering plank and tile flooring, resilient and soft flooring, and area rugs. Brief explanations of the products, product sizes, and packaging are intended to clarify the unique aspects of flooring. Included in the section are eight worksheets covering the various types of flooring products that are commonly used.

Section 3—Built-Ins

Section 3 focuses on countertops, with a brief explanation of cabinetry. The discussion of countertops explains the products, sizing, and packaging and includes four worksheets explaining calculations for several different types. Cabinetry is a distinct niche, and the interior designer calculates prices differently than most other products. Similar to case goods, the designer prices most cabinetry using pricing grids from the manufacturer. For this reason, pricing for cabinetry is not addressed in this book.

Section 4—Window Treatments

Section 4 consists of three chapters on curtains and draperies, top treatments and window shades, and hard window treatments. This section discusses some of the common types of window treatments, including the elements involved with specifications and pricing. Twelve worksheets are included showing the steps to calculate yardage.

Section 5—Soft Fabrications

Section 5 consists of two chapters—the first one on bedding and the second one on pillows and accent table coverings. Bedding includes spreads, coverlets, duvets, bedscarves, duvets, bedskirts, and shams. The most common products are discussed, and ten worksheets are included showing the steps in calculating yardage.

Section 6—Upholstery

Section 6 consists of two chapters; the first is on new upholstery, and the second is on reupholstered and slipcovered upholstery. The chapter on new upholstery shows the student how to calculate pricing from an upholstery manufacturer's price list, and the chapter on reupholstered and slipcovered upholstery explains the various issues that the designer must consider when creating an estimate. Two worksheets are included showing calculations for reupholstery with fabric and then fabric conversion to leather.

Epilogue

The epilogue takes the student through the process that occurs after the client decides he or she wants to go forward with the project. It briefly describes the process that occurs behind the scenes to the point of installation.

Text Features

Estimating and Costing for Interior Designers: A Step-by-Step Workbook provides a logical process for calculating costs of products. Terminology; explanations of the types, sizes, and packaging; cost factors; calculations; examples; worksheets; and practice lessons with answers are included to help the student fully grasp the information.

Terminology

The same word can be used a little differently depending upon which product is being discussed. The list of terms that begins each chapter gives the student a common vocabulary for each topic.

Types of Product

Certain products require explanation regarding the various types available. For example, the different types of plank flooring and tile flooring require specific considerations when they are being priced.

Sizes and Packaging

Each product is available in unique sizes, and some products are available only in certain quantities. These discussions provide the designer with an understanding of the units used in calculations and explain the minimums that the designer must consider when pricing so that all costs are covered in the final price.

Cost Factors

Most products have two different types of cost factors: materials and labor. These discussions describe some of the possible costs that can occur with each product. Understanding what these costs are allows the interior designer to have fewer unanticipated costs.

Calculations

Students are shown in a step-by-step style how to calculate the amount of materials needed for the product. These calculations are based on the worksheets that are included.

Step-by-Step Examples

The step-by-step examples give scenarios from the client for certain products. In the chapters that cover several different types of products, there are multiple examples. The worksheet is used, an explanation is given for the calculations, and additional tips are provided.

Manual Worksheets

Worksheets have been included specifically for each area. These worksheets can be copied and used multiple times. A total of 42 worksheets are included in this book to cover as many various products as is practical. These worksheets have been favorites of students.

Practice Lessons

Practice lessons have been created by giving certain scenarios, residential and commercial, and questions for the student to calculate and answer. There are three levels of lessons: basic, intermediate, and advanced.

In the chapters that have multiple variations, multiple lessons in these three levels are provided for the student. Also included in the advanced lessons is at least one lesson that integrates the quantities calculated with per-unit pricing to determine the total price of the product.

Practice Lesson Answers

Math can be confusing. Practice lesson answers are included for the students to self-check their understanding of the process. This is invaluable to students because sometimes their error is simple, and a way to check their answer and their process enables them to correct the error.

Insights from the Field

Sidebars appear throughout the book with advice from professionals from different aspects of the interior design field. These voices provide assurance to the student. Some advice relates to tricky areas when calculating material, some advice relates to working with the customers, and some advice is given in general for the design professional.

Instructor's Manual

The instructor's manual provides suggestions for organizing the material and additional information not included in the book. Suggestions for team projects and applied assignments are explained.

The practice lessons in the book are intended to help the student understand the process. For class assignments, additional problems, including those combining product quantity with costs, with answers are provided. Because there are regional differences in costs and some variations in practice across the country, the instructor may want to substitute local costs into the lessons provided in the instructor's manual. A test bank with an answer key is provided.

Acknowledgments

The idea for this book grew out of a class I taught for 11 years at Johnson County Community College in Overland Park, Kansas. The class focused on calculating materials and prices for walls, floors, upholstery, draperies, bedding, and area rugs. The only worksheet that was handed down to me to share with students was a basic one on calculating pinch-pleated draperies. The students in that class expressed how helpful that worksheet was and they wanted more!

From that point on I began creating handouts and worksheets. Those initial worksheets have changed over the years as I refined them and continued to produce more. Alumni of our program continually told me how they referred to the handouts and worksheets I created for that class as they worked on client projects. The department chair, Jan Cummings, told me I should write a book, and eventually I contacted Olga Kontzias.

I would like to thank Jan Cummings, Bobanne Kalkofen, Darla Green, Dalene Erwin, Jo Randolph, and Jo Wilson for their encouragement. I must thank my students as well because every student who has had class with me has taught me something! They inspired me to work harder to make the math aspect of this profession easier to understand.

There are innumerable others who helped supply information for this book: Brooke Nienstadt with Sherwin-Williams, Janie Gilbert, Jennifer Allred, Albert DeLeon, Jeff Bailey, Jim Martin of Hobson Interiors, Tony Shaefer, Kris Lance, Kathy Bryles, Lauren Wilkinson, Mark Quitno, Dan Edinger, Jenee Coleman, Craig Speer, Wayne Daugherty, Steven Smith, Dalene Erwin, and Sharon Hilt. Joy Smith was invaluable to me, and really helped when I was in a pinch. Many thanks also to those at Fairchild and Bloomsbury who were able to put all of this together in a cohesive package. Those that I worked closely with and who have my special thanks are:Olga Kontzias, Sylvia Weber, Stephen Pinto, Edie Weinberg, Kirsten Dennison, Charlotte Frost, and Sarah Silberg.

Most of all I thank my son, Joe Ingham, for putting up with me as I focused on this book. He is the reason I started teaching as an adjunct. He has been and continues to be my biggest supporter.

Chapter 1 | The Business of Interior Design

Chapter Outline

The Interior Designer as a Businessperson

When studying interior design, designers must keep in mind how easy it is to get caught up in the problem solving and the creativity of a design project. After all, this is what interior designers love! However, being an interior designer is about more than design. It also means being a professional businessperson and having authenticity, credibility/legitimacy, integrity, personality, and people skills. The ability to design, coordinate, project manage, and think outside of the box is important, but if the business aspects are not handled well, the chances of keeping a job and of having clients decrease drastically. Whether the designer is self-employed or employed by another doesn't matter; the client is looking for someone who is professional and ethical—someone who knows the field and is comfortable to work with. Clients are also looking for the interior designer to be their advocate, to look out for their best interests, and to be able to logically explain design decisions and the road blocks or issues that come with the project. The client is looking for the "added value"—that is, the intangible knowledge that the interior designer brings to any project. Designers must be compensated for this added value they bring whether it is by an hourly fee, a design fee, profit from products, or any combination of these.

Interior designers get to know their clients very well. Because they work so closely and intimately with their clients, discovering their needs and wants, it is sometimes possible to cross the line between working relationships and friendships. While this may be unavoidable, the interior designer who remembers to keep the working relationship separate from the friendship, realizing that this is first and foremost a business, should go far in this field. By acting in a professional manner, you will earn the respect and regard of your clients. This pays off with the hard-earned "client for a lifetime" and with referrals. Over the long run, the best clients usually come from word-of-mouth referrals.

Business Relationships

Vendors, contractors, subcontractors, workrooms, and installers are all looking for an interior designer who is professional and ethical, understands the way things occur in practice, and takes the business side of design seriously. As in most things, respect of colleagues in the field must be earned. Networking and earning respect start very early in interior design. Students sitting in a classroom sometimes forget that those they see in their classrooms and on field trips, including the vendors and manufacturers' representatives, are likely to be their colleagues in the field after graduation.

With this in mind, let's take a closer look at each of these professionals and businesses:

Contractor—The contractor is responsible for a project's costs, scheduling, and completion. Sometimes the interior designer works for the contractor, sometimes the interior designer works for the client who has hired the contractor, and sometimes the contractor is the interior designer. Check your state laws for the definition of a contractor, the qualifications of the contractor, and any required licensing and/or insurance contractors should have.

Subcontractor—Subcontractors generally specialize in a certain area of work, such as electrical work, plumbing, cabinetmaking, drapery workroom, and installation. Interior designers subcontract the majority of labor to these types of professionals while maintaining control of the project. Be sure to check subcontractors' credentials and to speak with others who have worked with them before you hire them. Check your state laws for any applicable licensing or insurance they should have.

Installer—The installer is usually a subcontractor and generally specializes in a specific area, such as flooring, window treatments, systems furniture, wallpaper, and so on. Installers can make or break a successful job by their creativity in problem solving on the job, their appearance, their communication with the client, and their attitude. You should take these things into consideration, along with credentials, when determining whom to hire for the job. Ultimately, they are one of the last faces the client sees representing you, the interior designer. The interior designer either gets the credit for the success or the blame for the failure of the installation.

Manufacturer's representative—The manufacturer's representative (rep) is a person hired by a company to promote the company's line to interior designers and interior design firms. Many times reps cover several states and are responsible for maintaining existing accounts and looking for potential new accounts. They can teach the interior designer about their line and how to sell it. Many times the interior designer will contact the rep for special pricing on a job with high volume potential or if the job is fairly intricate and the rep can help to confirm the correct specifications. The rep is also the person contacted when there are problems with the product. Reps can help you understand the issues and provide potential solutions.

Workroom—The workroom is generally where custom items are created. This includes window treatments, bedding, furniture, art/stained glass, cabinetry, and so on. Any specifications for construction of the product you have designed (furniture, cabinetry, window treatments, etc.) will be given to the workroom to create. Many times the interior designer and the workroom will discuss what is to be created, and the end product is a combination of the designer's vision and the workroom's construction knowledge (see Figure 1.1). The interior designer gets to know the workroom very well. Although workrooms can be found through a search on the Internet, most interior designers find workrooms from referrals from other interior designers and business colleagues. As with contractors and subcontractors, find out if there are any state laws that pertain to

a workroom, and make sure it has the applicable licenses and insurance.

Vendor—The vendor is the person or place where you purchase material and product. Usually the vendor requires an account to be established and asks for a sales tax or use tax certificate to be on file. Because the interior designer is purchasing at wholesale and is not the end user, the designer should not be charged sales tax by the vendor.

Showroom—The showroom is normally a "to the trade only" business. This means that as an interior designer in the trade, you can use the showroom to find items and materials for your clients. Many showrooms will represent multiple lines of manufacturers; for example, furniture, fabric, trim, and accessory lines, among others, will often be together in one showroom. Many interior designers have close working relationships

Figure 1.1 Interior designer collaborating with drapery workroom. (Courtesy of Jennifer Allred)

Figure 1.2 Showroom employee working with interior designer. (Courtesy of Lauren Wilkinson)

with their showrooms (see Figure 1.2). There is an unwritten rule when you use showrooms: If you find something there that you specify for a job, either order directly from the showroom or make sure the showroom gets the sales credit for the order. The easiest way to do this is to specify and order from the showroom even if you have a direct account with the line from which you purchase. This will go a long way toward establishing a good business relationship with that showroom.

With all of these different businesses, if you are perceived as a professional, ethical, and reasonable businessperson, and if you have shown them the respect they deserve, they will be more willing to go out of their way to work with you when you have questions or need a last-minute favor or if some part of the job has an issue.

Interior designers must be aware of the team aspect that is crucial for a project to be completed. For some, the team may begin at their firm as different professionals are brought together for their expertise on a particular project. This is not where the team ends. The other, sometimes unacknowledged, team members (workrooms, subcontractors, installers, and contractors) involved in completing the project are as important and sometimes more important because

they bring the vision to life, hopefully on time and in budget. It is vital to keep these relationships on good terms. If you are fair, knowledgeable, and reasonable with those you work with, when something goes awry, their willingness to help can be the difference in keeping the project on track and your clients happy.

Importance of Estimating and Calculating Costs

Why is it important to be able to do estimations? In large cities, workrooms and installers are available who can go to the site, take measurements, and do the calculations. The problem is that there are fewer and fewer workrooms and installers and the demand for their services is great. Do you or your client want to wait several weeks until someone can go out to measure and price the job? The ability for the interior designer to take measurements and calculate the costs of the job allows for a faster turnaround of the project and creates credibility in the client's eyes.

The quickest way to lose the respect of any of the professionals you work with is to send them out on multiple jobs to measure without knowing what the specifications are or whether it is within the client's budget. It is a best practice to do a quick estimate to "qualify" your client. An estimate allows the client to have an idea of how much the project will cost and be able to determine if it fits within the budget. An estimate is a win-win-win for all concerned because it saves you, your client, and the installer/workroom time if the client decides from the estimate that the project is more than he or she are willing to pay.

The client's budget is important and should not be ignored. An interior designer is able to look at the overall picture to balance the needs of the client with their wants within their budget. Life cycle costing comes into play. Life cycle costing is a way of looking at the price of a product over its life span. A product's life cycle cost is determined by adding all costs, including maintenance, and dividing by the estimated life of that product. Most durable products generally have a higher up-front cost; however, when spread over their life span, such products are much less expensive than those that initially have lower costs. This allows the interior designer, when dealing with conflicting information, such as quality and price, to determine where it is essential to budget for quality products. If a piece of furniture is never or seldom used, it is possible to select a less expensive piece of furniture, allowing more money to go to a well-constructed, more expensive piece that is heavily used. The same is true of flooring. If there are rooms that are used infrequently, a less expensive carpet can be used in these areas, allowing more money to go to areas like entries, halls, and kitchens that need more durable flooring, such as bamboo, hardwood, or tile. This allows the client to make more informed decisions on selections in a timely manner before the budget is blown.

If the client is ready to progress after this initial estimation, more time is taken to develop a quote for the work to be done. Before anything is ordered, a quote is given, a signature is obtained, and the appropriate deposit is collected. So, estimation also helps to determine the final "hard figures" quoted to the client. The ability to estimate quickly and correctly improves over time with practice.

Calculating Costs and Client Pricing

Once a price is quoted, the interior designer stands behind that price for better or worse. All foreseeable costs of the specific product need to be calculated before any price is quoted to the client. If the designer does not know the overall cost, the designer might quote the client a price that is too low. In the following chapters the various components of specific products are delineated so that the designer can include them in the calculations to find the overall cost. Various worksheets are included to help you calculate the amount of material needed, which can then be plugged into the costs. These worksheets allow for waste. While all pricing calculations will be based on the amount calculated from these worksheets, it is an acceptable industry practice to add additional quantity to the material needed, to allow for breakage, waste, and miscalculations. This amount varies based upon the product and the firm's policies.

Most firms have determined the type of markup or profit margin that is needed to cover overhead and built-in value added, and to stay profitable. This amount is added to the overall cost in order to determine the retail price to the client. Pricing calculations must begin with measurements and account for regional considerations.

Measuring and Take-Offs

Any interior designer responsible for specifications and pricing must obtain dimensions in order to do his or her job. Most nonresidential design work relies on contractors' or installers' dimensions and material amounts; however, there are still times when interior designers need to get their own measurements. A field measure whereby the actual space can be measured is ideal. A clipboard, pencil, graph paper, and a tape measure that is a minimum 25 feet long with a 1-inch-wide blade are the standard tools used for measuring (see Figure 1.3). This type of tape measure can extend over a large area, and the width of the tape makes it substantial enough to feed out over distances. Laser tape measures are useful for longer distances but currently are not helpful when trying to measure more detailed areas, such as around windows, doors, and fireplaces.

Figure 1.3 Different kinds of tape measures. (Courtesy of Diana Allison)

At times costs must be estimated before the actual space is built and take-offs must be done. A take-off is a calculation of the dimensions using a scaled drawing of the space along with an architect's scale. AutoCAD is helpful in calculating base numbers for some materials, but not all. Materials can be estimated this way, but it is important to get actual field measurements once the space is built and to closely watch the project in case there are changes to the structure and space that will influence the choice of materials ordered and overall costs.

Throughout this book you will be calculating the materials and costs of various products common in the interior design field. The costs of a product include the price you pay for the material, all material components, shipping of the material and components, fabrication, and installation. Be aware that no matter how carefully you have done your math or written your contract, there are always unexpected factors, such as indirect job costs or simple mistakes, that will eat into your profits. Do not feel guilty about marking up the product appropriately. Novice interior designers often forget or don't realize that the

markup isn't usually pure profit but must also cover overhead. They also must learn that what to them seems like an expensive item may actually be an appropriate price for what they have priced.

In most states clients are also charged sales tax for what they purchase. Sales tax is not considered a cost since you function as a collector of the sales tax for the city, county, and state. You basically pass this money on to the state, so sales tax does not factor into costs or profits. However, if the client's budget is accurate as to how much money must be spent, all monies the client will eventually pay need to be considered. At this point, sales tax must be calculated so the client can see what the bottom-line expenditure will be.

Regional Considerations

Getting to know the region and the design norms and expectations of that region is important when you are designing and calculating prices for your client. Different climates, building systems, and cultures have an impact not only on the interior design and specifications but also on how retail prices are calculated for the consumer. The cost of labor, installation, material, and shipping will vary greatly from one part of the United States to another. When becoming familiar with the region you work in, network with other design professionals in ASID (American Society of Interior Designers), IIDA (International Interior Design Association), NKBA (National Kitchen & Bath Association), AIA (The American Institute of Architects), NARI (National Association of the Remodeling Industry), and HBA (Home Builders Association). Attend continuing education events, and visit local vendors. Immerse yourself in the interior design community, and you will learn what you need to know.

Be aware that the costs and markups found in the exercises and examples in this book are not intended to represent any standards; rather, they are intended to help you learn the process of calculating and pricing.

Calculations and Pricing Terminology

You should be familiar with the following terms as we cover pricing concerns:

Cost price The actual price paid to buy the goods from the manufacturer or distributor. It may or may not include shipping.

Discounts A deduction, usually stated as a percentage, from the suggested retail price. This deduction will vary depending on the product and where you obtain it.

Multiple discounts A progression of discounts off of the list or suggested retail price. A 50/5 discount is calculated by taking a 50 percent discount off of the initial amount. From this figure, an additional 5 percent would be deducted. $100 less 50 percent = $50. $50 less 5 percent = $47.50. This is not the same as adding 50 percent + 5 percent. Do not add these percentages together because they will not give the correct discount. Sometimes for sales or very large orders a three-tiered discount is used—that is, 50/10/5. Again, each discount is calculated off of the previous resulting balance. $100 less 50 percent = $50. $50 less 10 percent = $45. $45 less 5 percent = $42.75.

Trade discount Discount given to people in the trade by local retail stores and establishments. These are generally not large discounts, usually from 10 to 40 percent off the retail price. Pier 1, Bed Bath & Beyond, Pottery Barn, Restoration Hardware, and so on extend these courtesies with proof of business credentials. They will also not charge sales tax if you are not the end user and have a sales or use tax certificate on file.

Freight The shipping costs (normally referring to semi-truck shipping) involved in the delivery of the goods from the manufacturer to the designer. Some companies have and use their own trucks on large orders, but most use independent carriers for their smaller orders.

Keystone A code to let a designer know that the price shown at retail is twice the wholesale price. When adding a 100 percent markup, the original amount (100 percent of the price) is added to the 100 percent markup. Cost is multiplied by 2 for a 100 percent markup because 100 percent + 100 percent = 200 percent, or 2.0 when shown as a decimal.

List price The manufacturer's suggested retail price for goods to be sold to the consumer.

Manufacturer's suggested retail price (MSRP) The manufacturer's suggested asking price for the goods to the consumer. It means the same as list price.

Net price Same as wholesale price. Net price can also be defined as a price to the designer that is lower than the item would cost the customer.

Number markup Also called keystone; a code way of saying that price at retail is twice the wholesale price.

Number + 10 markup A few showrooms may have added an additional amount to the doubled price to allow for such things as shipping or freight and will express it as *number + another number,* indicating the additional percentage. For example, number + 10 markup means that the wholesale price is doubled and then another 10 percent is added to obtain the suggested retail price shown on the price tag.

Price list This comes in two forms: the suggested retail price or the list price and the net or wholesale price list to the designer. Designers should always determine which price list they are working with before quoting a price to the customer or estimating a job.

Retail price The price the retailer decides to charge for the goods. This is not necessarily the same as MSRP.

Wholesale price Same meaning as net price. Depending on whether the interior designer has direct accounts with the manufacturers or is going through a showroom, this may be a 30 percent or more discount off of the suggested retail price list.

It is impossible to discuss calculating costs without a brief discussion of different methods of charging your client for product. The price to the client is dependent on the type of design work—that is, residential, commercial, hospitality, institutional, and so on—since each of these areas is approached a bit differently based on norms, volume, and region. The methods are as follows:

Discount from retail This is a certain discount given on the merchandise you sell your client. For some manufacturers that don't have an MSRP (such as carpet), a retail figure must be established before you can mark it down.

Markup from cost One way of calculating prices is by taking all costs of the product (material, freight, labor, etc.), adding them together to get the true cost of the job, and then adding on the markup percentage. This method gives a consistent percentage of profit.

Profit margin This is an amount that must be added to all sales to allow for compensation of overhead, miscellaneous costs, and unknown costs while still maintaining an acceptable percentage of profit. Markup and profit margin are not the same thing. When you are calculating prices by profit margin, your percentage of profit is higher. Say a $100 item has a 50 percent markup: $100 × 1.5 = $150. Consider the same item with a 50 percent profit margin: $100 ÷ 50 percent = $200.

Math in Interior Design

Frankly, math is math. Everyone makes mistakes, even the most experienced interior designers and installers. As you become more familiar with products and quantities needed for projects, it will be easier to know when the numbers are off because of a math error. Knowing how to calculate materials and prices allows the designer to double-check another's calculations. Because mistakes cost you or your firm money and sometimes credibility, having this knowledge will help to minimize this loss of profit.

Approach to Calculations Dictated by Product Size and Packaging

There are specific issues with each material and product relating to the manufactured size of the product and how it is packaged and shipped. For example, while many carpet stores today sell broadloom (wall-to-wall) carpet by the square foot instead of the square yard, it actually comes in a roll, approximately 12 feet wide. If someone were to order 6 square feet from a carpet manufacturer, he or she would receive a 12-foot-wide roll that is only 8 inches long. While it isn't common that anyone would want just 8 inches of carpet, this example makes the point that we must calculate material and then adjust the quantity according to the product dimensions.

Calculator Language

Interior designers become proficient in considering feet and inches in the traditional architectural scale manner—fractions—and the language of the calculator—decimals. Remember that math functions must be done using the same type of units, feet with feet and inches with inches. A room that is 12 feet 8 inches × 14 feet 6 inches is an example of combined units, feet and inches. These dimensions must be converted to either feet or inches; converting to feet creates a more manageable number. When you are converting to decimals in order to use most calculators, the feet in this example are the whole numbers, and the inches are a fraction of the whole.

To convert inches to a decimal, take the number of inches and divide by 12.

Table 1.1 shows inches to decimal conversion. Copy this and keep it handy until this information becomes second nature.

Business Math

The fewer math steps that can be taken to find the answer will lower the probability of a math mistake. Because discounts, markups, profit margins, and other percentage-driven items are common, a useful concept to remember when you are working with percentages is the complement of a percentage. If a 20 percent discount is given on a product, the long way of calculating this is as follows: $100 × .2 (20 percent) = $20. $100 − $20 = $80. A quicker way of arriving at the same solution is to consider the complement. The complement percentage is the number that added to the original percentage equals 100 percent. In this case, when there is a 20 percent discount, in essence taking away 20 percent, 80 percent is being kept. $100 × .8 = $80. This creates fewer steps to the right answer, minimizing the possibility of error.

Using the complement also works with multiple discounts. If a company gives a 40/20 discount, the complement, the amount being kept, is 60/80. $100 × 60 percent = $60 × 80 percent = $48.

Converting 12 feet 8 inches to a decimal: The inches must be converted to feet units from inch units. 8 inches divided by 12 inches (1 foot) equals .666 feet. Only two numbers are kept to the right of the decimal point. If the third number to the right of the decimal is less than 5, the second number remains as it is. If the third number is 5 or more, the second number should be rounded up. In this case, .666 becomes .67. Therefore, 12 feet 8 inches as a decimal is 12.67 feet.

Converting 14 feet 6 inches to a decimal: 6 inches divided by 12 inches equals .5 feet. Therefore, 14 feet 6 inches as a decimal is 14.5 feet.

Box 1.1 Converting Inches to Feet

1″	.08′
2″	.17′
3″	.25′
4″	.33′
5″	.42′
6″	.5′
7″	.58′
8″	.67′
9″	.75′
10″	.83′
11″	.92′
12″	1′

Table 1.1 Inches Converted to Decimals

Math Test

If you can calculate the following math problems, you can do the math found throughout this book. The answers are found on the following page.

1. $4 + 4 =$ _____

2. $18 + 18 =$ _____

3. $36 \div 12 =$ _____

4. $5 \times 8 =$ _____

5. $40 \div 9 =$ _____

6. $1.5 \times 4 =$ _____

7. Knowing that 12 in. = 1 ft., convert .5 ft. into inches.

8. Knowing that 12 in. = 1 ft., convert .75 ft. into inches.

9. Knowing that 12 in. = 1 ft., convert 3 in. into feet using a decimal.

10. $6 \times 12 =$ _____ $\div 9 =$ _____

11. Convert 9 ft. 9 in. to feet using a decimal.

12. 12 ft. – 8 ft. 3 in. = _____

13. What is the numeric equivalent of π?

14. What is the formula to find the circumference of a circle?

Math Test Key

1. $4 + 4 = \mathbf{8}$

   Most of the math interior designers use is simple math such as this.

2. $18 + 18 = \mathbf{36}$

   When working with fabrics, understand that 18 inches is ½ yard; 36 inches is 1 yard.

3. $36 \div 12 = \mathbf{3}$

   36 inches divided by 12 inches equals 3 feet.

4. $5 \times 8 = \mathbf{40}$

   A common bathroom size is 5 feet × 8 feet, which results in 40 square feet.

5. $40 \div 9 = \mathbf{4.44}$

   Sheet vinyl laid in that bathroom will require 4.44 square yards. 9 is used because there are 9 square feet in 1 square yard and the same units must be used in math.

6. $1.5 \times 4 = \mathbf{6}$

   Calculators work with decimals and not fractions.

7. Convert .5 ft. into inches = **6 in.**

   $.5 \times 12 = 6$ in.

8. Convert .75 ft. into inches = **9 in.**

   $.75 \times 12 = 9$ in.

9. Convert 3 in. into feet using a decimal = **.25 ft.**

   12 in. ÷ 3 in. = .25 ft.

10. $6 \times 12 = \mathbf{72} \div 9 = \mathbf{8}$

    A 6-foot × 12-foot space is 72 square feet, divided by 9 square feet is 8 square yards. When you are doing math, it is important to use the same units, in this case square feet.

11. Convert 9 ft. 9 in. to feet using a decimal = **9.75 ft.**

    .75 ft. × 12 = 9 in.

12. 12 ft. − 8 ft. 3 in. = **3 ft. 9 in.**

13. What is the numeric equivalent of π? **3.14**

14. What is the formula to find the circumference of a circle? **$2r \times 3.14$, where r represents the radius of the circle.**

    When working with round fabric products, such as table cloths or swags, you must sometimes know the perimeter, or circumference, so that you can order fringe or other trim.

Reference

Piotrowski, C. *Professional Practice for Interior Designers.* 4th ed. New York: Wiley, 2008.

Chapter 2 | Paint

Chapter Outline

Terminology

Base Generally a white paint to which colorants are added. When different colorant combinations are blended, all colors of the fan deck can be created. A clear base is without white and is used for ultra-deep colors, allowing a rich, deep, vibrant, and highly saturated color to be achieved.

Coat Each layer of paint applied to a surface is considered a coat of paint (Figure 2.1). For example, two layers of paint on a wall may be referred to as two coats of paint. Darker-colored (white base) paint will require more coats of paint than a lighter-colored (white base) paint. Ultra-deep colors (clear base) take even more coats of paint.

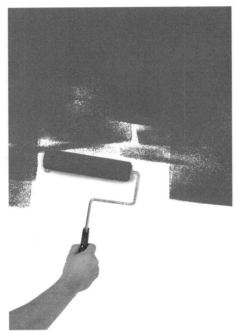

Figure 2.1 Coat of paint being applied. (© D. Hurst / Alamy)

Coverage The amount of square feet a can of paint will cover. The coverage varies among different paint types, colors, and paint manufacturers and is stated on the paint can as well as on the manufacturer's data sheets.

Faux finish Painting techniques that simulate the look of something else, such as marble, leather, or stucco, or other unique looks that have some texture or representational feature.

Finish/luster/sheen The different reflective values available in paint. Actual color and the purpose of the room are important considerations when selecting the finish. (See Figure 2.2.)

Flat A finish where there is little or no light-reflecting quality. Commonly used on walls and ceilings, flat tends to hide surface imperfections. However, flat finishes (especially dark colors) will burnish—showing a mark on the wall when someone brushes against it. Flat paints are more difficult to clean because of this.

Eggshell/satin A finish with a small amount of light reflection. Many designers prefer this finish because it gives a richness to the appearance of the room and because it is easier to clean than flat. Some wall imperfections will show with this finish, and many painters will charge a little more when using eggshell/satin since it can entail additional labor and material in correcting imperfections.

Semigloss A finish with a medium light reflection, but not total reflection. Commonly used for trim work, semigloss shows imperfections in the surface because of the amount of light reflection; however, it is very easy to clean. Painters will charge

more when painting a wall with a semigloss finish.

Gloss Has a high degree of light reflection and shows every imperfection in the surface. Gloss can create a beautiful look and is even easier to clean than semigloss. Painters will charge more for painting gloss because of the extra work necessary to correctly prepare the surface. Gloss is used for trim work, but not as often as semigloss is.

Latex A water-based paint, which is considered to be better for the environment. Latex has less odor than oil-based paint and is available in no- or low-VOCs (volatile organic compounds). Brushes and other equipment used can be cleaned with soap and water.

Milk paint A natural type of paint used for centuries made from milk protein and lime. It is nontoxic, considered very environmentally friendly, and has a limited range of colors. It is mixed from powder and can spoil several days after mixing.

Oil Oil-based paint is generally not considered good for the environment, as the brushes and tools must be cleaned with solvents. Oil paint is more durable, especially on trim, but has a strong odor because of VOCs.

Primer A product painted prior to the first paint coat. Primers have a number of different uses, such as preparing the wall for a darker paint, allowing for better adhesion of the paint to the wall for better coverage, and covering oils and other stains. They are also quick drying. Gray primers are used especially to prepare the wall for dark and ultra-dark paints.

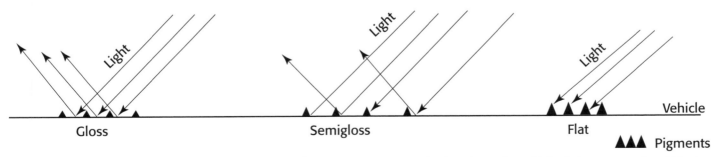

Figure 2.2 Basic types of paint finishes: As the points of the paint pigment rise higher above the vehicle, light gets caught within the peaks. A flat finish has higher peaks than a gloss finish.

Coverage and Packaging

Paint may be purchased in 1-quart, 1-gallon, and 5-gallon containers. Large commercial and residential contractor jobs will require the larger 5-gallon containers of paint. Homeowners, on the other hand, typically buy by the gallon or the quart. While the average coverage per gallon for paint is 350–400 square feet, other factors affect how much paint is needed, including wall type, paint color, and type of paint. Some paints require a coat of primer before the paint is applied. Dark paint usually needs a primer, as does light paint that is painted over a dark wall. Each type of paint has a data sheet available online that shows how many square feet it covers. The designer must reference this data sheet once the paint type and color are determined. Also on the paint companies'

websites are paint calculators that can be used to determine the quantity of paint needed.

Cost Factors

There is great variance in painting labor costs. Some painters charge by the hour; others charge by the job. Some cities require that painters belong to a union, which in turn will increase the labor cost. If faux finishing is involved, the price will vary from artist to artist and by the level of complexity. However, new technologies with paint have allowed paint manufacturers to create paint formulas that make the finish easier for the standard paint contractor to apply. Additional supplies that contractors need for the job, such as brushes, tape, plastic, paper, rags, paint thinner, and so on, are usually included in the labor cost quoted to the interior designer or the client.

Figure 2.3 Sherwin-Williams online paint calculator. (Sherwinwilliams.com)

Figure 2.4 Painting contractors. (© Jaubert Bernard / Alamy)

INSIGHT FROM THE FIELD

❝One of the quickest and potentially most dramatic changes you can make in design is with paint. While it can be one of the most cost-effective ways to make change, that is not always the case. Rooms and walls with a lot of architectural detail or windows require more taping off and cutting in. This increases cost. Also, changing paint colors can increase cost, as equipment will need to be rinsed or replaced with each color change.❞

Kathleen Ramsey, *Allied ASID, CAPS, owner of Ramsey Interiors, Overland Park, Kansas*

Painting Schedule						
Client:				Painter:		
Phone #s:				Phone #s:		
Address:						
Material Costs	**Quantity in Gallons**			**Amount**		
Primer	W:	T:	C:	W: $	T: $	C: $
Paint	W:	T:	C:	W: $	T: $	C: $
			Subtotal Cost for Material	**W: $**	**T: $**	**C: $**
Labor Costs	**Circle Areas Addressed**			**Amount**		
Repair	Wall	Trim	Ceiling	W: $	T: $	C: $
Prep	Wall	Trim	Ceiling	W: $	T: $	C: $
Priming	Wall	Trim	Ceiling	W: $	T: $	C: $
Painting	Wall	Trim	Ceiling	W: $	T: $	C: $
			Subtotal Cost for Material	**W: $**	**T: $**	**C: $**
Total Cost of Job (Material and Labor)				**$**		

Table 2.1 Painting: Calculating Total Cost

When determining the overall costs for the job, be sure to consider the following (see Table 2.1):

1. **Labor costs**
   A. Repair work
   B. Prep work
   C. Primer
   D. Painting
2. **Material costs**
   A. Primer
   B. Paint

Calculations

Calculations for determining the amount of paint to purchase are very straightforward and are some of the easiest calculations to make. Estimating paint is based on the square feet of wall or ceiling to be covered and then determining how many coats of paint are needed for the color to look its best. The steps are as follows:

1. Determine the perimeter of the room in feet.
2. Determine the height of the room in feet and multiply by the perimeter to find the square footage of the room.
3. Deduct the square footage of windows, doors, and openings from the total room square footage to find the adjusted square footage.
4. Divide the adjusted square footage by the estimated coverage of the paint selected.
5. Round up to the nearest whole number to determine gallons of paint needed for coverage.

Step-by-Step Examples

Example 1

Your client wants her teenager's room painted. The room is 12 feet wide × 10 feet long (see Figure 2.5) with a ceiling height of 8 feet. There is one door 36 inches wide × 84 inches tall, a closet door 72 inches wide × 84 inches tall, and two windows 42 inches wide × 54 inches long. It will take 2 coats of paint. Each gallon of paint specified covers 350 square feet.

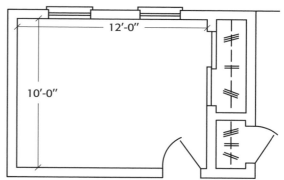

Figure 2.5 Example 1—floor plan.

Step 1: Find perimeter of room in feet (e.g., 65.3 ft.).

Wall A:	10	ft.
Wall B: +	12	ft.
Wall C: +	10	ft.
Wall D: +	12	ft.
Total perimeter:	44	ft.

Step 2: Find square footage of area to be covered.

Total perimeter from Step 1:	44	ft.
Height of area to be covered: ×	8	ft.
Total square feet:	352	sq. ft.

Step 3: Determine deductions.

Door width:	3	ft. (36 in. ÷ 12 in. = 3 ft.)
Closet door width: +	6	ft. (72 in. ÷ 12 in. = 6 ft.)
Total width:	9	ft.
Height: ×	7	ft. (84 in. ÷ 12 in. = 7 ft.)
Total square feet:	63	sq. ft.

Window width:	3.5	ft. (42 in. ÷ 12 in. = 3.5 ft.)
Window width: +	3.5	ft.
Total width:	7	ft.
Height: ×	4.5	ft. (54 in. ÷ 12 in. = 4.5 ft.)
Total square feet:	31.5	sq. ft.

Add all deductions together:

Doors:	63	sq. ft.
Windows: +	31.5	sq. ft.
Total deductions:	94.5	sq. ft.

Step 4: Determine square footage of paint needed.

Take total square feet from Step 2:	352	sq. ft.
Subtract total from Step 3: −	94.5	sq. ft.
Total square feet needed for 1 coat of paint:	257.5	sq. ft.
Multiply by anticipated coats of paint: ×	2	coats
Total square feet of paint needed:	515	sq. ft.

Step 5: Determine gallons of paint needed.

Take total from Step 4:	515	sq. ft.
Divide by square feet of coverage/gallon:	÷ 350	sq. ft.
Total gallons of paint needed:	1.47	gallons
Round up to whole number:	**2**	**gallons of paint needed to purchase**

Example 2

Your client has a great room that is 18 feet wide × 26 feet long (see Figure 2.6). The ceiling height is 12 feet, and the room has one cased opening 12 feet wide × 10 feet tall, a door 36 inches wide × 84 inches tall, and a bank of windows that has a total measurement of 12 feet wide × 8 feet tall. It will take 2 coats of paint. Each gallon of paint covers 350 square feet.

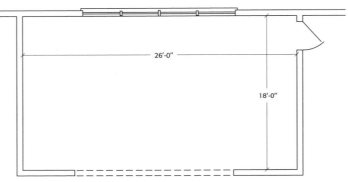

Figure 2.6 Example 2—floor plan.

Step 1: Find perimeter of room in feet (e.g., 65.3 ft.).

Wall A:	18	ft.
Wall B:	+ 26	ft.
Wall C:	+ 18	ft.
Wall D:	+ 26	ft.
Total perimeter:	88	ft.

Step 2: Find square footage of area to be covered.

Total perimeter from Step 1:	88	ft.
Height of area to be covered:	× 12	ft.
Total square feet:	1056	sq. ft.

Step 3: Determine deductions.

Cased opening width:	12	ft.
Multiply by height of opening:	× 10	ft.
Total square feet:	120	sq. ft.
Door width:	3	ft. (36 in. ÷ 12 in. = 3 ft.)
Multiply by height of opening:	× 7	ft. (84 in. ÷ 12 in. = 7 ft.)
Total square feet:	21	sq. ft.
Window width:	12	ft.
Multiply by height of opening:	× 8	ft.
Total square feet:	96	sq. ft.

Add all deductions together:

Cased opening:	120	sq. ft.
Door:	+ 21	sq. ft.
Windows:	+ 96	sq. ft.
Total deductions:	237	sq. ft.

Step 4: Determine square footage of paint needed.

Take total square feet from Step 2:	1056	sq. ft.
Subtract total from Step 3:	− 237	sq. ft.
Total square feet needed for 1 coat of paint:	819	sq. ft.
Multiply by anticipated coats of paint:	× 2	coats
Total square feet of paint needed:	1638	sq. ft.

Step 5: Determine gallons of paint needed.

Take total from Step 4:	1638	sq. ft.
Divide by square feet of coverage/gallon:	÷ 350	sq. ft.
Total gallons of paint needed:	4.68	gallons
Round up to whole number:	5	gallons of paint needed to purchase

Manual Worksheet

Paint Worksheet

Step 1: Find perimeter of room in feet (e.g., 65.3 ft.).

Wall A:	_____	ft.
Wall B:	+ _____	ft.
Wall C:	+ _____	ft.
Wall D:	+ _____	ft.
Wall E (if applicable):	+ _____	ft.
Total perimeter:	_____	**ft.**

Step 2: Find square footage of area to be covered.

Total from Step 1:	_____	ft.
Multiply by height:	× _____	ft.

Note: This may not be full height of wall.

Total square feet:	_____	**sq. ft.**

Step 3: Determine deductions.

Width of opening or cabinets w/same height:	_____	ft.
Width of opening or cabinets w/same height:	+ _____	ft.
Total width of openings:	_____	**ft.**
Multiply by height of opening/cabinets:	× _____	ft.
Total square feet:	_____	**sq. ft.**

Repeat the deduction process for total openings in room and add all deductions together.

Note: Do not use entire height of door, window, or cabinet when only a portion of the wall is being painted (as in above or below a chair rail). Add together the widths of all openings that have the same height and then multiply by the height. Repeat as needed until total square footage is found.

Step 4: Determine square footage of paint needed.

Take total square feet from Step 2:	_____	sq. ft.
Subtract total from Step 3:	− _____	sq. ft.
Total square feet needed for 1 coat of paint:	_____	**sq. ft.**
Multiply by anticipated coats of paint	× _____	coats
Total square feet of paint needed:	_____	**sq. ft.**

Step 5: Determine gallons of paint needed.

Take total from Step 4:	_____	sq. ft.
Divide by square feet of coverage/gallon:	÷ _____	sq. ft.
Total gallons of paint needed:	_____	**gallons**
Round up to whole number:	_____	**gallons of paint needed to purchase**

Paint estimating has been made easy by paint manufacturers such as Sherwin-Williams and Benjamin Moore. The companies' websites allow the user to choose colors, integrate them into an uploaded photo, and calculate paint for walls, ceiling, and trim. Both Sherwin-Williams and Benjamin Moore have smart phone applications. Look at the paint calculators for both companies. Input the same room dimensions into each one and see if there is a difference.

INSIGHT FROM THE FIELD

"There are two different ways of calculating paint for trim and woodwork: you use less paint when you do it by brush, you use more paint when you spray, so you're always going to figure in terms of the client and what's best for them. For example, a small kitchen will take five gallons if we spray and 3 gallons if we do it by brush."

Armando Guerrero, *owner of AMG Painting, Round Rock, Texas*

Practice Lessons: Paint

BASIC

Your client wants to paint a powder room that is 3 feet wide × 7 feet long (see Figure 2.7). The ceiling is 9 feet tall. There is one 30-inch-wide door that is 84 inches high. The existing paint color is light and similar in value to the color already on the walls and will take 1 coat of paint. Each gallon covers 350 square feet.

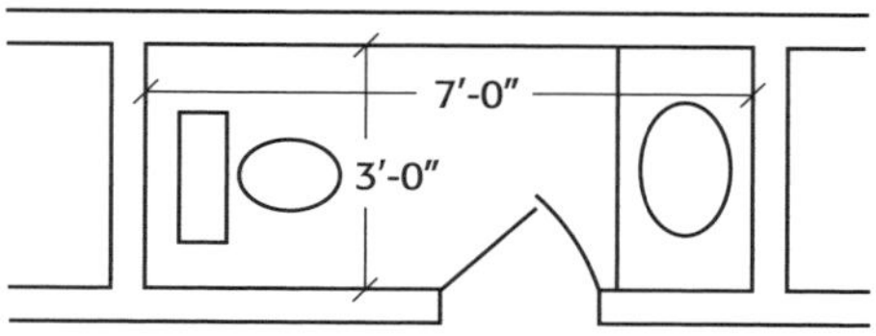

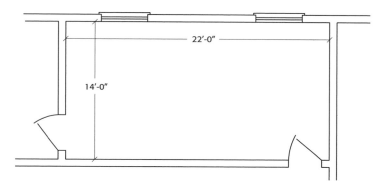

Figure 2.7 Practice lessons: Basic—Floor plan.

1. How many gallons of paint must be purchased to order to adequately cover the walls?

INTERMEDIATE

The bedroom she wants to paint is 22 feet wide × 14 feet long (see Figure 2.8). The ceiling is 9 feet tall. The room has two doors 36 inches wide × 84 inches tall. There are two windows. Each one is 44 inches wide × 66 inches long. Each gallon covers 350 square feet. A primer will be necessary. She is trying to decide between a light-colored paint and a medium-colored paint.

Figure 2.8 Practice lessons: Intermediate—Floor plan.

1. How many gallons of light-colored wall paint (needs 1 coat) are necessary to order to adequately cover the walls?
2. How many gallons of dark-colored wall paint (needs 2 coats) are necessary?
3. How many gallons of primer (needs 1 coat) are necessary to adequately cover the walls?

ADVANCED

The dining room is to be painted below the chair rail, which is at 3 feet. This room is 14 feet × 14 feet (see Figure 2.9). The ceiling is 9 feet tall. There are two cased openings 8 feet wide × 7 feet long. There is only one set of windows totaling 72 inches wide × 72 inches long (see Figure 2.10). Each gallon covers 350 square feet. A primer will be necessary.

1. How many gallons of medium-colored paint (2 coats) are necessary to order to adequately cover the walls below the chair rail?
2. How many gallons of dark-colored paint (2 coats) are necessary to order to adequately cover the walls above the chair rail?
3. What is the cost of the paint and primer? Use the following figures:

   Below chair rail—Medium-colored eggshell paint at $39.99 per gallon

   Above chair rail—Dark-colored eggshell paint at $47.99 per gallon

   Use 1 gallon of primer.

   Primer—$25.99 per gallon

4. Calculate the total cost of the job using the answer from 3 above, and labor as quoted by painting contractor—$1500.00

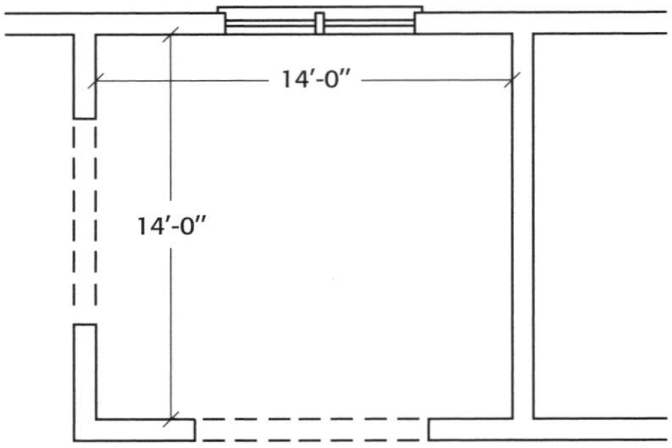

Figure 2.9 Practice lesson: Advanced—Floor plan.

Figure 2.10 Practice lesson: Advanced—Wall elevation.

References

Benjamin Moore: http://www.benjaminmoore.com.
Brook Nienstadt, personal interview.
Sherwin-Williams: http://www.sherwin-williams.com.

INSIGHT FROM THE FIELD

❝One tip I have for interior designers is to not rush the people working on the project. Designers need to discuss the time frame with the workers to ensure the project will be completed on time. Communication is very important. ❞

Armando Guerrero, *owner of AMG Painting, Round Rock, Texas*

Chapter 3 | Wallcoverings

Chapter Outline

Terminology

Bolt A continuous roll of wallcovering. Residential wallcoverings generally come in double-roll bolts 27 feet or 33 feet long. Commercial vinyl bolts are 54 inches wide and 30–35 yards long. Wallpapers imported directly from Europe are packaged and priced by the bolt. American wallpapers are priced by the single roll but packaged usually as a length of two single rolls in a bolt. (See Figure 3.1.)

Pattern repeat The dimension of a lengthwise or crosswise measurement of one design motif (pattern) to where that same design motif is again repeated. The longer the repeat, generally, the more paper needed to match the pattern.

Straight or horizontal repeat Repeat matches straight across. For example, when seen at the ceiling, every strip has the same pattern motif in the same spot. (See Figure 3.2.)

Drop match or half-drop repeat Repeat matches diagonally. For example, when seen at the ceiling, every other strip has the same pattern in the same spot. (See Figure 3.2.)

Random repeat Even though there may be a design, there is nothing to match because of the randomness of the pattern. Wallpaper installers should reverse-hang some wallcoverings such as grasscloth and some faux-look papers.

Reverse hang A technique used by wallpaper installers to ensure that wallcoverings with no repeats or random repeats have a uniform color and appearance. Sometimes during manufacturing the dyes and paints will be a little darker toward one side because the tension on the rollers may be off a little. This is more noticeable in paper with either no repeats or random repeats. Reverse hanging is accomplished by rotating every other strip cut from the bolt. For example, the top of the first strip is hung at the ceiling, the bottom of the second strip is hung at the ceiling, the top of the third strip is hung at the ceiling, and so on.

Roll A unit designation used to price wallpaper and to describe length of the roll. In the United States, wallpaper is priced and sold by the single roll but is commonly packaged by the double roll. A few wallcoverings, including custom wallcoverings, may be available by the triple roll. A triple roll allows for a longer length of paper that is very desirable for papering tall spaces, such as two-story entries. (See Figure 3.1.)

American-sized Wallcoverings that are approximately 27 inches or 28 inches wide and approximately 13.5 feet long per single roll (s/r).

Metric-sized (European-sized) Wallcoverings that are approximately 20–22 inches wide and approximately 16.5 feet long per single roll (s/r).

Sealer/primer A liquid applied to new or painted walls that seals the surface and helps create a smooth surface for papering.

Sizing A liquid that is painted on walls in preparation for wallpaper. Sizing makes it easier to apply wallpaper to the wall and provides something for the wallpaper paste to "grip" to and stay on the wall.

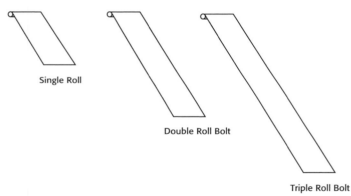

Single Roll

Double Roll Bolt

Triple Roll Bolt

Figure 3.1 Roll and bolt lengths.

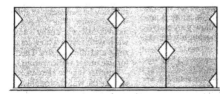

Straight Across Match
(Every strip is the same at the ceiling line)

Drop Match
(Every other strip is the same at the ceiling line.)

Figure 3.2 Straight and drop matches. (Paint & Decorating Retailers Association (1997). *Seabrook: How to Hang Wallcoverings*)

Types of Wallcoverings

The common types of wallcoverings are vinyl-coated, commercial vinyl, grasscloth, stringcloth, Mylar, and sand. Although there are other types, such as flocked and modular, these won't be discussed specifically.

Vinyl-coated papers, generally a residential type paper, differ from commercial vinyl in that vinyl-coated papers have a thin coating of vinyl on them for general protection and usually are too lightweight to use in commercial applications.

Commercial vinyl is a vinyl wallcovering that is used in commercial/contract settings. These wallcoverings have been tested and rated for flame spread and smoke. Class A wallcoverings have the best fire rating. Fabric-backed vinyl wallcoverings are also rated for use as either Type I (light duty) or Type II (medium duty). Generally, the class of wallcovering required for the commercial/contract setting is specified according to code.

Grasscloth and stringcloth are wallcoverings that have different types of grasses or strings adhered to the front of a paper backing. These papers traditionally came in 36-inch width; however, they can be found both American-sized and metric-sized today. Whenever there is a horizontal application of the grass or the string on the paper backing, seams *will* show. The customer needs to be aware of this when specifying this product. These papers are great to install on imperfect walls because the very nature of the grass and string texture will disguise the wall issues.

Mylar is a highly reflective polyester polymer used on a paper backing. Its reflective surface tends to show any imperfection in the wall on which it is installed. Sand has been used to create beautiful patterns in wallpaper. This paper tends to be stiffer. It generally shouldn't be used in areas like bathrooms where there is a lot of moisture in the air.

Sizes and Packaging of Wallcoverings

Written on the back cover of the wallcovering book and usually on the back of the wallcovering page within the book are the specifications for the wallcovering. These include width of the wallpaper, size of repeat if applicable, and yards per single roll. The width in feet times the length in feet equals the square feet per single roll. The width dimension can vary somewhat, but the wallpapers generally fall into four sizing categories: American-sized, metric-sized, grasscloth/stringcloth, and commercial vinyl (Table 3.1).

Cost Factors

Cost factors with wallcoverings include the wallcovering, labor (including wall preparation—sealing, priming, and sizing), and shipping (see Table 3.2). Following is a discussion of these factors in detail.

Wallcovering. The retail price of wallcoverings varies widely. Your cost will depend upon whether you purchase through a showroom, directly from the manufacturer, or with special pricing from the manufacturer because of purchasing commitments you have with that company.

Most metric, American, and grasscloth/stringcloth rolls are sold in double-roll bolts but *are always referred to and priced as single rolls.* Always round up the single rolls to an even number, since most (if not all) wallpaper companies will sell wallpaper only by the full bolt size. For example, if the room needs only 9 s/r, the client will order and pay for 10 s/r.

Commercial wallcoverings 54 inches wide are sold by the bolt and by the linear yard. If you order by the linear yard that is less than a bolt, it is considered cut yardage, and there is a cutting-per-yard charge when the full bolt isn't ordered.

	Width	Length	Square Feet	Priced	Packaged
Metric-Sized Roll	20–22 in.	16.5 ft. per single roll	Approximately 26.5 sq. ft. per single roll	By the single roll	In double-roll bolts
American-Sized Roll	27–28 in.	13.5 ft. per single roll	Approximately 30 sq. ft. per single roll	By the single roll	In double-roll bolts (sometimes triple-roll bolts)
Grasscloth and Stringcloth	36 in. (some are 20–28 in. wide)	13.5 ft. per single roll	40.5 sq. ft. per single roll	By the single roll	In double-roll bolts
Commercial Vinyl	54 in. (some are 20–28 in. wide)	Bolts are 30–35 linear yards long, but can be ordered by the cut yard	Approximately 13.5 sq. ft. per yard; approximately 472.5 sq. ft. per bolt	By the yard	By the yard

Note: Wallpapers imported directly from Europe are priced and sold by the bolt. This information can be found on the pricing page.

Table 3.1 Wallpaper Sizes and Packaging

Wallpaper Schedule												
Client:						Paper Hanger:						
Phone #s:												
Address:												
Material												
Room	Manufacturer/ Vendor	Pattern	Color	Width	Repeat	Qty.	Retail Per	Cost Per	Sub-total	Est. Ship.	Total	PO
										Material Subtotal	$	
Labor												
Room	Wall Prep	Sealing/Priming	Sizing	Paper Install	Vents	Covers	Scaffold Work	Hand Trim	Misc.		Total	WO
									Labor Subtotal		$	
Total (Material and Labor)											$	
Notes:												

Table 3.2 Wallpapering: Calculating Total Costs

Sometimes it is more economical to buy the whole bolt even when it is not needed. The additional material can be used for potential repairs.

Some manufacturers may take back unused and unopened wallpaper; however, fewer and fewer currently do this. If the manufacturer does accept returns, they must be returned within the required time frame from the invoice date, and the manufacturer will charge you a restocking fee.

Labor. Many wallpaper hangers charge by the number of single rolls ordered. In the example above, the client will pay for 10 s/r rolls to be installed instead of the 9 s/r needed. If you aren't hiring the wallpaper hanger for the job and will have the client hire the paperhanger directly, have

several paperhangers that you can refer if the client needs one. Currently, a paperhanger may charge $16 to $35 per single roll to hang depending on the type of paper and the complexity of the job. This per-single-roll charge will vary across the country, sometimes lower and sometimes higher. Commercial installers charge by the square foot—currently at approximately $1.00 to $2.50 per square foot, but again this will vary across the country. Any stripping or repair work is done on a bid basis. Most installers will also cover vents and wall plates for additional charges.

Wall preparation may be necessary. This includes sealing, priming, and sizing walls. New sheetrock or painted walls must be sealed and primed. All walls should be sized before wallpaper is hung. This makes the wallpaper easier to install and the removal much easier by allowing the wallpaper to release from the wall. Most installers will charge an additional amount that will include labor and material based on the number of single rolls.

Shipping. After the wallpaper is ordered, the length of time it takes to receive it will depend on whether it is in stock and where it is shipped from. Sometimes there are backorders whereby the wallpaper isn't in stock but is scheduled for production. The manufacturer will give the estimated date for shipping as the backorder date. It is important to get on the paperhanger's schedule. Sometimes it is necessary to get the wallpaper faster than regular shipping times allow. Overnight shipping and next-day shipping can be requested; however, this will add a significant amount to the shipping costs. It is up to the situation whether this is warranted.

Calculations

Methods

There are three common ways of calculating the quantity of wallcoverings: with a wallpaper book chart, the strip method, and the square footage method. The first method refers to a chart in the back of most wallpaper books that serves as a guide for how many single rolls are needed.

The strip method is used by most wallpaper hangers and many interior designers who become familiar with measuring wallcoverings. The strip method requires knowledge of how many strips of wallcoverings can be cut from a bolt. Once this is calculated, the perimeter of the room is determined and divided by the width of the wallcovering to determine the number of strips necessary. The number of strips necessary is then divided by the number of strips per bolt to find out how many bolts must be ordered. For a room with an 8-foot ceiling, only two or three strips of wallpaper will come from a double-roll bolt. This method can get a little complicated when there are multiple heights in the room, such as those found in bathrooms and kitchens.

The square footage method takes the perimeter of the room times the height to be covered to find the overall square feet. If the wallpaper has a repeat, the repeat must be factored into the height of the space to be covered before calculating the square footage of the area. Deductions will be made for openings in the space. Figure 3.3 shows how to calculate square footage for unusual areas. Any of these three methods can be used; however, for clarity in this chapter, the square footage method will be used.

Deductions

For European and American rolls, deduct only doors and windows 41 inches wide or wider. For

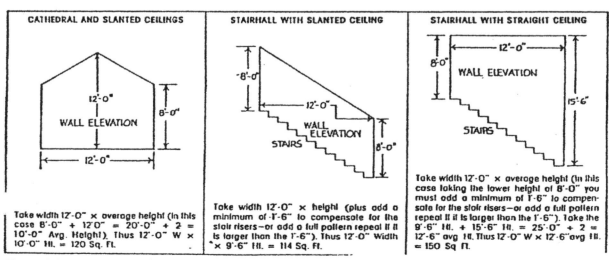

Figure 3.3 Measuring unusual areas for square footage. (Paint & Decorating Retailers Association (1997). *Seabrook: How to Hang Wallcoverings*)

commercial vinyl, the opening must be 108 inches or greater before deducting because of the 54-inch width of the paper.

After deductions are made, the final square footage is divided by the number of square feet in a single roll.

Square feet per single roll:

30 square feet = American

26.5 square feet = European

13.5 square feet = per linear yard for commercial 54-inch width paper

Estimating Wallpaper

Step 1. Find the total perimeter of the room or the width of the area to be papered. Add the width in feet of all walls to be papered. This may be one wall or more than four walls if the room has a lot of angles.

Step 2. To determine total square feet of the space, find the height of the area to be papered in feet. If there is a repeat, adjust the height to accommodate pattern matching.

Adjusting for pattern repeat. Divide the height to be covered by the height of the repeat. Usually, doing this will result in a fraction. To match repeats, it is necessary to have full repeats, so round this number up to a whole number to find the number of full repeats needed per cut. To determine the new length, multiply the number of

repeats by the height/length of the repeat. This is the new cut length/the adjusted cut length needed for the wallpaper repeat to be matched when it is installed. The adjusted cut length replaces the height in your calculations.

Multiply the perimeter of the room in feet by the height of the space to be covered or length of cut in feet. This will give you total square footage of the room.

Step 3. Determine square footage for any deductions. To find this number, if using metric-sized or American-sized wallpaper, add the width of all openings 41 inches wide or wider that are the same height together using feet increments, not inches. Multiply this total width by the height of the opening in feet to determine total square footage to be deducted. When calculating wallpaper in a kitchen, you can deduct cabinets from the overall total in this same manner.

Step 4. Determine total square footage for wallpaper. Take the total square footage of the room and deduct applicable square footage for doors and windows (or cabinets, Figure 3.4). This is the adjusted square feet needed for wallpaper.

Step 5. Take the adjusted square feet and divide by the amount of square feet in a single roll. If this number is a decimal or an odd number, round up to the nearest even number. This is the number of single rolls to be ordered.

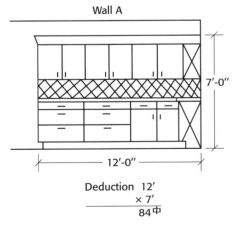

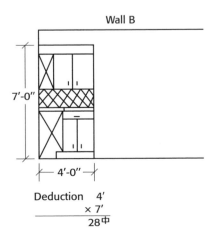

中 = Square Feet

Figure 3.4 Deducting square footage for cabinets.

Step-by-Step Examples

Example 1

Your client wants to wallpaper her guest room. The room is 12 feet × 9 feet with a ceiling height of 8 feet (see Figure 3.5). There are two 36-inch-wide doors and two 42-inch-wide windows that are each 66 inches long. The wallpaper is American-sized and has no repeat.

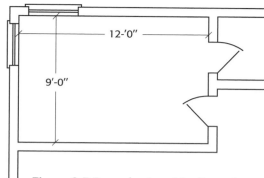

Figure 3.5 Examples 1 and 2—floor plan.

Step 1: Find perimeter of room in feet (e.g., 65.3 ft.).

Wall A:		12	ft.
Wall B:	+	12	ft.
Wall C:	+	9	ft.
Wall D:	+	9	ft.
Total perimeter:		42	ft.

Step 2: Find height of area.

Height of area to be wallpapered in feet:	8	ft.

Step 3: Determine base square feet of area.

Height, adjusted or otherwise, from Step 2:	8	ft.
Multiply by total perimeter from Step 1:	× 42	ft.
Total square feet:	336	sq. ft.

Step 4: Determine deductions.

Only deduct openings or cabinets 41 inches wide or wider.

Width of deduction in feet (e.g., 4 ft. for 48 in.):	7	ft. (42 in. ÷ 12 in. = 3.5 ft.; 3.5 ft. + 3.5 ft. for two windows)
Multiply by height of deduction in feet:	× 5.5	ft. (66 in. ÷ 12 in.)
Total square feet of deduction for windows:	38.5	sq. ft.

The doors are not 41 inches wide or wider, so they are not included in the deductions.

Step 5: Calculate adjusted square feet.

Take total square feet from Step 3:	336	sq. ft.
Subtract total square feet of openings from Step 4:	− 38.5	sq. ft.
Adjusted square feet of wallpaper:	297.5	sq. ft.

Step 6: Calculate number of rolls to be ordered.

Adjusted square feet of wallpaper from Step 5:	297.5	sq. ft.
Divide by square feet of single roll of wallpaper:	÷ 30	sq. ft.
Total number of single rolls:	9.92	s/r American-sized

Note: Most wallpaper sold today is packaged in double-roll bolts, so quantity must be an even number.

Round up to nearest even whole number: **10 total single rolls**

> **Using metric rolls:** 297.5 sq. ft. ÷ 26.5 sq. ft. = 11.23 s/r. Round this up to 12 s/r.
>
> **Using commercial roll bolts that are 35 linear yards:** 336 sq. ft. ÷ 472.5 sq. ft./bolt = .71 bolt. Round up to 1 bolt. **OR** 336 sq. ft. ÷ 13.5 sq. ft./yard = 24.88 yards. Round up to 25 linear yards.
>
> **Note:** The original square footage of the room is used, since the wallpaper is wider.

Box 3.1 Example 1—A Comparison with Other Types of Rolls

Example 2

Same room, but now she is considering a different wallpaper that has an 18-inch repeat and is metric-sized.

Step 1: Find perimeter of room in feet (e.g., 65.3 ft.).

Wall A:	12	ft.
Wall B:	+ 12	ft.
Wall C:	+ 9	ft.
Wall D:	+ 9	ft.
Total perimeter:	42	ft.

Step 2: Find height of area.

Height of area to be wallpapered in feet:	8	ft.
If the wallpaper has a repeat:		
Take the height of the area to be wallpapered:	8	ft.
Divide by the length of the repeat, in feet:	÷ 1.5	ft. (18 in. ÷ 12 in. = 1.5 ft.)
Note: Be sure to convert the repeat from inches to feet.		
Total number of repeats:	5.33	repeats
Round up to whole number:	6	repeats
Multiply by the length of the repeat:	× 1.5	ft.
This is the new adjusted height:	9	ft.

Step 3: Determine base square feet of area.

Height, adjusted or otherwise, from Step 2:	9	ft.
Multiply by total perimeter from Step 1:	× 42	ft.
Total square feet:	378	sq. ft.

Step 4: Determine deductions.

Only deduct openings or cabinets 41 inches wide or wider.

Width of deduction in feet (e.g., 4 ft. for 48 in.):	7	ft. (3.5 ft. + 3.5 ft. for two windows)
Multiply by height of deduction in feet:	× 5.5	ft. (66 in. ÷ 12 in.)
Total square feet of deduction:	38.5	sq. ft. for windows

The doors are not 41 inches wide or wider, so they are not included in the deductions.

Step 5: Calculate adjusted square feet.

Take total square feet from Step 3:	378	sq. ft.
Subtract total square feet of openings from Step 4:	− 38.5	sq. ft.
Adjusted square feet of wallpaper:	339.5	sq. ft.

Step 6: Calculate number of rolls to be ordered.

Adjusted square feet of wallpaper from Step 5:	339.5	sq. ft.
Divide by square feet of single roll of wallpaper:	÷ 26.5	sq. ft.
Total number of single rolls:	12.81	s/r metric-sized

Note: Most wallpaper sold today is packaged in double-roll bolts, so quantity must be an even number.

Round up to nearest even whole number:	**14**	**total single rolls**

Using American rolls: 339.5 sq. ft. ÷ 30 sq. ft. = 11.32 s/r. Round this up to 12 s/r.

Using commercial roll: 378 sq. ft. divided by 13.5 sq. ft. = 28 yards.

Box 3.2 Example 2—A Comparison with Other Types of Rolls

Manual Worksheet

Wallcovering—Square Footage Method Worksheet

Step 1: Find perimeter of room in feet (e.g., 65.3 ft.).

Wall A:	_____	ft.
Wall B:	+_____	ft.
Wall C:	+_____	ft.
Wall D:	+_____	ft.
Wall E:	+_____	ft. *Continue adding walls as necessary.*
Total perimeter:	_____	**ft.**

Step 2: Find height of area.

Height of the area to be wallpapered:	_____	**ft.**

If the wallpaper has a repeat:

Take the height of the area to be wallpapered:	_____	ft.
Divide by the length of the repeat in feet:	÷_____	ft. (**Important:** convert inches to feet)
Total number of repeats:	_____	**repeats**
Round up to whole number:	_____	**full repeats**
Multiply by length of the repeat:	×_____	ft.
This is the new adjusted height:	_____	**ft.**

For a drop match repeat:

Take the new adjusted height and add ½ the repeat back to it. For example, if the repeat is 18 inches, after finding the new adjusted height, add 9 inches to the total.

If drop match, add ½ the length of the repeat:	+_____	ft.
New total height for paper with drop match:	+_____	**ft.**

Step 3: Determine base square feet of area.

Height, adjusted or otherwise, from Step 2:	_____	ft.
Multiply by total perimeter from Step 1:	×_____	ft.
Total square feet:	_____	**sq. ft.**

Step 4: Determine deductions.

Only deduct openings or cabinets 41 inches wide or wider.

Width of deduction in feet (e.g., 4 ft. for 48 in.):	_____	ft.
Multiply by height of deduction in feet:	×_____	ft.
Total square feet of deduction:	_____	**sq. ft.**

Repeat this process for however many openings or cabinets are 41 inches or wider.

Note: Multiple areas that are the same height may be added together before multiplying by the height. Do not use entire height of door, window, or cabinet when only a portion of the wall is being papered (as in above or below a chair rail).

Step 5: Calculate total adjusted square feet.

Take total square feet from Step 3:	_____	sq. ft.
Subtract total square feet of openings from Step 4:	−_____	sq. ft.
Total adjusted square feet of wallpaper:	_____	**sq. ft.**

Step 6: Calculate number of rolls to be ordered.

Adjusted square feet of wallpaper from Step 5:	_____	sq. ft.
Divide by square feet of single roll of wallpaper:	÷_____	sq. ft.

- 27–28 in. wide—American-sized roll is 30 square feet per single roll.
- 20–22 in. wide—European/metric-sized roll is 26.5 square feet per single roll.
- 54 in. wide—Commercial roll has approximately 13.5 square feet per yard.

Total number of single rolls (or yards):	_____	**s/r (or yds.)**

Note: Most wallpaper sold today is packaged in double-roll bolts, so quantity must be an even number.

Round up to nearest even whole number:	_____	**total single rolls (or yards)**

Practice Lessons: Wallcoverings

BASIC

Your client wants to wallpaper her powder room that is 3 feet wide × 7 feet long (see Figure 3.6). The ceiling is 9 feet tall. There is one 30-inch door that is 84 inches high. The wallpaper is metric-sized with a 15-inch straight match repeat.

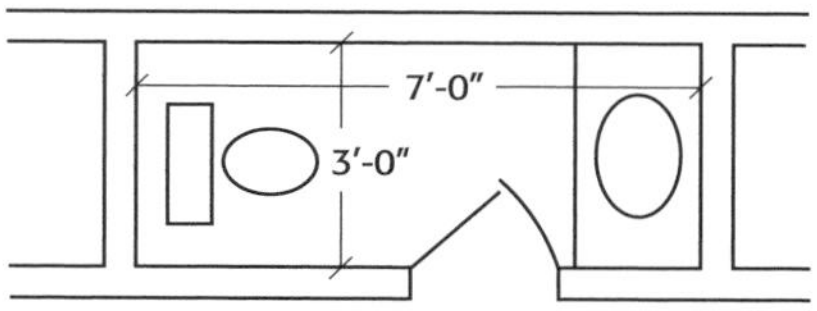

1. What is the total perimeter of the room?
2. What is the amount of square footage to be deducted for openings?
3. How many single rolls of wallpaper will be ordered?

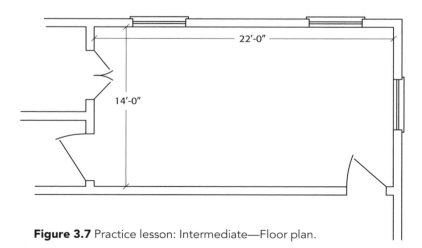

Figure 3.6 Practice lesson: Basic—Floor plan.

INTERMEDIATE

Another client wants to wallpaper a bedroom that is 14 feet wide × 22 feet long (see Figure 3.7). The ceiling is 9 feet tall. It has two doors 36 inches wide × 84 inches tall and one door 48 inches wide × 84 inches tall. Each of the three windows is 44 inches wide × 66 inches long. This wallpaper is American-sized with a 21-inch straight match. It retails at $45.95. The paperhanger will charge the client $30 per single roll to hang the wallpaper and $5 per single roll to size the walls. You will give your client a 20 percent discount on the wallpaper and charge shipping and handling based on $1.00 per single roll.

1. What is the total perimeter of the room?
2. What is the adjusted cut length of the wallpaper?
3. What is the amount of square footage to be deducted for openings?
4. How many single rolls of wallpaper will be ordered?
5. What is the single roll price the client will pay for the wallpaper (disregard shipping)?
6. What is the total for shipping and handling?
7. How much will be charged for labor/installation?
8. What is the total price, including material, labor, and shipping and handling (disregarding sales tax), the client will pay?

Figure 3.7 Practice lesson: Intermediate—Floor plan.

ADVANCED

A lawyers' office has initially contracted you to protect some of its halls with a heavy-duty, fire-rated wallpaper. The hall has a 9-foot ceiling, 4-foot-wide cased openings, and 3-foot-wide doors. See Figure 3.8 for the hall configuration and dimensions. Commercial 54-inch-wide wallpaper has been specified. This wallpaper has a 20.5-inch drop match repeat. The wallpaper retails at $18.95 per yard.

1. What is the total perimeter of the room?
2. What is the adjusted cut length of the wallpaper?
3. What is the amount of square footage to be deducted for openings?
4. How many yards of wallpaper will be ordered?
5. What is the total retail price (disregard shipping) for the wallpaper material?

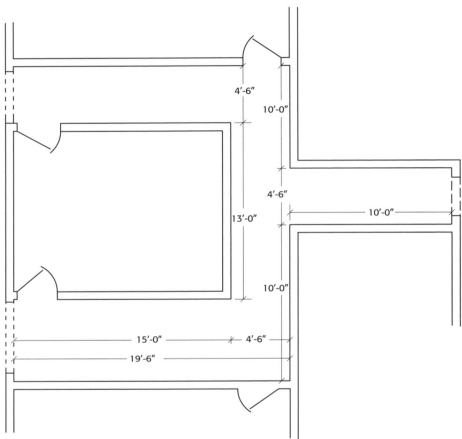

Figure 3.8 Practice lesson: Advanced—Floor plan.

Reference

Paint & Decorating Retailers Association. *Seabrook: How to Hang Wallcoverings, 1997.*

INSIGHT FROM THE FIELD

❝ Sizing is a must. A lot of people try to short cut that, but it is what allows the wallpaper to go up smoothly and to come down without destroying walls. But beyond sizing, the most important thing is to read the directions that come with the wallpaper. Each different type of wallpaper will have a different set of directions. If the specifications found in the directions aren't followed, you will be paying for and redoing that project. For example, if there is a problem such as wallpaper ink reacting to the sizing, the manufacturer has no liability or responsibility if the directions aren't followed. ❞

Janie Gilbert, *retired paper installer*

Chapter 4 | Other Wall Materials

This chapter focuses on paneling and wall tile, such as those found in kitchen backsplashes, bath walls, and other vertical placements. Vertical wall application of these materials isn't very different from floor application; however, there are enough differences for them to be discussed separately.

Chapter Outline

Terminology

Other Types of Wall Materials
Wall Tile
Paneling

Sizes and Packaging
Wall Tile
Paneling

Cost Factors
Wall Tile
Paneling

Calculations
Wall Tile
Paneling

Step-by-Step Examples
Example 1—Wall Tile
Example 2—Paneling

Manual Worksheets
Wall Tile Worksheet
Paneling Worksheet
Trim and Accent Worksheet

Practice Lessons
Basic
Wall Tile
Paneling
Intermediate
Wall Tile
Paneling
Advanced
Wall Tile
Paneling
Pricing of Wall Tile

References

Terminology

Accent tile Tile used to provide a decorative accent. This can be regular tile cut and placed to add a decorative element. Sometimes these are small pieces, and sometimes they are rectangular pieces, such as listello. They might be sold by the square foot or by the piece (see Figure 4.1).

Figure 4.2 Bullnose tile is finished on at least one side so that the raw edge of a tile is not seen. It provides a finished look. (Creative Commons)

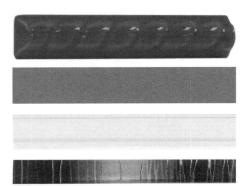

Figure 4.1 Accent tile comes in many shapes and sizes. (Courtesy of Dal-Tile Corporation)

Allowance Additional amount of material added to base calculations to allow for any pattern and waste from cutting the material.

Backsplash The vertical space above a countertop. In kitchens the upper limit of the backsplash is often defined by the upper cabinets.

Box/carton Most paneling and wall tile are priced by the square foot but sold by the full box or carton. Once the square footage needed for the material is calculated, this amount is divided by the square footage found in a box/carton. The subsequent number is rounded up to a whole number to give the actual number of boxes/cartons to be ordered.

Bullnose tile Tile trim piece that has a rounded edge to the side that is open to the wall. This provides a finished look (see Figure 4.2). When wall tile is used that doesn't have bullnose (commonly using floor tile for wall tile), sometimes you can find a local company that will create a bullnose to the tile.

Field tile The tile that covers the main portion of the wall. It normally refers to basic, unadorned tile that is used for wall surfaces.

Freight The cost of shipping. This cost may be factored into the price of material. Sometimes freight companies will add fuel surcharges that will increase this amount.

Grout A thin mortar used to fill the spacing between tiles. The size of this space factors directly into the amount of grout needed. Grout used for wall tile is not sanded.

Haul-off Term used to describe the removal of existing materials from the job site. This is usually an amount charged to the client—the haul-off fee.

Labor The cost per square foot of installing the material. This will include additional items such as staggered, diagonal, and herringbone design; accent pieces; moving large items such as refrigerators; pulling up toilets; and haul-off.

Listello Decorative tile border.

Minimums As this relates to labor, installers have a minimum charge for going to a job site to measure or install. As this relates to freight, there is a minimum charge to ship anything. If the amount shipped doesn't meet the minimum, the minimum charge is billed. As this relates to material, at times, there is a minimum amount of product that must be ordered. This depends on the manufacturer.

Out corner tile Tile trim piece that is bullnosed on two sides in order to provide a finished corner (see Figures 4.3 and 4.4).

Square foot Obtained by multiplying, in feet measurement, width times length (see Figure 4.5). Tile and panel goods are normally calculated, ordered, and priced by the square foot.

Thinset adhesive— A thin coating of mortar used to adhere tile to walls and floors, creating a strong adhesion.

Trim pieces Coordinating pieces that provide accent and or finished edges for paneling and tile. In wall tile they include items such as bullnose; in paneling they include quarter rounds and half rounds (see Figure 4.6).

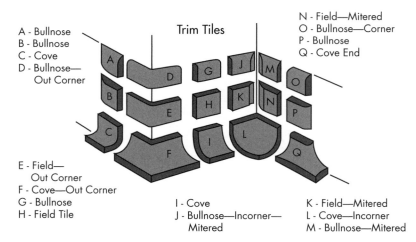

Figure 4.3 Especially when tile is exposed on the wall, as in an out corner, special bullnoses are made to accommodate and finish the look. (Source: Godsey, L. *Interior Design Materials and Specifications*. New York: Fairchild Publishing, 2008.)

Figure 4.4 The out corner bullnose tile is finished on two sides to finish the exposed edges of an out corner. (HeathCeramics.com)

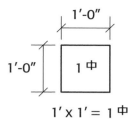

$$1' \times 1' = 1 \, 中$$

Figure 4.5 Square foot is obtained by multiplying feet times feet. If inches are multiplied by inches, the total must be divided by 144 square inches to obtain 1 square foot.

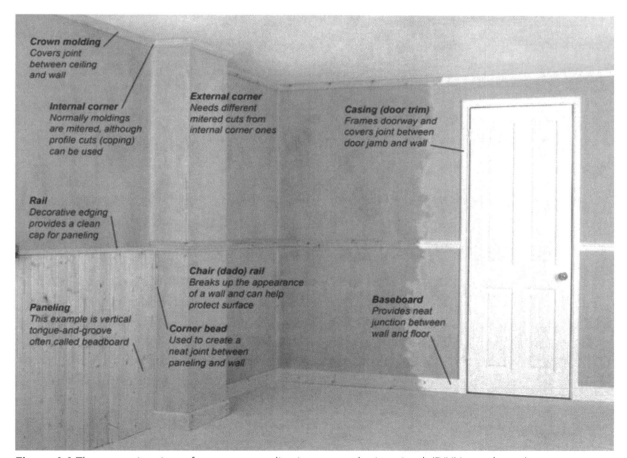

Crown molding
Covers joint between ceiling and wall

Internal corner
Normally moldings are mitered, although profile cuts (coping) can be used

External corner
Needs different mitered cuts from internal corner ones

Casing (door trim)
Frames doorway and covers joint between door jamb and wall

Rail
Decorative edging provides a clean cap for paneling

Chair (dado) rail
Breaks up the appearance of a wall and can help protect surface

Baseboard
Provides neat junction between wall and floor

Paneling
This example is vertical tongue-and-groove often called beadboard

Corner bead
Used to create a neat joint between paneling and wall

Figure 4.6 There are trim pieces for as many applications as can be imagined. (DIYNetwork.com)

Other Types of Wall Materials

Wall Tile

Wall tile can be made of natural and baked materials of innumerable shapes and sizes. Natural materials include granite, marble, slate, limestone, travertine, and sandstone, and baked materials include brick, quarry, Saltillo, ceramic, and porcelain. Wall tile is often thinner than floor tile and is not used for flooring; however, floor tile can be put on the wall. There are many accent pieces that are made to add the "jewelry" effect to these vertical surfaces (see Figure 4.7). Wall tile generally exists within our eye level and can emphasize focal areas in rooms such as bathrooms and kitchens. It can also be used to enhance other focal points, such as fireplaces.

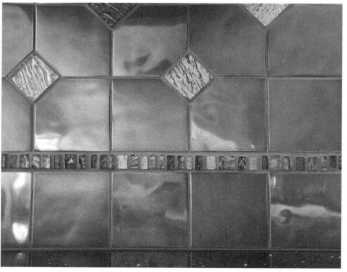

Figure 4.7 Some accent pieces are intended to be used just like jewelry, to enhance and draw attention. (Top: Courtesy of Diana Allison; bottom: LightStreamGlassTile.com)

INSIGHT FROM THE FIELD

"A shower has many components in a tile installation that are not required in a standard floor installation. If water is involved, hire a very qualified tile contractor. This will make all the difference in having a smooth installation and customer satisfaction in the end."

Steven M. Smith, *Owner, Custom Tile of Austin, Austin, Texas*

In vertical applications of wall tile, items such as light switches and electrical outlets in kitchens and shower heads and control fixtures in showers and tubs have an impact on the overall tile design. These items can be moved up and down and be placed vertically or horizontally. There are even electrical strips that can be placed directly under the upper cabinets that will leave the backsplash clear of electrical outlets. It is important to draw elevations of special tile designs in order to plan for these essential elements.

Bullnoses allow for a finished edge where the tile meets the wall. If the tile used doesn't have bullnose options, local companies can create these pieces from any tile whose color goes all the way through the tile, such as granite, marble, limestone, travertine, slate, and porcelain. Beginning interior designers sometimes forget these essential pieces when they are pricing wall tile.

Paneling

Paneling is traditionally known as thin sheets of wood used on vertical surfaces. It can be applied floor to ceiling or any height between. Some new products come in panels, and although not the same as wood, they can be calculated in the same manner. MDF board simulates wood for areas that are intended to be painted. As with tile, there are many different trim pieces that are used to create a beautiful, finished product. Crown and cove molding, chair rail, base cap, baseboard, quarter round, panel mold, picture rail, and corner blocks are a few of the trim pieces available to finish and enhance molding. It is common to see elevation drawings that detail the elements of a paneled room (see Figure 4.6).

Sizes and Packaging

Wall Tile

Tile comes in many sizes, from 1 inch × 1 inch (which is usually found in 12-inch × 12-inch sheets with mesh backing) to 18 inch × 18 inch or larger. It comes in squares, rectangles, octagons, and many other shapes. The accent and trim pieces also come in so many sizes and shapes that they can't be defined. The design of anything involving tile is unlimited! Basic wall tile, usually called field tile, normally comes packaged in boxes/cartons; however, there are many exceptions to this. Trim pieces and accent pieces are often priced individually and can be ordered individually.

Paneling

As with tile, paneling comes in many sizes. It may be planks, such as tongue and groove, or sheets (Figure 4.8). As a standard, strips/planks come 3½ inches wide in 32-inch, 6-foot, and 8-foot lengths. Some companies make planks that are 1 foot wide × 6 feet or 8 feet long. Some companies, such as Elmwood Reclaimed Lumber, carry planks from 3 inches to 12 inches wide and 2 feet to 12 feet long. Standard sheet size is 4 feet × 8 feet. Wainscoting and bead board, to be used up to a chair rail height, are 3 feet tall × 8 feet long. Most paneling can be purchased by the strip/plank, sheet, or trim piece. Trim pieces are normally sold by the length of the pieces.

Cost Factors

Cost factors for wall tile and paneling are very similar (Table 4.1). Regionally, there are differences regarding what the installers provide on the job.

Wall Tile

Wall tile is sold by the square foot and often by the full box. Accent and trim pieces, such as out corners, bullnoses, decorative rails, and decorative tiles, are often priced individually. Grout has a significant impact on the look of the tile and must be selected

Figure 4.8 There are several types of wall paneling, from planks, used to create tongue and groove, to larger panels, which create a paneled look. (Top: Ehow.com; bottom: iStockphoto/© Soubrette)

Wall Tile	Paneling
Material	Material
Trim pieces* (bullnose, out corners, accents, etc.)	Trim pieces* (base, chair rail, crown molding, picture rail, quarter round, half round, etc.)
Installation**	Staining or painting
Mastic	Installation**
Grout	Shipping*
Sealant*	
Shipping*	
*If necessary/applicable.	
**Installation cost is more than base cost when you are using intricate patterns.	

Table 4.1 Costs Involved with Wall Tile and Paneling

carefully. Installers must be consulted to determine if their labor charge will include mastic and grout. If sealant is to be used, ask whether they provide it or you need to provide it.

Paneling

Paneling is sold by the panel or by the square foot and must be calculated for full panels. Most paneling can be purchased as full sheets or planks and doesn't require full boxes or cartons to be purchased. The price of the paneling is determined by the type of wood or product used, how much detail there is, the finishing of the paneling, and the trim pieces needed to finish the look. Bear in mind that the person who installs the paneling may not be the person who finishes the paneling if it requires staining or painting. You may have a finish carpenter and a painter involved with this type of wall treatment. Trim pieces are usually sold by the linear foot of full pieces.

Calculations

Wall Tile

More tile must be allowed than the actual square footage of the space. When tile is installed, normally, pieces must be cut, creating waste. If there is a pattern, such as staggered placement for subway tile or diagonal placement, additional tile must be calculated because of the waste caused by the pattern. Regular, "straight" lay and staggered lay will require 10 percent additional tile. Diagonal placement will require 15 percent more tile. When calculating wall tile, find the square feet, and then determine how much more must be added for patterning and basic waste. The steps are as follows:

1. Calculate the base square footage. By multiplying width and height in feet, you can find square feet. If you are multiplying inches by inches, divide by 144 square inches to find square feet.
2. Add an additional 10 to 15 percent to the base amount, allowing for waste from cutting, to find total square feet needed for installation.

3. Determine how many full boxes/cartons are necessary if the product is sold by the full box/carton. Take the total square feet needed and divide by the number of square feet in a full carton. Round up to a whole number to determine how many full cartons must be ordered.
4. Determine how many total square feet the client will pay for based on the number of full cartons. Take the number of cartons, and multiply by the number of square feet in the carton. This is the total square feet to charge the client.

After you have determined the square feet for the base tile, calculate the number of trim or accent pieces that will be necessary. Bullnoses are needed where the tile edge is exposed on a wall. For example, if a backsplash is tiled from the counter to the upper cabinets, there is no exposed tile edge at the top or the bottom. However, the sides of the tile may require bullnose (Figure 4.9).

To calculate for bullnose or other accent pieces, add the linear feet together to find the total needed. Divide this number by the length of the trim or bullnose and round up to the nearest whole number. This will be the number of full pieces needed. Some designers will add several more pieces to this amount to allow for waste from cutting. This is something to carefully consider should the trim piece be expensive. Some trim pieces are in excess of $50 each. Calculating the number of out corners is usually just a matter of counting the number of exposed corners.

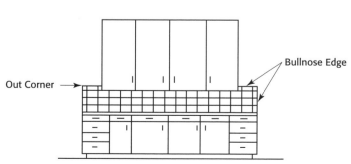

Figure 4.9 Backsplashes with exposed edges require bullnoses to finish the edge.

Paneling

Just as with wall tile, more paneling needs to be calculated than the actual square feet of space to allow for waste from cutting the product. An additional 10 percent is usually all that is required. The size of paneling material usually makes it unnecessary to deduct for door and window openings when estimating material.

1. Calculate the perimeter of the room.
2. Add an additional 10 percent to the base amount, allowing for waste from cutting, to find the total perimeter with waste allowance.
3. Calculate the total number of panels by dividing the total perimeter by the width of the panel.

Round up to a whole number to determine how many full panels must be ordered.

4. If the paneling is sold by the square foot, determine how many total square feet the client will pay for based on the number of panels. Take the number of panels, and multiply by the number of square feet in each panel. This is the total square feet to charge the client.

Trim pieces, such as baseboards, chair rails, and so on, are calculated the same way that wall tile is. Usually the trim pieces are 6- to 8-foot-long pieces instead of 4- or 6-inch for tile, but the process is exactly the same.

Step-by-Step Examples

Example 1—Wall Tile

You have selected tile for a one-wall butler's pantry (Figure 4.10). The space is 9 feet long and 1 foot 6 inches tall, and the tile will be laid straight. There are 4 inches of tile exposed beyond the cabinetry on both sides (included in the 9-foot length). The tile is a basic 6-inch × 6-inch field tile with 2-inch × 6-inch bullnose and 2-inch × 2-inch out corners. There are 10.01 square feet of field tile in a box.

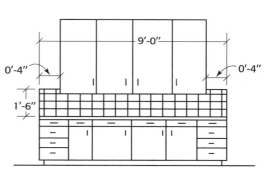

Figure 4.10 Example 1—wall tile.

The wall tile is calculated first.

Step 1: Calculate the base square footage of space.

Take width of area in feet:	9	ft.
Multiply by height of area in feet:	× 1.5	ft.
Total base square footage:	13.5	sq. ft.

Step 2: Calculate additional materials for waste allowance.

For wall tile laid straight:

Take square footage from Step 1:	13.5	sq. ft.
Multiply by 10 percent to allow for waste:	× 1.10	waste allowance
Total square footage needed:	14.85	sq. ft.

If tile material is sold by the full box/carton, proceed to Step 4 to determine amount needed.

Step 3: Calculate the number of full boxes/cartons to be ordered.

Take square footage needed from Step 2:	14.85	sq. ft.
Divide by square footage per box/carton:	÷ 10.01	sq. ft.
Equals total boxes/cartons needed:	1.48	boxes/cartons
Round up to whole number:	**2**	**full boxes/cartons to order**

Step 4: Calculate square feet in boxes/cartons ordered to calculate pricing to client for material.

Take number of boxes from Step 3:	2	boxes/cartons
Multiply by square feet per box/carton:	× 10.01	sq. ft.
Total square footage ordered:	**20.02**	**sq. ft.**

The installer will bill for 14.85 square feet of labor; however, the client will pay for 20.02 square feet of tile, since this is how it is packaged.

Next, calculate for the bullnose and the out corners. There are only two exposed corners, so you need to order only two out corners. For the bullnose, the exposed length and the height are added together and then the number of pieces is calculated.

Step 1: Calculate total length of accent or trim needed.

Add length of trim needed:	.33	ft.

Note: Convert the 4 inches into feet by dividing by 12 inches.

Add additional lengths:	+	.33	ft.
Add additional lengths:	+	1.5	ft.
Add additional lengths:	+	1.5	ft.
Total length needed for accent or trim:		3.66	ft.

Step 2: Deduct for openings.

This step is not needed, so we proceed to Step 3.

Step 3: Calculate the total number of pieces of trim to be ordered.

Take total from Step 1:	3.66	ft.
Divide by length of accent/trim piece:	÷ .5	ft.
Equals pieces of trim needed:	7.32	pieces
Round up to whole number:	**8**	**full pieces**

Step 4: Calculate total length to be ordered.

The trim is sold by the piece, so this step is not needed.

Example 2—Paneling

Your client is interested in changing a dining room into a library/study area and wants to panel it to give it more character. The room is 14 feet × 16 feet with two openings and a window (Figure 4.11). The openings are 7 feet tall; one is 2 feet 6 inches wide and one is 8 feet 6 inches wide. The ceiling is 9 feet tall. The window is 5 feet wide × 6 feet tall. Base and crown molding will finish the look. The paneling is prefinished tongue and groove 4-foot-wide × 10-foot-panels, which are sold by the square foot. The crown and base come in 8-foot lengths.

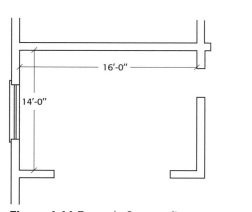

Figure 4.11 Example 2—paneling.

Step 1: Find perimeter of room in feet (e.g., 65.3).

Wall A:		14	ft.
Wall B:	+	14	ft.
Wall C:	+	16	ft.
Wall D:	+	16	ft.
Total perimeter:		60	ft.

Step 2: Calculate additional materials for waste allowance.

Total from Step 1:	60	ft.
Multiply by 10 percent to allow for waste:	× 1.10	waste allowance
Total perimeter needed:	66	ft.

Step 3: Calculate total number of panels to be ordered.

Take total from Step 2:	66	ft.
Divide by width of panel:	÷ 4	ft.
Total:	16.5	panels
Round up to whole number:	**17**	**full panels**

If items are sold by the piece, stop here. If items are sold by the square foot, continue to Step 4.

Step 4: Calculate square feet in panels ordered to calculate pricing to client for material.

Take number of panels from Step 3:	17	panels
Multiply by square feet per panel:	× 40	sq. ft.

4-ft. wide × 10-ft. long panel = 40 sq. ft. per panel.

Total square footage ordered:	**680**	**sq. ft.**

Next, the crown and base need to be calculated. The crown is determined by the width and length of the room. The base is calculated the same way, but the doorways are deducted from the total, since the base is not needed there. The base does exist under the window at the floor, so that dimension will not be deducted.

Calculate the crown first.

Step 1: Calculate total length of accent or trim needed.

Add length of trim needed:		14	ft.
Add additional lengths:	+	14	ft.
Add additional lengths:	+	16	ft.
Add additional lengths:	+	16	ft.
Total length needed for accent or trim:		60	ft.

Step 2: Deduct for openings. If this step is not needed, skip to Step 3.

There are no deductions for the crown, but there will be for the base. This step is skipped for now.

Step 3: Calculate total number of pieces of trim to be ordered.

Take total from Step 1 or Step 2:	60	ft.
Divide by length of accent/trim piece:	÷ 8	ft.
Total pieces of trim needed:	7.5	pieces
Round up to whole number:	8	full pieces

If items are sold by the piece, stop here. If items are sold by the foot, continue to Step 4.

Step 4: Calculate total length to be ordered.

Take total from Step 3:	8	pieces
Multiply by actual length of pieces:	× 8	ft.
Total feet actually ordered:	**64**	**ft.**

Next, calculate the base: Start with the total from Step 1 in which the crown was calculated.

Step 1: Calculate total length of accent or trim needed.

Total length needed for accent or trim:	60	ft.

Step 2: Deduct for openings. If this step is not needed, skip to Step 3.

Total length from Step 1:	60	ft.
Subtract opening:	− 2.5	ft.
Continue to subtract as needed:	− 8.5	ft.
Total adjusted length:	49	ft.

Step 3: Calculate total number of pieces of trim to be ordered.

Take total from Step 1 or Step 2:	49	ft.
Divide by length of accent/trim piece:	÷ 8	ft.
Total pieces of trim needed:	6.125	pieces
Round up to whole number:	7	full pieces

If items are sold by the piece, stop here. If items are sold by the foot, continue to Step 4.

Step 4: Calculate total length to be ordered.

Take total from Step 3:	7	pieces
Multiply by actual length of pieces:	× 8	ft.
Total feet actually ordered:	**56**	**ft.**

Materials to be ordered for this library include 680 square feet of paneling (17 panels), 64 linear feet of crown molding (8 pieces), and 56 linear feet of base molding (7 pieces).

Manual Worksheets

Wall Tile Worksheet

Step 1: Calculate base square footage of space.

Take width of area in feet:	_____	ft.
Multiply by height of area in feet:	× _____	ft.
Total base square footage:	_____	**sq. ft.**

Step 2: Calculate additional materials for waste allowance.

For wall tile laid straight:

Take square footage from Step 1:	_____	sq. ft.
Multiply by 10 percent to allow for waste:	× ____1.10____	waste allowance
Total square footage needed:	_____	**sq. ft.**

For wall tile laid diagonally and staggered:

Take square footage from Step 1:	_____	sq. ft.
Multiply by 15 percent to allow for waste:	× ____1.15____	waste allowance
Total square footage needed:	_____	**sq. ft.**

If tile material is sold by the full box/carton, proceed to Step 3 to determine amount needed.

Step 3: Calculate number of full boxes/cartons to be ordered.

Take square footage needed from Step 2:	_____	sq. ft.
Divide by square footage per box/carton:	÷ _____	sq. ft.
Total boxes/cartons needed:	_____	**boxes/cartons**
Round up to whole number:	_____	**full boxes/cartons to be ordered**

Step 4: Calculate square feet in boxes/cartons ordered to calculate pricing to client for material.

Take number of boxes/cartons from Step 3:	_____	boxes/cartons
Multiply by square feet per box/carton:	× _____	sq. ft.
Total square footage ordered:	_____	**sq. ft.**

Paneling Worksheet

Step 1: Find perimeter of room in feet (e.g., 65.3 ft.).

Wall A:	_____	ft.
Wall B: +	_____	ft.
Wall C: +	_____	ft.
Wall D: +	_____	ft.
Wall E: +	_____	ft. *Continue adding walls as necessary.*
Total perimeter:	_____	**ft.**

Step 2: Calculate additional materials for waste allowance.

Total from Step 1:	_____	ft.
Multiply by 10 percent to allow for waste: ×	1.10	waste allowance
Total perimeter needed:	_____	**ft.**

Step 3: Calculate total number of panels to be ordered.

Take total from Step 2:	_____	ft.
Divide by width of panel: ÷	_____	ft.
Total panels needed:	_____	**panels**
Round up to whole number:	_____	**full panels to be ordered**

If items are sold by the piece, stop here. If items are sold by the square foot, continue to Step 4.

Step 4: Calculate square feet in panels ordered to calculate pricing to client for material.

Take number of panels from Step 3:	_____	panels
Multiply by square feet per panel: ×	_____	sq. ft.
Total square footage ordered:	_____	**sq. ft.**

Accent and Trim Worksheet

Step 1: Calculate total length of accent or trim needed.

Add length of trim needed:	_____	ft.
Add additional lengths:	+ _____	ft.
Add additional lengths:	+ _____	ft.
Add additional lengths:	+ _____	ft.
Add additional lengths:	+ _____	ft.
Total length needed for trim:	_____	ft.

If there are more lengths to add, continue to do so to achieve the total length needed.

Step 2: Deduct for openings. If this step is not needed, skip to Step 3.

Total length from Step 1:	_____	ft.
Subtract opening:	– _____	ft.
Continue to subtract as needed:	– _____	ft.
Continue to subtract as needed:	– _____	ft.
Total adjusted length:	_____	**ft.**

Step 3: Calculate total number of pieces of trim to be ordered.

Take total from Step 1 or Step 2:	_____	ft.
Divide by length of accent/trim piece:	÷ _____	ft.
Total pieces of trim needed:	_____	**pieces**
Round up to whole number:	_____	**full pieces to be ordered**

If items are sold by the piece, stop here. If items are sold by the foot, continue to Step 4.

Step 4: Calculate total length to be ordered.

Take total from Step 3:	_____	number of pieces
Multiply by actual length of pieces:	× _____	ft.
Total feet actually ordered:	_____	**ft.**

Note: Some trim pieces, such as out corners, can be manually counted and calculated.

Practice Lessons: Other Wall Materials

BASIC
Wall Tile

Your client has added small 3-foot × 3-foot × 7-foot-tall shower walls in a laundry area off the garage (Figure 4.12). You have specified a basic 4¼-inch × 4¼-inch field tile, 2-inch × 6-inch bullnose, and 2-inch × 2-inch out corners. The field tile is sold and packaged 12.5 square feet per box. The bullnose and out corners are sold by the piece.

1. What is the base square footage of the shower?
2. What is the total square footage needed, including waste allowance, to ensure coverage?
3. How many boxes/cartons must be ordered, and what is the total square footage that must be ordered?
4. How many out corners are needed?
5. How many pieces of bullnose are needed?

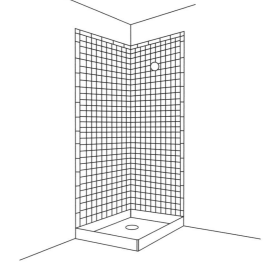

Figure 4.12 Practice lesson: Basic—Wall tile.

Paneling

In your client's breakfast area, you are adding bead board between the existing chair rail and baseboard (Figure 4.13). The space to be covered is 30 inches, so bead board paneling that is 8 feet wide × 4 feet tall (32 square feet) can be used. This paneling is sold by the full panel but priced by the square foot.

1. What is the perimeter after calculating for waste?
2. How many full panels are needed?
3. How many square feet must be ordered?

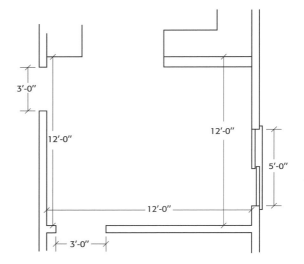

INTERMEDIATE
Wall Tile

You are using a 12-inch × 12-inch tile on the diagonal for an L-shaped kitchen in a corporate office (Figure 4.14). Each leg of the L is 10 feet. The backsplash is 18 inches (1.5 feet) tall. Although a window encroaches into the tile over the sink, this will be ignored, as it is not very large and the tile is large. The 2-inch × 6-inch bullnose starts at the countertop and ends at the cabinets, so corner bullnoses are not necessary. Each side of the window will require 2 inches for bullnose. The main tile is packaged 18 square feet to a carton, and the bullnose is sold by the piece.

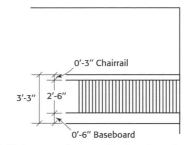

Figure 4.13 Practice lesson: Basic—Paneling.

1. What is the base square footage of the space?
2. What is the total square footage with the allowance for placing the tiles on the diagonal?
3. How many cartons/boxes must be ordered, and how many square feet is this?
4. How many pieces of bullnose must be ordered?

Paneling

A CPA desires her office to be paneled floor to ceiling. Her office is 12 feet × 18 feet, with one 48-inch × 54-inch window and two 36-inch × 80-inch doors (Figure 4.15). Her ceiling is 8 feet tall. You must also calculate the baseboard and the crown molding. The paneling comes in 4-foot-wide × 8-foot-long panels (32 square feet), and the base and crown come in 12-foot lengths.

1. What is the perimeter after calculating for waste?
2. How many full panels are needed?
3. How many square feet must be ordered?
4. How many feet of crown molding must be ordered, and how many pieces is this?
5. How many feet of baseboard must be ordered, and how many pieces is this?

ADVANCED
Wall Tile

Your client has a 4-foot × 6-foot × 7-foot-tall shower in her master bedroom that you have designed using tile (Figure 4.16). Three sides are to be tiled. The main tile is 8 inches × 12 inches and is packaged 13.4 square feet to the box. The accent liner is 3 inches × 8½ inches and can be purchased by the piece. The bullnose is 3 inches × 6 inches, and the corner bullnose is 3 inches × 3 inches and are purchased by the piece.

1. What is the base square footage of the space?
2. What is the total square footage, including waste allowance for the main tile?
3. How many boxes/cartons must be ordered, and what is the total square footage of this?
4. How many corner tiles are needed?
5. How many pieces of bullnose must be ordered?
6. How many pieces of accent liner must be ordered?

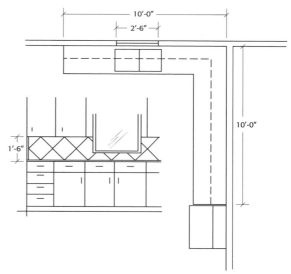

Figure 4.14 Practice lesson: Intermediate—Wall tile.

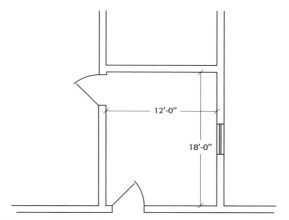

Figure 4.15 Practice lesson: Intermediate—Paneling.

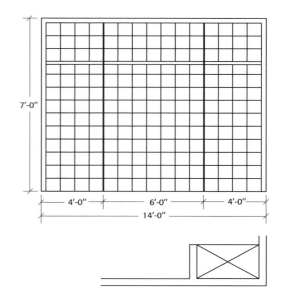

Figure 4.16 Practice lesson: Advanced—Wall tile.

Paneling

You have designed a 16-foot × 24-foot office for a psychologist in the Arts and Crafts style (Figure 4.17). To continue this look, you have specified the walls to be paneled. There is a 3-foot × 6-foot 8-inch door, two 3-foot × 4-foot 8-inch windows, and a wall of windows that covers 14 feet × 5 feet 6 inches. The paneling will be 1-foot × 8-foot tongue and groove, prefinished panels. Plate molding will be used to finish the top of the paneling at 6 feet 8 inches, and baseboard will finish the bottom. The plate and base molding come in 10-foot lengths.

1. What is the perimeter after calculating for waste?
2. How many full panels are needed?
3. How many square feet must be ordered?
4. How many feet of plate rail must be ordered, and how many pieces is this?
5. How many feet of baseboard must be ordered, and how many pieces is this?

Pricing of Wall Tile

Calculate pricing for the Advanced Wall Tile practice lesson. The builder has provided the shower pan. All material is available locally without additional shipping. The installer includes mastic and grout in his labor pricing, and there is no sealant being used.

Use the quantities calculated from the advanced wall tile practice lesson and the following prices:

Tile Pricing:

Main wall tile—$3.15 per square foot

Bullnose tile—$1.86 each

Corner bullnose tile—$3.98 each

Accent tile—$7.47 each

Labor Pricing:

Main tile installation—$15 per square foot

Bullnose and accent tile installation—$8.00 per linear (running) foot

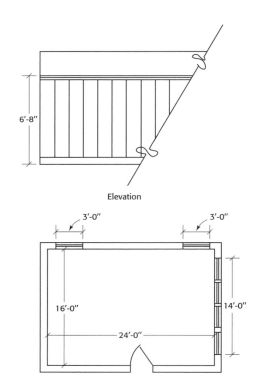

Figure 4.17 Practice lessons: Advanced—Paneling.

Then answer the following questions:

1. What is the price of all the tile before sales tax?
2. What is the price of labor?
3. What is the total price of this job (disregarding plumber, plumbing, and fixtures).

References

American Olean. Accessed September 1, 2012. http://americanolean.com/series.cfm?series=13&c=49

Smith, Steven. Personal interview. December 2012.

Chapter 5 | Suspended Ceilings

Chapter Outline

Terminology

Ceilings: Suspended and Decorative

Sizes and Packaging

Cost Factors and Calculations

Step-by-Step Examples
Example 1—Suspended Ceiling
Example 2—Decorative Ceiling

Manual Worksheets
Ceiling Panel/Tile Worksheet

Practice Lessons: Suspended Ceilings
Basic
Intermediate
Advanced
Pricing

References

Terminology

Allowance Additional amount of material added to base calculations to allow for any pattern and waste from cutting the material.

Ceiling grid system Used to hold ceiling panels/tiles in suspended ceiling applications (Figure 5.1). It consists of wall moldings, main beams, and cross tees in which ceiling panels/tiles will be set.

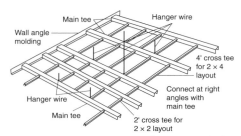

Figure references within figure:
Main tee
Hanger wire
Wall angle molding
4' cross tee for 2 × 4 layout
Connect at right angles with main tee
Hanger wire
Main tee
2' cross tee for 2 × 2 layout

Figure 5.1 Components of a suspended ceiling. (Al's Home Improvement Center)

Freight The cost of shipping. This cost may be factored into the price of material. Sometimes freight companies will add fuel surcharges that will increase this amount.

Haul-off Term used to describe the removal of existing materials from the job site. This is usually an amount charged to the client—the haul-off fee.

Labor The cost of installing the material.

Minimums As this relates to labor, installers have a minimum charge for going to a job site to measure or install. As this relates

to freight, there is a minimum charge to ship anything. If the amount shipped doesn't meet the minimum, the minimum charge is billed. As this relates to material, at times, there is a minimum amount of product that must be ordered. This depends on the manufacturer.

Reflected ceiling plan A plan that shows the ceiling and the items that exist from the ceiling, such as lighting, suspended ceilings, sprinkler systems, smoke detectors, air diffusers, and grilles (Figure 5.2).

Square foot Measurement obtained by multiplying, in feet, the width times the length (Figure 5.3).

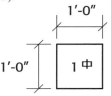

Figure 5.3 1 ft. × 1 ft. = 1 sq. ft. *or* 12 in. × 12 in. = 144 in. ÷ 144 in. = 1 sq. ft.

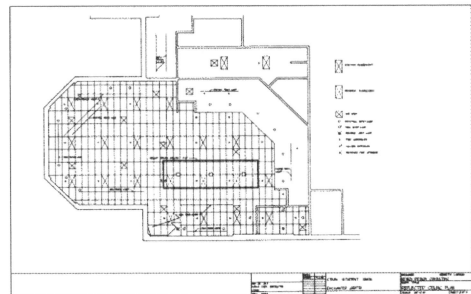

Figure 5.2 Reflected ceiling plan showing 2-foot × 4-foot ceiling tiles and fluorescent troffers. (Kenneth A. Larson Design)

Ceilings: Suspended and Decorative

This chapter focuses on suspended and decorative ceilings. Either ceiling can be found in residential and commercial applications. Suspended ceilings are made of acoustic-absorbing materials, wood, and tin and are suspended in grid systems (Figure 5.4). The decorative ceilings specifically discussed in this chapter refer to tin ceilings that can be suspended, glued, or nailed to the ceiling (Figure 5.5). In large commercial work, the interior designer often lays out the suspended ceiling by using a reflected ceiling plan

Figure 5.4 2-foot × 2-foot suspended ceiling. (© David Burton / Alamy)

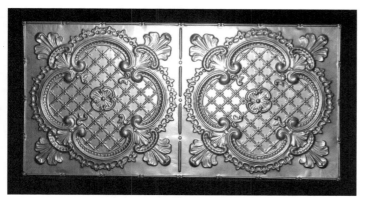

Figure 5.5 Close-up of a decorative tin panel. (Courtesy of W.F. Norman)

to show the positioning of the grids and anything else that comes from the ceiling. Interior designers are used mainly to establish the placement of ceiling tiles, but depending on their company and their scope of work, they may be required to determine quantity.

INSIGHT FROM THE FIELD

❝Tin ceiling and wall panels and moldings can add uniqueness to rooms of any size or style of décor, from classic to contemporary. These products make wonderful wainscotings, backsplashes, and even entire accent walls. On a ceiling you can simply trim around the perimeter with a cornice/crown molding and/or frieze. You can also use just a round, square, rectangular, or oval-shaped center medallion around a light fixture or up in a ceiling tray or coffer. And, of course, you can cover an entire ceiling wall-to-wall if you like in anything from one simple panel design to a fully elaborate design, including panels, moldings, borders, and cornices.

Help is available at no cost from the factory for designing the look you'll love, and also for planning the easiest, most finished-looking installation. Some of the more elaborate combinations of panels and moldings do require that a layout drawing be made to ensure you get a proper look, fit, and proportion of all of the elements used. The more simple one-pattern wall-to-wall installations are no more difficult than putting tiles on the floor. You center your panels on the ceiling in both directions (usually), then start in the center and work out in all four directions. All of these designs, from plain to fancy, can be installed by a homeowner with ordinary do-it-yourself skills.

These products often turn out to be one of the features in the room the home or building owner is most pleased with over time.❞

Mark Quito, *co-owner of the W. F. Norman Corporation in Nevada, Missouri*

Sizes and Packaging

Ceiling panels and tiles are sold by the piece. Common sizes are 16 inches × 16 inches (1.33 feet × 1.33 feet.), 2 feet × 2 feet, and 2 feet × 4 feet. Decorative tin panels and tiles include molding and cornice pieces, where sizes vary.

Cost Factors and Calculations

Cost factors include the product/material, shipping, labor to hang/install, and, with decorative tiles, painting or finishing (Table 5.1). Calculations for the quantity of materials share similarities with paint, wallpaper, and paneling.

The steps for calculation are as follows:

1. Calculate the base square footage by multiplying width and length of area to be covered in feet; this gives square feet. If you are multiplying inches by inches, divide by 144 square inches to find square feet.
2. Add an additional 10 percent to the base amount to allow for waste from cutting and fitting to find total square feet needed for installation.
3. Determine how many panels/tiles are needed. Take the total square feet needed, and divide by the square feet found in one panel/tile. Round up to a whole number to determine how many full panels/tiles must be ordered.

Suspended Ceilings	Decorative Tiles
Material	Material
Shipping	Shipping
Installation*	Installation*
	Painting
Installation cost is more than base cost when intricate patterns are involved.	

Table 5.1 Costs Involved with Suspended Ceilings and Decorative Tiles

Step-by-Step Examples

Example 1—Suspended Ceiling

A local community day-care center has a generous donor replacing the ceiling in the indoor play area with a suspended ceiling. You have specified a 2-foot × 4-foot suspended ceiling for this 36-foot × 42-foot area (Figure 5.6).

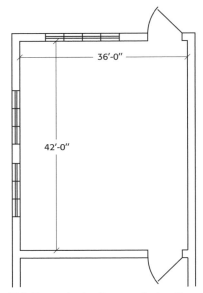

Figure 5.6 Example 1—Suspended ceiling.

Step 1: Calculate base square footage of space.

Take width of room in feet:	36	ft.
Multiply by length of room in feet:	× 42	ft.
Total base square footage of space:	1512	sq. ft.

Step 2: Calculate additional materials for waste allowance.

Take square footage from Step 1:	1512	sq. ft.
Multiply by 10 percent to allow for waste:	× 1.10	waste allowance
Total square footage needed:	1663.2	sq. ft.

Step 3: Calculate number of ceiling tiles to be ordered.

Take square footage needed from Step 2:	1663.2	sq. ft.
Divide by square footage of individual tiles:	÷ 8	sq. ft. per tile

Note: 2-foot × 4-foot tile = 8 square feet.

Total tiles needed:	207.9	tiles
Round up to whole number:	**208**	**tiles to order**

Example 2—Decorative Ceiling

A restaurant owner wants to replicate a decorative tin ceiling on the 12-foot-high ceiling of his dining area. This is a charming restaurant located in a downtown building in a small town. The overall space is 24 feet × 48 feet with two alcoves of 16 feet × 20 feet each (Figure 5.7). The decorative tin is 2 feet × 2 feet.

Step 1: Calculate base square footage of space.

Space #1—Take width of room in feet:	48	ft.
Multiply by length of room in feet:	× 24	ft.
Total base square footage of space:	1152	sq. ft. #1

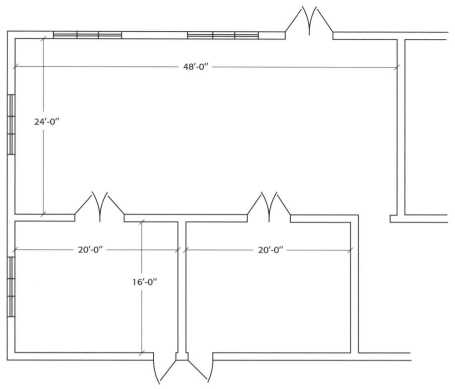

Figure 5.7 Example 2—Decorative ceiling.

Space #2—Take width of room in feet:	20	ft.
Multiply by length of room in feet:	× 16	ft.
Total base square footage of space:	320	sq. ft. #2
Space #3—Take width of room in feet:	20	ft.
Multiply by length of room in feet:	× 16	ft.
Total base square footage of space:	320	sq. ft. #3
Add all spaces together—Space #1:	1152	sq. ft.
Space #2:	+ 320	sq. ft.
Space #3:	+ 320	sq. ft.
Total Step 1:	1792	sq. ft.

Step 2: Calculate additional materials for waste allowance.

Take square footage from Step 1:	1792	sq. ft.
Multiply by 10 percent to allow for waste:	× 1.10	waste allowance
Total square footage needed:	1971.2	sq. ft.

Step 3: Calculate number of ceiling tiles to be ordered.

Take square footage needed from Step 2:	1971.2	sq. ft.
Divide by square footage of individual tiles:	÷ 4	sq. ft. per tile

Note: 2 feet × 2 feet = 4 square feet.

Total tiles needed:	492.8	tiles
Round up to whole number:	**493**	**tiles to order**

Manual Worksheet

Ceiling Panel/Tile Worksheet

Step 1: Calculate base square footage of space.

For odd-shaped rooms, divide room into geometric shapes and calculate for each space.

Space #1—Take width of room in feet:		_____	ft.
Multiply by length of room in feet:	×	_____	ft.
Total base square footage of space:		_____	**sq. ft. #1**
Space #2—Take width of room in feet:		_____	ft.
Multiply by length of room in feet:	×	_____	ft.
Total base square footage of space:		_____	**sq. ft. #2**
Space #3—Take width of room in feet:		_____	ft.
Multiply by length of room in feet:	×	_____	ft.
Total base square footage of space:		_____	**sq. ft. #3**
Add all spaces together—Space #1:		_____	sq. ft.
Space #2:	+	_____	sq. ft.
Space #3:	+	_____	sq. ft.
Total Step 1:		_____	**sq. ft.**

Step 2: Calculate additional materials for waste allowance.

Take square footage from Step 1:		_____	sq. ft.
Multiply by 10 percent to allow for waste:	×	1.10	waste allowance
Total square footage needed:		_____	**sq. ft.**

Step 3. Calculate number of ceiling tiles to be ordered.

Take square footage needed from Step 2:		_____	sq. ft.
Divide by square footage of individual tiles:	÷	_____	sq. ft. per tile
Total tiles needed:		_____	**tiles**
Round up to whole number:		_____	**tiles to order**

Practice Lessons: Suspended Ceilings

BASIC
Decorative Ceiling

You are working with a client designing the library/music room in their home. They want a painted tin ceiling of 2-foot × 2-foot tins. The space is 16 feet × 24 feet (Figure 5.8).

1. What is the base square footage of the ceiling?
2. What is the total square footage needed, including waste allowance, to ensure coverage?
3. How many tiles must be ordered?

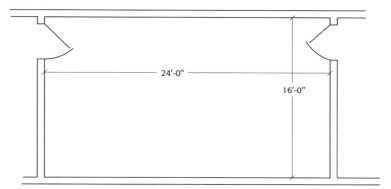

Figure 5.8 Practice lesson: Basic—Decorative ceiling.

INTERMEDIATE
Suspended Ceiling

Your mother is finishing the basement in your childhood home. The most economical way to finish the ceiling is with a 2-foot × 4-foot suspended ceiling. The overall dimension of the space being finished is 30 feet × 48 feet (Figure 5.9).

1. What is the base square footage of the ceiling?
2. What is the total square footage, including waste allowance, to ensure coverage?
3. How many tiles must be ordered?

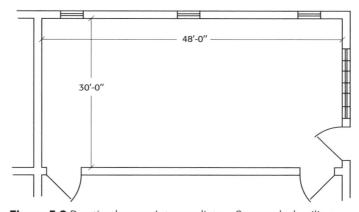

Figure 5.9 Practice lesson: Intermediate—Suspended ceiling.

ADVANCED

Suspended and Decorative Ceilings

You are planning to open your own interior design firm. The space consists of a reception area, a work area, and an office space for yourself and two other interior designers. You are using a 2-foot × 2-foot suspended ceiling tile in the office space and bathroom space and a 2-foot × 2-foot decorative tin in the reception and work areas (Figure 5.10).

1. What is the base square footage of the suspended ceiling?
2. What is the total square footage of the suspended ceiling, including waste allowance, to ensure coverage?
3. How many tiles must be ordered for the suspended ceiling?
4. What is the base square footage of the decorative tin ceiling?
5. What is the total square footage of the decorative tin ceiling, including waste allowance, to ensure coverage?
6. How many tiles must be ordered for the decorative tin ceiling?

Pricing

Refer to the Basic practice lesson. Your client wants to know what it will cost for the tin ceiling to be installed. They plan on painting it themselves. The subcontractor has quoted $770 for the installation. The tiles are $24.00 each. Shipping will be factored at $0.60 per tile so long as a $10.00 minimum shipping charge has been surpassed.

1. What is the price of the ceiling tiles plus shipping?
2. What is the price of the materials (including shipping) and installation combined?

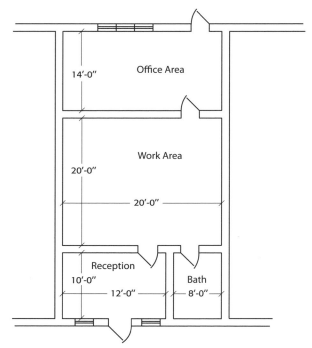

Figure 5.10 Practice lesson: Advanced—Suspended and decorative ceilings.

References

Al's Home Improvement Center Suspended Ceiling Components. Accessed September 13, 2012. http://alsnetbiz.com/homeimprovement/htseries/susceil.html.

Armstrong Ceiling Product. Accessed September 13, 2012. http://www.armstrong.com/resclgam/na/ceilings/en/us/select-a-product.html.

Kenneth A. Larson Design. Accessed September 13, 2012. http://www.kesigndesign.com/code/en_grot1.htm.

W.F. Norman Corporation Decorative Tin Ceilings. Accessed September 13, 2012. http://wfnorman.com/about/designs#2.

Chapter 6 | Plank and Tile Flooring

Plank and tile floor coverings are hard surface flooring. These surfaces are easy to clean and very durable. When compared to other flooring products such as broadloom carpet, their life cycle cost is usually less expensive because they last much longer than resilient or broadloom flooring; however, their immediate up-front costs are significantly higher.

Chapter Outline

Terminology

Types of Plank and Tile Flooring
Plank Flooring
Tile Flooring

Sizes and Packaging

Cost Factors

Calculations

Step-by-Step Examples
Example 1—Plank Flooring
Example 2—Tile Flooring
Example 3—Tile Flooring Diagonally Set

Manual Worksheets
Hard Flooring Material Worksheet
Flooring Transition Worksheet

Practice Lessons: Plank and Tile Flooring
Basic
Plank Flooring
Tile Flooring
Intermediate
Plank Flooring
Tile Flooring
Advanced
Plank Flooring
Pricing for Plank Flooring

References

Terminology

Allowance Additional amount of material added to base room dimension allowing for any pattern and waste from cutting the material (Figure 6.1).

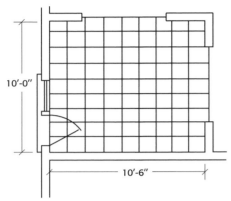

Figure 6.1 Tile must be cut to fit the room. This is more than the basic room dimension of 10 ft. × 10.5 ft. = 105 sq. ft. Add 10 percent to this to allow for the tile that will be cut. 105 sq. ft. × 1.1 = 115.5 total square feet needed.

Box/carton Most plank and tile floors are priced by the square foot but sold by the full box or carton.

Cement board Board made of cement and fibers used to make an inflexible flooring surface for tile installation, usually used on top of plywood subfloor. This helps to prevent flex under the tile that can pop or crack grout and tiles. It comes in 4-foot × 8-foot or 3-foot × 5-foot sheets in ¼-inch to ½-inch thicknesses. It is sometimes used under vertical wall tile for added strength.

Direct glue-down Type of flooring installation where the product is permanently attached to the subfloor or foundation with glue adhesive.

Floating floor Type of flooring installation whereby the product is not permanently attached to the subfloor or foundation. There is a distinct separation between the subfloor and the final flooring product. Floating floors tend to be modular and interlock with each other. Cork, laminate, Marmoleum, rubber, vinyl, and prefinished wood products may use floating-floor installation. Sometimes the product rests on a cushion on top of a moisture barrier.

Freight The cost of shipping. This cost may be factored into the price of material. Sometimes freight companies add fuel surcharges that will increase this amount.

Grout A thin mortar used to fill the spacing between tiles. The size of this space factors directly into the amount of grout needed. Grout used for most flooring tile is sanded, whereas grout used for wall tile is un-sanded. Grout joints of ⅛ inch and less, floor or wall, require un-sanded grout.

Haul-off The removal of old flooring material from the job site. This is usually an amount charged to the client—the haul-off fee.

Labor The cost per square foot of installing the material. This includes additional costs, such as staggered, diagonal, and herringbone design, moving large items such as refrigerators, pulling up toilets, and haul-off.

Minimums As this relates to labor, installers have a minimum charge for going to a job site to measure or install. As this relates to freight, there is a minimum charge to ship anything. If the amount shipped doesn't meet the minimum, the minimum charge is billed. As this relates to material, at times, there is a minimum amount of product that must be ordered. This depends on the manufacturer.

Nail down Type of flooring installation whereby the product is permanently attached to the subfloor or foundation by being nailed down.

Plank flooring Type of flooring whereby long rectangular strips of wood or bamboo are fitted together (Figure 6.2). The planks

Figure 6.2 Plank flooring. (iStockphoto/© Oksana Struk)

can be narrow or wide, as seen in 2¼- or 5½-inch-wide planks. Also referred to as strip floor covering.

Shipping See *freight*.

Square foot 12 inches by 12 inches is 1 square foot (Figure 6.3). Obtained by multiplying, in feet measurement, width times length. Should the space be calculated by

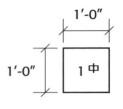

Figure 6.3 Square foot.

multiplying inches by inches, the total must then be divided by 144 inches to convert to square feet, as there are 144 square inches in 1 square foot. Tiles and plank goods are normally calculated, ordered, and priced by the square foot.

Strip floor covering See *plank flooring*.

Take-off Utilizing scaled drawings or floor plans instead of a site measure to calculate quantity of materials needed for a job, generally used for budgeting purposes.

Take up The cost of pulling up any existing flooring that must be removed and hauled off before new flooring is installed.

Thinset adhesive A thin coating of mortar used to adhere tile to walls and floors, creating a strong adhesion. Allows floor tile to be used in areas where the floor wasn't dropped for a mortar bed.

Tile flooring Hard flooring surface in geometric shapes, such as brick, granite, marble, slate, limestone, travertine, sandstone, quarry, Saltillo, and ceramic or porcelain tile, adhered to a floor.

Transition pieces Products made to finish exposed, raw edges and provide a smooth transition from one flooring surface to another, minimizing height differences between surfaces (Figure 6.4 and Figure 6.5).

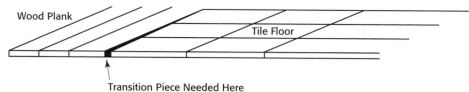

Wood Plank

Tile Floor

↑
Transition Piece Needed Here

Figure 6.4 Two different flooring surfaces sometimes need transition pieces to allow for slight differences in height or to finish the seam edge.

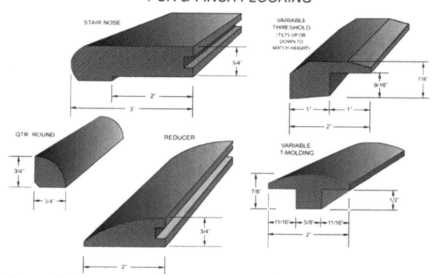

MOLDING SCHEMATICS
FOR 3/4 INCH FLOORING

Figure 6.5 Different types of transition pieces. (Mullican Flooring)

Types of Plank and Tile Flooring

Plank Flooring

Plank is most commonly seen as long, narrow strips of wood or bamboo that are fitted together in a staggered pattern and either nailed or glued down or installed as a floating floor (Figure 6.6). Depending on the region of the country, this flooring is also referred to as strip floor covering. Plank floors come in a variety of wood and bamboo cuts, widths of material, and finishes. Some plank floors are laid and finished on-site, while others are pre-stained and finished at the factory. Factory pre-finish allows better control over stain color and allows multiple finishes to be applied to make a stronger, more durable finish. Pre-finished floors are ideal in a situation where the environment isn't conducive for proper drying of the finish, the homeowner is staying in the home during

Figure 6.6 Plank flooring can be nail-down, glue-down, or floating. (Age Fotostock/Elena Elisseeva)

the renovation, or there are environmental concerns about finishing materials.

Nearly any wood species available can be used for flooring. Recently, hickory has become a very popular wood for the floor because of its grain and characteristics. Next popular, white oak has been preferred over red oak because it doesn't have a natural redness that can alter the color of stain. Pine is a look that is normally seen "distressed." It is especially expensive and shows imperfections in the wood and in its use, especially divots from high heels. It is possible to use wood that has been salvaged and reclaimed, from old warehouses and other buildings. Many large cities have local companies that specialize in reclaimed wood.

Plank flooring that is laid unfinished on the floor and then is sanded and stained allows the homeowner to customize the stain. The floor company will usually apply (lay up) different stain samples to a small area before the final sanding so that the designer and homeowner can determine which stain to use. Once the stain has been determined, the floor is sanded, stained, and sealed. Normally, floors stained in the home are sealed only two times. Additional layers of sealant or a harder finish involves more time and money. Each finish must dry before anyone can walk on it. If all entrances into the space are stained on-site, all work will need to be shut down while the floors are being finished. After the floors have dried, it takes four weeks before the finish is cured enough to lay an area rug on the wood. This type of floor works best in instances where the homeowner isn't in residence and wants to customize the stain color.

Do not install wood floors directly on concrete. The moisture, temperature variations, and wicking ability of the concrete will damage a wood floor. Most wood floors must be glued or nailed down. Recently, manufacturers have come out with "floating" wood floors that can be used on concrete so long as a moisture barrier and pad cushion are used. They basically snap together and don't need to be nailed down.

Tile Flooring

Hard tile floor covering can be made of natural or baked materials. Natural materials include granite, marble, slate, limestone, travertine, and sandstone, and baked materials include brick, quarry, Saltillo, ceramic, and porcelain. These materials can be laid on almost any floor surface so long as they have appropriate support for their weight and a rigid, non-flex floor. The larger the tile, the more important it is that the floor be rigid, since any shifting will cause larger tiles to "pop" and break. Concrete slabs are inherently rigid. For a rigid floor, either concrete board or a concrete subfloor can be used. Concrete board is ½ inch thick, 3 feet × 5 feet, and is nailed to a plywood subfloor to create rigidity. In new construction a concrete subfloor can be created on plywood subfloor with a lowered level of flooring that allows 2 inches of concrete to be poured. After the concrete dries, tile is set. Tile floors can be heated to be more comfortable for those in cold climates by the installer's laying a thin mat of wires under the tile in the thinset, which is wired to a thermostat and switch. Tubes that circulate hot water or antifreeze liquids can also be used, but more depth is necessary at the floor (see Figure 6.7). This alleviates the problem of cold, hard-surface floors. Keep in mind, however, that heated tiles to the cost of the project because of the cost of the wiring and an electrician to connect the wiring to a switch.

To protect the surface from stains from foods and liquids, brick, granite, marble, limestone, travertine,

Figure 6.7 Tubing for hot water or antifreeze ingredients used to heat tile flooring. (© Werner Otto / Alamy)

sandstone, slate, quarry, and Saltillo tiles must be sealed. The sealant is in liquid form and applied to the floor. Enhancement sealers are used to bring out inherent color in non-glazed materials, including slate, concrete, sandstone, quarry, and Saltillo tiles. With today's technology, ceramic and porcelain tiles have been made to replicate the look of these natural materials, including wood, and because of their inherent properties, they don't require sealing or as much maintenance as natural products do.

Spacing between the tiles is determined by the material used and the client's preference. Materials such as brick, quarry, ceramic, sandstone, or Saltillo tile are normally spaced between ⅜ inch and ½ inch. The sides of these particular tiles are not ruler-straight. Materials such as granite, marble, travertine, porcelain, limestone, and slate are cut more precisely and normally spaced between ¼ inch and ⅜ inch. Granite, marble, and travertine can be spaced as close as ⅛ inch. The width of this spacing and the color of the grout used to fill the spacing can drastically affect the look of the tile.

Grout is a thin mortar used to fill the spacing between tiles. Grout used for most flooring tile is sanded, whereas grout used for wall tile is un-sanded. Grout joints of ⅛ inch and less, floor or wall, require un-sanded grout. Many people have had experiences with grout whereby it has dirtied quickly or, in areas of high moisture, grown mold. Sealants are now available for grout to prevent mold and stains. Also, grouts have been developed that are antibacterial (mold and mildew resistant) and are made with acrylic, which is stain resistant and strengthens the grout, allowing it to bond better to the tile.

Sizes and Packaging

Bamboo planks generally come in widths of 3¾ inches or 5¼ inches and are normally pre-finished. Bamboo flooring offers much more variety than does wood flooring. Wood plank flooring comes in many different widths, from 2¼ inches up to 19 inches wide. Standard sizing has been 2¼ inches

wide; however, 6-inch-wide and wider sizes seem to be preferred. Tiles come in many sizes and shapes, from 1 inch × 1 inch to 30 inches × 30 inches. Plank and tile flooring are calculated by the square foot. Unless they are in stock at a local distributor, they must be ordered and purchased by the full carton or box. There is no common square footage number to use for the full cartons or boxes because there are so many varying sizes, even among product manufacturers. It is important to find out what the full box/carton quantity is for the products so that they can be ordered and priced accordingly.

Cement board is normally provided by the installer but must be accounted for in the costs.

Transition pieces are used to finish edges and transition from one type of flooring to another and come in many different lengths. They must be ordered by the whole length. Even if the total measurement of transitions needed at a doorway is only 3 feet 6 inches, if the length of the transition piece is 6½ feet, this is the amount that must be ordered.

Cost Factors

Cost factors for plank and tile flooring are almost identical (Table 6.1). Material, shipping, transition pieces, and installation are common for both. Tile has a few more costs that may need to be calculated, such as cement board, mastic, grout, and sealant. Be sure

Tile	Strip/Plank
Material	Material
Transition pieces*	Transition pieces*
Cement board*	Installation**
Installation**	Shipping*
Mastic	
Grout	
Sealant*	
Shipping*	
*If necessary/applicable. **Installation cost is more than base cost when diagonal, staggered, and herringbone patterns are used.	

Table 6.1 Costs Involved in Strip/Plank and Tile Flooring

to check with the installer to see if the price includes not only the labor to install but also the transitions, grout, and mastic. While the interior designer is usually responsible for ordering the transition pieces and sealant, most installers include the cost for the grout and mastic in their labor price. It is also important to see how much more the installer will add for labor if cement board is needed and whether the installer is responsible for bringing this material to the job.

The plank or tile floor installer will charge installation for the amount needed, base plus waste allowance, before you adjust for full boxes or cartons. Cement board is normally charged at the same amount that the installer charges labor (base plus waste allowance). Costs for tile or plank material must be adjusted to accommodate full boxes or cartons. Not included under each category are the miscellaneous charges for tear-out, haul-off, preparation, installing heated tile floors and the electrical work, toilet and pedestal removal and reinstallation, furniture moving (they generally don't move grand pianos or pool tables), and appliance moving.

Table 6.2 is an example of a cost worksheet/schedule that pulls all the various cost components of a job together.

Calculations

All hard flooring is ordered and sold by the square foot, so you must find the square footage of the space first. Square feet are found by multiplying the width in feet by the length in feet. This is easy if the room is square or rectangular. If the room has an angle, however, you must perform additional computations.

For example, suppose you have a room that is 15 feet × 17 feet and has an angled wall. To find the square footage:

1. Draw a diagram of the room (Figure 6.8). This doesn't have to be to scale, but you must have the measurements.
2. Divide the room into geometric shapes. You will probably be able to find a square or a rectangle, and if the room has one angle wall, you will have a triangle as well (Figure 6.9). Find the triangle's base and height.
3. Find the area for each geometric shape, and find the total square footage (Box 6.1).

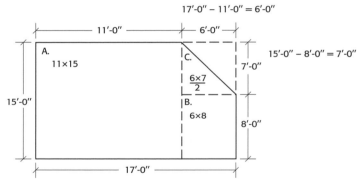

Figure 6.9 Dividing room into basic geometric shapes. Find area of each shape to discover total square feet of room.

To find the area of the triangular shape, multiply the base times the height and divide by 2.

A: Large Rectangular Area is 15 × 11 = 165

B: Small Rectangular Area is 6 × 8 = 48

C: Triangular Area is 6 × 7 = 42 ÷ 2 = 21

The total square footage is 165 + 21 + 48 = 234 square feet.

OR

15 feet × 17 feet = 255 square feet. Find area of triangular shape as above and subtract from the overall total.

255 sq. ft. − 21 sq. ft. = 234 sq. ft.

Box 6.1 Finding the Area of the Example

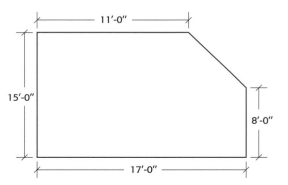

Figure 6.8 Example of room with angled wall.

Flooring Schedule

Client:
Phone #s:
Address:
Installer:

Room	Item	Mfr./Vendor	Pattern	Color	Size	Repeat	Quantity	Quantity per Box/Carton	Adjusted Quantity	Cost Per	Subtotal	Est. Ship.	Total	PO	Date
	Material														
	Transitions														
	Sealant														
	Labor	Description of work, pattern, and pattern direction							Quantity	Cost Per	Subtotal	Est. Ship.	Total	WO	Date
	Cement Board														
	Miscellaneous														
												Total Cost			
Room	Item	Mfr./Vendor	Pattern	Color	Size	Repeat	Quantity	Quantity per Box/Carton	Adjusted Quantity	Cost Per	Subtotal	Est. Ship.	Total	PO	Date
	Material														
	Transitions														
	Sealant														
	Labor	Description of work, pattern, and pattern direction							Quantity	Cost Per	Subtotal	Est. Ship.	Total	WO	Date
	Cement Board														
	Miscellaneous														
												Total Cost			

Table 6.2 Flooring Schedule

If you are multiplying feet by feet, you will already have square feet. If you are multiplying inches by inches, you will have to divide by 144 in order to convert to square feet. In general, when hard flooring is installed, it should come to the middle of a doorway unless the room dictates otherwise. Since additional material is always added to the base square footage, it is unnecessary to measure into the doorways.

Once you have found the base square footage, you must add an additional amount for waste allowance (Table 6.3); the amount depends on the pattern in which the material will be laid (Figure 6.10). Be sure to speak with your installer to confirm the additional amount required. The costs for installation and cement board, if needed, will be based on the base plus waste allowance. The costs for the material depend on how much you must purchase, including full box/carton square footage considerations. Any needed transitions, sealant, shipping costs, and miscellaneous charges will be added to this.

Waste Allowance for Plank and Tile Flooring			
This percentage will be added to the base square footage.			
Straight	**Diagonal/ Staggered**	**Herringbone**	**Cement Board**
10%	15%	25%	10%
Transition pieces are calculated by the linear foot and priced according to the full length totals.			

Table 6.3 Waste Allowances Based on Pattern Laid

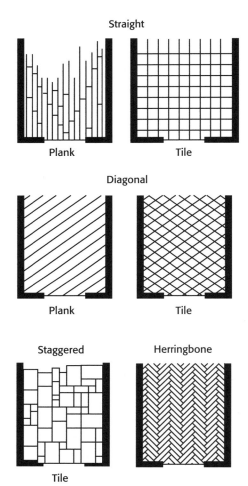

Figure 6.10 Wood and tile flooring patterns.

Step-by-Step Examples

Example 1—Plank Flooring

You are working with a client who is designing his office in his law firm's new space. You recommend a bamboo plank flooring to enhance the overall design you have created. The space is 16 feet × 30 feet (Figure 6.11), and the bamboo will be laid in a normal, straight pattern. There are 23.59 square feet in a carton. Transition pieces are 6 feet long.

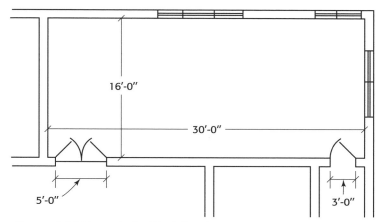

Figure 6.11 Example 1—Plank flooring.

Bamboo Material:

Step 1: Calculate base square footage of space.

16 ft. × 30 ft. = 480 sq. ft.

Step 2: Calculate for additional materials for waste allowance.

480 sq. ft. × 1.1 for waste = 528 sq. ft.

Step 3: Calculate number of full boxes/cartons to be ordered.

528 sq. ft. ÷ 23.59 sq. ft. per carton = 22.38 cartons needed
Round up to whole number = 23 cartons

Step 4: Calculate square feet in cartons ordered that client will be charged.

23 cartons × 23.59 sq. ft. per carton = 542.57 sq. ft. ordered

Transition Material:

Step 1: Calculate total length of transition needed.

3 ft. + 5 ft. = 8 ft. total for changes of flooring.

Step 2: Calculate total number of pieces of transition to be ordered.

8 ft. needed ÷ 6 ft. per transition piece = 1.33 pieces
Round up to find total pieces to order: 2 full pieces

Step 3: Calculate total feet ordered that client will be charged.

2 pieces × 6 ft. per piece = 12 ft. ordered

For this flooring the material and labor calculations are based on the following numbers in Table 6.4. The shipping cost must also be added. You can find the amount by calling the manufacturer from which the material is to be purchased.

Item	Quantity of Material
Bamboo flooring	542.57 sq. ft.
Labor to install	528 sq. ft.
Transition pieces	12 ft.

Table 6.4 Material Quantity Used for Pricing to the Client

Example 2—Tile Flooring

The dining area of your client's kitchen is to be tiled on the diagonal. Since there is a plywood subfloor, cement board will be used. The space is 14 feet × 18 feet, so the larger 16-inch × 16-inch tiles create a good sense of proportion (Figure 6.12). There are 15.5 square feet per carton. In two places the tile meets different flooring, cork in one and wood in another. This requires transition moldings, which come in 6-foot 6-inch lengths.

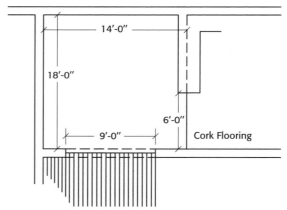

Figure 6.12 Example 2—Tile flooring.

Tile Material:

Step 1: Calculate base square footage of space.

14 ft. × 18 ft. = 252 sq. ft.

Step 2: Calculate for additional materials for waste allowance.

Since this is placed on the diagonal, an additional 15 percent will be necessary.

252 sq. ft. × 1.15 for waste = 289.8 sq. ft.

Step 3: Calculate number of full boxes/cartons to be ordered.

289.8 sq. ft. ÷ 15.5 sq. ft. per carton = 18.7 cartons needed

Round up to whole number = 19 cartons

Step 4: Calculate square feet in cartons ordered that client will be charged.

19 cartons × 15.5 sq. ft. per carton = 294.5 sq. ft. ordered

Transition Material:

Step 1: Calculate total length of transition needed.

9 ft. + 6 ft. = 15 ft. total for changes of flooring.

Step 2: Calculate number of pieces of transition to be ordered.

15 ft. needed ÷ 6.5 ft. per transition piece = 2.31 pieces

Round up to find total pieces to order: 3 full pieces

Step 3: Calculate total feet ordered that client will be charged.

3 pieces × 6.5 ft. per piece = 19.5 ft. ordered

For this flooring the material and labor calculations are based on the numbers shown in Table 6.5. The shipping cost must also be added. You can find the amount by calling the manufacturer from which the material is purchased.

Item	Quantity of Material
Tile flooring	294.5 sq. ft.
Labor to install	289.8 sq. ft.
Transition pieces	19.5 ft.

Table 6.5 Material Quantity Used for Pricing to the Client

Manual Worksheets

Hard Flooring Material Worksheet

Step 1: Calculate base square footage of space.

For odd-shaped rooms, divide room into geometric shapes and calculate for each space.

Take width of room in feet:	_____	ft.
Multiply by length of room in feet:	× _____	ft.
Base square footage of space:	_____	**sq. ft.**

Step 2: Calculate for additional materials for waste allowance.

For tile or plank flooring laid "straight":

Take square footage from Step 1:	_____	sq. ft.
Multiply by 10% to allow for waste:	× 1.10	waste allowance
Total square footage needed:	_____	**sq. ft.**

For tile and plank flooring laid diagonally and tile flooring staggered:

Take square footage from Step 1:	_____	sq. ft.
Multiply by 15% to allow for waste:	× 1.15	waste allowance
Total square footage needed:	_____	**sq. ft.**

For hard flooring laid in a herringbone pattern:

Take square footage from Step 1:	_____	sq. ft.
Multiply by 25% to allow for waste:	× 1.25	waste allowance
Total square footage needed:	_____	**sq. ft.**

If hard flooring material is sold by the full box/carton, proceed to Step 3 to determine amount needed.

Step 3: Calculate number of full boxes/cartons to be ordered.

Take square footage needed from Step 2:	_____	sq. ft.
Divide by square feet per box/carton:	÷ _____	sq. ft.
Boxes/cartons needed:	_____	**boxes/cartons**
Round up to whole number:	_____	**boxes/cartons to order**

Step 4: Calculate square feet in boxes/cartons ordered to calculate pricing to client for material.

Take number of boxes/cartons from Step 3:	_____	boxes/cartons
Multiply by square feet per box:	× _____	sq. ft.
Total square footage ordered:	_____	**sq. ft.**

Flooring Transition Worksheet

Step 1: Calculate total length of transition needed.

Add widths of flooring change:	_____	ft.
Continue to add additional widths:	+ _____	ft.
Total length needed for transition:	_____	**ft.**

Step 2: Calculate total number of pieces of transition to be ordered.

Take total from Step 1:	_____	ft.
Divide by length of transition piece:	÷ _____	ft.
Pieces of transition needed:	_____	**pieces**
Round up to whole number:	_____	**full pieces needed**

Step 3: Calculate total length of transition to be ordered.

Take total from Step 2:	_____	pieces
Multiply by actual length of pieces:	× _____	ft. per piece
Total feet actually ordered:	_____	**ft. ordered**

Practice Lessons: Plank and Tile Flooring

BASIC
Plank Flooring

In a home office, 2¼-inch-wide oak flooring will be installed in a regular and straight pattern. The room is 12 feet × 15 feet (Figure 6.13). The material is provided by a local flooring company, which will stain the floor on-site and use stock material so it doesn't have to be ordered by the box or carton. The office connects with the entry, which currently has wood flooring. Because the office will tie into the entry and the entire wood flooring in the home is being re-stained and refinished, there is no need for transition pieces.

1. What is the base square footage of the space?
2. How many square feet are needed?
3. How many square feet must be ordered?

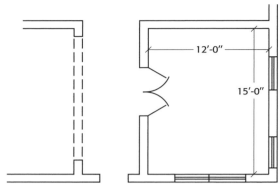

Figure 6.13 Practice lesson: Basic—Plank flooring.

Tile Flooring

The 10-foot × 8-foot closet of a home will have the carpet replaced with tile to match the tile in the bedroom (Figure 6.14). The porcelain tile is 15 inches × 15 inches and is stocked at a local distributor, so the exact amount needed can be ordered. There will be no transition pieces needed in this space.

1. What is the base square footage of the space?
2. How many square feet are needed?
3. How many square feet must be ordered?

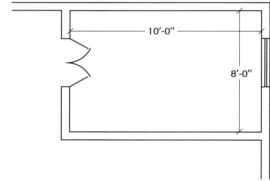

Figure 6.14 Practice lesson: Basic—Tile flooring.

INTERMEDIATE
Plank Flooring

A reception area in a furniture store is to have strand bamboo laid in a straight pattern. Overall, the room is 20 feet × 40 feet but includes several angles in the room (Figure 6.15). Each doorway is 12 feet 9 inches wide and will require a transition. The strand bamboo is packaged 23.65 square feet per carton. The transition pieces are 6 feet long.

1. What is the base square footage of the space?
2. How many square feet are needed?
3. How many square feet must be ordered?
4. How many full boxes/cartons must be ordered?

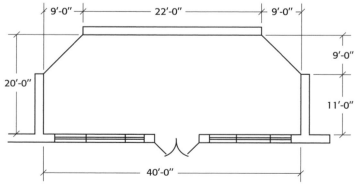

Figure 6.15 Practice lesson: Intermediate—Plank flooring.

5. How many feet of transition are needed?
6. How many feet of transition must be ordered?

Tile Flooring

Your client has fallen in love with a tile you have recommended for her great room. The tile will be laid in a diagonal pattern. It is an 18-inch × 18-inch porcelain tile packaged 18 square feet per carton. The room is 19 feet × 22 feet with one 20-foot-wide cased opening and another 9-foot-wide opening, which will require transition pieces (Figure 6.16). The transition pieces are 6.5 feet long.

1. What is the base square footage of the space?
2. How many square feet are needed?
3. How many square feet must be ordered?
4. How many full boxes/cartons must be ordered?
5. How many feet of transition are needed?
6. How many transition pieces must be ordered?

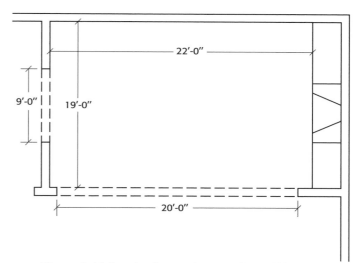

Figure 6.16 Practice lesson: Intermediate—Tile flooring.

ADVANCED
Plank Flooring

The entry and path to the kitchen will have 4¾-inch-wide hand-scraped hickory flooring installed in a herringbone pattern. The overall size of the entry is 7 feet × 22 feet with a 4-foot × 14-foot path to the kitchen extending from it (Figure 6.17). The flooring comes packaged 24.94 square feet to a carton. There are three openings that will require transition pieces. Two openings are 12 feet each and the other one is 9 feet. The transition pieces are 6.5 feet long.

1. What is the base square footage of the space?
2. How many square feet are needed?
3. How many square feet must be ordered?
4. How many full boxes/cartons must be ordered?
5. How many feet of transition are needed?
6. How many feet of transition must be ordered?

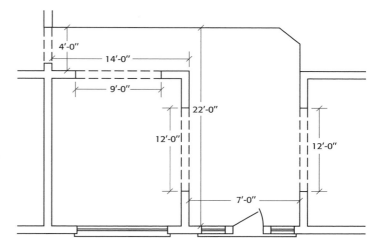

Figure 6.17 Practice lesson: Advanced—Plank flooring.

Pricing for Plank Flooring

Use the quantities found in the Advanced Plank Flooring practice lesson and the following prices to calculate pricing for your client.

Hickory flooring—$4.30 per square foot

Hickory transition pieces—$55.98 each piece

Shipping per box is $22.00

Shipping for the transition pieces is $15.00

Installation of the floor—$11.00 per square foot (This price already includes 25 percent additional labor for the herringbone pattern.)

1. What is the price for the hickory flooring including shipping?
2. What is the price for the hickory transition pieces including shipping?
3. What is the price for installation?
4. What is the total price for this project?

References

American Olean. Accessed online September 1, 2012. http://americanolean.com.

Martin, Jim. Personal communication. July 1, 2012.

Smith, Steve. Personal communication. December 16, 2012.

Walker Zanger. Accessed September 2, 2012. http://walkerzanger.com.

Chapter 7 | Resilient and Soft Flooring

Resilient and soft floor covering are two of the most affordable types of flooring. Most resilient floor covering allows a surface that is easy to keep clean and yet is easier to stand on over time than wood, tile, or concrete flooring. Resilient floor covering includes vinyl, linoleum/Marmoleum, cork, and rubber. Soft floor covering, carpet, is appealing to many people for its softness, warmth, and style. These types of flooring materials are specified in nearly every residential and commercial setting.

Chapter Outline

Terminology

Allowance Additional amount of carpet and vinyl added to width and length of room to allow for straightening edges for seaming, width or length adjustments within room, and extra material to run to center of doorway.

Birdcage Carpet installation terminology referring to the spindles circling a newel post and the newel post itself on a staircase. There is usually an upcharge per birdcage to install, since there is much cutting and stapling involved in the fit.

Box/carton Most tile and modular floors are priced by the square foot but sold by the full box or carton. Once the square footage needed for the room has been calculated, this amount is divided by the square footage found in a box/carton. The subsequent number is rounded up to a whole number to give the actual number of boxes/cartons to be ordered.

Broadloom Carpet that is made on a very wide loom and comes on a roll. The most common broadloom carpet is 12 feet wide.

Carpet tile Carpet that is made in modular sizes, allowing easier installation than broadloom and the ability to replace damaged or worn pieces without replacing the entire space. Sizes of carpet tile will vary by pattern and by manufacturer. Some are metric sizes. See also *modular flooring*.

Carpet upholstery Any exposed flooring edge where carpet is wrapped, for example, the sides of stairs or a second floor landing that overlooks another area.

Carpet/vinyl width The actual width of the roll (broadloom or sheet) goods. Most carpet is 12 feet wide; however, it can be manufactured in 13-foot 6-inch and 15-foot widths. Rarely does it come in widths different from these, but it is possible. Most vinyl is manufactured 12 feet; 6 feet 6 inches; and 6 feet wide. The more rigid the vinyl material, the narrower the roll will be.

Churn The amount of downtime created when a space for a business or institution is remodeled or reconfigured. It can also be considered the turnaround time from physically starting work on a space to finishing the work. The less amount of churn, the happier the client. It is not unusual for businesses open during daytime hours to have flooring installations done at night to reduce the amount of churn.

Direct glue-down Type of flooring installation whereby the product is permanently attached to the subfloor or foundation with glue adhesive.

Fill Rooms wider than the width of carpet must be seamed so that another piece of carpet can fill the rest of the space. Fill refers to the carpet in a room or on a seaming diagram that is not covered by the first full width of carpet or vinyl (Figure 7.1).

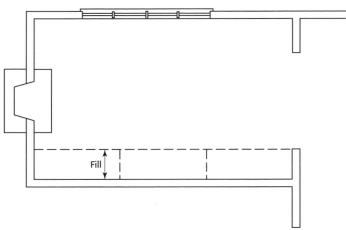

Figure 7.1 Carpet fill is the amount of carpet needed to complete the room width.

Floating floor Type of flooring installation where the product is not permanently attached to the subfloor or foundation. There is a distinct separation between the subfloor and the final flooring product. Floating floors tend to be modular and interlock to each other. Cork, laminate, Marmoleum, rubber, vinyl, and wood materials may use floating floor installation. Sometimes the product rests on a cushion on top of a moisture barrier.

Freight The cost of shipping carpet or vinyl. Many times this cost is factored into the price of the carpet as per square yard or per square foot price. Sometimes freight companies will add fuel surcharges that will increase this amount.

Haul-off The removal of old carpet and pad from the job site. This is usually an amount charged to the client—the haul-off fee.

Labor The cost per square yard or per square foot of installing the material. This includes additional items such as birdcages, upholstering stairs, moving large items such as refrigerators, pulling up toilets, and haul-off.

Minimums As this relates to labor, installers have a minimum charge for going to a job site to install. If a small room is getting carpet or vinyl, sometimes the minimum installation amount must be charged instead of the square yardage or square footage labor amount.

As this relates to material, at times, there is a minimum amount of product that must be ordered. This depends on the manufacturer. For example, some manufacturers

might require a minimum of 3 inches or 6 feet of carpet to be ordered.

As this relates to freight, there is a minimum charge to ship anything. If the amount shipped doesn't meet the minimum, the minimum charge is billed.

Modular flooring Flooring that is made in a particular size unit that is meant to fit easily together. Some modular flooring units interlock with each other. Carpet tile, Marmoleum interlocking tile, Cork tile, and rubber tile are examples of soft and resilient modular flooring. See also *carpet tile*.

Nap/pile Just like velvet fabric has a direction to the fabric, called nap, carpet has a nap/pile. Carpet fibers reflect light differently when looked at from different directions. The pile (nap) runs the length, not the width, of the carpet roll in one direction. For carpet to have a uniform look, the pile must run the same direction for all carpet that is seamed together.

Pad A layer of cushioning beneath the carpet. The most common densities and heights are:

- 6-pound density, ½-inch high (6 lb., ½″)
- 6-pound density, ⅞-inch high (6 lb., ⅞″)
- 8-pound density, ¼-inch high (8 lb., ¼″)
- 8-pound density, ⅜-inch high (8 lb., ⅜″)

These are not the only densities and heights available. Carpet manufacturers will recommend the specific height and density of the pad for the carpet under consideration. Variation from the manufacturer's recommendation will void the product warranty. New pads should always be installed under new carpet. There are few exceptions to this.

Pile See *nap/pile*.

Resilient flooring Flooring that is firm when walked on but has some resilience, such as vinyl, linoleum/Marmoleum, cork, and rubber. It is not as soft and as giving as carpet, but it is softer than wood, tile, and concrete.

Roll balance The amount of carpet left on a roll after exact, or "cut," orders are cut from the roll. Many times manufacturers will honor the roll price if the roll balance is taken.

Roll goods Broadloom carpet and sheet goods that are rolled around a core and can be ordered in necessary lengths. Although the technical name is "rolled goods," "roll goods" has become the commonly used term. A whole roll of carpet or sheet goods will come in a specific length. For example, 125 feet may be the length of a roll of carpet. Although roll goods can be ordered in amounts less than a full roll, there is a price break if a full roll is ordered.

Room length When roll goods are calculated, the length of the room is determined to be the direction in which the material comes off of the roll (Figure 7.2).

Room width When roll goods are calculated, the width of the room is determined to be the direction of the width of the material as it rests. It is the room width that determines whether a seam is necessary (Figure 7.2).

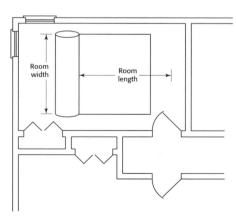

Figure 7.2 Room width and length are determined by how the carpet will come off the roll for the room.

Seam When the width of the carpet or vinyl will not entirely fill the space from side to side, a seam is necessary in order to fill the space. It is possible to get several fill pieces out of a carpet width. If the fill is 6 feet or less, two pieces or more can be utilized from the same length. This reduces the amount of carpet or vinyl that must be ordered for the fill. The main seam runs the length of the carpet. The two types of seams are as follows:

Cross seam When more than one fill piece is needed, the fill pieces must be seamed together. The carpet seam perpendicular to the length seam of the carpet is the cross seam. Depending on the application, it is preferable to have no more than three or four cross seams (Figure 7.3).

Length seam This is the main seam along the length of the carpet (Figure 7.3).

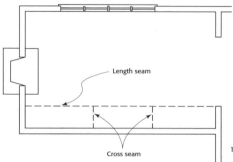

Figure 7.3 Length and cross seams.

Seaming diagram A diagram of the area to be covered showing carpet direction, length seams, and cross seams (Figure 7.4). The diagram can be created on a scaled floor plan, or it can be a sketch, usually not to scale, and generally in proportion to the rooms nearby. This diagram is used by the flooring installers.

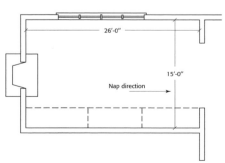

Figure 7.4 Seaming diagram showing nap direction.

Seaming tape A tape used on the underside, or jute side, of the carpet to seam two pieces of carpet together. A carpet iron is used to melt the adhesive on the tape to the carpet. Seaming tape comes in various widths and with various features.

Sheet goods Flooring, such as vinyl linoleum/Marmoleum, and rubber, that comes on a roll. See *roll goods*.

Soft flooring Flooring that is soft to walk on, generally carpeting.

Square foot Obtained by multiplying, in feet measurement, width times length (Figure 7.5). Tiles and plank goods are normally calculated, ordered, and priced by the square foot.

Square yard Obtained by multiplying, in feet measurement, width times length to find square feet, then dividing by 9 to find square yards. There are 9 square feet in 1 square yard (Figure 7.5). Carpet and vinyl roll goods have traditionally been calculated, ordered, and priced by the square yard.

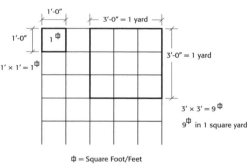

Figure 7.5 1 ft. × 1 ft. = 1 sq. ft.; 3 ft. = 1 yd.; 3 sq. ft. × 3 sq. ft. = 9 sq. ft. in 1 sq. yd.

Stair nose The part of the stair tread that extends past the stair riser (Figure 7.6).

Stair riser The vertical portion of a stair—that is, the portion that rises (Figure 7.6).

Stair tread The horizontal portion of a stair—that is, the portion that is tread upon (Figure 7.6).

Take-off Utilizing floor plans instead of a site measure to calculate quantity of materials needed for a job, generally used for budgeting.

Take-up An installation term referring to the cost of pulling up any existing flooring that must be removed before new flooring is installed.

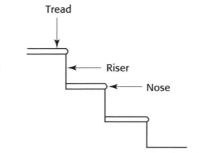

Figure 7.6 Stair parts: Riser, tread, and nose.

Transition pieces Products made to finish exposed raw edges and provide a smooth transition from one flooring surface to another, minimizing height differences between surfaces.

Underlayment A firm and smooth material that will provide support underneath vinyl flooring. Underlayment helps to smooth out any imperfections in the subflooring material.

Waste Portions of roll and tile goods that are left over on a project and usually left with the client/customer.

Types of Soft and Resilient Flooring

Soft and resilient flooring can be found as roll goods, sheet goods, and modular tiles. Many types of soft flooring, such as broadloom carpet, are available on the market: cut pile, loop pile, or a combination of cut and loop. Common fiber contents of carpets are nylon, olefin, polyester, wool, acrylic, and various blends. Resilient flooring is available as sheet goods as well as modular tiles. Common examples of resilient flooring include vinyl, linoleum/Marmoleum, cork, and rubber. Carpet most commonly comes in roll goods (broadloom carpet), but the popularity and availability of modular carpet tiles is starting to make an impact on the market.

Carpet Tile and Resilient Tile

Most carpet tiles are commercial carpet. A few residential carpet offerings come as carpet tile; however, commercial carpet can be used in residential settings. Commercial carpet tiles have a very firm feel, since a very firm pad is part of the carpet tile. Most people are used to a softer feel in their homes than what commercial carpet tiles create. Many carpet tiles are laid so that each tile is turned 90 degrees when no pattern match is necessary. Some carpet tiles can be

installed without glue by using the manufacturer's recommended glue-free adhesive squares.

Vinyl, linoleum/Marmoleum, cork, and resilient flooring tiles may come as either individual tiles that glue directly to the floor or as pieces that interlock with each other to create a floating floor. Interlocking tile is sometimes referred to as "click tile," since they make a clicking noise as they are locked together. Depending on the subfloor and the product, a cushion and moisture barrier may be needed.

Sheet Goods

The most common sheet goods used in residential and commercial settings are vinyl, linoleum/Marmoleum, and rubber. Sheet vinyl flooring is often found residentially in kitchens and bathrooms. While linoleum/Marmoleum can be used in homes, currently it is found more often in commercial settings. Rubber sheet goods are very popular in exercise spaces.

Broadloom Carpet

Broadloom carpet is sold as residential or commercial. While commercial grade carpet can be used residentially, residential grade carpet should not be used commercially. A "high traffic" residential carpet is not appropriate for commercial applications.

The majority of residential carpet sold is in solid or duo colors; however, the popularity of carpet selections with a pattern has grown over the years. Where once it was important that all carpet be the same in a home, today carpet is selected based on anticipated use of the space. For example, denser carpeting, perhaps with a woven pattern, is better for stairs and hallways, to accommodate and hide the wear common in these heavily trafficked spaces.

The majority of commercial carpet sold is patterned. Commercial spaces get heavier wear than residential spaces, and patterned carpet helps to disguise wear and stains.

Pad for carpet is dependent on the type of carpet and the manufacturer's specifications. Unless a special type of pad is specified, pads that currently meets manufacturers' warranties for residential carpets are normally ⁷⁄₁₆-inch 6-pound or ¼-inch 8-pound.

Sizes and Packaging

Depending on which product you are considering, sizing and packaging will vary. Note that products change rapidly and sizes that are common today may change. Once the product is selected, download the specification sheet and follow the dimensions and information given. Carpet and resilient tiles must be ordered by the full box or carton, which will vary from style to style and manufacturer to manufacturer. Broadloom and sheet goods are ordered either as a cut length or by the roll. The width of the product will depend on the style selected.

Carpet Tile and Resilient Tile

Carpet tiles have a broad range of sizes: 12 inches × 12 inches, 18 inches × 18 inches, 19.7 inches × 19.7 inches (50 cm × 50 cm), and 24 inches × 24 inches (60.96 cm × 60.96 cm). Vinyl resilient tiles come in many sizes, including 12 inches × 12 inches, 12 inches × 24 inches, 16 inches × 16 inches, 16.5 inches × 16.5 inches, 18 inches × 18 inches, and 18.5 inches × 18.5 inches. Linoleum/Marmoleum

direct glue-down resilient tiles commonly come in sizes 13 inches × 13 inches and 20 inches × 20 inches. The click tiles commonly are sized as 13 inches × 13 inches and 12 inches × 36 inches. Cork also comes as a direct glue-down or interlocking tile. The direct glue tiles are approximately 12 inches × 12 inches and 24 inches × 24 inches. The interlocking tiles are normally 12 inches × 36 inches. Rubber tiles are generally interlocking and sized as 12 inches × 12 inches and 24 inches × 24 inches.

Sheet Goods

Vinyl sheet goods generally come in 6-foot and 12-foot widths. The 6-foot-wide sheet vinyl is more rigid than the 12-foot-wide sheet vinyl. Vinyl roll length is anywhere from 110 feet to 150 feet. Unless the interior designer has a contract with a large housing complex or other type of commercial project that uses a lot of sheet vinyl, he or she will never have a single job that will take a whole roll of vinyl. Linoleum/Marmoleum comes in widths of 6 feet 7 inches, with rolls that are 105 feet long. Rubber comes in 4-foot-wide rolls that are 25 feet or 50 feet long. As mentioned earlier, all of these items can be ordered to the exact length needed if you don't need a full roll.

Most 12-foot-wide sheet vinyl is not as durable as 6-foot-wide sheet vinyl. The more durable and rigid the sheet vinyl is, the narrower the product is made for the roll. As vinyl gets more rigid and durable, it becomes more fragile in the installation process, and the narrower widths are necessary to prevent it from breaking easily.

Broadloom Carpet

Most carpet comes as rolls in three common widths: 12 feet, 13 feet 2 inches, and 15 feet. The most common width of roll goods is 12 feet. Carpet manufacturers will sometimes offer their carpet in 12-foot and 15-foot widths. This helps minimize seams in situations in which room widths are greater than 12 feet but less than 15 feet. The width of the carpet is important in the seaming diagram and the computations. Each manufacturer will have a minimum length of carpet that can be ordered. This may be less than 1 foot. Carpet roll length may vary from 100 feet to 150 feet. The length of carpet needed to meet roll lengths can vary with each manufacturer and each style. It is possible to ask about roll balances when ordering. A roll balance is the amount of carpet left on a roll after "cut" orders are cut from the roll.

Cost Factors

Although these types of flooring are uniquely different from each other, they share common cost factors (Table 7.1). The basic components to be considered are material, pad/cushion/underlayment, transition pieces, shipping, installation, and labor extras. Note that there are different costs for residential and commercial projects. Usually these costs depend on the scale and complexity of the project and the labor laws in the state.

Material costs depend on the quality and quantity of material ordered, especially when pricing roll goods, resilient or broadloom. The price for roll quantity is less than the exact yardage price. Freight figures will differ from region to region and year to year and are always dependent on the price of gas. Most freight companies have minimum charges for shipping roll goods.

Direct glue-down installations are usually less expensive than other floor installations because there is usually not as much complexity (Table 7.2). Extra labor costs beyond the base installation may be incurred for moving furniture or appliances, taking up and disposing of previous flooring material, pulling and reseating toilets, and any stair work. Installers limit their cleanup to removing carpet scraps, tools, and equipment. Small yarn cuttings need to be vacuumed by a cleaning crew or the homeowner.

The amount of estimated time to complete a project depends on size of the project, type of installation, and availability of the installers. Large, new homes may take only two days to install; however, it usually takes at least a week for carpet to be shipped to the destination city. Commercial installations may take from several days to several weeks. If the commercial building is currently occupied, installation sometimes must occur in the evening or on weekends. Holidays slow everything down.

The quantity of material may differ from the quantity for which labor is charged. The client will be charged for the amount of material that is actually ordered even though more may have to be ordered than will be installed because of how it is cartoned or packaged. Pad will be charged based on the same quantity as the main material ordered. Labor charges for sheet goods and broadloom will be based on the amount

Carpet Tile & Resilient Tile	Sheet Goods	Broadloom Carpet
Tile material	Sheet material	Carpet material
Cushion, if applicable	Underlayment, if applicable	Pad, if applicable
Moisture barrier, if applicable		
Transition pieces, if applicable	Transition pieces, if applicable	Transition pieces, if applicable
Freight/shipping	Freight/shipping	Freight/shipping
Installation	Installation	Installation
Labor extras*	Labor extras*	Labor extras*
*Labor extras: New or existing construction, take-up and haul-off of existing flooring, repair of existing flooring, moving furniture, moving appliances, stair work, amd pulling and reseating toilets. In general, flooring installers will not move grand pianos or pool tables.		

Table 7.1 Cost Components for Carpet Tile and Resilient Tile, Sheet Goods, and Broadloom Carpet

Direct Glue-Down Installation	Modular Tile Floating Floor	Sheet Goods with Underlayment	Stretched Carpet over Pad
Material	**Material**		
	Cushion & Moisture Barrier, If Applicable	**Underlayment**	**Pad**
Transition pieces, if applicable	Transition pieces, if applicable		
Freight/shipping	Freight/shipping		
Installation	Installation		
Labor extras, if applicable	Labor extras, if applicable		

Table 7.2 Comparison of Cost Components between Direct Glue-Down and Other Installation

of material ordered, even when there is waste. Labor charges for tile products are based on the base amount plus the waste allowance. Table 7.3 on page 78 shows a cost worksheet/schedule that pulls all the various cost components of a job together.

Carpet Tile and Resilient Tile

Cost variables for carpet tile and resilient tile start with the material costs and the type of installation. Depending on the product and the surface upon which it is installed, you may not have a choice as to which installation can be used. If the tiles are directly glued down, the costs include the material, possible transition pieces, shipping/freight, installation, and possible labor extras. The glue or other adhesive is usually included in the installation cost; however, some installers may charge separately for this. If the tiles are laid as a floating floor, costs include the material, possible transition pieces, products serving as a cushion and moisture barrier, shipping, installation, and possible labor extras (see Table 7.2). Carpet tile and resilient tile labor is charged per square foot.

Most carpet tile installations are for commercial areas. Depending on the type of company, installation may have to be scheduled for evenings or weekends to minimize churn. This will impact the installation charge. Commercial carpet tiles can be recycled. Carpet manufacturers will take back used carpet tiles as long as you can get them to a facility where they are accepted. This may involve shipping the carpet tile to a different state.

Sheet Goods

The cost of the material varies with quality and quantity. The cost of sheet goods installation varies depending on whether it is a direct glue-down installation or whether the installation involves underlayment (see Table 7.2). Sheet goods must be laid on "perfect" floors—that is, floors that don't have any blemishes. They can be installed directly on a smooth, clean, concrete floor, but with plywood subfloors, underlayment must be installed to smooth out any rough places. Underlayment is a material that is screwed down to provide this smooth base. In a few instances, sheet vinyl or linoleum/Marmoleum can be laid over existing vinyl floors or linoleum if the underlying product doesn't have a deep pattern that will "telegraph," or show through. The installer must confirm this decision.

Labor charges can be per square foot or per square yard. Additional labor costs will apply if installation is in an existing kitchen and appliances must be moved. Underlayment is charged per square foot. If installation is in an existing residential bathroom, there will also be costs for pulling and reseating the toilet and any pedestal sink. Freight costs will vary. Distributors in many cities generally have vinyl in stock and have already factored the freight cost into your cost per square yard of the material. In cases for which the product (vinyl, rubber, or linoleum/Marmoleum) must be special-ordered, freight must be calculated.

Flooring

Client:
Phone #s:
Address:
Installer:

Room	Item	Mfr./Vendor	Pattern	Color	Size	Repeat	Quantity	Quantity per Box/Carton	Adjusted Quantity	Cost Per	Subtotal	Est. Ship.	Total	PO	Date
	Material														
	Pad/Cushion/Moisture Barrier/ Underlayment														
	Transitions														
	Labor	Description of Work							Quantity	Cost Per	Subtotal	Est. Ship.	Total	WO	Date
												Total Cost			

Room	Item	Mfr./Vendor	Pattern	Color	Size	Repeat	Quantity	Quantity per Box/Carton	Adjusted Quantity	Cost Per	Subtotal	Est. Ship.	Total	PO	Date
	Material														
	Pad/Cushion/Moisture Barrier/ Underlayment														
	Transitions														
	Labor	Description of Work							Quantity	Cost Per	Subtotal	Est. Ship.	Total	WO	Date
												Total Cost			

Room	Item	Mfr./Vendor	Pattern	Color	Size	Repeat	Quantity	Quantity per Box/Carton	Adjusted Quantity	Cost Per	Subtotal	Est. Ship.	Total	PO	Date
	Material														
	Pad/Cushion/Moisture Barrier/ Underlayment														
	Transitions														
	Labor	Description of Work							Quantity	Cost Per	Subtotal	Est. Ship.	Total	WO	Date
												Total Cost			

Table 7.3 Flooring Cost Worksheet

Broadloom Carpet

Carpet has five main costs to be calculated: carpet material, pad, shipping/freight, installation, and labor extras (see Table 7.1). There is a price break if a roll of carpet can be ordered. The length of carpet needed to meet roll lengths can vary with each manufacturer and style. A good idea is to ask about roll balances when ordering. If a roll balance meets your length requirements, the mill will usually give a roll price on it instead of the cut price. Not all carpet jobs require pad. Just like the other products, broadloom carpet can use a direct glue-down installation, which would not require pad (see Table 7.2). When pad is used, it is common industry practice to price and order the same amount of pad as carpet.

When you are ordering through a carpet broker or showroom, carpet will have a freight allowance for shipping. This means that there is a monetary amount assigned per square yard to be added to the totals to cover shipping. So long as the minimum freight cost has been met, this amount per square yard times the number of square yards shipped is what you will pay for freight. In the past this per-square-yard freight allowance has been less than a dollar. Carpet pad is often stocked locally and the shipping cost already incorporated into the price.

Sometimes multiple styles and colors of carpet are ordered from the same manufacturer. It is important to realize from a freight perspective that the different styles and colors may be manufactured at different mills or shipped at different times, and each style and color will need to meet the minimum shipping charge. This can sometimes be verified when you are ordering. Some companies will charge a cut fee for carpet less than 6 feet long and a minimum shipping charge. Smaller pieces of carpet, for example, smaller than 1 foot, can be shipped via a delivery service (e.g., UPS or Federal Express) for much less than a trucking company would charge.

Most carpet installations are based on a per-square-foot or per-square-yard price; however, there are minimum charges for installation just as there are for freight. Be aware of these charges in case the trip charge applies instead of the per-square-yard charge. When furniture needs to be moved, some installers charge per room, and some charge by the square yard. Carpet and pad removal can be charged as a flat amount, an amount per layer (with carpet counted as one layer and pad counted as a second layer), or an amount per square yard.

Calculations

The basic method for calculating quantity of material needed is common across the country. The costs of material will vary from year to year, and the costs of freight and labor will vary regionally. All tile materials are calculated and ordered based on square feet. Sheet goods and broadloom carpet can be calculated by the square foot or square yard; however, the material comes in specific widths from 4 feet to 15 feet and is normally ordered based on these widths and ordered in square yards. When doing the math, always keep two places to the right of the decimal. If the third number to the right of the decimal is 5 or greater, the second number is rounded up.

Over the years, a number of residential carpet stores have started selling broadloom carpet by the square foot, allowing the consumer to readily compare flooring products to each other, since hard flooring materials are priced and sold by the square foot. The material must still be ordered by the full width of the carpet. Carpet manufacturers now show a square foot and square yard for their goods. Calculating a room on the square footage of the room will not determine the quantity of roll goods that need to be ordered. Whatever product is considered, you will need to understand the basic issues with calculating the amount of material needed.

Carpet Tile and Resilient Tile

When you are calculating carpet tile or resilient tile, the base square footage of the installation is calculated like it is for plank and tile materials. Ten percent additional material is added to allow for waste and precise placement. Because one of the main selling points for using carpet tile is the ease of replacing damaged carpet, an additional 15 to 20 percent of carpet tile must be calculated for the replacement in addition to the 10 percent for cuts and precise placement. This is the only difference between carpet tile and resilient tile calculations. Note that this product must be ordered by the full box. Common practice is to bill the client by the square footage of material ordered. In order to bill correctly, the total square footage represented by full boxes must be calculated. The square footage amounts in full boxes vary by manufacturer and by carpet style. Once the total square footage is determined, costs for the total project can be calculated.

Sheet Goods

Sheet goods are calculated by the square yard; however, any necessary underlayment is calculated by the square foot. When calculating sheet goods material, make sure to add 6 inches to both the length and width of the room. Rooms can vary by several inches from the width or length at one end to the width or length at the other end of the room. The 6 inches will allow for squaring the materials within the room and allow for doorways where the material should go to the center of the doorway. The center of the doorway is approximately 3 inches outside the room dimensions. This dimension can vary depending on wall thicknesses. Because there is no nap to consider, sheet goods can be run in the most efficient way or the most logical way to view the pattern, keeping seams of sheet vinyl out of doorways and walkways when possible. Watch where the seams will be placed, since they can be somewhat visible. The room length is determined as the dimension that the goods will come off the roll; the opposite dimension is the width of the goods.

The number of cuts of material necessary to cover the space is calculated by dividing the adjusted room width by the width of the material (remember that this may be 4 feet, 6 feet, 6.58 feet, or 12 feet, so adjust accordingly) and rounding up to a whole number. Take the number of cuts times the length of the material and divide by 9 to get the square yardage. Underlayment is calculated by determining the base square feet of the space and adding 10 percent more to the original square-foot total.

When calculating sheet goods for rooms with cabinets, use the measurement to the front of the cabinet under the toe kick. When you are estimating for underlayment, it is easier to use the room dimensions and not worry about subtracting the amount under the cabinets. In most cases, an installer will also measure to confirm amounts. Your measurements are used to determine whether the prices are appropriate for your client's budget. When designers are experienced, they are able to measure and close the sale in the same visit if they choose to.

Broadloom Carpet

It takes more steps to calculate the material needed for broadloom carpet. Rigid carpet width dictates that there will be carpet seams in any installation larger than 11 feet 6 inches wide, and nap requires more thought as to how the carpet is laid. A seaming diagram (see Figure 7.4) is necessary to communicate to the installers and to efficiently calculate the material to be ordered. When you are calculating for square yardage, the number of carpet cuts are multiplied by the length of the carpet cut and divided by 9 to determine square yards. There are 9 square feet in 1 square yard (see Figure 7.5).

Broadloom carpet has several important considerations that must be determined before you proceed with square yardage calculations. The first consideration is that carpet can't be turned one way in the hall and another way in the adjoining room that is seamed to the hall (Figure 7.7). The change of nap direction will make it look as if there is a dye lot issue—a color change (Figure 7.8). The first major step in calculating carpet yardage in the home is determining carpet pile direction.

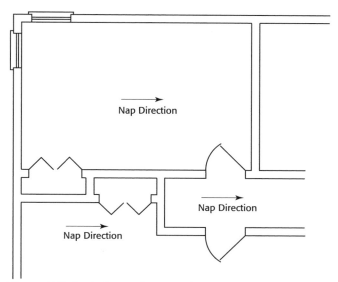

Figure 7.7 The hall nap direction determines the nap direction of the bedrooms that use the same carpet as the hall.

1) Carpet width
2) Pile direction
3) Seam placement
   a. Natural light source
   b. Traffic pattern
   c. Furniture arrangement

Box 7.1 Considerations for Determining Carpet Direction

PILE DIRECTION GUIDELINES

Normally, the carpet nap runs the length of the room—length as it is determined by carpet direction. Ideally, one will walk into the nap of the carpet, with these exceptions:

1. When carpet is not seamed to other carpet outside the space, the area is not a highly public area, and there is no way to use the extra carpet for fill, resulting in too much carpet waste.
2. When the rest of the home is the same carpet and the carpet will be seamed together. The public areas of the home dictate the carpet nap direction for the rest of the rooms. In this case, in some rooms, usually bedrooms seamed at the doorway

Figure 7.8 The same carpet laid with the nap in opposite directions. Notice the color difference. (Courtesy of Craig Speer, The Flooring Guy, Austin, TX, www.austinfloorsandmore.com)

into the hall, the carpet length may run the opposite direction than would normally be calculated. The hall carpet nap direction is set by the nap direction in the public areas, which in turn sets the nap direction in the adjoining bedrooms (see Figure 7.7).

3. When the seam would fall in an awkward area of the traffic pattern, the carpet may need to be turned, so that one walks into the side of the nap

instead of into the nap (Figure 7.9). This is not always necessary, since the seam is strong and should not open; however, if the seam is likely to show, it is better to avoid placing it in a highly visible place, such as the entry to the room.

While the following is not an exception, it is a situation to consider. Imagine entering a home where the entry and major traffic patterns to the kitchen and bedrooms are a hard surface. The living room/office is to the left and the dining room is to the right of the entry, with a great room straight ahead. The carpet may need to be considered differently if it has a **strong nap.** In order for the carpet to visually look the same color, the nap should run toward the direction you walk into the room—in this case the entry. This means that the carpet is not laid with the nap so that it lines up in the same north/south (or east/west) direction in the three rooms. This is probably unusual for the carpet installer to consider, so the designer must insist upon it (Figure 7.10).

SEAM PLACEMENT

It is common for rooms to have seams. Many rooms are wider than the width of the carpet, and additional carpet must be seamed together to finish covering the floor. When additional carpet used is less than the width of the carpet roll, the additional carpet is called fill. The main seam runs the length of the carpet at the side (see Figure 7.3). It is common to have cross seams. With cross seams, a shorter length of carpet can be ordered and cut into strips—still respecting the carpet nap—so that less carpet can be ordered for the fill (Figure 7.11).

Carpets that are plush, looped, and patterned are more likely to show seams than are frieze carpets. This doesn't mean that the seam will show for the plush, looped, and patterned. It is not possible to guarantee that the seams won't show, but there are ways to minimize the appearance of a seam. Careful consideration of natural light sources, furniture

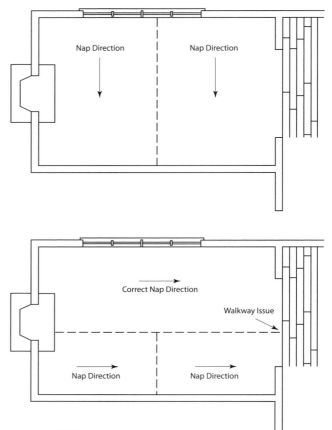

Figure 7.9 Carpet seams.

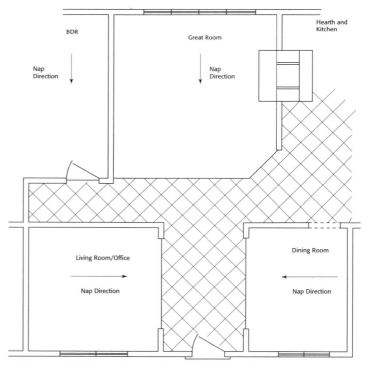

Figure 7.10 Room layout in public areas of home can determine pile direction because of the desired visual appearance.

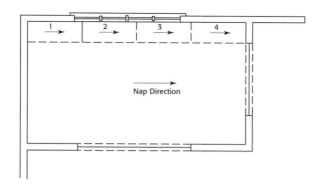

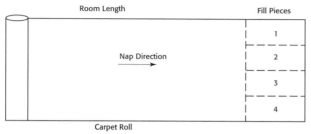

Figure 7.11 Seam and fill placement in room and from roll of carpet

Furniture Arrangement. When a room is totally bare of furniture, it is easier to find seams than when furniture is in the room. Furniture will break up light as it comes into a room and will change the shadow pattern. So, even when the seam is parallel to a window, furniture placed in the room may cover the seam or just change the light pattern being cast on the carpet enough to hide the seam (Figure 7.12).

Traffic Patterns. Carpeted areas in traffic patterns are likely to show wear over time. When a seam is placed in a traffic pattern, it is more likely that the seam over time will be seen. Seamed carpet is strong and should not split or break open, but continued traffic over the same area can cause the seam to be visible. It is preferable not to have a seam in a major traffic pattern, such as to the center of the doorway.

Even though a designer can calculate carpet and determine square yardage, carpet installers will also measure to confirm square yardage and to

arrangements, and traffic patterns will help to minimize seams.

Natural Light Sources. To create a seam, seaming tape is placed under the seam, and a carpet iron is used to heat up the adhesive through the carpet to bind the two pieces together. The seaming tape adds another layer at this point, causing the seam to be almost imperceptibly taller than the other area. Strong light coming through windows and doors can throw shadows on seams that are parallel to the light because of this height variance. Northern light is weaker light but should still be considered. When there are windows on adjacent walls and cross seams, it is impossible to make sure all seams are perpendicular to the light. Consideration must be given to the window treatment and what is going to sit on the carpet near the window that will create other shadows that will help to hide seams. Draperies and sheers can help to diffuse strong light.

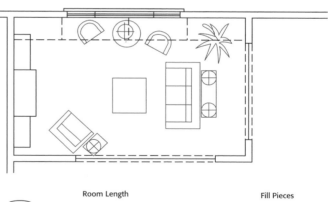

Figure 7.12 The furniture arrangement can disguise seams by covering them and changing the light pattern that hits them.

determine their carpet cuts. A reputable carpet installer will take into consideration light sources, furniture arrangements (if they know it), and traffic patterns when they measure. If there is concern about the seam being visible, the installer has different types of seaming tape that may cost more but can be helpful. It is very important to communicate to your installer if your client is expressing concern from the beginning about seams showing. While it is not possible to guarantee that seams won't show, it is possible to educate the client about this so that should seams show, the client isn't taken by surprise.

GENERAL NOTES FOR CARPET CALCULATIONS

1. Make a diagram of space showing dimensions in feet and inches—for example, 10 feet 3 inches. Normally this is not drawn to scale.

2. Determine length and width direction of carpet and draw arrows indicating nap direction.

3. Remember to add 6 inches to the room length and width to allow for fitting the carpet to the room and for carpet to go to the center of doorways.

4. Determine seam placement.

5. When calculating for fill pieces, keep the number of fill pieces to four or fewer. More cross seams will greatly increase the possibility that a seam will show.

6. If the carpet has a repeat, remember that the length of each carpet cut must be adjusted to accommodate pattern matching in the same way it is done with wallpaper and fabric.

7. Determine how transitions from one flooring material to another will be treated. Transition thresholds may need to be ordered.

8. To accurately measure stairs, take measurements from under the stair nose, down the riser, across the tread, and under the nose again. This number will probably be somewhere between 18 inches and 22 inches (Figure 7.13). Then add 3 inches to this. Determine how many cuts can come from one carpet width. Take the total number of treads, and divide by how many cuts come from the carpet width. Multiply this number by the length needed for each stair. Pieces of 12-foot-wide carpet that normally cover stairs, depending on the number of treads and the stair width, are 12 feet × 8 feet, 12 feet × 10 feet, or 12 feet × 16 feet.

9. Once you know the width and length in feet of carpet to be ordered, multiply them together to get square feet and then divide by 9 to find square yards. Keep two decimals to the right of the decimal point.

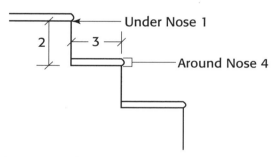

Figure 7.13 When you are measuring stairs for carpet, keep in mind that the carpet dimension for each step begins under the nose (1), comes down the riser (2), goes across the tread (3) and around the nose (4), and ends under the nose at the top of the next riser.

Step-by-Step Examples

Example 1—Resilient Tile

Your client is going to use a Marmoleum tile for a 50-foot × 30-foot multipurpose room of a community building (Figure 7.14). The Marmoleum will be direct glued down, is 20 inches × 20 inches, and comes in boxes containing 53.82 square feet.

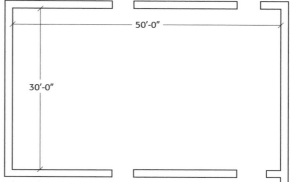

Figure 7.14 Example 1—Resilient tile.

Step 1: Draw diagram of room and take room dimensions.

Do not use inches. Convert everything to feet. A room 13 feet 8 inches converted to feet will be 13.67 feet.

Step 2: Calculate base square footage of space.

Take width of room in feet:	50	ft.
Multiply by length of room in feet: ×	30	ft.
Total base square footage of space:	1500	sq. ft.

Step 3: Calculate additional materials for waste allowance.

Take square footage from Step 2:	1500	sq. ft.
Multiply by 10 percent to allow for waste allowance: ×	1.10	waste allowance
Total square footage needed:	1650	sq. ft.

Note: This is usually the square footage amount the installer will use to bill for labor.

Step 4: Calculate additional materials for replacement allowance.

The Marmoleum tiles will not have a replacement allowance, so we are skipping to Step 5.

Step 5: Calculate the number of full boxes/cartons to be ordered.

Take square footage needed from Step 3 or 4:	1650	sq. ft.
Divide by square feet per box/carton: ÷	53.82	sq. ft.
Total boxes/cartons needed:	30.66	boxes/cartons
Round up to whole number:	31	full boxes/cartons to order

Step 6: Calculate actual square feet in boxes/cartons ordered.

Take number of boxes from Step 5:	31	boxes/cartons
Multiply by square feet per box/carton: ×	53.82	sq. ft.
Total square footage ordered:	**1668.42**	**sq. ft.**

Most installers will charge for 1650 square feet, the square footage plus waste allowance. This is important to be aware of when you calculate your costs. The client is usually charged for 1668.42 square feet in material cost.

Example 2—Sheet Goods

An existing bathroom in a home, originally carpeted, is going to have sheet vinyl installed and will need underlayment (Figure 7.15). The floor space measures 5 feet × 5 feet, and the vinyl material is 6 feet 6 inches wide.

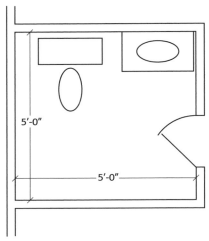

Figure 7.15 Example 2—Sheet goods.

Step 1: Draw diagram of room and take room dimensions.

    Do not use inches. Convert everything to feet.

Step 2: Determine width with allowance.

Take width of room in feet (e.g., 15.5):	5	ft.
Add 6 inches (.5 feet):	+ .5	ft.
Total cut width:	5.5	ft.

Step 3: Determine number of cuts based on material width.

Take total cut width from Step 2:	5.5	ft.
Divide by width of vinyl:	÷ 6.5	ft.
Total:	.85	cut
Round up to whole number:	1	cut

Note: With sheet goods it is desirable to have only a lengthwise seam, if any at all.

Step 4: Determine cut length.

Take length of room in feet (e.g., 9.25 feet):	5	ft.
Add 6 inches (.5 feet):	+ .5	ft.
Total length of cuts:	5.5	ft.

Step 5: Determine length to order.

Take total from Step 3:	1	cut
Multiply by the total from Step 4:	× 5.5	ft.
Total length of material to be ordered:	5.5	ft.

Step 6: Determine square feet and square yards.

Take length from Step 5:	5.5	ft.
Multiply by width of material:	× 6.5	ft.
Total square feet:	35.75	sq. ft.
Divide by 9 to convert to square yards:	÷ 9	
Total square yards needed:	3.972	sq. yd.
Round to two numbers to right of decimal point:	**3.97**	**sq. yd. needed to order**

Determine underlayment, if necessary.

Step 1: Determine base square footage of room.

Take exact width of room:	5	ft.
Multiply by exact length of room:	× 5	ft.
Base square feet of room:	25	sq. ft.

Step 2: Determine square footage of underlayment needed.

Take total from Step 1:	25	sq. ft.
Multiply by 1.10 to allow for waste:	× 1.10	waste allowance
Total for underlayment:	27.5	sq. ft.
Round to two numbers to right of decimal point:	**27.5**	**sq. ft. needed to order**

When the vinyl is ordered, it will be ordered as a 6.5-foot × 5.5-foot piece; 3.97 square yards. Just as the underlayment is calculated differently than vinyl, the price charged to install it will also be different. In this case, vinyl is priced by the square yard and underlayment is priced by the square foot.

Example 3—Broadloom Carpet

Your client has decided to re-carpet her son's bedroom. The room is 10 feet × 13 feet with a 2-foot-deep closet. The carpet is a 12-foot-wide broadloom (Figure 7.16).

Step 1: Draw diagram of room and take room dimensions.

Do not use inches. Convert everything to feet.

Step 2: Determine carpet direction in room.

Decide which way the carpet will run. The length dimension of the room is determined by the direction the carpet will come off the roll. The width dimension of the room is the other dimension. In this specific problem, the width is the short dimension of the room and will result in no seams (Figure 7.17).

Step 3: Determine overall width with allowance.

Take width of room in feet (e.g., 15.5):

	10	ft.
Add 6 inches (.5 feet):	+ .5	ft.
Total cut width:	10.5	ft.

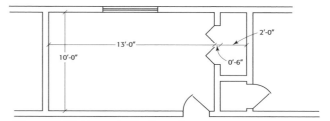

Figure 7.16 Example 3—Broadloom carpet.

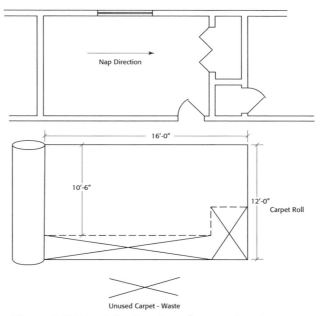

Figure 7.17 Nap/pile direction of room related to the roll of carpet. Not all carpet is needed; some will be waste. The client still pays for all the carpet, and normally all carpet is left with the client after installation.

Step 4: Determine whether fill is necessary.

Take total cut width from Step 3:	10.5 ft.
Subtract width of carpet in feet	− 12 ft.

Note: This will probably be 12-foot-, 13.17-foot-, or 15-foot-wide carpet.

Total:	− 1.5 ft.

If this is a positive number (greater than 0), you have to determine seam placement and possible fill.

Step 5: Determine fill width.

Because this is a negative number, this tells you that the carpet width is sufficient and won't need a seam. Since no fill is needed, Step 5 is skipped.

Step 6: Determine length of first cut.

Take length of room in feet (e.g., 9.25 feet):	15.5 ft.

Note: The room length is 13 feet + 6-inch wall depth + 2-foot closet depth.

Add 6 inches (.5 foot):	+ .5 ft.
Total length of first cut:	16 ft.

Step 7: Determine fill length.

Because there is no fill, Step 7 is skipped.

Step 8: Determine total length to be ordered.

Take length of first cut from Step 6:	16 ft.
Add length of fill from Step 7:	+ 0 ft.
Total length of carpet to be ordered:	16 ft.

Step 9: Determine square feet and square yards.

Take length of carpet from Step 8:	16 ft.
Multiply by width of carpet:	× 12 ft.

Note: Even though 10.5 feet of carpet is needed for the room, you must use the full width of the carpet material.

Total square feet:	192 sq. ft.
Divide by 9 to convert to square yards:	÷ 9 sq. ft.
Total square yards of carpet:	**21.33 sq. yd.**

Example 4—Carpeted Stairs

Along with an upper hall and bedrooms, your client has a run of stairs that will be carpeted (Figure 7.18). The stairs are 44 inches wide and the carpet is 12 feet wide. In this exercise, just calculate carpet for the run of stairs.

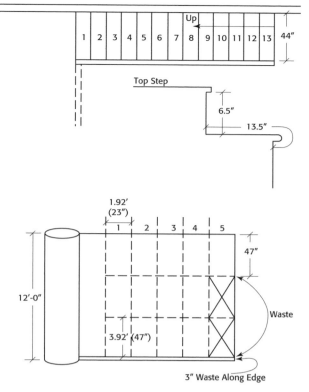

Figure 7.18 Example 4—Carpeted stairs.

Step 1: Determine cut width.

Measure width of stair in inches:	44	in.
Add 3 inches cut allowance:	+ 3	in.
Total:	47	in.
Convert to feet:	÷ 12	in.
Total in feet:	3.92	ft.

Step 2: Determine number of cuts from carpet width.

Take width of carpet in feet:	12	ft. (12 ft., 13.17 ft., or 15 ft.)
Divide by total from Step 1:	÷ 3.92	ft.
Total:	3.06	cuts
Round down to nearest whole number:	3	vertical cuts from carpet width

For best wearability, the nap will always run the length of the stairs.

This tells you how many full strips will come out of the width of a 12-foot-wide piece of carpet.

Step 3: Determine total number of cuts for carpet length.

Take total number of treads:	13	treads
Divide by total from Step 2:	÷ 3	cuts
Total:	4.33	cuts
Round up to whole number:	5	total carpet cuts needed

Hint: 13 to 15 treads will need 5 cuts of carpet.

Step 4: Determine length of cuts.

Take length of stair cut (riser + tread + around nose)	20	in.
Add 3 inches cut allowance:	+ 3	in.
Total:	23	in.
Convert to feet:	÷ 12	in.
Total length of carpet cuts:	1.92	ft.

Step 5: Determine total length of carpet.

Take total from Step 3:	5	cuts
Multiply by total from Step 4:	× 1.92	ft.
Total length of carpet needed:	9.6	ft.

Step 6: Determine square feet and square yards.

Take length of carpet from Step 5:	9.6	ft.
Multiply by width of carpet:	× 12	ft.
Total square feet:	115.2	sq. ft.
Divide by 9 to convert to square yards:	÷ 9	
Total square yards of carpet to order:	**12.8**	**sq. yd.**

Quick Estimate

To quickly estimate stairs that meet the basic code of 18 inches for tread plus riser, allow 24-inch cuts of carpet per tread. Unless the stairs are more than 45 inches wide, allow 48 inches per vertical cut, and consider that you will have 3 carpet cuts from a width. Take the number of treads, divide by 3, and round up to the nearest whole number to find the number of horizontal cuts. Multiply this number of horizontal cuts by 2 feet to find the length of carpet ordered. Multiply the length by the carpet material width (the assumption is that this is 12-foot-wide carpet), and divide by 9 for square yards.

Using the same scenario as above, we can use the quick estimate process to calculate the square yardage needed.

Step 1: Determine cuts of carpet.

Take number of treads:	13	treads
Divide by 3:	÷ 3	widths from 12-ft. carpet
Total:	4.33	ft.
Round up to whole number:	5	cuts of carpet

This tells you how many cuts will be needed in the length of a piece of carpet. (Hint: 13 to 15 treads will need 5 cuts of carpet.)

Step 2: Determine total length of carpet.

Take total from Step 1:	5	cuts of carpet
Multiply by length of cut:	× 2	ft.
Total:	10	ft.

Step 3: Determine square feet and square yards.

Take length of carpet from Step 2:	10	ft.
Multiply by width of carpet:	× 12	ft.
Total square feet:	120	sq. ft.
Divide by 9 to convert to square yards:	÷ 9	
Total square yards of carpet to order:	**13.33**	**sq. yd.**

Note that when compared to the expanded carpeted stair worksheet, the quick estimate requires approximately 5 inches more carpet to be ordered (10 feet compared to 9.6 feet). Even in a hard measure, this is within industry standards.

Manual Worksheets

<table>
<tr><td colspan="3" align="center">Carpet Tile and Resilient Tile Worksheet</td></tr>
<tr><td colspan="3">

Step 1: Draw diagram of room and take room dimensions.

Do not use inches. Convert everything to feet. A room 13 feet 8 inches converted to feet will be 13.67 feet.

Step 2: Calculate base square footage of space.

Take width of room in feet:	_____	ft.
Multiply by length of room in feet:	× _____	ft.
Base square footage of space:	_____	**sq. ft.**

Step 3: Calculate additional material for waste allowance.

Take square footage from Step 2:	_____	sq. ft.
Multiply by 10 percent to allow for waste:	× _____1.10_____	waste allowance
Total square footage needed:	_____	**sq. ft.**

If material being calculated will not need additional replacement tiles ordered, skip to Step 5.

Step 4: Calculate additional materials for replacement allowance.

Take square footage from Step 2:	_____	sq. ft.
Multiply by 20 percent to allow for replacement:	× _____1.20_____	replacement allowance
Total square footage needed:	_____	**sq. ft.**

Step 5. Calculate number of full boxes/cartons to be ordered.

Take square footage needed from Step 3 or 4:	_____	sq. ft.
Divide by square feet per box/carton:	÷ _____	sq. ft.
Total boxes/cartons needed:	_____	**boxes/cartons**
Round up to whole number:	_____	**full boxes/cartons to order**

Step 6. Calculate actual square feet in boxes/cartons ordered.

Take number of boxes/cartons from Step 5:	_____	boxes/cartons
Multiply by square feet per box/carton:	× _____	sq. ft.
Total square footage ordered:	_____	**sq. ft.**

</td></tr>
</table>

Sheet Goods Worksheet

Step 1: Draw diagram of room and take room dimensions.

Do not use inches. Convert everything to feet. A room 13 feet 8 inches, converted to feet, will be 13.67 feet.

Step 2: Determine width with allowance.

Take width of room in feet (e.g., 15.5 ft.): _____ ft.

Add 6 inches (.5 ft.): +_____.5_____ ft.

Total: _____ **ft.**

Step 3: Determine number of cuts based on material width.

Take total from Step 2: _____ ft.

Divide by width of material: ÷_____ ft.

Note: 4 ft. rubber, 6 ft. vinyl, 6.58 ft. linoleum/Marmoleum, or 12 ft. vinyl width.

Total: _____ **cuts**

Round up to whole number: _____ **cuts**

Note: With vinyl it is desirable to have only one lengthwise seam, if any at all.

Step 4: Determine cut length.

Take length of room in feet (e.g., 9.25 ft.): _____ ft.

Add 6 inches (.5 ft.): +_____.5_____ ft.

Total length of cuts: _____ **ft.**

Note: If more than one cut is necessary and the material has a repeat, divide this length by the length of the repeat to find full repeats necessary. Round up to a full number, and multiply by the length of the repeat. This will be the adjusted cut length.

Step 5: Determine length to order.

Take total from Step 3: _____ cuts

Multiply by the total from Step 4: ×_____ ft.

Total length of material to be ordered: _____ **ft.**

Step 6: Determine square feet and square yards.

Take length of material from Step 5: _____ ft.

Multiply by width of material: ×_____ ft. (4 ft., 6 ft., 6.58 ft., or 12 ft. width)

Total square feet: _____ **sq. ft.**

Divide by 9 to convert to square yards: ÷_____9_____ sq. ft.

Total square yards needed: _____ **sq. yd.**

Round to two numbers to right of decimal point: _____ **sq. yd. needed to order**

Determine underlayment if necessary:

Step 1: Determine base square footage of room.

Take exact width of room: _____ ft.

Multiply by exact length of room: _____ ft.

Base square feet of room: _____ **sq. ft.**

Step 2: Determine square footage of underlayment needed.

Take total from Step 1: _____ sq. ft.

Multiply by 1.10 to allow for waste: ×_____ waste allowance

Total for underlayment: _____ **sq. ft.**

Round to two numbers to right of decimal point: _____ **sq. ft.**

Broadloom Carpet Worksheet

Step 1: Draw diagram of room and take room dimensions.

Do not use inches. Convert everything to feet. A room 13 feet 8 inches, converted to feet will be 13.67 feet.

Step 2: Determine carpet direction in room.

Decide which way the carpet will run. The length dimension of the room is determined by the direction the carpet will come off the roll. The width dimension of the room is the other dimension.

Step 3: Determine overall width with allowance.

Take width of room in feet (e.g., 15.5 ft.):	_____	ft.
Add 6 inches (.5 ft.): +	_____.5_____	ft.
Total cut width:	_____	**ft.**

Step 4: Determine whether fill is necessary.

Take cut width from Step 3: −	_____	ft.
Subtract width of carpet in feet: −	_____	ft.

Note: This will probably be 12-foot, 13.17-foot, or 15-foot-wide carpet.

Total:	_____	**ft.**

If this is a positive number (greater than 0), you have to determine seam placement and possible fill.

Step 5: Determine fill width.

Take width of carpet in feet:	_____	ft.
Divide by total from Step 4: ÷	_____	ft.
Total:	_____	cuts
Round down to nearest whole number:	_____	**full pieces from carpet width**

This tells you how many full strips will come out of a 12-foot-wide piece of carpet.

Step 6: Determine length of first cut.

Take length of room in feet (e.g., 9.25 ft.):	_____	ft.
Add 6 inches (.5 ft.): +	_____.5_____	ft.
Total length of the first cut.	_____	**ft.**

If carpet has a repeat, divide this length by the length of the repeat to find full repeats necessary. Round up to a whole number and multiply by the length of the repeat. This will be the adjusted cut length.

Step 7: Determine fill length.

Take length of room in feet + 6 inches (.5 ft.):	_____	ft.
Divide by total from Step 5: ÷	_____	full pieces from carpet width
Total length of second cut:	_____	**ft.**

Step 8: Determine total length to be ordered.

Take length of first cut from Step 6:	_____	ft.
Add length of second cut from Step 7: +	_____	ft.

If more rooms with same carpet, continue to add as many lengths as needed.

Total length of carpet to be ordered:	_____	**ft.**

Step 9: Determine square feet and square yards.

Take length of carpet from Step 8:	_____	ft.
Multiply by width of carpet: ×	_____	ft.
Total square feet:	_____	**sq. ft.**
Divide by 9 to convert to square yards: ÷	_____9_____	sq. ft.
Total square yards of carpet:	_____	**sq. yd.**

Note: When ordering carpet, you not only need to have square yards, but also the exact width and length of the cut. Convert any decimal total in Step 8 to inches. For example, to find how many inches are represented in the decimal, multiply the decimal by 12. For carpet that is 9.25 feet long, multiply .25 × 12 = 3 inches. The carpet length is 9 feet 3 inches. This would be ordered as 12 × 9 ft. 3 in., a total of 12.33 square yards.

See Carpeted Stairs Worksheet to determine amount of carpet needed for stairs.

Carpeted Stairs Worksheet

Step 1: Determine cut width.

Measure width of stair in inches: _____ in.

Note: If any side is upholstered, add 3 inches for each side to the width measurement.

Add 3 inches cut allowance: +_____3_____ in.

Total cut width: _____ **in.**

Convert to feet: ÷_____12_____ in.

Total cut width in feet: _____ **ft.**

Note: Sometimes stair widths will change from the top of the run to the bottom. In this case, write down the width measurements and how many treads this affects.

Step 2: Determine number of cuts from carpet width.

Take width of carpet in feet: _____ ft. (12 ft., 13.17 ft., or 15 ft.)

Divide by total from Step 1: ÷_____ ft.

Total: _____ **cuts**

Round down to nearest whole number: _____ **vertical cuts from carpet width**

This tells you how many full strips will come out of a 12-foot-wide piece of carpet.

Step 3: Determine total number of cuts for carpet length.

Take total number of treads: _____ treads

Divide by total from Step 2: ÷_____ cuts

Total: _____ **cuts**

Round up to whole number: _____ **total carpet cuts needed**

Step 4: Determine length of cuts.

Take length of stair cut (riser + tread + around nose) _____ in.

Add 3 inches cut allowance: +_____3_____ in.

Total: _____ **in.**

Convert to feet: ÷_____12_____ in.

Total: _____ **ft.**

Note: If carpet has a repeat, divide this length by the length of the repeat to find full repeats necessary. Round up to a full number and multiply by the length of the repeat. This will be the adjusted cut length.

Step 5: Determine total length of carpet.

Take total from Step 3: _____ cuts

Multiply by total from Step 4: ×_____ ft.

Total length of carpet needed: _____ **ft.**

Note: Landing space might be able to be found in carpet waste, if there is any, or will be added at the end of this step.

Step 6: Determine square feet and square yards.

Take length of carpet from Step 5: _____ ft.

Multiply by width of carpet ×_____ ft. (12 ft., 13.17 ft., or 15 ft.)

Total square feet: _____ **sq. ft.**

Divide by 9 to convert to square yards: ÷_____9_____ sq. ft.

Total square yards of carpet to order: _____ **sq. yd.**

Carpeted Stairs Worksheet—Quick Estimate

This can be used as long as the tread and riser measurements are equal to or less than 18 inches and the stair width is not more than 45 inches.

Step 1: Determine cuts of carpet.

Take number of treads:	_____	treads
Divide by 3: ÷	_____3_____	widths from 12-ft. carpet
Total:	_____	**ft.**
Round up to whole number:	_____	**cuts of carpet**

This tells you how many cuts will be needed in the length of a piece of carpet. (Hint: 13 to 15 treads will need 5 cuts of carpet.)

Step 2: Determine total length of carpet.

Take total from Step 1:	_____	cuts of carpet
Multiply by 2 ft.: ×	_____2_____	ft.
Total:	_____	**ft.**

Step 3: Determine square feet and square yards.

Take length of carpet from Step 2:	_____	ft.
Multiply by width of carpet: ×	_____	ft. (12 ft., 13.17 ft., or 15 ft.)
Total square feet:	_____	**sq. ft.**
Divide by 9 to convert to square yards: ÷	_____9_____	sq. ft.
Total square yards of carpet to order:	_____	**sq. yd.**

Note: If there is a pattern, the 2 ft. cut will need to be adjusted according to the pattern.

Practice Lessons: Resilient and Soft Flooring

Resilient Tile

A living room is being converted to a home office, with cork tile as the flooring selection (Figure 7.19). The tiles are 12 inches × 12 inches and come packaged 36 square feet to a carton. They will be laid using direct glue-down installation.

1. What is the base square footage of the room?
2. What is the total square footage needed to ensure coverage?
3. How many boxes/cartons must be ordered, and what is the total square footage that is ordered?

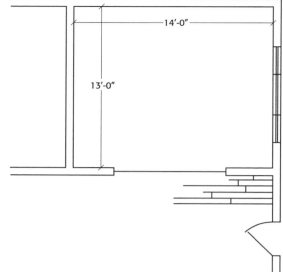

Figure 7.19 Practice lesson: Basic—Resilient tile.

Sheet Goods

Sheet vinyl is going to be used in the utility/laundry room of a new home (Figure 7.20). The sheet vinyl is 12-foot-wide and will need underlayment. The pattern in the vinyl is non-directional, so it can be laid in any direction.

1. What is the total length of the material to be ordered?
2. How many square yards must be ordered?
3. What is the total underlayment square footage to be charged?

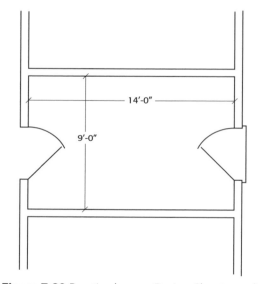

Figure 7.20 Practice lesson: Basic—Sheet goods.

Broadloom Carpet

A frieze carpet and the appropriate pad have been selected for the living room in your client's home (Figure 7.21). The carpet is 12 feet wide and will butt into wood flooring in the entry and hall.

1. What direction does the pile run?
2. What is the total length of carpet to be ordered?
3. How many square yards must be ordered?

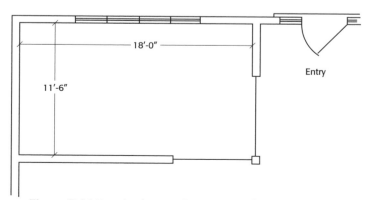

Figure 7.21 Practice lesson: Basic—Broadloom carpet.

Carpeted Stairs

Your client wants to carpet stairs into her lower level. It is a straight run to a space with 13-foot ceilings, with a total of 15 treads. The stair width is 40 inches, and the carpet width is 12 feet (Figure 7.22).

1. How long is each cut of carpet for each step?
2. How many cuts of carpet are needed?
3. How many full widths can be cut from a 12-foot-wide piece of carpet?
4. What is the length of carpet to be ordered for the stairs?

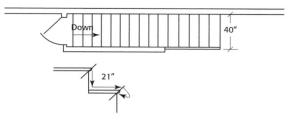

Figure 7.22 Practice lesson: Basic—Carpeted stairs.

INTERMEDIATE
Resilient Tile

Carpet tiles will be used in a reception area that gets a lot of use and has had issues with stains in the past (Figure 7.23). Carpet tiles have been chosen because they can be replaced easily if they become stained or worn. The carpet tiles are 2 feet × 2 feet and are packaged 48 square feet in a box.

1. What is the base square footage of the space?
2. What is the total square footage including replacement tiles?
3. How many boxes/cartons must be ordered, and what is the total square footage ordered?

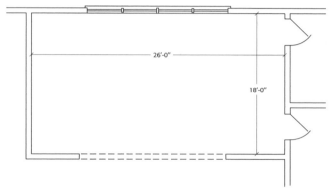

Figure 7.23 Practice lesson: Intermediate—Resilient tile.

Sheet Goods

Your client wants to use sheet Marmoleum for her kitchen and eating area (Figure 7.24). The material is 79 inches wide and will be installed as a direct glue-down. Any seams should run parallel to the sink run of cabinets.

1. Which direction in the room will the Marmoleum run, and how many seams will this be?
2. What is the total length of material to be ordered?
3. How many square yards must be ordered?

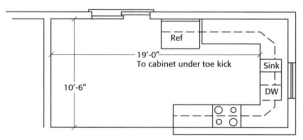

Figure 7.24 Practice lesson: Intermediate—Sheet goods.

Broadloom Carpet

This room will be carpeted in 12-foot-wide cut/loop broadloom, the same as found in the hall (Figure 7.25).

1. What direction does the pile run?
2. What is the total length of carpet to be ordered?
3. How many square yards must be ordered?

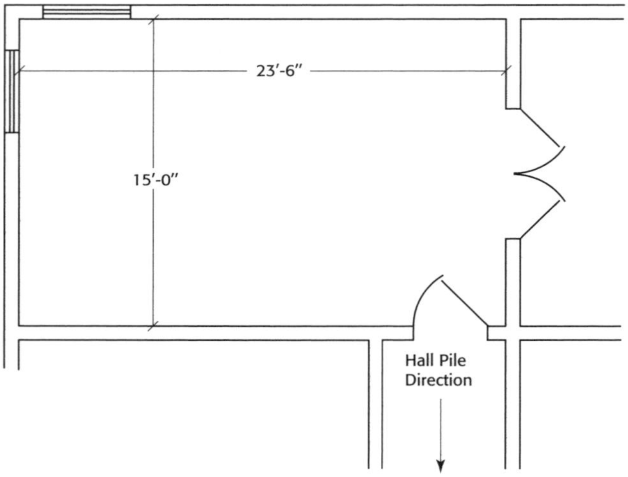

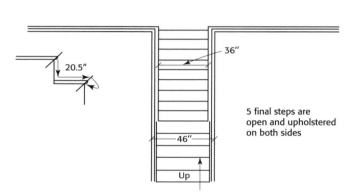

Figure 7.25 Practice lesson: Intermediate—Broadloom carpet.

Carpeted Stairs

The stairs in this space have two different width dimensions. The first 5 treads are 46 inches wide and are upholstered to each side. The remaining treads are 36 inches wall to wall (Figure 7.26). The carpet material is 12 feet wide.

1. How long is each cut of carpet for each step?
2. How many vertical cuts of carpet are needed?
3. How many full widths can be cut from a 12-foot-wide piece of carpet for the first five steps? How many full widths can be cut from a 12-foot-wide piece of carpet for the remaining steps?
4. What is the total length of carpet to be ordered for the stairs?

Figure 7.26 Practice lesson: Intermediate—Carpeted stairs.

ADVANCED
Resilient Tile

The hall and copy room area of lawyers' offices will be covered with carpet tile (Figure 7.27). They want to be able to replace worn and stained squares, as they like to keep their space looking pristine. The carpet tile is 18 inches × 18 inches and is packaged in cartons containing 42.84 square feet.

1. What is the base square footage of the space?
2. What is the total square footage including replacement tiles?
3. How many boxes/cartons must be ordered, and what is the total square footage ordered?

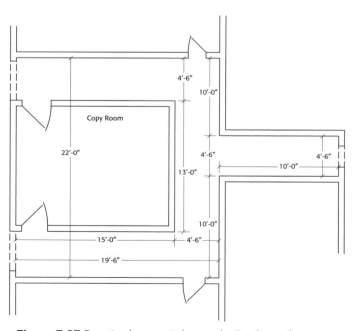

Figure 7.27 Practice lesson: Advanced—Resilient tile.

Sheet Goods

Sheet rubber will be used in a workout facility (Figure 7.28). The rubber is 4 feet wide.

1. Which direction in the room will the rubber run, and how many seams will this be?
2. What is the total length of material to be ordered?
3. How many square yards must be ordered?

Broadloom Carpet

Your client is re-carpeting her living room with a 12-foot-wide, cut pile carpet (Figure 7.29). The wood floor meets the carpet at the opening into the living room.

1. What direction does the pile run?
2. How many fill pieces will be used?
3. What is the length of the fill piece?
4. What is the total length of carpet to be ordered (including the fill)?
5. How many square yards must be ordered?

Pricing Broadloom Carpet

Use the square yardage found in the Advanced Broadloom Carpet practice lesson and the prices below to calculate the price of this job for your client.

Carpet—$38.49 per square yard

Freight—$0.85 per square yard (Minimum shipping charge is $60.00. If the square yardage times the freight charge doesn't meet the minimum, the minimum shipping charge is used.)

Pad—$4.00 per square yard (material is stocked locally and doesn't have any additional freight charges)

The existing transition piece will be used, so no cost is incurred.

Installation—$12.00 per square yard

Take-up charge—$2.50 per square yard for carpet and pad

Haul-off charge—$85.00 total

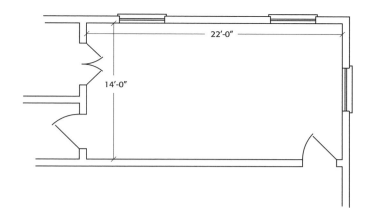

Figure 7.28 Practice lesson: Advanced—Sheet goods.

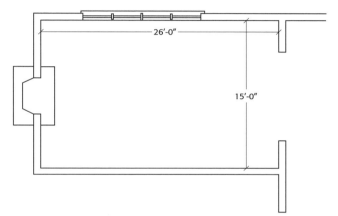

Figure 7.29 Practice lesson: Advanced—Broadloom carpet.

Your clients will move the furniture from the room themselves.

1. What is the price of materials: carpet, pad, and freight?
2. What is the price of labor: installation, take-up, and haul-off?
3. What is the total price of this job?
4. What is the price per square yard?

References

Godsey, L. *Interior Design Materials and Specifications.* New York: Fairchild Publishing, 2008.

Martin, Jim. Personal communication. July 1, 2012.

Chapter 8 | Area Rugs

Area rugs are important design elements for many spaces, and interior designers make great use of them. It is not always easy or possible to find area rugs of the right size, colors, and style for a project. While those that provide oriental and patterned area rugs urge us to start with the area rug, this isn't always possible or practical.

Several area rug manufacturers, such as Fabrica, Shaw, Schumacher, and Merida, make rugs to designer specifications, including style, design, and color. However, it is sometimes possible to save time and money by having a basic bound piece of carpet or a two- or more pieced bordered carpet made locally. This chapter deals specifically with the bordered rugs that are generally fabricated locally.

INSIGHT FROM THE FIELD

❝❝ I discovered bound rugs can be designed in any way imaginable. They can have a contrasting carpet border, a leather border, or even a monogram laser cut into the center. The sky is the limit. Bound carpet remnants are a great option for a client on a budget.❞❞

Kathy Bryles, *owner of Kathy Bryles Interiors in Kansas City, Missouri*

Chapter Outline

Terminology

Allowance Additional amount of carpet, 3 inches, added to each cut of carpet to allow for straightening edges for seaming.

Backing Material applied to the back of the area rug to create a finished look. Cotton monk cloth is sometimes used. The fabricator normally charges by the square foot for the labor including the material (Figure 8.1). The square feet are found by taking the overall width in feet times the overall length in feet of the area rug.

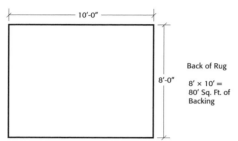

Figure 8.1 Backing charge for area rugs is calculated by multiplying, in feet, the overall width and length of the area rug.

Bevel A 45-degree angle cut into the carpet either where two pieces of carpet are seamed or into the field of the carpet to create a pattern.

Binding Commonly, cotton tape of varying widths that is either color-matched or contrasted sewn to the raw edge of the area rug to finish the edges. This is a labor charge that is calculated by the running foot (Figure 8.2). The running feet are found by adding all sides, in feet, together.

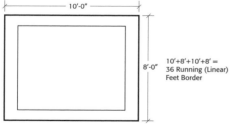

Figure 8.2 Binding is applied to the perimeter of the area rug to finish the raw edges. It is calculated by adding, in feet, all sides together.

Border When an area rug is made of two or more pieces of carpet, the outer part of the area rug is the border. If the area rug is made of three or more pieces of carpet, it will have an outer border and one or more inner borders (Figure 8.3).

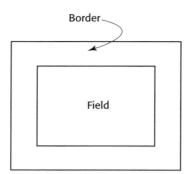
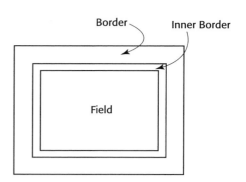

Figure 8.3 Borders and field.

Broadloom Carpet that is made on a very wide loom and comes on a roll. The most common broadloom carpet is 12 feet wide.

Carpet width The actual width of the broadloom roll of goods. Most carpet is 12 feet wide; however, it can come in widths of 13 feet 2 inches and 15 feet. Rarely does it come in sizes different from these.

Field When an area rug has a border, the field is the innermost part of the area rug (see Figure 8.3).

Freight The cost of shipping carpet. Sometimes the carpet must be shipped via regular trucking companies; however, sometimes the carpet can be packaged and shipped via a delivery service such as UPS or Federal Express, which will have lower shipping costs.

Labor The cost of fabricating an area rug, which can include binding or serging, seaming, backing, and beveling.

Minimums As this relates to material, there is a minimum amount of product that must be ordered. This depends on the manufacturer. For example, some manufacturers might require a minimum of 3 inches or 6 feet of carpet to be ordered. If less than this is ordered, a cut charge will be added to the total. As this relates to freight, there is a minimum charge to ship anything. Usually, each carpet piece for area rugs must have the minimum shipping charge factored into the cost.

Nap/pile As with velvet fabric, which has a direction to the fabric, called nap, carpet has a nap, usually referred to as pile. Carpet fibers reflect light differently when viewed from different directions. The pile runs the

length, not the width, of the carpet roll in one direction. For area rugs to have a uniform look, the nap/pile of all borders must run toward the field (Figure 8.4).

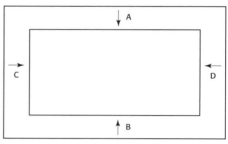

Arrows Represent Nap Direction

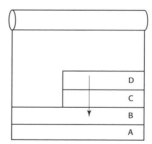

Figure 8.4 The nap/pile of the borders must run toward the center of the carpet so that it has a uniform appearance where it meets in the corners.

Pad A layer of cushioning beneath the area rug. Different types of pad are used depending on the type of area rug and the flooring on which the rug will lay. A 21-pound, ⅛-inch or ¼-inch pad will provide appropriate support to area rugs and the furnishings placed upon them.

Pile See *nap/pile*.

Seam Where two pieces of carpet come together, a seam is created. In an area rug

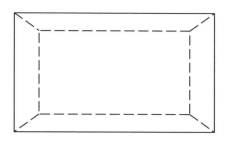

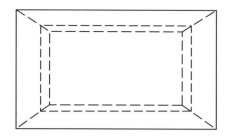

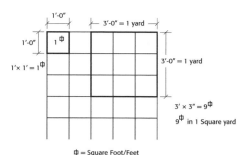

Φ = Square Foot/Feet

Figure 8.7 Square yards.

— — — — Seams

Figure 8.5 Seams occur where two pieces of carpet meet. They are generally found at the corners and where borders meet inner borders or the field.

there are seams at the mitered corners and where the borders meet each other and the field (Figure 8.5).

Seaming The fabricator charges by the running foot for seaming the borders and field together (Figure 8.6). This is calculated by adding, in feet, all seams together.

Serging A way of finishing the raw edges of area rugs by using a large sewing machine that sews back and forth, perpendicular to the edge, using thread as the finish. This is

commonly found in inexpensive area rugs that are mass-produced.

Square yard Obtained by multiplying, in feet measurement, width times length to find square feet, then dividing by 9 to find square yards. There are 9 square feet in 1 square yard (Figure 8.7). Broadloom goods have traditionally been calculated, ordered, and priced by the square yard.

Waste Parts of the carpet roll that are not used for the border or the field (Figure 8.8).

Sometimes the waste can be bound and used for small throw rugs in other parts of the home.

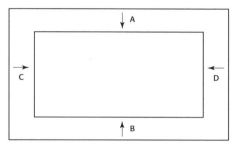

Arrows Represent Nap Direction

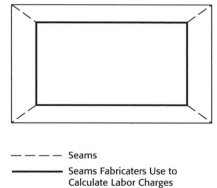

— — — — Seams

———— Seams Fabricaters Use to Calculate Labor Charges

Figure 8.6 Fabricators will charge for seaming where the borders meet borders or the field. The seam at the mitered corners is not calculated. The perimeter of these areas, in feet, are added together to determine the charge.

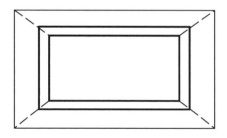

Figure 8.8 It is common that there is carpet waste, sometimes just scraps, when carpet is used in area rugs. If the waste is large enough, it can be bound and used as smaller throw rugs in other areas of the home.

Types of Custom Area Rugs

Because this chapter focuses on bordered area rugs, it will not discuss every type of area rug that can be found. Common types of custom area rugs are one-piece bound, two-piece bordered and bound, and three-piece bordered and bound (Figure 8.9). While there can be more than three pieces (a rug with an

outer border, an inner border, and a field), it isn't common; however, the method of determining labor and material quantity is the same.

Area rugs can be made of any type of carpet. Sisal, cable, frieze, residential, and commercial—all have a role to play in the design that is desired for the space. Interior designers have been known to take heavy

A

B

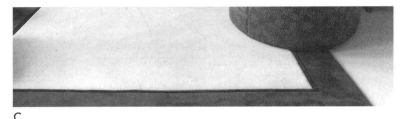

C

Figure 8.9 Interior designers can create many different types of area rugs. Sisal bound with a wide tape (A) differs greatly in style from bound (B) and bordered (C) area rugs made from residential carpet. (Courtesy of Diana Allison)

tapestry fabrics, have them upholstered around tight loop commercial carpet, and then use them for 1-inch to 6-inch inner borders. The look created by the various types of carpets is unlimited.

Sizes and Packaging

As stated in the previous chapter, most carpet comes as rolls in three common widths: 12 feet, 13 feet 2 inches, and 15 feet. The most common width of roll goods is 12 feet. When designing area rugs, we sometimes need pieces as small as 10 inches × 12 feet. Each manufacturer will have a minimum length of carpet that can be ordered without an additional cut charge. This amount may be smaller than 1 foot or as large as 6 feet.

Cost Factors

Custom area rugs have four to seven costs to be calculated. Materials include carpet material (however many pieces there are), shipping/freight for each piece of carpet, pad, binding, seaming, backing, and delivery (Table 8.1). An area rug schedule allows all specifications and costs to be pulled together into one place (Table 8.2).

Sometimes multiple styles and colors of carpet are ordered from the same manufacturer. It is important to realize, from a freight/shipping perspective, that the different carpets may be manufactured at different mills or shipped at different times, and each style and color will need to have the minimum shipping

Material	Labor
Carpet—Field	Binding
Freight/shipping	Seaming—1st border*
Carpet—Outer border*	Seaming—2nd border*
Freight/shipping*	Backing*
Carpet—Inner border*	Delivery
Freight/shipping*	
Pad**	
*If applicable. **Sometimes the fabricator will supply the pad, in which case the cost comes on that invoice.	

Table 8.1 Cost Components for Custom Area Rugs

Custom Area Rug

Client:
Phone #s:
Address:
Designer:
Fabricator:

Item	Mfr./Vendor	Pattern	Color	Repeat	Quantity	Cost Per	Subtotal	Est. Ship.	Total	PO	Date
Carpet—Field											
Carpet—Outer border											
Carpet—Inner border											
Carpet—Inner border											
Pad											
Miscellaneous											
								Total Cost			

Labor	Description	Quantity	Cost Per	Subtotal	Est. Ship.	Total	WO	Date
	Binding							
	Seaming							
	Seaming							
	Seaming							
	Backing							
	Miscellaneous							
	Delivery							
				Total Labor Cost				
				Total Material Cost				
				TOTAL COMBINED COSTS FOR AREA RUG				

Table 8.2 Custom Area Rug Cost Worksheet

charge calculated. This can sometimes be verified when ordering. As stated, some companies charge a cut fee for carpet less than 6 feet long and also a minimum shipping charge. If the carpet ordered is short enough, the carpet manufacturer may roll it the short direction and ship it via a delivery service, saving shipping costs.

Calculations

Carpet can be made any size and of any carpet material. In order to price an area rug, you must know what size to make it. In a living area, ideally the area rug is sized so that all conversation furniture sits on the rug and the rug then extends at least 3 inches beyond the furniture (Figure 8.10). For dining room area rugs, where the size of the dining room and placement of the floor vents allow, add 5 feet to the overall width and length of the dining table (Figure 8.11). This allows 30 inches on each side beyond the table and should ensure that people at the table will remain on the area rug when chairs are slightly pushed back from the table. Two feet will not allow this. In a bedroom the area rug needs to be large

enough (or use runners) that extend 24 inches to 30 inches on each side of the bed where people will put their feet (Figure 8.12).

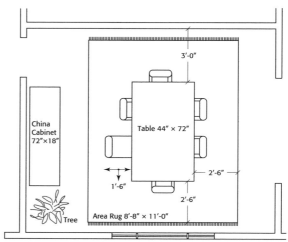

Figure 8.11 If the room allows, an area rug for a dining room should extend at least 30 inches (2.5 feet) beyond each side of the table to allow for chair legs to remain on the rug when the chairs are occupied.

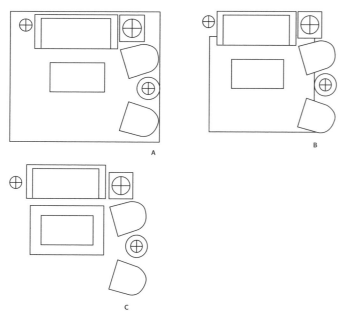

Figure 8.10 Note how the area rug can effectively pull the grouping together. (A) Area rug with all furniture legs on rug. (B) Area rug with only the fronts of chairs on area rug. (C) Incorrect placement. Don't use an area rug to anchor only a coffee table.

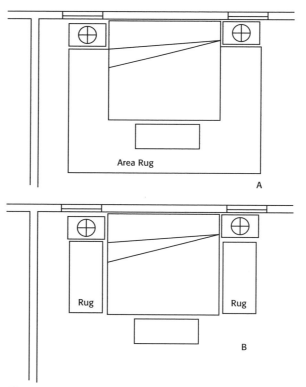

Figure 8.12 (A) Area rug that is positioned under the bed to allow approximately 30 inches each side of the bed. (B) Area rug runners positioned on each side of the bed.

For bordered rugs, the nap/pile direction must run toward the center field. Because of this the carpet border length is factored up the roll (Figure 8.13). The nap direction of the field is an arbitrary decision made by the designer and often determined by which direction takes the least amount of carpet (see Figure 8.13). To each cut of carpet material for an area rug, 3 inches must be added to allow for straightening the cut. This means that if the border is 12 inches, 15-inch cuts are required when you are calculating the amount of material needed (see Figure 8.13). Keep in mind when ordering that if the border is less than 6 feet wide, two sides can be obtained from one cut. If the border is more than 12 feet, an additional cut may be necessary to provide the fill for those sides. If the field is 4 feet 6 inches × 7 feet 0 inches with 4 feet 6 inches as the shortest side, 4 feet 9 inches is the length of the 12-foot-wide carpet.

When calculating square yardage, you multiply the number of carpet cuts by the length of each carpet cut. This length is multiplied by the width of the carpet, normally 12 feet, and divided by 9 to determine square yards. The length of the border in Figure 8.13 is 12 inches, but each cut will have 3 inches added and equal 15 inches. Convert this to feet by dividing by 12 inches to equal 1.25 feet. 1.25 feet × 4 cuts = 5 feet. So 5-foot × 12-foot-wide carpet = 60 square feet. Convert this to square yards by dividing by 9 and you will get 6.67 square yards of carpet for the border.

The field in Figure 8.13 is found by taking the overall dimension of the carpet and subtracting the borders from it. 9 feet – 1 foot – 1 foot = 7 feet wide. 6.5 feet – 1 foot – 1 foot = 4.5 feet long. 4.5 feet is the short side, and this will be used for the length, since the 7 feet fits within the 12-foot-wide carpet width. Add 3 inches to 4.5 feet and the cut will be 4.75 feet (3 inches must be converted to feet by dividing by 12, which equals .25 feet; 4.5 feet + .25 feet = 4.75 feet). 4.75 feet × 12 feet = 57 square feet. Convert this to square yards by dividing by 9 = 6.33 square yards for this field.

Waste is a common component of creating area rugs. There will usually be extra carpet that can't be used for the specific area rug being created. Sometimes some of the waste pieces can be bound to be used in other areas.

Labor costs include binding/serging, seaming, backing, pad, beveling if applicable, and delivery.

- Binding/serging is calculated on the perimeter of the area rug. All sides are added together. In Figure 8.13, 9 feet + 9 feet + 6.5 feet + 6.5 feet = 31 feet for binding/serging.

- Seaming is calculated on the perimeter of the areas where the different carpets meet. It is not calculated on the corner seams or cross seams in the case of large rugs. All sides are added together. In Figure 8.13, the seam perimeter

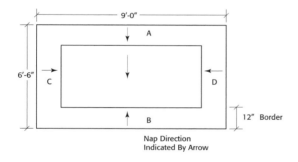

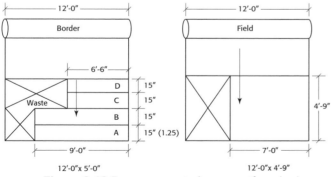

Figure 8.13 For area rugs to have a uniform look at the corner miter and when viewed from different directions, the nap of the borders must run toward the field. Generally, the nap direction of the field can be in the direction that takes the least amount of carpet. The fabricator needs 3 inches more than the actual length specified for each border cut or the field in order to straighten the cuts for seaming and binding.

is found by subtracting the border from the perimeter. As mentioned, the actual field is 7 feet × 4 feet 6 inches. 7 feet + 7 feet + 4.5 feet + 4.5 feet = 23 feet for seaming.

- Backing is calculated on the actual square feet of the area rug. The overall width and length of the rug in feet are multiplied together: Width in feet × Length in feet = Square feet of rug. In Figure 8.13, 9 feet × 6.5 feet = 58.5 square feet of backing.

- Pad is calculated on the square yardage of area

rug pad used. This pad may be 6 feet or 12 feet wide and is calculated in the same manner that carpet square yardage is. In Figure 8.13, if the pad width is 12 feet, a 6.5-foot × 12-foot piece of pad will be ordered. 6.5 feet × 12 feet = 78 square feet. Convert this to square yards by dividing by 9 = 8.67 square yards.

- Beveling is calculated on the perimeter of the areas being beveled, usually where the carpet is seamed. All sides that are beveled are added together.

Step-by-Step Examples

Example 1—One-Piece Custom Area Rug

Your client has a 60-inch round table in her breakfast area, and an 8-foot × 8-foot area rug will work best for the space and for the table (Figure 8.14). The carpet is 12-foot-wide synthetic sisal and will look great and clean up well in the area it is to be used. A backing is required, but no pad is going to be used for the area rug.

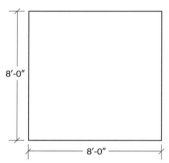

Figure 8.14 Example 1—One-piece custom area rug.

Labor:

Step 1: Draw diagram.

Step 2: Find the perimeter of the area rug for binding.

Add length of all sides together:	Side 1 in feet:	8 ft.
	Side 2 in feet:	+ 8 ft.
	Side 3 in feet:	+ 8 ft.
	Side 4 in feet:	+ 8 ft.
Total perimeter of area rug for binding:		**32 ft.**

Steps 3 and 4: Find perimeters of first and second seams.

There are no seams, so Steps 3 and 4 are bypassed.

Step 5: Calculate for backing.

Take overall width of area rug in feet:	8 ft.
Multiply by overall length of area rug in feet:	× 8 ft.
Total square feet of area rug for pad:	**64 sq. ft.**

Material:

Steps 1 and 2: Determine yardage needed for outer and inner borders.

There are no borders, so bypass Steps 1 and 2 and go directly to Step 3.

Step 3: Determine yardage needed for field.

Take shortest side of field + .25 ft.. (3 in.) for total length:	8.25	ft.
Multiply by width of carpet in feet:	× 12	ft.
Equals:	99	sq. ft.
Divide by 9 to convert to square yards:	÷ 9	sq. ft.
Total square yards to be ordered for field:	**11**	**sq. yd.**

Step 4: Calculate for area rug pad.

There is no area rug pad used, so Step 4 is skipped.

Binding: 32-foot perimeter

Seaming: Does not apply since there is no seam

Backing: 64 square feet

Carpet material: 11 square yards of carpet

Pad: No pad will be used.

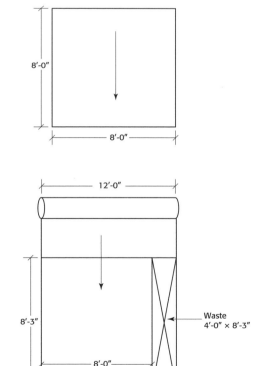

Figure 8.15 Example 1 Answer—One-piece custom area rug.

Example 2—Two-Piece Custom Area Rug

A 10-foot × 12-foot bordered area rug will be used in a great room under the main conversational pieces (Figure 8.16). The border is 15 inches. The two different carpets are 12-foot-wide broadloom goods. The area rug will have a backing. A 12-foot-wide high-density pad will be used under the carpet.

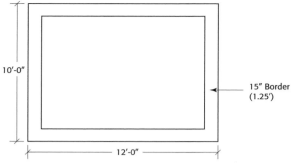

Figure 8.16 Example 2—Two-piece custom area rug.

Labor:

Step 1: Draw diagram.

Step 2: Find the perimeter of the area rug for binding.

Add length of all sides together:	Side 1 in feet:	12 ft.
	Side 2 in feet:	+ 12 ft.
	Side 3 in feet:	+ 10 ft.
	Side 4 in feet:	+ 10 ft.
Total perimeter of area rug for binding:		**44 ft.**

Step 3: Find perimeter of first seam.

Total width of area rug in feet:	12	ft.
Subtract exact size of top border in feet:	− 1.25	ft.
Subtract exact size of bottom border in feet:	− 1.25	ft.
Subtotal A—width of field:	9.5	ft.
Total length of area rug in feet:	10	ft.
Subtract exact size of right side border in feet:	− 1.25	ft.
Subtract exact size of left side border in feet:	− 1.25	ft.
Subtotal B— length of field:	7.5	ft.
Take Subtotal A:	9.5	ft.
Add to Subtotal B:	+ 7.5	ft.
Total:	17	ft.

Note: 17 ft. represents one-half of the perimeter of the rectangle. We multiply by 2 to get the entire perimeter of the 4 sides.

	× 2	
Total perimeter for seaming first seam:	**34 ft.**	

Step 4: Find perimeter of second seam.

There is only one seam, so Step 4 is skipped.

Step 5: Calculate for backing.

Take overall width of area rug in feet:	12	ft.
Multiply by overall length of area rug in feet:	× 10	ft.
Total square feet of area rug for backing:	**120**	**sq. ft.**

Material:

Step 1: Determine yardage needed for outer border.

Add length of border in feet + .25 ft. (3 in.):	Top:	1.5	ft.
	Bottom:	+ 1.5	ft.
	Side:	+ 1.5	ft.
	Side:	+ 1.5	ft.
Total length of carpet needed for outer border:		6	ft.
Multiply length by width of carpet in feet (normally 12 ft.)		× 12	ft.
Total square feet:		72	sq. ft.
Divide by 9 to convert to square yards:		÷ 9	sq. ft.
Total square yards to be ordered for outer border:		**8**	**sq. yd.**

Step 2: Determine yardage needed for inner border.

Step 2 is skipped, as there is no inner border.

Step 3: Determine yardage needed for field (length and width can be found under labor calculations).

Take shortest side of field + .25 ft. (3 in.) for total length:	7.75	ft.
Multiply by width of carpet in feet (normally 12 ft.):	× 12	ft.
Total square feet:	93	sq. ft.
Divide by 9 to convert to square yards:	÷ 9	sq. ft.
Total square yards to be ordered for field:	**10.33**	**sq. yd.**

Note: If the field is wider than 12 ft. in both directions, it will need to have a fill piece and a seam for either the width or the length. With area rugs, we want only lengthwise seams, not cross seams. A second cut the length of this seam + .25 ft. will have to be ordered in addition to the first cut.

Step 4: Calculate for area rug pad.

Take dimension that is 12 feet wide or less. Round up to 12 feet:	12	ft.

Note: If pad is 6 feet wide, substitute 6 feet here.

Multiply by other dimension of area rug in feet:	× 10	ft.
Total square feet of pad:	120	sq. ft.
Divide by 9 to convert to square yards:	÷ 9	sq. ft.
Total square yards of pad:	**13.33**	**sq. yd.**

Binding: 44 feet

Seaming: 34 feet

Backing: 120 square feet

Carpet material: 10.33 square yards for the field; 8 square yards for the border

Pad: 13.33 square yards

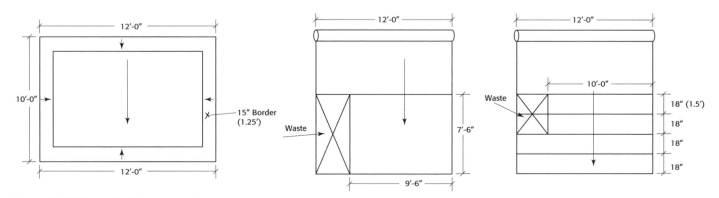

Figure 8.17 Example 2 Answer—Two-piece custom area rug.

Example 3: Three-Piece Custom Area Rugs

You have designed a large area rug for a client who loves bright colors. This area rug will be a three-piece rug; the outer border is violet, the inner border is orange, and the field is green (Figure 8.18). This area rug will be backed and will have a pad. Both the carpet material and the pad are 12 feet wide.

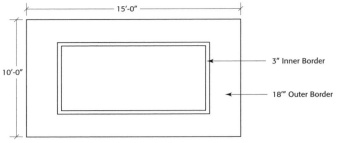

Figure 8.18 Example 3—Three-piece custom area rug.

Labor:

Step 1: Draw diagram.

Step 2: Find the perimeter of the area rug for binding.

Add length of all sides together:	Side 1 in feet:	15	ft.
	Side 2 in feet:	+ 15	ft.
	Side 3 in feet:	+ 10	ft.
	Side 4 in feet:	+ 10	ft.
Total perimeter of area rug for binding:		50	ft.

Step 3: Find perimeter of first seam.

Total width of area rug in feet:	15	ft.
Subtract exact size of top border in feet:	− 1.5	ft.
Subtract exact size of bottom border in feet:	− 1.5	ft.
Subtotal A—width of inner border:	12	ft.
Total length of area rug in feet:	10	ft.
Subtract exact size of right side border in feet	− 1.5	ft.
Subtract exact size of left side border in feet	− 1.5	ft.
Subtotal B—length of inner border:	7	ft.
Take Subtotal A:	12	ft.
Add to Subtotal B:	+ 7	ft.
Total:	19	ft.

Note: 19 ft. represents one-half of the perimeter of the rectangle. We multiply by 2 to get the entire perimeter of the 4 sides.

	× 2	
Total perimeter for seaming first seam:	38	ft.

Step 4: Find perimeter of second seam.

Take Subtotal A—width of inner border:	12	ft.
Subtract exact size of top border in feet:	− .25	ft.
Subtract exact size of bottom border in feet:	− .25	ft.
Subtotal C—width of field:	11.5	ft.
Take Subtotal B—length of inner border:	7	ft.
Subtract exact size of top border in feet:	− .25	ft.
Subtract exact size of bottom border in feet:	− .25	ft.
Subtotal D—length of field:	6.5	ft.

Take Subtotal C:	11.5	ft.
Add to Subtotal D:	+ 6.5	ft.
Total:	18	ft.
	× 2	
Total perimeter for seaming second seam:	**36**	**ft.**

Step 5: Calculate for backing.

Take overall width of area rug in feet:	15	ft.
Multiply by overall length of area rug in feet:	× 10	ft.
Total square feet of area rug for backing:	**150**	**sq. ft.**

Material:

Step 1: Determine yardage needed for outer border.

Add length of border in feet + .25 ft. (3 in.):	Top:	1.75	ft.
	Bottom:	+ 1.75	ft.
	Side:	+ 1.75	ft.
	Side:	+ 1.75	ft.

Since this area rug is wider than 12 feet, there will need to be seams in the outer border. To calculate how many more carpet cuts are necessary for the border, take the width of the area rug 15 feet and subtract the width of the carpet – 12 feet = 3 feet. In this example, the shorter side of the outer border is 10 feet, which will have 2 feet of waste. This isn't enough to cover the 3 feet for the top and 3 feet for the bottom. This 3 feet is considered fill. Both pieces of fill can be taken off the same cut. Only 1 fill cut is needed.

	Fill:	+ 1.75	ft.
Total length of carpet needed for outer border:		8.75	ft.
Multiply length by width of carpet in feet (normally 12 ft.):		× 12	ft.
Total square feet:		105	sq. ft.
Divide by 9 to convert to square yards:		÷ 9	sq. ft.
Total square yards to be ordered for outer border:		**11.67**	**sq. yd.**

Step 2: Determine yardage needed for inner border.

Add length of inner border in feet + .25 ft. (3 in.):	Top:	.5	ft.
	Bottom:	+ .5	ft.
	Side:	+ .5	ft.
	Side:	+ .5	ft.

The inner border is not wider than 12 feet, so there is no need for a fill cut.

Total length of carpet needed for inner border:	2	ft.
Multiply by width of carpet in feet (normally 12 ft.):	× 12	ft.
Total square feet:	24	sq. ft.
Divide by 9 to convert to square yards:	÷ 9	sq. ft.
Total square yards to be ordered for inner border:	**2.67**	**sq. yd.**

Step 3: Determine yardage needed for field (length and width can be found under labor calculations).

Take shortest side of field + .25 ft. (3 in.) for total length:	6.75	ft.
Multiply by width of carpet in feet (normally 12 ft.):	× 12	ft.
Total square feet:	81	sq. ft.
Divide by 9 to convert to square yards:	÷ 9	sq. ft.
Total of square yards to be ordered for field:	**9**	**sq. yd.**

Step 4: Calculate for area rug pad.

Take dimension that is 12 feet wide or less. Round up to 12 feet:	12	ft.

Note: If pad is 6 feet wide, substitute 6 feet here.

Multiply by other dimension of area rug in feet:	× _____ 15	ft.
Total square feet of pad:	180	sq. ft.
Divide by 9 to convert to square yards:	÷ _____ 9	sq. ft.
Total square yards of pad:	**20**	**sq. yd.**

Binding: 50 feet

Seaming: 36 feet + 38 feet = 74 feet

Backing: 150 square feet

Carpet material:

9 square yards for the field

11.67 square yards for the outer border

2.67 square yards for the inner border

Pad: 20 square yards. The pad is 12 feet wide and has no nap or direction. There doesn't need to be a seam if 10 feet is used for the width and the length is 15 feet. This will result in only 2 feet of waste.

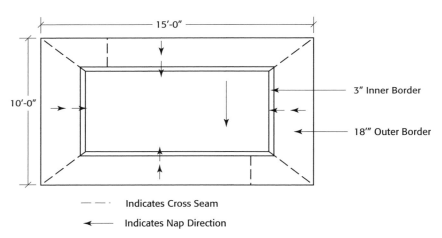

— — — Indicates Cross Seam

◄——— Indicates Nap Direction

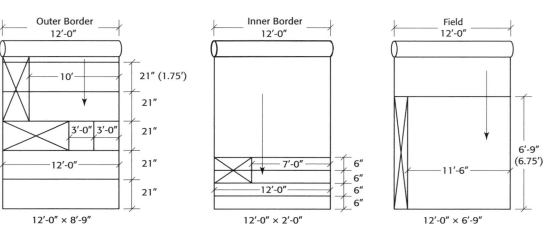

Figure 8.19 Example 3 Answer—Three-piece custom area rug.

Manual Worksheets

Area Rug Worksheet—Part One: Labor

Step 1: Draw the diagram.

Draw diagram of area rug and determine finished size of total rug (including size of borders, if applicable).

Step 2: Find the perimeter of the area rug for binding.

Add length of all sides together:

Side 1 in feet:	_____	ft.
Side 2 in feet:	+_____	ft.
Side 3 in feet:	+_____	ft.
Side 4 in feet:	+_____	ft.
Total perimeter of area rug for binding:	_____	**ft.**

If there are more than 4 sides, continuing adding sides.

Step 3: Find perimeter of first seam, if applicable.

Total width of area rug in feet:	_____	ft.
Subtract exact size of top border in feet:	−_____	ft.
Subtract exact size of bottom border in feet:	−_____	ft.
Subtotal A—width of inner border or field:	_____	**ft.**
Total length of area rug in feet:	_____	ft.
Subtract exact size of right side border in feet:	−_____	ft.
Subtract exact size of left side border in feet:	−_____	ft.
Subtotal B—length of inner border or field:	_____	**ft.**
Take Subtotal A:	_____	ft.
Add to Subtotal B:	+_____	ft.
Total:	_____	**ft.**

Note: Total represents one-half of the perimeter of the rectangle. Multiply by 2 to get the entire perimeter of the 4 sides.

	×_____2_____	
Total perimeter for seaming first seam:	_____	**ft.**

Step 4: Find perimeter of second seam, if applicable.

Take Subtotal A—width of inner border or field:	_____	ft.
Subtract exact size of top border in feet:	−_____	ft.
Subtract exact size of bottom border in feet:	−_____	ft.
Subtotal C—width of next border or field:	_____	**ft.**
Take Subtotal B—length of inner border or field:	_____	ft.
Subtract exact size of top border in feet:	−_____	ft.
Subtract exact size of bottom border in feet:	−_____	ft.
Subtotal D—length of next border or field:	_____	**ft.**
Take Subtotal C:	_____	ft.
Add to Subtotal D:	+_____	ft.
Total:	_____	**ft.**
	×_____2_____	
Total perimeter for seaming second seam:	_____	**ft.**

Step 5: Calculate for backing.

Not all area rugs will be backed.

Take overall width of area rug in feet:	_____	ft.
Multiply by overall length of area rug in feet:	×_____	ft.
Total square feet of area rug for backing:	_____	**sq. ft.**

Use diagram from Part One.

If area rug is one piece, not bordered, skip to Step 3.

Step 1: Determine yardage needed for outer border.

Add length of border in feet + .25 ft. (3 in.):   Top: _____ ft.

Note: If any side of the area rug is less than 6 feet, 2 sides can be obtained from 1 cut. Adjust as needed:

Bottom: +_____ ft.

Side: +_____ ft.

Side: +_____ ft.

Note: If any side of the area rug is wider than 12 feet, take total width − 12 feet = fill width. Take width of carpet, subtract fill to determine if more than 1 fill can come from a cut of carpet:

Fill: +_____ ft.

Fill: +_____ ft.

Total length of carpet needed for outer border: _____ **ft.**

Multiply by width of carpet in feet (normally 12 ft.): ×_____ 12 _____ ft.

Total square feet: _____ **sq. ft.**

Divide by 9 to convert to square yards: ÷_____ 9 _____ sq. ft.

Total square yards to be ordered for outer border: _____ **sq. yd.**

Step 2. Determine yardage needed for inner border.

Note: If area rug does not have an inner border, skip to Step 3.

Add length of inner border in feet: + .25 ft. (3 in.):   Top: _____ ft.

Note: If any side of the area rug is less than 6 feet, 2 sides can be obtained from 1 cut. Adjust as needed.

Bottom: +_____ ft.

Side: +_____ ft.

Side: +_____ ft.

Note: If any side of the area rug is wider than 12 ft., take total width − 12 ft. = fill width. Take width of carpet, subtract fill to determine if more than 1 fill can come from a cut of carpet.

Fill: +_____ ft.

Fill: +_____ ft.

Total length of carpet needed for inner border: _____ **ft.**

Multiply by width of carpet in feet (normally 12 ft.): ×_____ 12 _____ ft.

Total square feet: _____ **sq. ft.**

Divide by 9 to convert to square yards: ÷_____ 9 _____ sq. ft.

Total square yards to be ordered for inner border: _____ **sq. yd.**

If more inner borders are used, continue this same process.

Step 3: Determine yardage needed for field (length and width can be found under labor calculations).

Take shortest side of field + .25 ft. (3 in.) for total length: _____ ft.

Multiply by width of carpet in feet (normally 12 ft.): ×_____ 12 _____ ft.

Total square feet: _____ **sq. ft.**

Divide by 9 to convert to square yards: ÷_____ 9 _____ sq. ft.

Total of square yards to be ordered for field: _____ **sq. yd.**

Step 4: Calculate for area rug pad.

Take dimension that is 12 feet wide or less. Round up to 12 feet: _____ 12 _____ ft.

Note: If pad is 6 feet wide, substitute 6 feet here.

Multiply by other dimension of area rug in feet: ×_____ ft.

Total square feet of pad: _____ **sq. ft.**

Divide by 9 to convert to square yards: ÷_____ 9 _____ sq. ft.

Total square yards of pad: _____ **sq. yd.**

Note: Ideally there is no seam in the pad. Since the pad has no nap or direction, it can be laid in the most ideal direction to prevent a seam. However, if both sides are more than 6 feet or 12 feet (depending on type of area rug and type of pad), two or more pieces of pad will be used.

Practice Lessons: Area Rugs

BASIC

Your client wants an area rug 8 feet × 10 feet (Figure 8.20). She likes a shaggy frieze and just wants it bound and backed. She doesn't want a pad. The carpet is 12 feet wide.

1. How many square yards must be ordered?
2. What is the size of carpet that will be waste?
3. How many feet are there in binding the area rug?
4. How many square feet are there in backing the area rug?

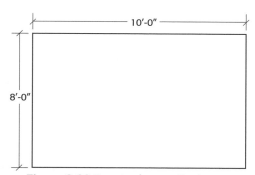

Figure 8.20 Practice lesson: Basic.

INTERMEDIATE

A large great room requires an odd-sized rug of 11 feet × 14 feet to best balance the space and accommodate the seating (Figure 8.21). You have specified two different types of carpet for this area rug with one of them as the border. You will back this rug and use a pad. It will have a 15-inch border. The carpet material and the pad are both 12 feet wide.

1. How many square yards must be ordered for the border?
2. How many square yards must be ordered for the field?
3. How many feet are there in binding the area rug?
4. How many feet are there in seaming the area rug?
5. How many square feet are there in backing the area rug?
6. How many square yards must be ordered for the pad?

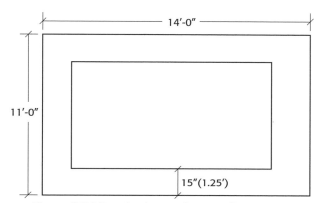

Figure 8.21 Practice lesson: Intermediate.

ADVANCED

Another bordered area rug is needed for the dining room. This rug will be 9 feet × 11 feet 6 inches with a 12-inch border and a 3-inch inner border (Figure 8.22). The area rug will be backed and will require a dense area rug pad. All three carpets and the pad are 12 feet wide.

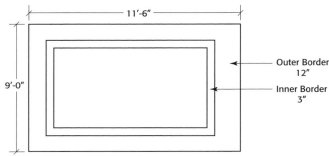

Figure 8.22 Practice lesson: Advanced.

1. How many square yards must be ordered for the field?
2. How many square yards must be ordered for the outer border?
3. How many square yards must be ordered for the inner border?
4. How many feet are there in binding the area rug?
5. How many feet are there in seaming the area rug?
6. How many square feet are there in backing the area rug?
7. How many square yards must be ordered for the pad?

Pricing of Intermediate Two-Piece Area Rug

Use the quantities found in the Intermediate Area Rug practice lesson and the prices below to calculate the price of this two-piece area rug for the client.

Border carpet material—$33.69/square yard

Field carpet material—$40.99/square yard

Carpet freight/shipping—$0.85/square yard with a minimum charge of $60.00

Pad—$8.50/square yard

Backing—$1.75/square foot

Binding—$2.00 per lineal foot

Seaming—$3.00 per lineal foot

Delivery—$50.00

1. What is the total for material: carpet material, freight, and pad?
2. What is the total for labor: binding, seaming, backing, and delivery? (Backing is provided by and applied by the workroom.)
3. What is the total price for this area rug?

Reference

Merida Sisal Rugs. Accessed September 26, 2012. http://www.meridameridian.com/area-rugs/seagrass.cfm

Chapter 9 | Countertops and Cabinetry

Interior designers are often involved in selection and specifications of cabinetry and countertops. Interior designers involved in health care, hospitality, and kitchen and bath design are most often involved in pricing countertops. The different materials that can be specified have greatly increased with technological inventions.

Chapter Outline

Terminology

Cubic yard A unit of measurement determined by multiplying in feet the width by the length by the depth. To convert to cubic yards, you then divide this amount by 27. There are 27 cubic feet in a cubic yard.

Cultured marble Man-made product, normally for bathrooms, made to look like marble consisting of polymer/filler matrix to which colorant and a high-gloss gel coat are added. This material is poured into a mold that includes a sink form and creates a seamless vanity top.

Custom cabinets Cabinets that are made from working drawings for a specific space and job.

Decorative laminate Created from layers of papers that are saturated with resin and compressed under heat. The exact process used depends on the type of laminate needed. This product comes in sheets and is less expensive than most other countertop surfaces.

Edge The finished front edge of countertops (Figure 9.1). Usually a number of different edge profiles can be shaped from or molded into the material. Other products, such as natural stone, have their edges finished, but additional material may be laminated to the edge to give it a different profile and a thicker appearance.

Engineered stone This product uses quartzite or another substance, such as glass, mixed with a polymer/filler matrix, which is then made into slabs. It is handled in much the same way as is natural stone slab.

Fabricator The subcontractor who actually makes the countertop.

Natural materials Whether in slab or in tiles, natural materials refer to stone that comes out of the ground, such as granite, marble, travertine, limestone, and soapstone. The expected use of the countertop will determine which natural materials are appropriate.

Semi-custom cabinets Made on the assembly line but can be ordered with some customization of sizes and interior accessories.

Slab Natural stone, recycled glass, solid surface, and engineered stone slabs are available. Depending on the location and the type of natural stone, these slabs will vary greatly in size. There is no standard. Recycled glass, solid surface, and engineered stone slabs are man-made and are produced in consistent sizes.

Square feet A unit of measure obtained by multiplying in feet width by length.

Solid surface Hallmarks of this type of countertop are color all the way through the material and the ability to form it into accessory pieces, including sinks, that can be bonded in a seamless look to the countertop. Solid surface is usually made of acrylic and/or polyester polymers, various fillers, and resin. Many solid-surface materials can be shaped with heat.

Stock cabinets Cabinets made in standardized sizes on the assembly line in quantity, not for any specific job.

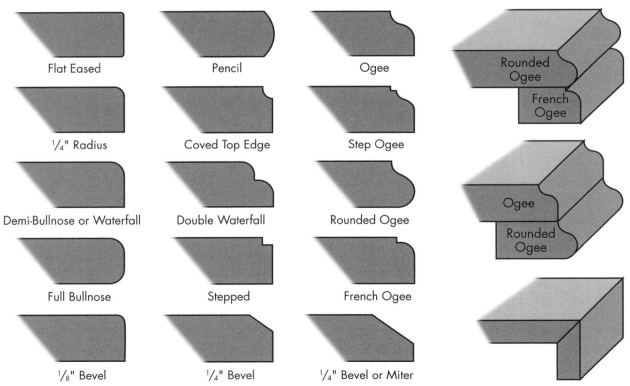

Figure 9.1 Examples of the various edges that can be selected for counters. Not all profiles are available for all materials. (From Godsey, L. *Interior Design Materials and Specifications*. New York: Fairchild Publishing, 2008.)

Cabinetry

Interior designers heavily involved in this type of design often have cabinet companies whose products they specify and price on a daily basis. This is not much different from an interior designer specifying and pricing case goods from a furniture manufacturer.

There are three basic types of cabinets to specify: stock, semi-custom, and custom. Stock cabinets can be found in catalogues and on the shelves in large box stores and are available quickly. Semi-custom cabinets have some of the benefits of the stock cabinets in that they are manufactured on the assembly line, which helps reduce the cost. However, with semi-custom cabinets, the client/designer has some flexibility in specifying sizes and usually has many options for the interior accessories. Custom cabinets are made specifically for a space and to the client's specifications. These are made one space at a time, tailored to the exact dimensions. The type of cabinets specified is dependent on the space and the client's budget.

Cost Factors

The following information is intended to be a simple guide to help you understand the fundamentals that contribute to the cost of cabinetry, allowing you to better inform your client regarding options. Cost factors with cabinets include the type of cabinet, the type of material, the type of door, the amount of detail, hardware, finish, and installation (Table 9.1). Stock cabinets are the least expensive type of cabinet, and custom cabinets are the most expensive. The use of wood, wood veneer, MDF board, melamine, laminate, or particleboard will also factor into the price. Melamine, laminate, MDF board, and particleboard are inexpensive and not as durable as wood and wood veneer. MDF board is not in itself a sign of poor quality, but the way that it is engineered and used in the cabinets may be. Door styles can be as simple as a plain panel or as elaborate as a cathedral raised panel. The details of joint construction, drawer guides and glides, door hinges, and knobs and pulls factor into

Cost Factors	Options
Type of Cabinet	Custom Semi-custom Stock
Type of material	Wood—type of wood Wood veneer—type of wood MDF board Particleboard Laminate Melamine
Construction style	Framed —Standard overlay —Full overlay Frameless, also known as European and full access
Door style	Arched Cathedral Mission Plain Recessed Raised
Detail	Joint construction
Hardware	Drawer guides Drawer glides Knobs and pulls Interior cabinet accessories
Finish	Stained Painted Specialty Melamine Laminate
Installation	

Table 9.1 Cabinet Cost Factors—Not Inclusive of All Aspects

the quality and durability of the cabinets. The cabinets can be finished by wrapping them in melamine or laminate, or they can be painted and stained. The number of finishing layers again will add cost, but also add durability. Finally, cabinets must be installed. An experienced installer can solve small problems and issues that crop up on-site, knowing how to hang and level the cabinets so that they are secure.

Calculations

Some firms have determined a ballpark price given as a dollar number per running foot. This is helpful when you are qualifying the client and then determining the client's budget. Unless the interior designer owns or works for a firm that prices cabinetry every day, the usual way designers determine prices is to get a quote from those supplying the cabinets. Some interior designers have access to certain cabinet companies that they will specify and price. Most cabinet companies have programmed their specific product into a computer program for use in design and pricing.

Countertops

Countertop materials range from natural stone slabs to solid-surface materials, engineered stone, recycled glass, stainless steel, copper, zinc, wood, bamboo, paper, tile, cultured marble, and laminate sheets. Depending on the location and use of the countertop, some materials will be more appropriate than others. For instance, a kitchen countertop must hold up to a different type of use than would a countertop in a guest bathroom, and it must be able to hold up to food preparation. Whichever material is selected, there are several common denominators to be found among sizing and pricing.

Sizing can be divided into four categories: slab, sheet, modular tiles, and poured material (Table 9.2). Slab material includes granite, marble, travertine, soapstone, limestone, and other natural materials, as well as man-made solid-surface and engineered stone products. The sizes of the slabs will vary in length, width, and thickness. The pattern and color of the material will vary from slab to slab. On long runs of cabinets, there will be a seam or seams where two different slabs are joined. Since slab edges are raw, they must be finished. This is normally done by selecting an edge profile and sometimes by laminating additional thickness to the edge.

Sheet goods include stainless steel, copper, zinc, paper, bamboo, wood, and laminate. Just as with slabs, different sizes in width, length, and thickness are available. For long runs of cabinets, there will be a seam or seams where two sheets meet. Different edge profiles can be routed, molded, or applied

by the fabricator to give a finished look. The interior designer specifies this profile.

Tile is a modular product that has been discussed in Chapters 4 and 6. Tiles can be made of nearly any product suitable for a countertop, such as granite, marble, engineered stone, ceramic, and porcelain. Tile can be found in innumerable sizes, with accent tiles and finishing pieces, such as in corners, out corners, bullnoses, cove bases, curbs, beads, and counter trims.

Several types of counter surfaces are poured either on-site or in molds and brought to the site. The most common products that are poured are concrete and cultured marble. There is also a recycled glass/engineered product for kitchens and bathrooms that is poured in a similar manner. Of all these kitchen products, the only ones that are able to have the sink as a "seamless" extension of the countertop are solid surface and cultured marble.

When replacing existing countertops, keep in mind the differences in heights of the materials. Laminate countertops are thicker than granite countertops. If there is a backsplash that your client doesn't intend to replace, the client needs to understand that an additional transition tile or granite liner/lip must be added to cover the exposed wall.

INSIGHT FROM THE FIELD

66 There is no substitute for client education! Prepare them for where seams will be and how the countertop will react. Concrete patinas, honed surfaces show fingerprints, soapstone is generally oiled for a couple months, acids can etch marble, and so on. An informed client can make choices that will work for his or her lifestyle and be delighted, not disappointed, in the outcome. With digital templating you can now view and approve seam placement and even where the pattern in the granite will be placed prior to fabrication. 99

Kris Lance, *AKBD, with Armstrong Kitchens of Overland Park, Kansas*

| | Material | Approximate Sizes | |
		Thickness	Width × Length
SLAB	Granite	2 cm, 3 cm (¾ in., 1¼ in.)	Varies greatly Examples: 56–74 in. wide 64–131 in. long
	Marble		
	Limestone		Varies greatly Examples: 51–70 in. wide 100–107 in. long
	Travertine		
	Soapstone	3 cm (1¼ in.)	Varies greatly Examples: 56–70 in. wide 105–115 in. long
	Recycled glass	1 in. 1¼ in.	27 in. × 84 in. 60 in. × 108 in.
	Solid surface	2 cm (¾ in.)	30 in. × 144 in.
	Engineered stone	1 cm, 2 cm, 3 cm (½ in., ¾ in., 1¼ in.)	54 in. × 120 in. 63 in. × 120 in. 54 in. × 128 in. 63 in. × 128 in.
SHEET	Stainless steel		In 6-in. increments from 24 in. to 144 in.
	Copper		36 in. × 96 in. 36 in. × 120 in.
	Zinc		28 in., 36 in., 39.4 in., and 44.75 in. wide 120 in. long
	Paper	¼ in., ½ in., ¾ in., 1 in., 1¼ in., 1½ in., 1¾ in., 2 in., 2½ in., 3 in.	48 in. × 96 in. 48 in. × 120 in. 48 in. × 144 in. 60 in. × 120 in. 60 in. × 144 in.
	Bamboo	1.5 in.	36 in. × 96 in.
	Wood		Up to 14–16 ft.
	Laminate		W: 36 in., 48 in., and 60 in. L: 96 in., 120 in., and 144 in.
MODULAR	Tile		Many sizes and shapes; varies by tile company
POURED	Concrete	2 in.	96 in. before seam
	Cultured marble		For bath use only
NOTE: Most fabricators specify thickness of material by centimeters.			

Table 9.2 Countertop Material Sizes

Cost Factors

In many areas, the countertop fabricator provides a price that includes templates, material, construction, cutouts, shipping of materials, and edge profile, and, in some instances, the sink and its installation. Understanding the factors the fabricator considers when pricing the countertop helps you when explaining options to your client. Tile countertops have cost factors that are the same as those for wall tile and floor tile, which include material, labor, grout, mastic, and sealer if sealer is appropriate.

As with other products you have studied, cost factors fall into the categories of materials and labor (Table 9.3). Cost factors of countertops made from slabs and sheets start with the material. There is a broad range

Material	Labor
Countertop surface	Site measure and template
Accessories (e.g., sink)	Construction of countertop, including substrate
Sealant (if applicable)	Cutouts for sinks, appliances, access to trash, etc.
Shipping costs	Counter edge profile
	Installation

Table 9.3 Fabricator and Countertop Cost Factors

of pricing between slab-granite and laminate countertops. Depending on the material selected, the type of substrate and support required will vary. Countertops in kitchens, bathrooms, and bar areas need sinks. If the sink is solid surface or cultured marble, it can be made seamlessly, bonded to the countertop from the same material, or poured in the same mold. Sinks that are undermount or drop-in have to be purchased separately, and they will have shipping costs to consider. Confirm with the fabricator whether he or she will install these.

When considering labor costs, the fabricator will begin with the site measurements to create the template for the counter and continue to the basic cost of the countertop construction. Countertops frequently require holes to be cut (referred to as cutouts) for appliances, sinks, and trash receptacles, requiring additional costs. The type of counter edge chosen may also add to the cost, especially if it is a stacked type of edge. Finally, there are installation charges.

Calculations

Prices for countertops are quoted to the client usually as a finished project. Costs for most material are quoted by the square foot, whereas the labor costs may be priced by the running foot. This may vary somewhat by region.

Calculations for material depend on the type of material being selected. Slab and sheet goods are normally sold by the entire slab or sheet, priced by the square foot. However, depending on the size of the fabricator's business, the designer or client may not always have to purchase entire slabs, only the square footage required. Tile has been explained in Chapters 4 and 6 as being priced by the square foot depending on tile size and carton size. Concrete is sold by the cubic foot and the cubic yard. Cultured marble is sold by the piece and is quoted by the contractor.

Step-by-Step Examples

Example 1—Tile Countertop

Your client wants a diagonally set tile countertop in his great room built-in bar (Figure 9.2). The base cabinet is 42 inches wide × 24 inches deep with a 1-inch overhang. A different material will be used for the backsplash. The tile is 6-inch × 6-inch porcelain that is stocked locally and can be purchased in the amount needed. The counter edge tile trim is 6 inches wide.

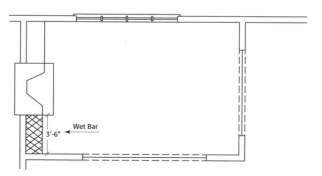

Figure 9.2 Example 1—Tile countertop.

Step 1: Calculate base square footage of space for tile.

Take depth of counter in feet:	2.08	ft.

24-in.-deep counter + 1-in. overhang = 25 in. ÷ 12 in. = 2.08 ft.

Multiply by length of counter in feet:	× 3.5	ft.
Base square footage of space:	7.28	sq. ft.

Step 2: Calculate additional materials for waste allowance.

For tile laid diagonally:

Take square footage from Step 1:	7.28	sq. ft.
Multiply by 15 percent to allow for waste:	× 1.15	waste allowance
Total square footage needed:	8.37	sq. ft.

Step 3: Calculate square feet to be ordered.

Divide by tile unit (width × length):	÷ .25	sq. ft.

Tile is 6 inches × 6 inches, so convert to feet to find this number: .5 ft. × .5 ft. = .25 sq. ft.

Total tiles:	33.48	tiles
Round up to whole number:	34	full tiles
Multiply by the tile unit:	× .25	sq. ft.
Total square feet ordered:	**8.5**	**sq. ft.**

For the counter edge:

Step 1: Calculate total length of counter edge, accent, or trim needed.

Depending on the different trims (including edge and accent) needed, this process may need to be done several times.

Total length needed for accent or trim:	3.5	ft.

If there are more lengths to add, continue to do so to achieve the total length needed.

Step 2: Calculate total number of pieces of trim to be ordered.

Take total from Step 1:	3.5	ft.
Divide by length of trim piece:	÷ .5	ft.
Pieces of trim needed:	7	pieces
Round up to whole number:	7	pieces to order
Add 2 to allow for breakage:	+ 2	breakage allowance
Total:	**9**	**pieces**

Base square feet: 7.28 square feet

Tiles ordered: 34 tiles

Total square feet needed after calculating for waste and tile size: 8.5 square feet

Pieces of counter edge trim ordered: 9 pieces

Example 2—Engineered Stone Countertop

You have designed a custom counter for a retail store and have specified an engineered stone to be used (Figure 9.3). The length of both counters is 9.16 feet. This allows for 1-inch overhangs on both sides. The depth of the front counter is 2.16 feet (overhangs on both sides again), and the depth of the back counter is 2.08 feet (one overhang to the front). There is no backsplash. This counter will be 2 centimeters thick. The fabricator sells this product by the full slab.

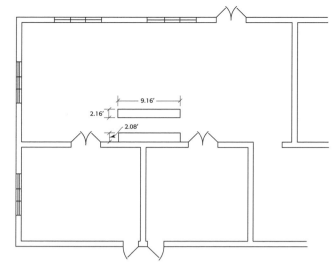

Figure 9.3 Example 2—Engineered stone countertop.

Step 1: Determine width of slabs or sheets to be used.

Width of slab or sheet being used in feet:	4.5 ft.
Divide by depth of counter in feet:	÷ 2.16 ft.

Note: The counter depth must include cabinet depth, overhangs (normally 1 inch each overhang) and any integrated, seamless backsplash (normally 4 inches to 6 inches tall and 1 inch deep).

Total number of counter cuts possible from slab/sheet:	2.08 cuts
Round down to nearest whole number:	2 cuts per slab/sheet

Step 2: Determine number of slabs to be used.

Length A of counter to counter/wall in feet:	9.16 ft.

Note: Counter length must include cabinet length plus overhangs.

Divide by length of slab/sheet being used in feet:	÷ 10 ft.
Total:	.92 slab/sheet
Round up to whole number: Total A:	1 slab/sheet

Note: If this number is greater than 1, seam placement must be considered.

This step may need to be repeated for additional counters; continue adding as needed.

Length B of counter to counter/wall in feet:	9.16 ft.

Note: Counter length must include cabinet length plus overhangs.

Divide by length of slab/sheet being used in feet:	÷ 10 ft.
Total:	.92 slab/sheet
Round up to whole number: Total B:	1 slab/sheet

Step 3: Determine total number of slabs/sheets needed.

Take Total A from Step 2:	1 slab/sheet
Add Total B from Step 2:	+ 1 slab/sheet
Total:	2 slabs/sheets
Divide by total from Step 1:	÷ 2 cuts per slab/sheet
Total:	1 slab/sheet

Step 4: Find square feet of material.

Width of slab or sheet being used in feet:	4.5	ft.
Multiply by slab/sheet length:	× 10	ft.
Total:	45	sq. ft.
Multiply by total from Step 3:	× 1	slab/sheet
Total square footage priced:	**45**	**sq. ft.**

Size slab to be used: 54 inches × 120 inches (2.16-foot + 2.08-foot counter depths = 4.24 foot; closest slab width = 54 inches wide)

Counter length is 9.16 feet; closest slab length = 120 inches long

Slabs ordered: One slab, as both counters can be cut from one slab.

Square feet to be charged: 45 square feet

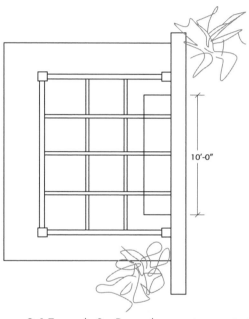

Example 3—Concrete Countertop

Your client lives in a warm climate year-round and wants a concrete countertop for an outside kitchen under his lanai (Figure 9.4). The metal cabinet base is 10 feet wide and 24 inches deep. The concrete will be 2 inches thick and will have a 1-inch overhang and a 6-inch backsplash 1-inch deep.

Figure 9.4 Example 3—Poured concrete countertop.

Step 1: Running length of counter in feet (do not add in counter depth or island depth).

Length A of counter to counter/wall:	10.17	ft.

The base cabinet is 10 feet long. There are 1-inch overhangs on each side.

2 in. ÷ 12 in. = .16666 ft. Round this up to .17 ft.

Total length:	10.17	ft.

Step 2: Determine depth of countertop.

Take depth of cabinet in feet:	2	ft.
Add overhang (normally 1 in. = .08 ft.):	+ .08	ft.
If applicable, add height of backsplash:	+ .58	ft.

Note: Normally, backsplash is approximately 4 inches to 6 inches tall + 1 inch deep. For this example, 6-in. backsplash + 1 in. deep = 7 in. ÷ 12 in. = .58 ft.

Total depth of counter material:	2.66	ft.

Step 3: Find cubic yards to order.

Total from Step 1:	10.17	ft.
Multiply by total from Step 2:	× 2.66	ft.
Total:	27.05	sq. ft.
Multiply by thickness of counter:	× .17	ft.

2-in. thickness ÷ 12 in. = .166666 ft. Round up to .17 feet.

Total:	4.60	cu. ft.

Running length of counter: 10.17 feet

Total depth of counter material: 2.66 feet

Cubic feet needed: 4.6 cubic yards

Manual Worksheets

Slab/Sheet Countertop Worksheet

Step 1: Determine width of slabs or sheets to be used.

Width of slab or sheet being used in feet: _____ ft.

Divide by depth of counter in feet: ÷ _____ ft.

Note: The counter depth must include cabinet depth, overhangs (normally 1 inch each overhang from base cabinet but can be more for counter and bar overhangs), and any integrated, seamless backsplash (normally 4 inches to 6 inches tall and 1 inch deep).

Total number of counter cuts possible from slab/sheet: _____ **cuts**

Round down to nearest whole number: _____ **cuts per slab/sheet**

Step 2: Determine number of slabs/sheets to be used.

Length A of counter to counter/wall in feet: _____ ft.

Note: Counter length must include cabinet length plus overhangs.

Divide by length of slab/sheet being used in feet: ÷ _____ ft.

Total: _____ **slabs/sheets**

Round up to whole number—Total A: _____ **full slabs/sheets**

Note: If this number is greater than 1, seam placement must be considered.

This step may need to be repeated for additional counters; continue adding as needed.

Length B of counter to counter/wall in feet: _____ ft.

Note: Counter length must include cabinet length plus overhangs.

Divide by length of slab/sheet being used in feet: ÷ _____ ft.

Total: _____ **slabs/sheets**

Round up to whole number—Total B: _____ **full slabs/sheets**

Note: If this number is greater than 1, seam placement must be considered.

Step 3: Determine total number of slabs/sheets needed.

Take Total A from Step 2: _____ slabs/sheets

Add Total B from Step 2: + _____ slabs/sheets

Continue adding lengths as necessary.

Total: _____ **slabs/sheets**

Divide by total from Step 1: ÷ _____ cuts per slab/sheet

Total: _____ **slabs/sheets**

Step 4. Find square feet of material.

Width of slab or sheet being used in feet: _____ ft.

Multiply by slab/sheet length: × _____ ft.

Total square footage of slab or sheet: _____ **sq. ft.**

Multiply by total from Step 3: × _____ slabs/sheets

Total square footage priced: _____ **sq. ft.**

Tile Countertop Worksheet

Step 1: Calculate base square footage of space.

Take depth of counter in feet: _____ ft.

Note: The counter depth must include cabinet depth, overhangs (normally 1 inch each overhang from base cabinet but can be more for counter and bar overhangs).

Multiply by length of counter in feet: × _____ ft.

Base square footage of space: _____ **sq. ft.**

Step 2: Calculate additional materials for waste allowance.

For tile laid straight:

Take square footage from Step 1: _____ sq. ft.

Multiply by 10 percent to allow for waste: × _____1.10_____ waste allowance

Total square footage needed: _____ **sq. ft.**

For tile laid diagonally or staggered:

Take square footage from Step 1: _____ sq. ft.

Multiply by 15 percent to allow for waste: × _____1.15_____ waste allowance

Total square footage needed: _____ **sq. ft.**

For tile laid in a herringbone pattern:

Take square footage from Step 1: _____ sq. ft.

Multiply by 25 percent to allow for waste: × _____1.25_____ waste allowance

Total square footage needed: _____ **sq. ft.**

Step 3: Calculate square feet to be ordered.

Total from Step 2: _____ sq. ft.

Divide by tile unit (width × length): ÷ _____ sq. ft.

Total tiles: _____ **tiles**

Round up to whole number: _____ **full tiles**

Multiply by the tile unit: × _____ sq. ft.

Total square feet ordered: _____ **sq. ft.**

If tile material is sold by the full box/carton, proceed to Step 4 to determine amount needed.

Step 4. Calculate number of full boxes/cartons to be ordered.

Take square footage needed from Step 3: _____ sq. ft.

Divide by carton square footage: ÷ _____ sq. ft. per box/carton

Boxes/cartons needed: _____ **boxes/cartons**

Round up to whole number: _____ **full boxes/cartons to order**

Step 5. Calculate square feet in boxes/cartons ordered to calculate pricing to client for material.

Take number of boxes/cartons from Step 4: _____ boxes/cartons

Multiply by square feet per box/carton: × _____ sq. ft. per box/carton

Total square footage ordered: _____ **sq. ft.**

Tile Countertop—Trim Worksheet

Step 1: Calculate total length of counter edge, accent, or trim needed.

Depending on the different trims (including edge and accent) needed, this process may need to be done several times.

Add length of trim needed:	_____	ft.
Add additional lengths: +	_____	ft.
Add additional lengths: +	_____	ft.
Add additional lengths: +	_____	ft.
Add additional lengths: +	_____	ft.
Total length needed for accent or trim:	_____	**ft.**

If there are more lengths to add, continue to do so to achieve the total length needed.

Step 2: Calculate total number of pieces of trim to be ordered.

Take total from Step 1:	_____	ft.
Divide by length of trim piece: ÷	_____	ft.
Equals pieces of trim needed:	_____	**pieces**
Round up to whole number:	_____	**full pieces**
Add 2 to allow for breakage: +	2	breakage allowance
Total:	_____	**pieces to be ordered**

If items are sold by the piece, stop here. If items are sold by the foot, continue to Step 3.

Step 3: Calculate total length to be ordered.

Take total from Step 2:	_____	pieces
Multiply by actual length of pieces: ×	_____	ft.
Total feet actually ordered:	_____	**ft.**

Note: Some trim pieces, such as out corners, can be counted and should just be manually calculated.

Poured Countertop Worksheet

Step 1: Determine running length of counter in feet (do not add in counter depth or island depth).

Length A of counter to counter/wall: _____ ft.
Length B of counter to counter/wall: + _____ ft.

Continue adding lengths as necessary.

Length C of counter to counter/wall: + _____ ft.
Length D of counter to counter/wall: + _____ ft.
Length E of counter to counter/wall: + _____ ft.
Total length: _____ **ft.**

Note: Don't forget to include 1-inch overhang in the length. Counter to counter will have a 2-inch overhang. Counter to wall will have a 1-inch overhang.

Step 2: Determine depth of countertop.

Take depth of cabinet in feet: _____ ft.
Add overhang (normally 1 in. = .08 ft.): + _____ ft.
If applicable, add height of backsplash: + _____ ft.

Note: Normally, backsplash is approximately 4 inches to 6 inches tall + 1 inch deep.

Total depth of counter material: _____ **ft.**

Note: This backsplash is one that is a seamless continuation of the counter material. A separate backsplash does not need to be calculated here. Use the Wall Tile Worksheet on page 43 in Chapter 4 for a tiled backsplash.

Step 3: Find cubic feet to order.

Take total from Step 1: _____ ft.
Multiply by total from Step 2: _____ ft.
Total: _____ **sq. ft.**
Multiply by thickness of counter: × _____ ft.

Note: Remember to divide inches by 12 to get feet.

Total: _____ **cu. ft.**

Practice Lessons: Countertops

BASIC

Laminate Countertop

The dentist you are working with has requested laminate countertops in the kitchen of his new office (Figure 9.5). The cabinet is 108 inches wide and 24 inches deep, and will have a 1-inch overhang to the front and a 4-inch seamless backsplash that is 1 inch deep. There is no overhang to the side.

1. What is the overall depth of the counter?
2. What is the overall length of the counter?
3. Using Table 9.2, what is the width and length of the laminate to be ordered?
4. How many square feet of laminate will be purchased?

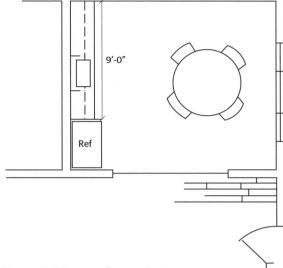

Figure 9.5 Practice lesson: Basic— Laminate countertop.

INTERMEDIATE

Tile Countertop

Your client loves the look of tile countertops for her master bathroom (Figure 9.6). Vessel-type sinks will be used on top of the counter. The cabinets are 18 inches deep with a 1-inch overhang to the front and no overhang to the side. The tile is a glass mosaic sold in 12-inch × 12-inch sheets, stocked locally, and laid in a straight pattern. The counter edge trim is 8 inches wide. A decorative trim will be used for the backsplash. This trim is 6 inches tall × 12 inches wide. Both trims are sold by the piece.

1. How many square feet of tile must be ordered for the countertop?
2. How many pieces of counter edge must be ordered?
3. How many pieces of accent trim must be ordered?

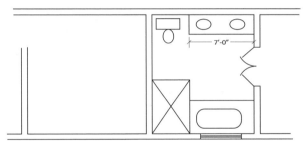

Figure 9.6 Practice lesson: Intermediate—Tile countertop.

ADVANCED
Granite Countertop

You have specified a granite countertop for a client's kitchen (Figure 9.7). The granite slabs you have found are 66 inches wide × 126 inches long. The cabinet is 24 inches deep and has a 1-inch overhang to the front and no overhangs to the side. A 6-inch backsplash made from the same slab will be used.

1. What is the overall depth of the counter including overhang?
2. How many slabs of granite must be used?
3. How many square feet will be purchased?

Pricing for Advanced Granite Countertop

Use the quantity found for the Advanced Granite Countertop practice lesson to calculate pricing for your client. You have spoken with a granite fabricator and have received purchase and installation prices for the granite countertop. There are no additional fees for measuring and templating, as it is built into the price of the granite. There will be two holes cut out, one for the sink and one for the stove. She has requested an ogee edge for the countertop.

Price per square foot	$ 96.00 granite installed
Price per hole cut out	$ 75.00
Price for ogee edge	$625.00

1. What is the overall price of the installed countertop?

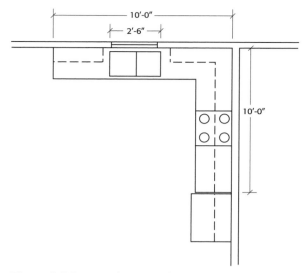

Figure 9.7 Practice lesson: Advanced—Granite countertop.

References

Eagle Group Stainless Steel Countertops Catalog Specification Sheet No. EG004.12. Accessed December 26, 2012. http://www.eaglegrp.com/LitLib/eg04.12.pdf.

Elements of Green Countertops. Accessed December 26, 2012. http://www.elements-of-green.com.

Formica Laminate by Formica Group Technical Data. Accessed December 26, 2012. http://www.formica.com/trade/Documents.aspx.

Godsey, L. *Interior Design Materials and Specifications.* New York: Fairchild Publishing, 2008.

International Cast Polymer Alliance. Accessed December 27, 2012. http://www.icpa-hq.org/consumers/cultured marble.cfm.

National Kitchen and Bath Association. *The Essential Kitchen Design Guide.* New York: Wiley, 1996.

Silestone by Cosentino Countertops, Floors, Walls, Partitions. Accessed December 27, 2012. http://www.silestoneusa.com.

Chapter 10 | Curtains and Draperies

Chapter Outline

Terminology

Curtains and Draperies
Gathered Curtains
Stationary Side Panels
Traversing, Pleated Draperies

Cost Factors

Calculations

Step-by-Step Examples
Example 1—Gathered Curtains
Example 2—Stationary Side Panels
Example 3—Traversing, Pleated Draperies

Manual Worksheets
Gathered Curtains
Stationary Side Panels
Traversing, Pleated Draperies
Seamless, Traversing Draperies

Practice Lessons: Curtains and Draperies
Basic
Gathered Curtains
Stationary Side Panels
Traversing, Pleated Draperies
Intermediate
Gathered Curtains
Stationary Side Panels
Traversing, Pleated Draperies
Advanced
Gathered Curtains
Seamless, Traversing Draperies and Traversing,
Pleated Draperies
Pricing for Intermediate Gathered Curtains
Pricing for Intermediate Stationary Side
Panels

References

When people think about curtains and draperies, many times they envision them in a residential setting. Many commercial settings use curtains and draperies (window treatments) as well. Consider hotels, country clubs, banks, small professional offices, and other similar businesses that use curtains and draperies to establish a style, control glare and acoustics, and give privacy. While code issues must be addressed and met when you are working in a commercial setting, the same types of window treatments are used commercially as are used residentially.

Most interior designers who have gone through a two-, three-, or four-year interior design program know the difference between drapery and drape. Drapery is a noun. Drape is a verb. As interior designers we work with drapery. Our drapery installers perform the action of draping. When selecting fabrics for custom drapery treatments we routinely look at color, pattern, texture, fiber content, width, repeat, and cost. Many times we use a specific fabric because of the way the fabric hangs or drapes. When you begin designing and creating window treatments and draperies, it is important to establish your team: drapery workroom and installer. When choosing a workroom or an installer to use, ask interior design colleagues if they have a workroom and an installer they like and if they will share that information with

you. It is not uncommon to have several different workrooms that you use for different treatments. Drapery construction is commonly found as a cottage industry. There are many fine seamstresses who work out of their homes.

There will be much teamwork with your workroom and your installer. If you feel intimidated by draperies, the best way to learn what you can and can't do with draperies is to spend several days with an installer and several days with a workroom, physically helping do the work. You will be immersed in the world of window treatments and will quickly learn essential information.

When you are beginning to specify window treatments, creating a book of ideas for your clients is often helpful. Cut window treatment pictures out of magazines and place in your own booklet to be an idea generator for your client and yourself, or create a Pinterest page to which you can direct your clients.. Make sure to be aware of current styles. Attend the different sessions on window treatments that local distributors offer so that you are knowledgeable about these styles. *Window Coverings* online magazine is another way of staying current with not only the styles but also with new technology. Look at the pictures of rooms in magazines, focusing on the window treatment.

Terminology

Allowance The amount added for hems, headings, overlaps, and returns in draperies. It also refers to the amount in inches taken as a deduction to allow for clearance at the top or bottom of draperies or at the sides for other window treatments such as blinds and shades that will allow them to function without dragging on floor, ceiling, or sides of window.

Apron Wood facing below the sill on a double hung window.

Buckram Also called crinoline. This is a stiff fabric used at the top of the drapery to stiffen the pleats.

Carriers Plastic devices in a traverse rod to which draperies are hooked or snapped. They are frequently called slides.

Clearance The portion of a window treatment that is airspace: behind, beside, above, below, and in front of it.

Cut length Total length of fabric needed per width of fabric to create a window treatment. The cut length includes the desired finished length of drapery plus the allowances needed for hems, headings, and pattern repeat.

When you are creating a layered window treatment, an additional allowance must be made for each layer to hang appropriately. Generally, add 3 inches to 3½ inches to the return for each additional layer. A window treatment that consists of a traversing sheer drapery, stationary side panels, and swags and cascades may have the following specified returns: the traversing sheer drapery, a 3-inch return; the stationary side panels, a 6½-inch return; and the swags and cascades, a 10-inch return.

It is common that subsequent layer is 1 inch to 2 inches longer than the previous layer.

Box 10.1

Decorative rod A rod, traversing or stationary, made of wood or metal (Figure 10.1). Since it is exposed and not hidden by any window treatment, the finish of the rod is attractive. It is completed at the ends with finials. Rings on the rod are often used to hold the drapery or the valance.

Figure 10.1 The type of decorative rod selected for the treatment should enhance the style being created. There are four basic components of decorative rods: pole, finials, brackets, and rings. Many designers will add batons that are placed to the backside of the first pleat to be used to open and close the treatment. Not shown, but an alternative to the utility rods and decorative rods, are cable systems that consist of cable, supports/brackets, and rings. (© BUILT Images / Alamy)

Drape This is a verb. It refers to how the drapery hangs.

Drop Depth (length) of a valance. For a standard 8-foot ceiling, a 16-inch to 18-inch drop is proportionate for most fabrics and treatments.

Dye lot Variation in intensity of color from one batch of fabric (or wallpaper, carpet, etc.) to the next.

Finished length The total finished length of drapery after the workroom is finished creating it.

Finished width The width of the rod plus the returns and plus the overlap (if applicable).

Flat measure The total width of the drapery treatment as it hangs on the wall; the actual width measurement of area to be covered.

Flaws Holes, heavy slubs, misweaves, or misprints in fabrics that make it unacceptable to use. The drapery workroom must inspect fabric before cutting for flaws. This fabric must be sent back to the manufacturer for replacement before it is cut.

Fullness Amount of fabric used in a drapery treatment as compared to the finished width. Interior designers prefer to use 2½ to 3 times fullness for pinch pleated treatments; however, some other treatments require only 1½ times fullness. Many ready-made pinch pleated treatments are only 1½ to 2 times fullness and may seem skimpy.

Grommet A circular metal piece that is attached to the top of a drapery or curtain that allows it to hang from a rod. Commonly seen in shower curtains and cubicle curtains.

Hand Feel of a fabric.

Heading Top of the curtain or drapery, sometimes pleated and with stiffening. It also refers to the part of a gathered curtain or valance that will project above the rod (Figure 10.2).

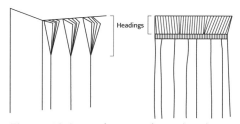

Figure 10.2 Headings in pleated and gathered window treatments. In a pleated treatment, the heading is the depth of the pleat. In a gathered treatment, the heading is the amount of fabric above the rod pocket.

Hems The finished sides and bottoms of draperies. These are usually double turned to hide shadowing of the raw edges.

Double hem Hem turned twice to eliminate shadows and raw edges and to add weight for hanging (Figure 10.3). For draperies, no less than a double 4-inch hem (8 inches total) is recommended. A double 6-inch to 12-inch hem is sometimes better because of the proportion to the overall length of the drapery.

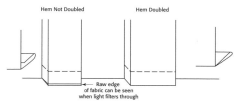

Figure 10.3 Double hems provide a finished weighted bottom to draperies and valances. If the fabric doesn't terminate in the bottom crease, a line will be created when light shines through.

Shirt-tail hem Hem, similar to that found in shirts, that is turned twice using less than 1-inch fabric and top stitched. When finished, hem is ¼ inch to ½ inch.

Interlining Flannel fabric placed between face fabric and regular lining to add richness and bulk to lightweight fabrics. It also provides additional protection from the sun for fabrics such as silk.

Lining Fabric used as a back layer for draperies. Be careful to use a similar weight and content lining fabric as the face fabric. Many interior designers use a challis lining.

At the window, as the light comes in, the lining seam lines can be seen. Most lining is white or off-white in order to provide a uniform appearance from the outside of the home. Blackout lining, while it does block light, will allow light to penetrate everywhere a pin was stuck or the needle went through the fabric when sewing. Some workrooms won't use blackout lining because it dulls their needles quickly and is hard on their sewing machines.

Box 10.2

Master carriers Carrier arms that overlap, holding the first two drapery pins of the treatment, to the center of a traverse rod (Figure 10.4).

Over-drapery Heavier drapery, to the room side, over a lighter drapery. The over-drapery may traverse or be stationary. A longer return of at least an additional 3 inches to 3½ inches is required to clear the lighter drapery.

Overlap The center portion of a traversing drapery that rides on the master carrier and overlaps the back carrier arm to make a neat closing.

Panel One or more widths of fabric finished as one unit. A pair of draperies used for a center draw drapery consists of two panels.

Pattern repeat Lengthwise or crosswise measurement of one design motif to where that same pattern is again repeated.

Straight match Repeat matches straight across.

Drop match or half drop Repeat is staggered so that only every other width matches along the same line. The match runs diagonally (see Figure 3.2 on page 22 in Chapter 3 for an example).

Projection The measurement from the wall out into the room. This is different from clearance since the projection goes to the most forward point and the clearance stops at the back of the rod or treatment (Figure 10.5).

Railroaded fabric The vertical pattern of regular rolled fabric runs up the bolt. The vertical pattern of a railroaded fabric runs side to side, selvage to selvage. A vertical stripe will run horizontally, like railroad tracks, when the fabric is made railroaded (Figure 10.6).

Return The part of the drapery treatment that returns to the wall. See Figure 10.5 for clarification. With multiple treatments, the return will increase usually by 3 inches to 3½ inches. The sheer close to the window may have a return of 3 inches. The side panels over the draperies may then have a return of at least 6 inches to 7 inches. The valance over all of this may then have a return of 9 inches to 10 inches.

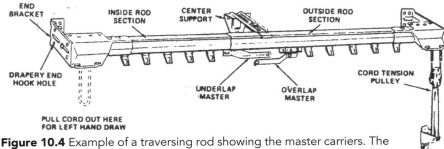

Figure 10.4 Example of a traversing rod showing the master carriers. The carrier that stays to the front is the overlap master. The carrier that goes behind the overlap is called the underlap master. (National Decorating Products Association)

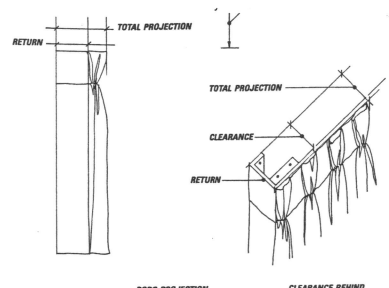

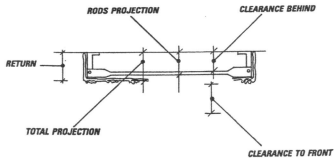

Figure 10.5 Drapery clearance, projection, and returns. (*Window Fashions*, February 1990)

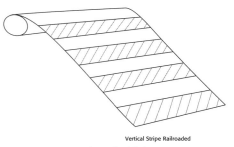

Vertical Stripe Railroaded

Figure 10.6 Railroaded fabric.

Rod pocket Hem at the top or bottom of curtain through which a rod is inserted for a shirred treatment. The rod pocket is used frequently at the top and bottom of shirred door panels (Figure 10.7).

Sash Window framework that holds the panes in place.

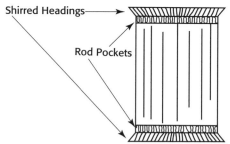

Figure 10.7 Treatment gathered (shirred) top and bottom showing rod pockets and headings.

Sash curtains Gathered treatment normally installed on the window framework with tautness between the top and bottom rods.

Seamless drapery A seamless drapery is made when using fabric that is 118 inches wide or wider (e.g., 124 inches, 130 inches, etc.). Fabric that is this wide is intended to be railroaded at the window, resulting in no vertical seams. The fabric and yardage for this type of treatment is calculated differently from all other treatments that are not railroaded.

Selvage Edge of fabric formed on the loom when the fabric is woven. It is frequently woven tighter than the fabric body.

Sheer See-through fabric for curtains or draperies. It filters light and controls glare.

Shirr Another name for gather. Sash curtains are shirred on the rod.

Side panels Stationary, decorative panels of draperies that hang on each side of a window, and sometimes between windows. They do not move and can be tied back.

Sill Horizontal piece of wood that is the bottom of the window.

Stack Area covered by the window treatment when the treatment is open. Allow 15 percent stack for very lightweight fabric, 25 percent stack for regular/medium-weight fabric, and up to 33 percent stack for heavy fabric, such as velvet.

Traversing drapery This is a drapery that moves on rings or carriers to open and close. Traversing draperies can be a one-way draw or a two-way draw, also called center draw.

One-way draw draperies Draperies, made as a panel, which move in only one direction to stack to one side. This is the most common type of drapery seen at a sliding glass door.

Two-way/center draw Draperies that open from and close to the center of the window.

Under-drapery Usually unlined sheers or casements that hang behind heavier draperies to help diffuse light.

Valance Horizontal top treatment used to conceal rod and give a finished appearance to a window. Valance styles can be used to create distinct period looks.

Width[1] Distance from one side of the window to the other or one side of a drapery treatment to the other.

Width[2] Single width of fabric of the cut length required to make a drapery, sometimes referred to as a cut. One or more widths are required to make a panel. Most fabric is 48 inches or 54 inches wide. Seamless draperies are made of fabric that is 118 inches wide. Other less common widths of fabric are 36 inches, 45 inches, 60 inches, 106 inches, and 130 inches. It is important to check the width of fabric used in the drapery treatment.

Curtains and Draperies

Curtains and draperies are in a category called soft window treatments, which will also include top treatments and fabric shades. To the general public there is no difference between curtains and draperies. In the interior design field, curtains are less formal and simpler window coverings than draperies. Curtains are fabric coverings, usually at the window, that are gathered on a rod. Normally curtains are two panels that may meet in the center, usually meant to be stationary, and often are not full length to the floor, but hang just below the window. They usually stay within the basic trim/framework of the window, and can even be mounted on the window trim. Other types of curtains meant to traverse are shower curtains and cubicle curtains, often used in hospitals to separate beds and patients. These may be grommeted

or have a snap system at the heading and are not floor length. Many times cubicle curtains hang from a track attached to the ceiling.

Draperies usually are made to be drawn across a window (traverse) to cover it, and are often hung several inches above the window frame, hanging to the floor. Most draperies have some kind of pleat in the heading.

Gathered Curtains
While gathered curtains can be found readymade in stores, many times, whether for size, color, pattern, or style, they are custom made. Gathered curtains have a rod pocket at the top of the treatment whereby the fabric can be shirred onto the rod. If there is fabric above the rod pocket, the heading, when shirred on the rod, can look like a ruffle. Sometimes the rod

pocket is in the form of fabric tabs. Unless they are made of a sheer or lace fabric, the curtains should be lined. Sash curtains are gathered curtains, normally found on or beside doors. They have a rod pocket at the top and the bottom and are installed so there is tautness between the rods.

Stationary Side Panels

The look of traversing draperies can be achieved with stationary side panels. Better window construction and hard window treatment options have minimized the use of traversing draperies for insulation; however, the look of floor-length draperies on either side of a window is appealing. They can help to create balance and grounding of pattern, texture, and color; and help with acoustical issues found in many open-design homes today. Stationary side panels will also minimize the amount of fabric needed to create the look of traversing panels. Stationary side panels are often floor length and can be either gathered or pleated. It is important that the width of the stationary side panels be proportionate to the window width and height.

Traversing, Pleated Draperies

Traversing, pleated draperies are a classic type of window treatment and are very popular today. Pleated draperies have an even, consistent depth and hang that gathered curtains can't achieve. Some pleated draperies are created and hung on decorative rods that don't require anything else for the treatment. Others are hung on standard white metal rods that require some type of top treatment to hide the rod. Using a top treatment hides the pleats at the top, but doesn't hide the way the pleat makes the drapery hang.

Cost Factors

Factors that impact the cost of curtains and draperies are fabric, lining, rod, shipping, labor, and installation (see Table 10.1).

When ordering fabric, check with the manufacturer to see if there is more than a 1-yard minimum order. Sometimes for more expensive fabric they require a minimum 2- or 3-yard order. Once the minimum amount has been reached, fabric must then be ordered by the ½ yard, for example, 1½ yards, 2 yards, 2½ yards, 3 yards, 3½ yards, and so on.

Make sure that the lining you specify for the job is as close as possible to the fiber content of and is the same width as the face fabric, usually 54 inches. Many interior designers will purchase an entire bolt of ivory or white lining, 60+ to 100+ yards, and have it shipped to their workroom. This gives them better pricing on the lining and makes it available for the workroom to use when the face fabric arrives. Most workrooms will gladly store the designer's lining.

The traditional way of installing draperies is with a rod. The rod can be decorative, meant to be seen, or purely functional, meant to be hidden by a valance or top treatment. Recently the use of cables as a rod has given a contemporary twist to traditional drapery styles. Some rods are sold in a set that includes return brackets and supports. Many decorative rods require specifying not only the rod, but the specific brackets, supports, finials, and rings. Since decorative rods are meant to be seen, this type of customization is important.

Labor for making the curtains and draperies is usually priced per width of fabric. This price includes sewing panels together, creating the hem and heading, and setting the pins. Additional labor charges will be found for lengths beyond a certain number (sometimes 120 inches), lined panels, sewing on trim, utilizing multiple fabrics, and any unusual add-on to the treatment. When pricing curtains and drapery labor, it is important to remember that any panel that consists of a fraction of a width will be rounded up to the full width. When a two-panel drapery, gathered, stationary, or traversing, uses an odd number of widths for calculating yardage, the labor price will increase. A two-way draw drapery or a pair of stationary or gathered side panels that use 3 or 5 (or any odd number) widths of fabric means the

Soft Window Treatment										
Client:						Workroom:				
Phone #s:						Installer:				
Address:										
Room/Window:										
Finished Dimensions:										

Materials										
	Mfr./ Vendor	**Pattern**	**Color/ Finish**	**Width**	**Repeat**	**Qty.**	**Cost Per**	**Sub-total**	**Est. Ship.**	**Total**	**PO**
Fabric										
Lining										
Hdwr.										
Rod										
Brackets										
Supports										
Finials										
Batons										
							Subtotal for Materials			

Labor & Installation								
Labor						**Qty.**	**Cost Per**	**Sub-total**	**Total**	**WO**
Install								
				Subtotal for Labor & Installation		
				Overall Total		

Diagram:

Table 10.1 Window Treatment: Specifying and Calculating Total Cost

workroom will use 1½ or 2½ widths (etc.) per side. In the case of 3 widths of fabric ordered, the workroom, sewing 1½ widths per side, will do the same amount of work as it will for 2 widths per side. The drapery workroom will charge you labor for 4 widths of fabric, reflecting the number of seams and amount of work that is actually done. When ordering fabric, the amount necessary for 3 widths is ordered, but the labor amount must be rounded up to 4 widths. This is a common area in which beginning interior designers will lose money because they forget to adjust for the labor. For one-panel or one-way draw draperies, labor is charged for the number of widths used, rounded up to a full number. Until you are very comfortable with pricing window treatments, speak to the workroom to confirm your estimate before giving your client a quote.

There are many variables that determine the installation charge of draperies and window treatments: measuring, making templates, trip charge for outside of accepted installation area, widths per treatment, number of rods per treatment, type of rod installed, customization of rod (cutting and assembling), minimum trip charge, working above floor beyond an acceptable number of feet (sometimes over 10 feet), and steaming draperies.

Most installers begin by charging per width of draperies they hang. They charge the same for two-panel window treatments as do workrooms; any partial widths are rounded up to a full width. Don't hesitate

to call the installer to be sure all required costs have been calculated for the job.

Calculations

Because window treatments are custom made, nearly any size of window or circumstance can be accommodated. The more limiting issue with window treatments are how they can be installed. For the majority of window installations, this isn't an issue; for those where it is, you should get your installer involved immediately.

All measurements and calculations for window treatments are done in inches. It is helpful to know what type of window treatment is being planned when taking measurements. Keep in mind the type of window, whether it is a sliding door, atrium door, double hung window, casement window, etc., so that inherent qualities of the window can be accounted for in the design of the window treatment. When measuring for window treatments, get a digital camera and take a picture to help remember small details. The final step after measuring is determining how far above the window trim you will install the treatment and how far to each side of the window trim the treatment will cover. Remember that curtains, stationary side panels, and traversing pleated draperies are meant to cover the window trim but as little window as possible when they're opened or, in the case of stationary side panels, as they hang. This final step will give you the flat measure and finished length.

While it is possible to pay for an installer to measure, knowing how to do this is helpful when time is of the

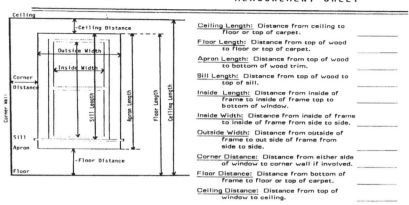

Ceiling Length: Distance from ceiling to floor or top of carpet. _____

Floor Length: Distance from top of wood to floor or top of carpet. _____

Apron Length: Distance from top of wood to bottom of wood trim. _____

Sill Length: Distance from top of wood to top of sill. _____

Inside Length: Distance from inside of frame to inside of frame top to bottom of window. _____

Inside Width: Distance from inside of frame to inside of frame from side to side. _____

Outside Width: Distance from outside of frame to out side of frame from side to side. _____

Corner Distance: Distance from either side of window to corner wall if involved. _____

Floor Distance: Distance from bottom of frame to floor or top of carpet. _____

Ceiling Distance: Distance from top of window to ceiling. _____

Figure 10.8 Example of a workroom's dimension sheet and terminology. (Courtesy of Jennifer Allred, Allred-Y-Made)

essence to the client and to be able to communicate properly with your workroom and installer. It is helpful to make an elevation of the window wall and take several measurements and notations. Many drapery workrooms utilize terminology a little differently. Some will have specific worksheets/work orders to be used to specify the treatment.

Use the workroom's specific terminology. Figure 10.8 is an example of one workroom's suggested measurement sheet.

1. Above the window to crown or ceiling (nearest height obstruction).

2. Overall width dimension of window—outside trim to outside trim.

3. Wall space to each side of the window to nearest obstruction (e.g., wall, cabinet, light switch).

4. Top of trim to floor—note whether flooring is wood, tile, or carpet, and so on.

5. Top of trim to bottom of window trim (sometimes necessary).

6. Any air vents in floor.

7. For a bay (Figure 10.9): Overall width of bay, depth of bay, and angles of bay. It is useful to have a protractor for this. Kirsch makes one especially for this purpose (Figure 10.10). If you don't have this protractor, take 4-inch × 6-inch

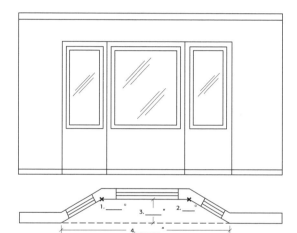

Figure 10.9 When measuring for a window treatment in a bay window, the following information must also be provided to the workroom: (1) left-angle degree, (2) right-angle degree, (3) depth of bay, (4) overall width of bay opening.

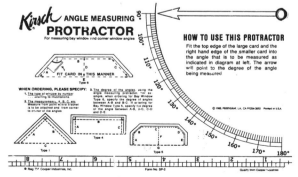

Figure 10.10 A Kirsch protractor can be used to determine degree of angle for window treatments, which is important for boarded treatments. This provides the most accurate information for your workroom. (Courtesy of Kirsch)

index cards, place one on each wall at the corner where they overlap, and staple them together. This will give the workroom or the installer the angle they need. Be sure to indicate which are the top and bottom of the cards and the right-side and left-side angles of the bay.

8. Anything else that might create an obstruction for the treatment.

Ten different designers or drapery workrooms will probably have ten different, however similar, methods for calculating curtain and drapery yardage. There are two separate sets of calculations necessary to determine yardage. One set of calculations determines the number of widths of fabric necessary to cover the appropriate width with the proper amount of fullness. The second set of calculations determines how long in inches (cut length) each of these cuts must be. Multiplying the number of widths by the length of each cut will result in the total number of inches necessary for the drapery. This number, divided by 36, will yield the number of yards, rounded up to the nearest ½ to full yard, needed to order. There are a few differences between gathered and/or stationary side panels and traversing/draw draperies that reflect rods with master carriers and undercarriers. All calculations, except for seamless draperies, will follow this format:

1. Determine the flat measure of the treatment, which includes stack. In the case of a gathered curtain, the finished width will include returns since the returns need to have fullness.

2. Determine number of widths to be used by adding in fullness and appropriate hems and overlaps, dividing by the width of fabric being used,

and rounding up to the next whole number.

3. Determine the cut length by adding appropriate headings and hems to the finished length and adjusting for any repeat.

4. Find yardage to price and order by multiplying the number of widths × the cut length (adjusted cut length if repeat is used), dividing by 36 inches to find yards, and rounding up to the nearest half yard.

Note: Lining for the treatment is the number of widths × the cut length before adjusting for any repeats, then, if necessary, rounding up to the nearest half yard.

When calculating for seamless draperies, you must determine the length first to see if the fabric width is wide enough to result in a seamless drapery. Seamless draperies will follow this format:

1. Determine the cut length by adding appropriate headings and hems to the finished length and adjusting for any repeat.

2. Determine if the cut length differs from the fabric width. If it does, continue to next step. If it doesn't, the treatment must be reconsidered, since it won't be seamless.

3. Determine the flat measure of the treatment, which will include stack.

4. Find yardage to price and order by adding in fullness and appropriate hems and overlaps, dividing by 36 inches to find yards, and rounding up to the nearest half yard.

5. Determine number of widths the workroom will charge to make the treatment by dividing the total amount of fabric in inches by 48 inches and then rounding up to the next *even* whole number.

Step-by-Step Examples

Example 1—Gathered Curtains

Your client has a breakfast room that she wants to use curtains, center split (two panels), lined and gathered on an oval curtain rod, to cover the lower portion of the window (Figure 10.11). They will be mounted just to the outside of the window frame.

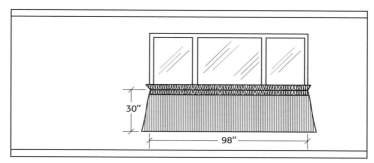

Figure 10.11 Example 1—Gathered curtains.

Flat measure of treatment: 98 inches

Finished length: 30 inches. This includes a ¾-inch oval rod and a 1-inch heading.

Returns: 2 inches

Hems: Double 2 inch

Desired fullness: 2½ times fullness

Fabric: 54 inches wide; 9-inch repeat

Step 1: Calculate finished width of treatment.

Take flat measure of the window:	98	in.
Add right return:	+ 2	in.
Add left return:	+ 2	in.
Total finished width (FW) to be gathered:	102	in.

Note: The returns in a gathered treatment need to be factored into the overall width, since they will need to be gathered.

Step 2: Calculate number of widths of fabric.

Take total finished width from Step 1:	102	in.
Multiply for fullness:	× 2.5	fullness
Total:	255	in.
Add side hems:	+ 6	in.
Total:	261	in.

Note: Side hems are added in after fullness because there is no fullness to a hem.

Divide by width of fabric:	÷ 54	in.
Total widths:	4.83	widths
Round up to whole number:	5	full widths

Note: Only full widths of fabric can be ordered.

Step 3: Calculate length of each width.

Desired finished length (FL):	30	in.
Add seam allowances:	+ 2	in.
Add bottom double 2-inch hem, as given:	+ 4	in.
Add rod pocket size with take-up allowance:	+ 1¾	in.

Note: See Table 11.2 on page 173 for rod pocket allowances.

Add heading:	+ 1	in.
Total cut length (CL):	38.75	in.

Note: The heading and the rod dimensions that are added here represent the fabric that goes to the back of the treatment. The finished length shown already includes the dimensions for the front of the rod and heading.

Calculate for repeat.

Take cut length:	38.75	in.
Divide by length of repeat:	÷ 9	in.
Number of repeats:	4.31	repeats
Round up to whole number:	5	full repeats

Note: In order to match the repeat when sewing, it is necessary to have fabric cuts that have full repeats.

Multiply by length of repeat:	× 9	in.
Adjusted cut length (ACL):	45	in.

Note: If it is a pattern for which you want to control which part of the repeat is at the top or bottom, add another full repeat to the adjusted cut length.

Step 4: Combine Steps 2 and 3.

Take ACL from Step 3:	45	in.
Multiply by total widths from Step 2:	× 5	widths
Total fabric required:	225	in.
Divide by 36 inches to find number of yards:	÷ 36	in.
Total yards:	6.25	yd.

Note: Fabric yardage must be ordered in ½-yard increments. If resulting yardage is not at full- or ½-yard amounts, round up to the next ½ yard.

Round up to nearest ½ yard:	**6.5**	**yd. to order**

To find yardage for lining: Multiply CL × W = Total inches. Divide by 36 inches to find yards, and round up or stay at the nearest yard or ½ yard.

Take CL from Step 3:	38.75	in.
Multiply by total widths from Step 2:	× 5	widths
Total fabric required:	193.75	in.
Divide by 36 to convert inches to yards:	÷ 36	in.
Total yards:	5.38	yd.
Round up to nearest ½ yard:	**5.5**	**yd. lining to order**

Note: In this scenario, you must order 6.5 yards of the decorative fabric and 5.5 yards of the plain lining.

Example 2—Stationary Side Panels

In the same client's family room, you have put cellular shades at the window to control privacy and glare, but you need fabric at each side of the window to help absorb sound and to provide balance in the room through the use of color and pattern. Fully traversing draperies aren't necessary, so you choose to specify stationary side panels with a pleated heading (Figure 10.12). They will be mounted above the window frame.

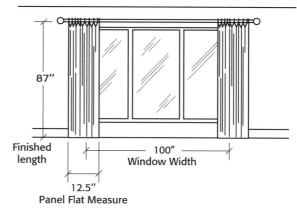

Figure 10.12 Example 2—Stationary side panels.

Window width from trim to trim: 100 inches

Finished length: 87 inches

Returns: 4 inches

Hems: Double 6 inch

Desired fullness: 3 times fullness

Fabric: 54 inches wide; 27-inch repeat

Step 1: Calculate flat measure of treatment.

Take trim-to-trim window measurement:	100 in.
Multiply by 25 percent to determine flat measure:	× .25
Total:	25 in.

Note: 25 percent is used to determine an appropriate width for stationary side panels. Sometimes 30 percent is used, especially if the window is taller than the normal 84 inches. This helps with the balance and proportion of the window treatment.

Divide by 2 to determine flat width per side:	÷ 2
Total flat measure (FM) of each panel:	12.5 in.

Note: Anything less than 12 inches seems to be skimpy. If there is room and the flat measure is less than 12 inches, use 12 inches as the minimum width measurement.

Step 2: Calculate number of widths of fabric.

Take total flat measure from Step 1:	12.5 in.
Multiply for fullness:	× 3 fullness
Total:	37.5 in.
Add side hems:	+ 6 in.
Add return:	+ 4 in.

Note: Side panels generally have one return.

Total:	47.5 in.

Note: Side hems are added in after fullness because there is no fullness to a hem.

Multiply by desired number of side panels:	× 2 side panels
Total:	95 in.
Divide by width of fabric:	÷ 54 in.
Total widths:	1.76 widths
Round up to whole numbers:	2 full widths

Note: Only full widths of fabric can be ordered.

Step 3: Calculate length of each width.

Desired finished length (FL):	87	in.
Add 18 inches for hems and heading:	+ 18	in.
Total cut length (CL):	105	in.

Calculate for repeat.

Take cut length:	105	in.
Divide by length of repeat:	÷ 27	in.
Number of repeats:	3.89	repeats
Round up to whole number:	4	full repeats

Note: In order to match the repeat when sewing, it is necessary to have fabric cuts that have full repeats.

Multiply by length of repeat:	× 27	in.
Adjusted cut length (ACL):	108	in.

Note: If it is a pattern for which you want to control which part of the repeat is at the top or bottom, add another full repeat to the adjusted cut length.

Step 4: Combine Steps 2 and 3.

Take ACL from Step 3:	108	in.
Multiply by total widths from Step 2:	× 2	widths
Total fabric required:	216	in.
Divide by 36 to convert inches to yards:	÷ 36	in.
Total yards:	**6**	**yd. to order**

Note: Fabric yardage must be ordered in ½-yard increments. Because the fabric calculated is an even 6 yards, nothing else needs to be done.

To find yardage for lining: Multiply CL × W = total inches, divide by 36 inches to find yards, and round up or stay at the nearest yard or ½ yard.

Take CL from Step 3:	105	in.
Multiply by total widths from Step 2:	× 2	widths
Total fabric required:	210	in.
Divide by 36 to convert inches to yards:	÷ 36	in.
Total yards:	5.83	yd.
Round up to nearest ½ yard:	**6**	**yd. lining to order**

Note: In this scenario, you must order 6 yards of the decorative fabric and 6 yards of the plain lining.

Example 3—Traversing, Pleated Draperies

You will be providing privacy draperies for bedrooms in a bed and breakfast. The pinch-pleated draperies are lined, traversing, and installed on a decorative rod (Figure 10.13). They will be mounted above the window frame.

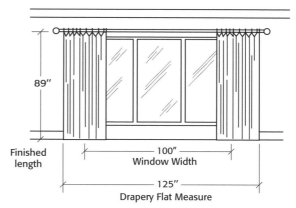

Figure 10.13 Example 3—Traversing, pleated draperies.

Window width from trim to trim: 100 inches

Finished length: 89 inches

Returns: 3 inches

Hems: Double 6 inch

Desired fullness: 3 times fullness

Stack: 25 percent

Fabric: 54 inches wide, 15-inch repeat

Step 1: Calculate flat measure of treatment.

Take trim-to-trim window measurement:	100 in.
Multiply by 25 percent to allow for stack:	× 1.25
Total flat measure (FM):	125 in.

Note: Stack is the space the drapery takes up when pulled open. Additional space is needed to allow for the drapery to hang over wall space instead of window space when it is pulled open. Stack ranges from 15 percent for lightweight fabrics to 33 percent for heavier weight fabrics.

Step 2: Calculate number of widths of fabric.

Take total flat measure from Step 1:	125 in.
Multiply for fullness:	× 3 fullness
Total:	375 in.
Add for master carrier overlap and side hems:	+ 20 in.
Total:	395 in.

Note: Master carrier overlap and side hems are added in after fullness because there is no fullness necessary for them.

Divide by width of fabric:	÷ 54 in.
Total widths:	7.31 widths
Round up to whole number:	8 full widths

Note: Only full widths of fabric can be ordered.

Step 3: Calculate length of each width.

Desired finished length (FL):	89 in.
Add 18 inches for hems and heading:	+ 18 in.
Total cut length (CL):	107 in.

Note: 18 inches for hems and headings represents a double 6-inch hem plus an additional 6 inches of fabric doubled over a 3-inch crinoline at the top of the drapery.

Calculate for repeat.

Take cut length:	107	in.
Divide by length of repeat:	÷ 15	in.
Number of repeats:	7.13	repeats
Round up to the nearest whole number:	8	full repeats

Note: In order to match the repeat when sewing, fabric cuts must have full repeats.

Multiply by length of repeat:	× 15	in.
Adjusted cut length (ACL):	120	in.

Note: If it is a pattern for which you want to control which part of the repeat is at the top or bottom, add another full repeat to the adjusted cut length.

Step 4: Combine Steps 2 and 3.

Take ACL from Step 3:	120	in.
Multiply by total widths from Step 2:	× 8	widths
Total fabric required:	960	in.
Divide by 36 to convert inches to yards:	÷ 36	in.
Total yards:	26.67	yd.

Note: Fabric yardage must be ordered in ½-yard increments. If resulting yardage is not at full- or ½-yard amounts, round up to the next ½ yard.

Round up to whole number:	**27**	**yd. to order**

To find yardage for lining: Multiply CL × W = total inches, divide by 36 inches to find yards, and round up or stay at the nearest yard or ½ yard.

Take CL from Step 3:	107	in.
Multiply by total widths from Step 2:	× 8	widths
Total fabric required:	856	in.
Divide by 36 to convert inches to yards:	÷ 36	in.
Total yards:	23.78	yd.
Round up to nearest ½ yard:	**24**	**yd. lining to order**

In this scenario, you must order 27 yards of the decorative fabric and 24 yards of the plain lining.

Manual Worksheets

Gathered Curtains Worksheet

Step 1: Calculate finished width of treatment.

Take flat measure of treatment:	_____	in.
Add right return: +	_____	in.
Add left return: +	_____	in.
Total finished width to be gathered:	_____	**in.**

Step 2: Calculate the number of widths of fabric.

Take total finished width from Step 1:	_____	in.
Multiply for fullness: ×	_____	fullness

Note: If this is a heavy-weight fabric, × 2; standard is × 2.5 or × 3; very lightweight is × 3 or × 4.

Total fullness:	_____	**in.**
Add 6 inches for side hems: +	6	in.
Total:	_____	**in.**
Divide by width of fabric: ÷	_____	in.
Total widths:	_____	**widths**
Round up to whole number:	_____	**full widths**

Step 3: Calculate length of each width.

Finished length:	_____	in.
Add for seam allowances (this number may vary): +	2	in.
Add bottom hem: +	_____	in.

- For double 2-inch hem, add 4 inches.
- For double 4-inch hem, add 8 inches.

Add additional amount for rod pocket and/or header (if rod and header are applicable):

Add rod pocket size w/take-up allowance: +	_____	in.
Add header height: +	_____	in.
Total cut length (CL):	_____	**in.**

If there is a repeat involved, continue with the following step. If not, skip to Step 4.

Take cut length:	_____	in.
Divide by length of repeat: ÷	_____	in.
Resulting number is the number of repeats:	_____	**repeats**
Round up to whole number:	_____	**full repeats**
Multiply by the length of repeat: ×	_____	in.
Adjusted cut length (ACL):	_____	**in.**

Step 4: Combine Steps 2 and 3.

Take cut length or ACL from Step 3:	_____	in.
Multiply by total widths from Step 2: ×	_____	widths
Total fabric required:	_____	**in.**
Divide by 36 to convert inches to yards: ÷	36	in.
Total yards:	_____	**yd.**

Note: Fabric yardage must be ordered in ½-yard increments.

Round up to nearest ½ yard:	_____	**yd. to be ordered**

To find yardage for lining: Multiply CL × W = total inches, divide by 36 inches to find yards, round up or stay at the nearest yard or ½ yard.

Note: Should the center draw traversing drapery consist of panels that use a portion of a width, the workroom will charge as if it is a whole width. For example: Center draw traversing draperies require 3 widths of fabric. There are 2 panels in a center draw. 3 widths ÷ 2 panels = 1½ widths per panel. Fabric will be ordered for 3 widths. Labor will be calculated as 4 widths, since there is the same amount of labor for a 1½-width panel as for a 2-width panel.

Stationary Side Panel Worksheet

Step 1: Calculate flat measure of stationary side panels.

Take trim-to-trim measure of window:		in.
Multiply by 25 percent: ×	.25	
Total:		**in.**
Divide by 2 to determine width per side: ÷	2	sides
Total flat measure each side of window:		**in.**

Note: Minimum flat measures for most windows needs to be 12 inches.

If less than 12 inches, round up to 12 inches:		**in.**

Step 2: Calculate the number of widths of fabric.

Desired flat measure of side panel:		in.
Multiply for fullness (× 2.5 or 3): ×	3	fullness

Note: If this is a heavy-weight fabric, × 2; standard is × 2.5 or 3; very lightweight is × 3 or × 4.

Total fullness:		**in.**
Add 6 inches for side hems: +	6	in.
Add depth of return: +		in.
Total:		**in.**
Multiply by number of side panels desired: ×		side panels
Total:		**in.**
Divide by width of fabric (normally 48 or 54 in.): ÷		in.
Number of widths of fabric:		**widths**
Round up to whole number:		**full widths**

Step 3: Calculate length of each width.

Take the finished length (FL) of drapery:		in.
Add 18 in. for hems and heading: +	18	in.

Note: 18 inches allows for double 6-inch hem; if narrower or wider hem, this number will change.

Total cut length (CL):		**in.**

If there is a repeat involved, continue with the following step. If not, skip to Step 4.

Take cut length:		in.
Divide by length of repeat: ÷		in.
Resulting number is the number of repeats:		**repeats**
Round up to whole number:		**full repeats**
Multiply this number by the length of the repeat: ×		in.
Adjusted cut length (ACL):		**in.**

Step 4: Combine Steps 2 and 3.

Take cut length or ACL from Step 3:		in.
Multiply by number of widths from Step 2: ×		widths
Total fabric required:		**in.**
Divide by 36 to convert inches to yards: ÷	36	in.
Total yards:		**yd.**

Note: Fabric yardage must be ordered in ½-yard increments.

Round up to nearest ½ yard:		**yd. to be ordered**

To find yardage for lining: Multiply CL × W = total inches, divide by 36 inches to find yards, and round up or stay at the nearest yard or ½ yard.

Note: Should side panels consist of 1½ or 1¾ widths, workroom will charge for 2 widths per panel since they involve the same amount of labor as 2 widths.

Traversing, Pleated Draperies Worksheet

Step 1: Calculate flat measure of treatment.

Take trim-to-trim measure of window: _____ in.

Multiply to allow for stack (15 to 33 percent): ×_____ (1.15 to 1.33)

Note: This explains why we are multiplying × 1.15 to 1.33.

Total flat measure (FM) of treatment: _____ **in.**

Step 2: Calculate the number of widths of fabric.

Total flat measure from Step 1: _____ in.

Multiply for fullness: × ____3____ fullness

Note: If this is a heavy-weight fabric, × 2; standard is × 2.5 or × 3; very lightweight is × 3 or × 4.

Total fullness: _____ **in.**

Add 20 in. for overlaps and returns for center draw (10 in. if a 1-way draw): +____20____ in.

Note: This allows for 3-inch to 4-inch returns.

If returns are deeper, add additional beyond amount allowed: +_____ in.

Total: _____ **in.**

Divide by width of fabric (normally 48 or 54 in.): ÷_____ in.

Widths of fabric: _____ **widths**

Round up to whole number: _____ **full widths**

Step 3: Calculate length of each width.

Take the finished length (FL) of drapery: _____ in.

Add 18 in. for hems and heading: +____18____ in.

Note: 18 inches allows for double 6-inch hem; if narrower or wider hem, this number will change.

Total cut length (CL): _____ **in.**

If there is a repeat involved, continue with the following step. If not, skip to Step 4.

Take cut length: _____ in.

Divide by length of repeat: ÷_____ in.

Resulting number is the number of repeats: _____ **repeats**

Round up to whole number: _____ **full repeats**

Multiply this number by the length of the repeat: ×_____ in.

Adjusted cut length (ACL): _____ **in.**

Note: If it is important to control where the pattern starts at the top, add another full repeat to ACL.

Step 4: Combine Steps 2 and 3.

Take cut length or ACL from Step 3: _____ in.

Multiply by number of widths from Step 2: ×_____ widths

Total length of fabric required: _____ **in.**

Divide by 36 to convert inches to yards: ÷____36____ in.

Total yards: _____ **yd.**

Note: Fabric yardage must be ordered in ½-yard increments.

Round up to nearest ½ yard: _____ **yd. to be ordered**

To find yardage for lining: Multiply CL × W = total inches, divide by 36 inches to find yards, and round up or stay at the nearest yard or ½ yard.

Note: Should the center draw traversing drapery consist of panels that use a portion of a width, the workroom will charge as if it is a whole width. For example: Center draw traversing draperies require 3 widths of fabric. There are 2 panels in a center draw. 3 widths ÷ 2 panels = 1½ widths per panel. Fabric will be ordered for 3 widths. Labor will be calculated as 4 widths since there is the same amount of labor for a 1½-width panel as for a 2-width panel.

Seamless, Traversing Draperies (118+ inches wide) Worksheet

Step 1: Calculate length of each width.

Take the finished length (FL) of drapery:	_____	in.
Add 18 inches for hems and heading: +	18	in.

Note: 18 inches allows for double 6-inch hem; if narrower or wider hem, this number will change.

Total cut length (CL): _____ **in.**

If there is a repeat involved, continue with the following step. If not, skip to Step 2.

Take cut length:	_____	in.
Divide by length of repeat: ÷	_____	in.
Resulting number is the number of repeats:	_____	**repeats**
Round up to nearest whole number:	_____	**full repeats**
Multiply this number by the length of the repeat: ×	_____	in.
Adjusted cut length (ACL):	_____	**in.**

Note: If it is important to control where the pattern starts at the top, add another full repeat to ACL.

Step 2: Determine if selected fabric will railroad.

If the cut length is the same or less than the fabric width, it can be used as intended. If the cut length is more than the fabric width, it can't be used as seamless.

If the fabric width is more than the cut length, proceed to the next step.

Step 3: Calculate flat measure of treatment.

Take trim-to-trim measure of window:	_____	in.
Multiply to allow for stack (15–33 percent): ×	_____	(1.15 to 1.33)
Total flat measure (FM) of treatment:	_____	**in.**

Step 4: Calculate yardage.

Total from Step 3:	_____	in.
Multiply for fullness: ×	3	fullness

Note: If this is a heavy-weight fabric, × 2; standard is × 2.5 or × 3; very lightweight is × 3 or × 4.

Total fullness:	_____	**in.**
Add 20 in. for overlaps and returns for center draw (10 in. if a 1-way draw): +	20	in.

Note: This allows for 3-inch to 4-inch returns.

If returns are deeper, add additional beyond amount allowed: +	_____	in.
Total fabric required:	_____	**in.**
Divide by 36 to convert inches to yards: ÷	36	in.
Total yards:	_____	**yd.**

Note: Fabric yardage must be ordered in ½-yard increments.

Round up to nearest ½ yard: _____ **yd.**

Step 5. Calculate number of labor widths of fabric the workroom will charge

Total of fabric in inches:	_____	in.
Divide by 48 inches to find labor widths: ÷	48	in.
Widths of fabric:	_____	**widths**
Round up to the nearest even whole number:	_____	**labor widths**

Note: Should the center draw traversing drapery consist of panels that use a portion of a width, the workroom will charge as if it is a whole width. For example: Center draw traversing draperies require 3 widths of fabric. There are 2 panels in a center draw. 3 widths ÷ 2 panels = 1½ widths per panel. Fabric will be ordered for 3 widths. Labor will be calculated as 4 widths since there is the same amount of labor for a 1½-width panel as for a 2-width panel.

Practice Lessons: Curtains and Draperies

BASIC

Gathered Curtains

Gathered curtains are being used in an 8-year-old girl's bedroom to provide privacy. The curtains will be center split (two panels), lined, and gathered on a ¾-inch oval rod (Figure 10.14). They will be mounted just to the outside of the window frame. She is going to use ribbons to tie back the window treatment.

Flat measure of treatment: 36 inches

Finished length: 56 inches; this includes a ¾-inch rod and 2-inch heading (see Table 11.2 on page 173).

Returns: 3 inches

Hems: Double 2 inch

Desired fullness: 2½ times fullness

Fabric: 48 inches wide; no repeat

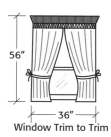

Figure 10.14 Practice lesson: Basic—Gathered curtains.

1. How many widths of fabric are needed?
2. How many widths will the workroom charge?
3. What is the cut length?
4. How many yards of decorative fabric must be ordered?
5. How many yards of lining must be ordered?

Stationary Side Panels

Stationary side panels will be used to frame a shuttered window in a media room. The side panels will be lined (Figure 10.15). They will be mounted 5 inches above the window frame.

Window trim-to-trim measurement: 66 inches

Finished length: 89 inches

Returns: 4 inches

Hems: Double 6 inch

Desired fullness: 2½ times fullness

Fabric: 54 inches wide; 16-inch repeat

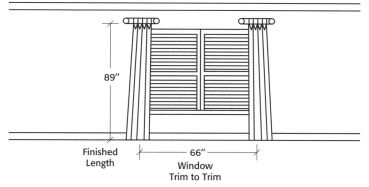

Figure 10.15 Practice lesson: Basic—Stationary side panels.

1. What is the desired flat measure for the side panels?
2. How many widths of fabric are needed?
3. How many widths will the workroom charge?
4. What is the adjusted cut length?
5. How many yards of decorative fabric must be ordered?
6. How many yards of lining must be ordered?

Traversing, Pleated Draperies

Traversing, pleated draperies will be used in a living room. The treatment will be a floor-length, pinch-pleated, unlined, center draw, traversing drapery. The client wants the sheer to stack off of the window. (Figure 10.16). The draperies will be mounted so that the top of the sheer will be 5 inches above the window trim.

Window trim-to-trim measurement: 50 inches

Top of window trim to floor: 84 inches

Returns: 3 inches

Hems: Double 6 inch

Desired fullness: 3 times fullness

Fabric: sheer; no repeat; 54 inches wide

Stack: 15 percent

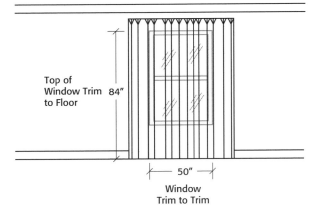

Figure 10.16 Practice lesson: Basic—Traversing, pleated draperies.

1. What is the flat measure of the drapery?
2. How many widths are needed?
3. How many widths will the workroom charge?
4. What is the finished length?
5. What is the cut length?
6. How many yards must be ordered?

INTERMEDIATE
Gathered Curtains

Gathered curtains that are center split (two panels), lined, and gathered on a 2-inch decorative rod with a 2-inch heading (see Table 11.2 on page 173) are being used on two windows on either side of a bed in a boy's bedroom (Figure 10.17).

They will be mounted 1 inch beyond the frame to each side and 6 inches above the window frame.

Window trim-to-trim measurement: 42 inches each window

Top of window trim to floor: 84 inches

Returns: 3 inches

Hems: Double 4 inch

Desired fullness: 3 times fullness

Fabric: 54 inches wide; 19-inch repeat

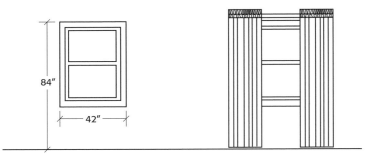

Figure 10.17 Practice lesson: Intermediate— Gathered curtains.

1. What is the flat measure?
2. How many widths of fabric are needed per window?
3. How many widths will the workroom charge per window?
4. What is the finished length?
5. What is the adjusted cut length?
6. How many yards of decorative fabric must be ordered for both windows?
7. How many yards of lining must be ordered for both windows?

Stationary Side Panels

Stationary side panels will be used in a spa lobby to break up a wide horizontal space and to provide sound absorption. You have decided to use stationary side panels on each side and between the three windows (Figure 10.18). They will be lined and installed 5 inches above the window trim on a decorative rod.

Window trim-to-trim measurement: 30 inches

Top of window trim to floor: 96 inches

Returns: 4 inches

Hems: Double 6 inch

Desired fullness: 3 times fullness

Fabric: 54 inches wide; 27-inch repeat

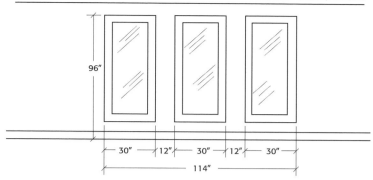

Figure 10.18 Practice lesson: Intermediate—Stationary side panels.

1. What is the desired flat measure for the side panels?
2. How many side panels will be made?
3. How many widths of fabric are needed for all side panels?
4. How many widths will the workroom charge for all side panels?
5. What is the finished length
6. What is the adjusted cut length?
7. How many yards of decorative fabric must be ordered?
8. How many yards of lining must be ordered?

Traversing, Pleated Draperies

A traversing, pleated drapery is one solution for your client who doesn't like vertical blinds for her patio door. The lined treatment will be a one-way draw to the right on a decorative rod. Because the patio door is at a lower height than the other windows, you have decided to install the treatment at the same height as the other windows (Figure 10.19).

Patio door trim-to-trim measurement: 84 inches

Top of trim to floor: 80 inches. Finished length of other treatments in the same room is 87 inches.

Returns: 3½ inches

Hems: Double 6 inch

Desired fullness: 3 times fullness

Fabric: 54 inches; 18-inch repeat

Stack: 25 percent

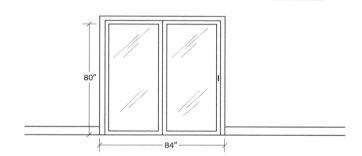

Figure 10.19 Practice lesson: Intermediate—Traversing, pleated draperies.

1. What is the flat measure of the drapery?
2. How many inches are added for overlap and return?
3. How many widths are needed?
4. How many widths will the workroom charge?
5. What is the finished length?
6. What is the adjusted cut length?
7. How many yards of decorative fabric, must be ordered?
8. How many yards of lining must be ordered?

ADVANCED
Gathered Curtains

Gathered curtains, specifically sash curtains, gathered top and bottom on ¾-inch sash rods with 1-inch headings (see Table 11.2 on page 173) will be made for your client's atrium door (Figure 10.20). They will be mounted 1 inch to each side and 1 inch above and 1 inch below the top and bottom of the window.

Window trim-to-trim width measurement: 24 inches each window

Window trim-to-trim length measurement: 72 inches

Returns: 1 inch

Hems: Not applicable because of headings

Desired fullness: 3 times fullness

Fabric: 54 inches wide; no repeat

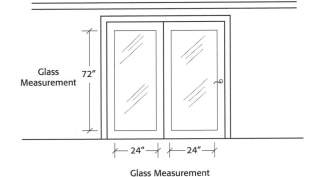

Figure 10.20 Practice lesson: Advanced—Gathered curtains (sash curtains).

1. What is the flat measure of each window?
2. What is the finished width of each window?
3. How many widths of fabric are needed per window?
4. How many widths will the workroom charge per window?
5. What is the finished length?
6. What is the cut length?
7. How many yards of sheer fabric must be ordered for both windows?

Seamless, Traversing Draperies and Traversing, Pleated Draperies

Traversing draperies, seamless sheer and pleated over-drapery, will be used in the lobby of lawyers' offices. Seamless, traversing, pleated, sheer draperies will be used closer to the window to help control glare, and traversing, pleated, lined draperies will be used for the outer layer (Figure 10.21). The top of the sheers will be 3 inches above the trim, and the top of the draperies will be 5 inches above the trim.

Window trim-to-trim measurement: 110 inches

Top of trim to floor: 84 inches

Returns: Sheer—3 inches; traversing drapery—6½ inches

Hems: Double 6 inches

Desired fullness: 3 times fullness

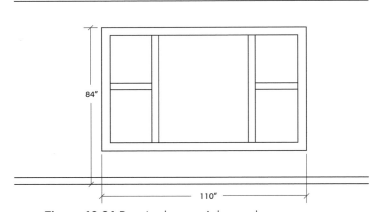

Figure 10.21 Practice lesson: Advanced—Traversing, pleated draperies.

Sheer fabric: 118 inches wide; no repeat

Traversing drapery fabric: 54 inches wide; 21-inch repeat

Stack: Sheer—15 percent; traversing drapery—25 percent

1. What is the flat measure of the sheer?
2. What is the flat measure of the traversing drapery?
3. How many widths are needed for the traversing drapery?
4. How many widths will the workroom charge for the traversing drapery?
5. How many widths will the workroom charge for the sheer?
6. What is the finished length for the sheer?
7. What is the finished length for the traversing drapery?
8. What is the adjusted cut length for the traversing drapery?
9. How many yards of decorative fabric must be ordered?
10. How many yards of lining must be ordered?
11. How many yards of sheer must be ordered?

Pricing for Intermediate Gathered Curtains

Use the scenario, labor, and fabric quantity found for the Intermediate Gathered Curtains practice lesson and the prices listed below to calculate pricing for your client. These are being made by a local workroom and will be picked up when they are finished. The lining is purchased from your workroom and doesn't have any additional shipping costs.

Fabric: $36.00/yard

Fabric shipping: $27.00 total

Lining: $8.00/yard

Hardware: $150.00 each (includes pole, brackets, finials, and rings)

Hardware shipping: $35.00 total

Labor: $58.00 per width

Installation: $85.00 each window (All aspects of the installation are included in this price.)

1. What is the subtotal for materials?
2. What is the subtotal for labor and installation?
3. What is the overall price for these two windows?

Pricing for Intermediate Traversing, Pleated Draperies

Use the scenario, labor, and the fabric quantity found for the Intermediate Traversing, Pleated Draperies practice lesson and the prices listed below to calculate pricing for your client. These draperies are being made by a local workroom and will be picked up when finished. The lining is purchased from your workroom and doesn't have any additional shipping costs.

Fabric: $62.00/yard

Fabric shipping: $27.00 total

Lining: $8.00/yard

Hardware: $325.00 (includes pole, brackets, finials, and rings)

Hardware shipping: $46.00 total

Labor: $60.00 per width

Installation: $130.00 (all aspects of the installation are included in this price)

1. What is the subtotal for materials?
2. What is the subtotal for labor and installation?
3. What is the overall price for this window?

References

National Decorating Products Association. *The New Guide to Soft Window Treatments*. St. Louis, MO: National Decorating Products Association, 1993.

Neal, M. *Custom Draperies in Interior Design*. Norwalk, CT: Appleton & Lange, 1982.

Robert Allen Design Hardware, accessed June 29, 2012, at http://www.robertallendesign.com/hardware/collection_ra.aspx.

Von Tobel, J. *The Design Directory of Window Treatments*. Layton, UT: Gibbs Smith Publisher, 2007.

Window Fashions, February 1990.

Chapter 11 | Top Treatments and Window Shades

Top treatments and custom window shades play very important roles in the design and coordination of interiors. They can provide simple solutions at the window to accentuate style, cover non-decorative rods for draperies, and, in the case of window shades, provide privacy and insulation value at the window. Styles and fabrics are limitless.

Chapter Outline

Terminology

Types of Top Treatments and Window Shades
Top Treatments
Custom Window Shades

Cost Factors

Calculations
Top Treatments
Cornice/Lambrequin
Gathered/Tabbed/Pulled-Up Valances
Swags, Cascades, and Jabots
Custom Window Shades

Step-by-Step Examples
Example 1—Gathered Valance
Example 2—Swags and Cascades
Example 3—Roman Shade
Example 4—Balloon Shade

Manual Worksheets
Cornice and Lambrequin Worksheet
Gathered Valance Worksheet
Tabbed Valance Worksheet

Pulled-Up Valance Worksheet
Swags, Cascades, and Jabots Worksheet
Roman/Hobbled Shade Worksheet
Balloon and Austrian Shade Worksheet
Mock Roman/Hobbled Shade Worksheet

Practice Lessons—Top Treatments and Custom Window Shades
Basic
Cornice
Gathered Valance
Roman Shade
Intermediate
Lambrequin
Tabbed Valance
Mock Hobbled Shade
Balloon Shade
Advanced
Pulled-Up Valance
Swags and Cascades
Austrian Shade
Pricing for Basic Gathered Valance
Pricing for Basic Roman Shade
Pricing for Advanced Swags and Cascades

References

Terminology

Allowance The amount added for hems, headings, overlaps, and returns in window treatments. It is also used to refer to amount in inches taken as a deduction to allow for clearance at the top or bottom or at the sides that will allow them to function without dragging on floor, ceiling, or sides of window.

Banding Flat strips of fabric, usually sewn at or near the edge of a top treatment or shade, used to create a contrast and accent. Banding is normally created from fabric cut on the bias.

Cascades Shaped, pleated ends for valances. They hang in zigzag folds to a point. They are used in other ways, but most often with swags. The underside of cascades is visible because of the zigzag.

Clearance The portion of a window treatment that is airspace: behind, beside, above, below, and in front of it.

Cornice Decorative top treatment, usually constructed of plywood, with a dust cap (top). It is shaped, padded, and covered in fabric (see Figure 11.4).

Cut length Total length of fabric needed per width of fabric to create a window treatment. The cut length includes the desired finished length of treatment plus the allowances needed for hems, headings, and pattern repeat.

Decorative rod A rod, traversing or stationary, made of wood or metal. Because it is exposed and not hidden by any window treatment, the finish of the rod is attractive. It is finished at the ends with finials. Rings on the rod are often used to hold the drapery or the valance.

Drape This is a verb. It refers to how the fabric hangs.

Drop Depth (length) of a valance. For a standard 8-foot ceiling, a 16-inch to 18-inch drop is proportionate for most fabrics and treatments.

Dye lot Variation in intensity of color from one batch of fabric (or wallpaper, carpet, etc.) to the next.

Empire valance Top treatment that uses narrower swags and horns/cones. This is a very traditional treatment (Figure 11.1).

Finished length The total finished length of treatment after the workroom is finished creating it.

Figure 11.1 Formal Empire valance with tassel trim mounted to a 1-inch x 6-inch board. The horns and swags are fabricated separately and then sewn together. (Courtesy of Diana Allison)

Finished width The width of the rod plus the returns.

Flat measure The total width and length of the drapery treatment as it hangs on the wall, the actual width and length measurement of the area to be covered.

Flaws Holes, heavy slubs, misweaves, or misprints in fabrics that make it unacceptable to use. The drapery workroom must inspect the fabric for flaws before cutting it. This fabric must be sent back to the manufacturer for replacement before it is cut.

Fullness Amount of fabric used in a window treatment as compared to the finished width. Interior designers prefer to use 2½ to 3 times fullness for most gathered top treatments; however, some other treatments require only 1½ times fullness.

Hand Feel of a fabric.

Heading Top of the curtain or drapery, sometimes pleated and with stiffening. It also refers to the part of a gathered curtain or valance that will project above the rod.

Hems The finished sides and bottoms of window treatments. These are usually double turned to hide shadowing of the raw edges (Figure 11.2).

  Double hem Hem turned twice to eliminate shadows and raw edges and to add weight for hanging.

  Shirt-tail hem Hem, similar to that found in shirts, that is turned twice, using less than 1 of inch fabric, and topstitched. When finished, the hem is ¼ inch to ½ inch.

Interlining Flannel fabric placed between face fabric and regular lining to add richness and bulk to lightweight fabrics. It also provides additional protection from the sun for fabrics such as silk.

Jabot A decorative cone or double-sided cascade used between sections of a valance.

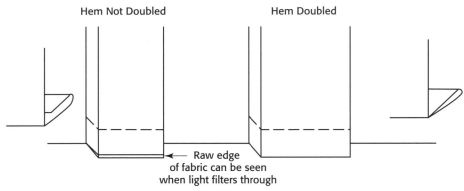

Figure 11.2 Hems are often doubled over to create weight for the treatment, to keep light from coming through and exposing the raw edge, and to create a professionally finished look.

Kingston valance A variation of the Empire valance that also uses swags and horns/cones. The main difference is that the Empire valance swags are attached and swag from the top of the treatment, whereas the Kingston swags are attached vertically from side to side like an Austrian shade (Figure 11.3).

Figure 11.3 Kingston valance installed on board. Like the Empire valance, the horns and swags are created separately before being sewn together. (© BUILT Images / Alamy)

Lambrequin Usually defined as a cornice that frames a window. Many times it has "legs" at the sides that go all the way to the floor (Figure 11.4).

Lining Fabric used as a back layer for window treatments. Be careful to use a weight and content lining fabric similar to that of the face fabric. Many interior designers seem to use a challis lining.

Pattern repeat Lengthwise or crosswise measurement of one design motif to where that same pattern is again repeated. (See Figure 3.2 on page 22 for examples.)

Straight match Repeat matches straight across.

Drop match or half drop Repeat is staggered so that every other width matches along the same line. The match runs diagonally.

Projection The measurement from the wall out into the room. This is different from clearance, since the projection goes to the most forward point and the clearance stops at the back of the rod or treatment.

Railroaded fabric The vertical pattern of regular rolled fabric runs up the bolt. The vertical pattern of a railroaded fabric runs side to side. A stripe will run like railroad tracks.

Return The part of the window treatment that returns to the wall. With multiple treatments, the return will increase, usually by 3 to 4 inches per layer. The sheer close to the window may have a return of 3 inches. The side panels over the draperies may then have a return of at least 6 to 7 inches. The valance over all of this may then have a return of 9 to 10 inches.

Rod pocket Hem at the top or bottom of a curtain through which a rod is inserted for a shirred heading.

Sash Window framework that holds the panes in place.

Seam Where two pieces of fabric are sewn together, a seam is created. When the fabric has a pattern, the pattern must be matched at the seam.

Selvage Edge of fabric formed on the loom when the fabric is woven. It is frequently woven tighter than the fabric body.

Shade A fabric window treatment that provides coverage for the glass area of the window and operates vertically up and down. The styles made by drapery workrooms are commonly Roman, hobbled, balloon, and Austrian (Figure 11.5).

Roman A window shade that is flat when it is fully down.

Hobbled A window shade that has fullness in the length, resulting in soft folds when the shade is fully down.

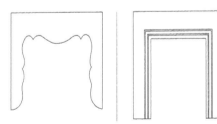

Figure 11.4 Cornices and lambrequins can be made almost any size and shape that an interior designer can imagine. While cornices create a treatment at the top, lambrequins provide a treatment at the top and down the sides, often to the floor. (Neal, M. (1982). *Custom Draperies in Interior Design*. Norwalk, CT: Appleton & Lange)

A.

Figure 11.5 Common types of custom shades: (A) Roman, (B) hobbled, (C) balloon, and (D) Austrian. (A: iStockphoto/© Peter Mukherjee; B–C: Courtesy of Diana Allison; D: Creative Commons)

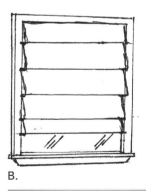

B.

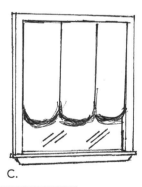

C.

D.

Balloon A shade that has fullness in the width and fullness at the very bottom, resulting in a shade that is gathered at the bottom in soft scallops and has fullness from either pleats or gathering along the top.

Austrian A shade that has fullness in the width and length. This type of treatment uses the most fabric of any window shade and results in soft scalloped gathers in the length when it is down and gathered fabric in the width.

Shirr Another name for gather. Sash curtains are shirred on the rod.

Sill Horizontal piece of wood that is the bottom of the window.

Swags Draped valance, pleated into a scalloped effect, usually overlapped. This creates a formal treatment (Figure 11.6).

Figure 11.6 Swags and cascades with side panels. (Courtesy of Diana Allison)

Top treatment Valance or cornice used to add decoration and conceal rods at the top of a window or window treatment.

Valance Horizontal top treatment used to conceal a rod and give a finished appearance to a window. Valances styles can be used to create distinct period looks.

Width[1] Distance from one side of the window to the other or one side of a drapery treatment to the other.

Width[2] Single width of fabric of the cut length required to make a window treatment, sometimes referred to as a cut. One or more widths are required to make a panel. Most fabric is 48 inches or 54 inches wide.

Types of Top Treatments and Window Shades

This chapter covers cornices, lambrequins, gathered/tabbed/pulled-up valances, swags and cascades, and mock shade valances. Mock shade valances are a shortened and stationary version of custom window shades. Custom window shades addressed here are Roman, hobbled, balloon, and Austrian shades. These are the basic types of treatments from which every other treatment is modified.

Top Treatments

Top treatments are either board, rod (decorative or functional), or hook mounted (installed). When valances are stapled to a 1-inch × 4-inch or 1-inch × 6-inch (or deeper) board, the board is wrapped with either lining or valance fabric before the treatment is attached to the wall with angle irons (Figure 11.7). With a hooked treatment, hooks are attached to wall and loops attached to valances are hooked over them to hold the treatment up (Figure 11.8). Rods are either decorative and exposed or more functional and covered by the fabric, usually using a treatment with rod pockets (Figure 11.9). Top treatments need to extend at least a total of 2 inches

Figure 11.7 Top treatment: swags and cascades attached to a board. (Courtesy of Diana Allison)

Figure 11.8 Top treatment: pulled-up valance with side panels attached to hooks. (Courtesy of Diana Allison)

Figure 11.9 Top treatment: swags with side panels attached to rod. (Courtesy of Diana Allison)

A.

B.

Figure 11.10 Cornice (A) and lambrequin (B). (A: Courtesy of Diana Allison; B: © Elizabeth Whiting & Associates / Alamy)

Figure 11.11 Gathered and shaped valances on 2½-inch flat rod with 2-inch header. (Courtesy of Diana Allison)

wider than the under-treatment and sometimes a total of 4 to 6 inches wider. Following are types of top treatments.

Cornices and lambrequins are upholstered and padded board treatments. Sometimes the cornice and lambrequin are made at the upholsterer's workroom. The bottom of the cornice and inside legs of the lambrequin are most often shaped to follow a specific style (Figure 11.10).

Gathered valances are created by using fabric gathered, usually 2 to 3 times the width of the window, on a rod or board. The bottom of the treatment can be straight or have a shape to it. The heading and the hem treatment changes the look of this type of valance (Figure 11.11).

Tabbed and pulled-up valances are also created using using more fabric width than the window itself. These valances are usually around 1½ to 2 times fuller than the window. They aren't gathered along the top with rod pockets or shirring tape like gathered valances. Instead, they are achieved by tabs that are sewn at regular intervals and held up by a rod or by "pulling up" the fabric and stapling it to a board at regular intervals. This is usually a more casual look (Figure 11.12). The width of the tabs and the spacing between them have a significant effect on the overall look of tabbed treatments.

Swags and cascades are a very traditional type of top treatment that has had numerous variations created to make it less formal and traditional. It is composed of fabric that swags from one point to another with angle-cut pleated widths of fabric at each end of the treatment. This treatment traditionally is board-mounted; however, decorative rods and hooks have also been used to attach this treatment to the wall

(Figure 11.13). When rods are used, there is airspace created between the swag and the rod. Designers must be careful to place the treatment far enough above the window so that the window or its trim isn't seen. The back sides of the cascades are revealed with the angle cut. This is an opportunity for contrast fabric to be used.

Custom Window Shades

Custom window shades generally work best when they are attached to a board where all the controlling mechanisms and eye rings for cords can be secured.

A.

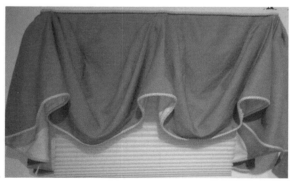

B.

Figure 11.12 (A) Tabbed top drapery panels. (B) Pulled-up valance. (A: iStockphoto/© stocknroll; B: Courtesy of Diana Allison)

A.

B.

Figure 11.13 (A) Casual swag and cascade attached to rod. (B) Formal swags, cascades, and jabot attached to board in bay window. (A–B: Courtesy of Diana Allison)

Common board thicknesses are 1 inch × 2 inches and 1 inch × 3 inches. These shades can be installed either inside or just on the outside of the window frame or the window on a door. When they are inside-mounted, make sure that the workroom takes the appropriate side allowances so that the shade will operate up and down easily.

Remember that all the cords and mechanisms that allow the shade to operate are generally seen from the outside of the house. Depending on the position of the window on the house, this may be an issue to the client. Another important point to consider is the physical ability of the client to raise the shade. For instance, balloon or Austrian shades have a lot of fabric, which increases the weight of the shade. A wide and long window may need to be made as several less-wide shades in order to be operated easily. This is a concern for anyone who has limited upper body strength. It is possible to get motorized and remote-controlled mechanisms for these shades, which will address this issue.

As with top treatments, the look of each of these shades can be greatly modified not only by the fabric specified but by the details added to them, including banding, cording, and shaped bottom designs. One other note is that when these custom shades are raised, they need a little attention to arrange the pleats or gathers so that they lay attractively. This doesn't take much time or effort, but the client will need to be made aware of this and shown how to do it.

Mock shade valances look as if they could be fully working custom shades (Figure 11.14). They don't take as much fabric as a working shade does, since they are stationary at the top. They can be made to look like any of the working shades, with all the different decorative details that can be added to them.

Roman shades lie flat when they are down (Figure 11.15). There are several variations, one of which is a hobbled shade. There is no fullness in the width in any of these variations. This type of treatment allows a beautiful pattern to be fully seen. However,

A.

B.

Figure 11.14 (A) Mock Roman shade. (B) Mock balloon shade. (A–B: Courtesy of Diana Allison)

Figure 11.15 Roman shade. (Courtesy of Diana Allison)

a solid fabric can also be beautiful. Many interior designers will add a contrast banding inset from the sides and the bottom to add interest.

A *hobbled shade* has a little fullness in the length at each row where the rings are located. The rings on the back are where the cords are guided through to pull the shade up, and they are placed in rows. Each hobble can add anywhere from 6 to 12 inches to the length of the fabric cut when making the shade. This dimension sometimes coincides with ring spacing. This creates a softened look to the Roman shade (Figure 11.16). Another variation of the Roman that is more tailored than the hobbled shade involves narrow wood slats, approximately 1 inch to 1½ inches, sewn into the fabric where the rings are placed (Figure 11.17).

Balloon shades have fullness in the width and about 20 inches added to the bottom length in order to give them a fuller look at the bottom. This fullness can be achieved either with a pleated or a gathered top (Figure 11.18). Either type of top will take the same amount of fabric in the width.

The *Austrian shade* takes the most fabric yardage of any of these shades because it has fullness in the width and the length. The Austrian is usually seen gathered across the top and all the way down (Figure 11.19). These used to be very popular in sheer fabric. This treatment is often seen in stage curtains.

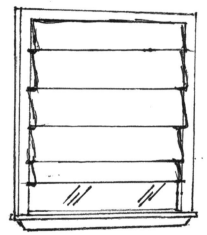

Figure 11.16 Hobbled shade. (Courtesy of Diana Allison)

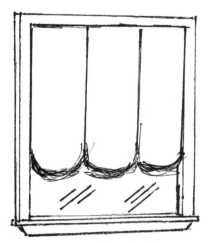

Figure 11.18 Balloon shade. (Courtesy of Diana Allison)

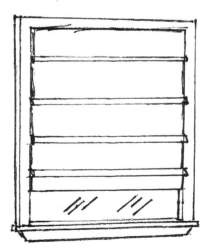

Figure 11.17 Slatted Roman shade. (Courtesy of Diana Allison)

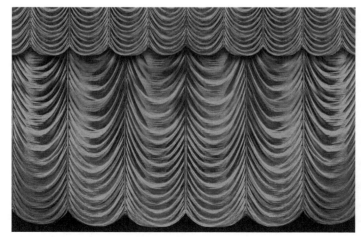

Figure 11.19 Austrian shade. (iStockphoto/© ginosphotos)

Cost Factors

Factors that impact the cost of top treatments and custom window shades are fabric, lining, rod (if applicable), shipping, labor, and installation (Table 11.1).

Most manufacturers require a 1-yard or 2-yard minimum order. Once the minimum is satisfied, fabric can be ordered in ½-yard increments. Make sure that the lining you specify for the job is the same width as the face fabric, usually 54 inches wide.

Window Treatment Schedule											
Client: Phone #s: Address:								Workroom: Installer:			
Room/Window: **Finished Dimensions:**											
Materials											
	Mfr./ Vendor	**Pattern**	**Color/ Finish**	**Width**	**Repeat**	**Qty.**	**Cost Per**	**Subtotal**	**Est. Ship.**	**Total**	**PO**
Fabric											
Lining											
Hdwr.											
Rod											
Brackets											
Supports											
Finials											
Batons											
								Subtotal for Materials			
Labor and Installation											
Labor						**Qty.**	**Cost Per**	**Subtotal**	**Est. Ship.**	**Total**	**WO**
Install											
							Subtotal for Labor and Installation				
							Overall Total				
Diagram:											

Table 11.1 Top Treatments and Custom Window Shades: Specifying and Calculating Total Cost

Top treatments require rods, hooks, or boards to attach the treatment to the wall. The rod can be decorative, meant to be seen, or purely functional, whereby the treatment slides onto the rod. Some rods are sold in a set that includes return brackets and supports. Many decorative rods require specifying not only the rod but the specific brackets, supports, finials, and rings. Because decorative rods are meant to be seen, this type of customization is important.

Decorative metal hooks are sometimes used to support looped or ringed top treatments. When a top treatment is attached to a board, the board will be wrapped in either lining or the fabric being used, to give it a finished look if viewed from the top or from underneath. Boards are used with custom window shades. It is important to find out from the workroom if the labor charge includes the costs of the boards.

Labor for making top treatments is dependent on the type of treatment. A gathered valance can be priced per width of fabric. This price includes sewing widths together and creating the hem and heading. There often are different charges for a lined or unlined valance. Keep in mind that any gathered valance that consists of a fraction of a width will be rounded up to the full width. A tabbed valance may be priced by the width and then additional amounts added for the number of tabs used. A cornice and lambrequin may be priced by the linear foot.

Swags and cascades are priced by the number of swags and cascades. Empire and Kingston valances are often charged the same way. Custom window shades are charged by the square inch or the square foot of the shade. Mock shade valances may be charged by the linear foot of the treatment width or by the square inch or square foot of the finished valance. Additional labor charges will be found for making and sewing banding, sewing on trim, utilizing multiple fabrics, and any unusual add-on to the treatment. Until you are comfortable with pricing window treatments, speak to the workroom to confirm your estimate before giving your client a quote.

Installers may charge for valances by the foot and custom window shades by the number of total shades. There are many variables that determine the final installation charge: measuring, making templates, trip charge for outside of accepted installation area, widths per treatment, number of rods per treatment, type of rod installed, customization of rod (cutting and assembling), minimum trip charge, working above floor beyond an acceptable number of feet (sometimes greater than 10 feet), and steaming. Don't hesitate to call the installer to be sure all required costs have been calculated for the job.

Calculations

Because these top treatments and custom window shades are custom made, nearly any size of window or circumstance can be accommodated. The more limiting issue with window treatments is how they can be installed. For the majority of window installations, this isn't an issue. For those situations where it is an issue, you should get your installer involved immediately.

All measurements and calculations for window treatments are done in inches. When taking measurements, you should know what type of window treatment is being planned. Keep in mind the type of window, whether it is a sliding door, atrium door, double-hung window, casement window, and so on, so that inherent qualities of that type of window can be accounted for in the design of the window treatment. When measuring for window treatments, take a digital photo to help you remember small details. The step after measuring is determining how far above the window trim you will install the treatment and how far to each side of the window trim the treatment will cover.

While it is possible to pay an installer to measure, knowing how to do this is helpful when the schedule is tight. In addition, it will allow you to communicate properly with your workroom and installer. A good idea is to make an elevation of the window wall, take

ALLRED - Y - MADE

CUSTOM WINDOW TREATMENTS
INTERIOR DESIGN & ACCESSORIES

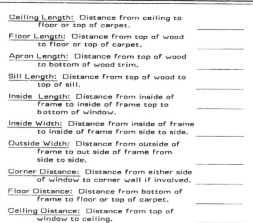

MEASUREMENT SHEET

Ceiling Length: Distance from ceiling to floor or top of carpet.

Floor Length: Distance from top of wood to floor or top of carpet.

Apron Length: Distance from top of wood to bottom of wood trim.

Sill Length: Distance from top of wood to top of sill.

Inside Length: Distance from inside of frame to inside of frame top to bottom of window.

Inside Width: Distance from inside of frame to inside of frame from side to side.

Outside Width: Distance from outside of frame to out side of frame from side to side.

Corner Distance: Distance from either side of window to corner wall if involved.

Floor Distance: Distance from bottom of frame to floor or top of carpet.

Ceiling Distance: Distance from top of window to ceiling.

Figure 11.20 Workroom measurements sheet. (Courtesy of Jennifer Allred)

several measurements, and make notations. Many drapery workrooms have slight differences in their use of terminology. Use the workroom's specific terminology to ensure you get what you are requesting. Some workrooms have specific worksheets/work orders to be used to specify the treatment. Figure 11.20 is an example of one workroom's suggested measurement sheet. This measurement sheet asks for more measurements than are necessary for a top treatment, but since top treatments are many times part of a full window treatment, these are the dimensions necessary for the whole treatment. The measurements are as follows:

1. Above the window to crown or ceiling (nearest height obstruction).
2. Overall width dimension of window—outside trim to outside trim.
3. Wall space to each side of the window to nearest obstruction (e.g., wall, cabinet, light switch).
4. Top of trim to floor—notate whether flooring is wood, tile, carpet, and so on.
5. Top of trim to bottom of window trim (sometimes necessary).

6. Any air vents in floor.
7. For a bay: Overall width and depth of bay, and angles of bay (Figure 11.21). It is useful to have a protractor for this. Kirsch makes one especially for this purpose (Figure 11.22). If you don't have this protractor, take 4-inch × 6-inch index cards,

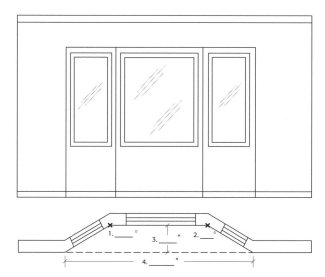

Figure 11.21 When measuring a bay window, be sure to measure each angle of the bay (1 and 2), the overall width of the bay (4), and the depth of the bay (3).

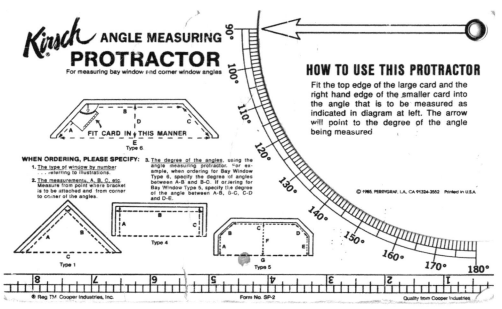

Figure 11.22 A Kirsch protractor is useful to obtain accurate bay angles. (Kirsch Protractors)

place one on each wall at the corner where they overlap, and staple them together. This will give the workroom or the installer the angle they need if necessary. Be sure to indicate which are the top and bottom and the right-side and left-side angles on the cards.

8. Anything else that might create an obstruction for the treatment.

For top treatments, an additional 1 to 2 inches on each side (2 to 4 inches total) of the under-treatment must be allowed. The return brackets need to extend 3 to 4 inches beyond the under-treatment. The type of top treatment or custom window shade will determine which calculation method should be used.

Top Treatments
CORNICE/LAMBREQUIN

Cornices and lambrequins are upholstered treatments (see Figure 11.10). Either the drapery workroom or the upholstery workroom will make these. A cornice or lambrequin is made of plywood, from which the top, face, returns, and legs (if it is a lambrequin) are made. Next, lightweight batting is applied to this frame, and the frame is upholstered with the fabric. Normally these top treatments don't have fullness.

The inside of the cornice or lambrequin, while not necessarily batted, will be upholstered in lining.

Labor charges for cornices are calculated by the foot and are based on the finished width. Lambrequins are normally calculated by the foot and are based on the outside perimeter dimension of the treatment. The basic steps in calculating material for cornices/lambrequins are as follows:

1. Determine the number of fabric widths needed by taking the finished width of treatment and adding to it the length of the right and left return. Add 6 inches for pulling, wrapping, and upholstering (3 inches each side). It is possible to reduce this amount after checking with your workroom. Finally, divide this total by the width of the fabric, and round up to the nearest whole number, since fabric can be ordered only by the whole width. This tells you how many widths are necessary.

2. Next, determine the cut length. This can be a little tricky if there is a shaped bottom edge to the cornice or if it is a lambrequin. With a shaped cornice, the longest point of the cornice is used as the finished length. For a lambrequin,

the finished length is the entire length of the leg. Commonly the legs of lambrequins take less than 1 width each. If the lambrequin is wider than 2 widths of fabric, 2 widths will be calculated for the legs, and the remaining widths will be calculated for the longest point of the horizontal mid-section of the lambrequin. Add 6 inches to the finished length dimension to obtain the cut length. It may be possible to get both lambrequin legs out of one width, depending on the size of the lambrequin and the fabric's width and repeat.

3. If there is a repeat, divide the cut length by the length of the repeat. This is the raw number of repeats. If this is a fraction, round up to a whole number and multiply by the length of the repeat. The resulting number is the adjusted cut length. The fabric must be calculated with whole repeats for the repeat to be matched.

4. Take the cut length, or adjusted cut length if there is a repeat, and multiply by the number of widths required. Divide this total by 36 inches and round up to the nearest ½ yard or full yard if the total isn't already a ½ yard or full yard. If this is a lambrequin with more than 2 widths, multiply the length of the lambrequins by 2 widths. Then multiply the remaining number of widths by the length of the mid-section. Add these two totals together and divide by 36 inches, following the process just described. Add 1 to 1½ yards to this amount if self-welt is being used. If manufactured cording is being used, add all sides together and divide by 36 inches, rounding up to the nearest ½ yard to determine the amount to order.

GATHERED/TABBED/PULLED-UP VALANCES

Gathered valances are usually gathered on some type of rod but can also be stapled to a board. This type of valance is found readymade in stores; however, it does have its applications for custom-made window treatments and is normally constructed with a 2½ or 3 times fullness. A rod and header require more fabric because of the diameter or depth of the rod and

Rod	Rod Pocket Size	Take-Up Allowance	Total Rod Pocket with Allowance
¾-in. Curtain Rod	1¼ in.	½ in.	1¾ in.
1-in. Round Pole	2 in.	1 in.	3 in.
1⅜-in. Round Pole	3 in.	1½ in.	4½ in.
2-in. Round Pole	4½ in.	2 in.	6½ in.
3-in. Round Pole	6 in.	2½ in.	8½ in.
2½-in. Flat Rod	3½ in.	½ in.	4 in.
4½-in. Flat Rod	5½ in.	½ in.	6 in.

Table 11.2 Rod Pocket Allowance

the fabric that wraps around to the back side of the header ending at the bottom of the rod on the back (Table 11.2). Lining is calculated from the bottom of the rod to the bottom of the treatment, allowing for hems. Keep in mind that heavier fabrics require less fullness in these treatments.

A tabbed valance has fullness like a gathered valance, but it has strips of fabrics—tabs—at the top at regular intervals that loop over a rod or hook for installation. This will not hang in quite the same way as a gathered valance does because of the tabs, and it usually requires less fullness, such as a 2 times fullness. After calculating fabric for the valance, you must then calculate fabric for the tabs. Lining is calculated only from the top of the treatment to the bottom, allowing for hems.

Pulled-up valances create an informal swag and bell (Kingston) appearance. They can be tabbed at the top or stapled to a board. In order to create that casual Kingston look, the tabs are spaced much farther apart than those found on tabbed valances. Fullness for pulled-up valances is normally 1½ or 2 times fullness. With a pulled-up valance, the back of the lining is always seen along the bottom edge. If this valance is attached to a pole with air between the tabs, the back of the lining is also seen at the top. Consider using a contrast lining for this treatment. Lining will be seamed to the face fabric—pillow cased—so hems do not need to be calculated for either the face fabric or the lining.

The fundamentals for calculating labor and fabric for gathered, tabbed, and pulled-up valances are the same. The main exception is with the gathered valance. Because the returns of a gathered valance are gathered as well, the returns are added to the finished width before the fullness is added. Every other treatment requires the returns to be added after fullness, since returns on other treatments do not have fullness.

To determine widths:

1. Width of finished treatment: For gathered treatments, add the right and left return at this point.
2. Multiply this by the desired fullness.
3. Add 6 inches for side hems.
4. Divide by width of fabric to find the number of widths required (remember to round up so the widths are whole numbers and not fractions).

Example 1—Gathered valance with 3-inch returns:
Finished width = 86 in.
+ 3 in. × 2 returns (6 in.) = 92 in.
× 3 fullness + 6 in. for side hems = 282 in.
÷ 54 in. = 5.22 widths
Round up to 6 widths needed.

Example 2—Pulled-up valance with 3-inch returns:
Finished width = 86 in.
× 1.5 fullness = 129 in.
+ 6 in. for returns + 6 in. for side hems = 141 in.
÷ 54 in. = 2.61 widths
Round up to 3 widths needed.

To determine cut length:

1. Decide on overall length and add 2 inches for seam allowance and add for hem. Gathered and tabbed valances may have a double 2-inch or a shirt-tail hem, whereas the pulled-up valance doesn't have a hem, since the lining is usually sewn in—pillow cased. A double 2-inch hem requires 4 inches and a shirt-tail hem requires 1½ inches of fabric.

2. If the treatment is gathered on a rod and has a header, additional fabric must be added for the fabric that wraps to the back of the header and the rod. Rods have dimension and so will take up more fabric than their basic measure. For instance, a 2½-inch flat rod needs a 3½-inch rod pocket plus ½ inch added to allow for the length the rod will pull up the treatment from the original flat measure (see Table 11.2). In this instance, if the take-up allowance wasn't added back in, a treatment you wanted to have a finish length of 18 inches will only have a finish length of 17½ inches with a 2½-inch flat rod. If this were a 3-inch round pole, it would be even shorter than that. A heavy fabric is more affected by this take-up than lightweight fabric. The rod pocket, take-up, and header must be added to the length (Figure 11.23). These dimensions added together give the cut length.

3. If there is a repeat, divide the cut length by the length of the repeat and round up to a whole number. To find the new adjusted cut length (ACL), multiply this whole number by the length of the repeat. In order to match repeats, there must be whole repeats to match.

4. The cut or adjusted cut length is multiplied by the number of widths. Divide this number by 36 inches to find yards. If there is a repeat, some interior designers will add one more repeat in at

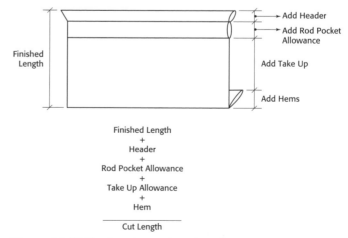

Figure 11.23 The header, rod pocket allowance, take-up allowance, and hem must be added to the overall finished length to obtain the raw cut length.

this point to give flexibility for where the repeat starts and stops. The total must be rounded up to the nearest ½ yard.

5. When calculating the number of tabs needed for a treatment, determine desired spacing. Divide the flat measure of the treatment by the desired spacing. If this is a fraction, round up. To this amount add 1 more tab.

SWAGS, CASCADES, AND JABOTS

Traditional swags and cascades are made of several pieces that are stapled on a board. It is possible to create swags and cascades that can be attached to rods. Swags traditionally are cut on the bias for better drapeability unless there is agreement with your workroom to not do this. For example, it may be desirable for stripes and distinctive patterns to be seen in a vertical placement, so in these cases they can't be cut on the bias.

The size and number of swags used are dictated by style and fabric width. Swags that are small and close together are reminiscent of a very traditional 18th-century style. If they are very wide, there is the possibility that the pleats will fall out. The popular look for this treatment today is 30-inch to 42-inch swags. Swags overlap when they are hung. Each swag may overlap the next by 3 to 9 inches depending on the look and the hardware holding the swag in place. Swags at the end of a run will only overlap a swag on one side and a cascade on the other. Often the cascade is under the swag, which will allow the cascade to fall or drape smoothly.

Figure 11.24 Even-numbered and odd-numbered swags on same window treatment width.

For example, a 120-inch overall width may take 3 to 5 swags. An odd number of swags allows the middle swag ends to be fully on top or behind so that it looks like the other swags flow from it; however, sometimes an even number of swag works better with the width of the treatment (Figure 11.24). After you determine overall width of the treatment, you can more easily determine how many swags are needed, since they should stay in the acceptable range of width for them to hang properly (Table 11.4).

Cascades are used to provide a finished look to the ends, and jabots are used to provide a finished look at the inside corners of bay windows and where two swags meet but don't overlap. Cascades have one side that is cut on a 45-degree angle. This angle allows the lining of the cascade to show, so the fabric selected for this should be given careful thought. It is advisable for the lining to be of a similar weight and fiber composition as the face fabric so that it hangs smoothly. Over time, some fabric can "grow" and roll a bit around the front angled seam of the cascade.

Swag Width before Overlap	Swag Width after Overlap	Effect Achieved
40 in.	43–49 in.	Probably too wide, pleats can fall out
30 in.	33–39 in.	Good dimension for draping and hanging
24 in.	27–31 in.	On narrow end; 18th-century style

Table 11.3 Swag Sizes and Effect Achieved

Overall Width of Window Treatment	Number of Swags	Increments	Swag Width with Overlap	Determine Which Works Best
120 in.	3	40 in.	43–49 in.	Too wide, pleats fall out
120 in.	4	30 in.	33–39 in.	Good dimension for hang
120 in.	5	24 in.	27–31 in.	On narrow end of good hang

Table 11.4 120-inch-wide Window Treatment and Number of Swags

This is due to varying fiber composition between the face fabric and the lining fabric. A jabot is angle cut on both sides and is much shorter than a cascade. The jabot lining shows in the same manner that the cascade lining shows.

The cascade length should be above or below the ½ mark of the window. Visually appealing lengths are ⅓ and ⅔ of the entire treatment. The ⅓ length is often used when there is a drapery or stationary side panel behind it. Jabot lengths are often longer than the drop of the swag by 3 to 6 inches.

To calculate for material:

1. Swags: Generally are cut on the bias and take 1½ yards. Occasionally the swag is wider than normal and will take 2 yards. There should be discussion with your workroom for wider than normal swags. Multiply the number of swags by 1½ yards for total swag yardage. Use this same yardage amount for the lining.

2. Cascades and jabots: 1 width of fabric is commonly used per cascade or jabot. Multiply the number of cascades (usually 2) or jabots by 1 width to determine number of widths. Take the finished length and add 4 inches for hems and allowance for attaching to treatment. This gives the cut length. If there is a repeat, divide the cut length by the length of the repeat. Round up to the nearest whole number and multiply by the length of the repeat to get the adjusted cut length. Multiply the cut length or the adjusted cut length by the number of widths (usually 2) and divide by 36 inches. Round up to the nearest ½ yard. Use this same amount of yardage for lining.

Be sure to keep track of the different fabrics to be ordered, since multiple fabrics are often used in this type of treatment (Table 11.5). This type of window treatment may use the same fabric for the swag face and cascade lining. The cascade face and drapery or side panel fabric may be the same. Lining for swags and draperies is normally the same challis-type

Fabric	A	B	C
Width	54 in.	54 in.	54 in.
Type	Solid	Floral pattern	Chamois lining
Repeat	None	27 in.	None
Retail	$32.00	$58.00	$8.00
Use	Side panel face	Swag face fabric	Swag lining
Yards	7.5 yd.	4.5 yd.	4.5 yd.
Use	Cascade lining	Cascade face fabric	Side panel lining
Yards	4 yd.	4.5 yd.	7.5 yd.
Total yards	**11.5 yd.**	**9 yd.**	**12 yd.**

Table 11.5 Organization for Multi-Fabric Window Treatments

lining, which is often different from the decorative cascade lining.

Custom Window Shades

Mock shades are made to look like custom window shades except that they are inoperable. Calculations for the width are exactly the same as they are for the shade style they represent. The only difference is in the length. Each of the following treatments will address the length calculation for a mock shade specific to the shade.

Roman shades/hobbled Roman shades are the most tailored shades. The basic Roman shade doesn't have any fullness in its width or length. A hobbled Roman shade has some fullness in its length. To calculate yardage for these treatments:

1. Add 6 inches to the finished width of the shade to obtain the cut width.
2. Most Roman shades are one width or less. To confirm this, divide the cut width by the fabric width. If this is a fraction, round up to the nearest whole number. This is the number of widths needed.
3. Add 10 inches to the finished length of the shade for hems and board allowance.* This gives the cut

*For a hobbled Roman, multiply the finished length by 2 before adding the 10 inches to the length.

length. If there is a repeat, divide the cut length by the length of the repeat. Round up to the nearest whole number and multiply by the length of the repeat to get the adjusted cut length in inches.

4. Multiply the number of widths by the cut or adjusted cut length and divide by 36 inches, rounding up to the nearest ½ yard.

If the window is narrow, it may be possible to get more than one from a width of fabric. If there is a valance that will hang to the front of the shade, additional fabric may be required. This is dependent on the look and how and where the workroom places the mechanisms for raising and lowering the shade. Because lining has no repeat, lining will be calculated from the original cut length amount.

For a mock shade, determine the finished length, multiply by 2, and add 10 inches. The workroom will make the shade to the desired length, making it look as if it has been pulled up.

Balloon shades/Austrian shades have fullness in the width and the length. A balloon shade has a ballooned look to the hem. This is where the additional length fullness is. An Austrian shade has fullness that remains gathered the entire length even when it

---

INSIGHT FROM THE FIELD

❝Nothing takes the place of good pictures and clear communications between designer-workroom-installer.❞

Jennifer Allred, *owner of Allred-Y-Made custom window workroom*

---

is lowered. The additional fabric in these treatments can make the shade heavy to operate if the window is overly large. Motorized headrails can be used for raising and lowering the shade, although they will add a considerable amount of money to the treatment. To calculate yardage for these treatments:

1. To the finished width of the shade, add the returns if it is an outside mount and then multiply by 2½ to 3 times fullness. This is dependent on the weight of the fabric. Add 6 inches to this total for side hems. Divide by the width of the fabric and round up to the nearest whole number to determine the total number of widths needed.

2. To the finished length of the shade, add 20 to 30 inches for a balloon shade.* Add 10 inches for hem and board allowance to obtain the cut length. If there is a repeat, divide the cut length by the length of the repeat and round up to the nearest whole number. Multiply this number for the length of the repeat. This is the adjusted cut length of the shade.

3. Multiply the number of widths by the cut or adjusted cut length and divide by 36 inches, rounding up to the nearest ½ yard.

Since the lining has no repeat, it will be calculated from the original cut length amount.

For a mock shade, determine the finished length, multiply by 3, and add 10 inches. The workroom will make the shade to the desired length, making it look as if it has been pulled up.

---

*For an Austrian shade, multiply the finished length by 2½ or 3 times fullness before adding the 10 inches for hem and board allowance.

Step-by-Step Examples

Example 1—Gathered Valance

You are specifying a gathered/shirred valance using 3 times fullness on an oval curtain rod for a bathroom with a 44-inch finished width, a 2-inch header, a double 2-inch hem, and 3-inch returns (Figure 11.25). The finished length is 16 inches. The fabric is 54 inches wide, with no repeat.

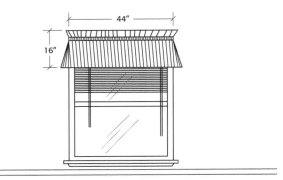

Figure 11.25 Example 1—Gathered valance.

Step 1: Determine total width dimension requiring fullness.

Take flat measure of treatment:	44	in.
Add right return:	+ 3	in.
Add left return:	+ 3	in.
Total width:	50	in.

Note: If this is the first window treatment layer, the return is 3 inches; if it is the second, it is 6 to 6.5 inches; if it is the third, it is 9 to 10 inches.

Step 2: Determine widths.

Total from Step 1:	50	in.
Multiply for fullness; allow 2.5 or 3 times fullness:	× 3	fullness
Total:	150	in.
Add 6 inches for side hems:	+ 6	in.
Total:	156	in.
Divide by width of fabric:	÷ 54	in.
Total widths of fabric:	2.89	widths
Round up to whole number:	3	full widths

Step 3: Determine cut length.

Take finished length:	16	in.
Add for seam allowances (this number may vary):	+ 2	in.
Add bottom hem (1.5 in. for shirt-tail hem; 4 in. for double 2-in. hem):	+ 4	in.
Add rod pocket size with take-up allowance:	+ 1.75	in.
Add header height:	+ 2	in.
Total cut length:	25.75	in.

There is no repeat for this fabric. If there were, it would be calculated at this point.

Step 4: Determine yardage.

Take cut length or ACL from Step 3:	25.75	in.
Multiply by total widths from Step 2:	× 3	widths
Total:	77.25	in.
Divide by 36 to convert inches to yards:	÷ 36	in.
Total yards needed:	2.15	yd.
Round up to nearest ½ yard:	**2.5**	**yd. to be ordered**

To find yardage for lining: 25.75 in. CL × 3 W = 77.25 in. Divide by 36 inches = 2.15 yards, and round up to the nearest yard or ½ yard. 2.5 yd. to be ordered for lining.

In this example, since there was no repeat to the fabric, it will be the same amount of lining as face fabric.

Fabric widths required: 3 widths

Cut or adjusted cut length: 25.75 inches

Yards required for the face fabric: 2.5 yards

Yards required for the lining: 2.5 yards

Example 2—Swags and Cascades

The best treatment for your client's window will consist of swags and cascades over existing stationary side panels (Figure 11.26). The finished width is 100 inches. The cascades will have a finished length of 66 inches.

Swags:

Face fabric is floral pattern B.

Lining is chamois lining C.

Cascades:

Use 1 width per cascade.

Cascade face fabric is floral pattern B.

Cascade lining is solid fabric A.

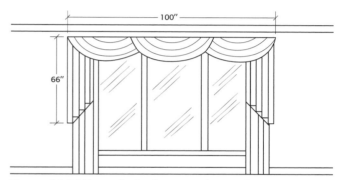

Figure 11.26 Example 2—Swags and cascades.

Fabric A: Solid, 54 inches wide, no repeat

Fabric B: Floral pattern, 54 inches wide, 27 inches repeat

Fabric C: Chamois lining, 54 inches wide, no repeat

Swags:

Step 1: Determine number of swags.

Total width of treatment:	100	in.
Divide by 30 inches:	÷ 30	in.
Number of swags:	3.33	swags
Round up or down to whole number:	3	total number of swags

Note: The .33 can be absorbed among the three swags. Choosing to do 3 swags is a judgment call dependent on the fabric and the look to be created.

Step 2: Determine yardage for swags.

Total number of swags:	3	swags
Multiply by 1.5 to 2 yards:	× 1.5	yd.
Total yardage for swags:	**4.5**	**yd. to order**

Note: This same amount will be needed for the lining.

Cascades:

Step 1: Determine widths.

Commonly, 1 width of fabric is needed per cascade:	1	width
Multiply by number of cascades (normally 2 per window):	× 2	cascades
Total number of widths necessary for treatment:	2	total widths

Step 2: Determine cut length.

Finished length of cascade:	66	in.
Add 4 inches for hems and placement:	+ 4	in.
Total cut length of cascade:	70	in.

If there is a repeat, factor for the repeat. If lining is solid, calculate from the cut length.

Take cut length:	70	in.
Divide by length of repeat:	÷ 27	in.
Resulting number is number of repeats:	2.59	repeats
Round up to whole number:	3	full repeats
Multiply full repeats by the length of the repeat:	× 27	in.
Adjusted cut length (ACL) in inches:	**81**	**in.**

Step 3: Determine yardage.

Cut length or adjusted cut length from Step 1:	81	in.
Multiply by widths from Step 2:	× 2	in.
Total:	162	in.
Divide by 36 to convert inches to yards:	÷ 36	in.
Total yards:	4.5	yd.
Round up to nearest ½ yard:	**4.5**	**yd. to order**

Yards required for the face of swags: 4.5 yards

Yards required for the face of cascades: 4.5 yards

Yards required for the lining of cascades:
4 yards
The lining is a solid.
70 in. cut length × 2 cascades = 140 in. ÷ 36 in. =
3.89 yd., round up to 4 yd.

Amount of each fabric to be ordered:
Fabric A: 4 yards; Fabric B: 9 yards;
Fabric C: 4.5 yards (Table 11.6)

Fabric	A	B	C
Width	54 in.	54 in.	54 in.
Type	Solid	Floral pattern	Chamois lining
Repeat	None	27 in.	None
Use		Swag face fabric	Swag lining
Yards		4.5 yd.	4.5 yd.
Use	Cascade lining	Cascade face fabric	
Yards	4 yd.	4.5 yd.	
Total yards	**4 yd.**	**9 yd.**	**4.5 yd.**

Table 11.6 Yardage Totals for Example 2

Example 3—Roman Shade

A lined, Roman shade will be used for a window in a laundry area. The finished inside measurement is 35 inches wide × 66 inches long (Figure 11.27). The fabric is 54 inches wide with a 27-inch repeat.

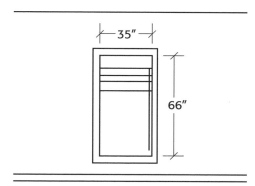

Figure 11.27 Example 3—Roman shade.

Basic Flat Roman Shade:

Step 1: Calculate cut width.

> **Note:** Unlike most other treatments, shades have a cut width.

Finished width of shade:	35	in.
Add 6 inches for side hem:	+ 6	in.
Total cut width:	41	in.

Step 2: Determine widths.

Take cut width from Step 1:	41	in.
Divide by fabric width:	÷ 54	in.
Total widths needed:	.76	widths
Round up to whole number:	1	full widths

Step 3: Determine cut length.

Take finished length of shade:	66	in.
Add 10 inches for hem and board allowance:	+ 10	in.
Total cut length:	76	in.

If necessary, calculate for repeat in the length at this point. Normally a repeat doesn't affect the width. If there is no repeat, proceed to Step 4.

Total cut length from Step 3:	76	in.
Divide cut length by length of repeat:	÷ 27	in.
Resulting number is the number of repeats:	2.81	repeats
Round up to whole number:	3	full repeats
Multiply by the length of the repeat:	× 27	in.
Adjusted cut length (ACL) in inches:	81	in.

Note: Even though this isn't sewn to other fabric so it is essential for the repeats to match, it is important to have full repeats calculated so that you can determine where the repeat will fall in the treatment. Some interior designers will add one more repeat than necessary when the pattern is very distinctive and they want to have flexibility for pattern placement.

Step 4: Determine yardage.

Cut length or adjusted cut length:	81	in.
Multiply by number of widths:	× 1	in.
Total:	81	in.
Divide by 36 to convert inches to yards:	÷ 36	in.
Total yards:	2.25	yd.
Round up to nearest ½ yard:	**2.5**	**yd. to be ordered**

Cut width: 41 inches

Cut or adjusted cut length: 76 inches

Yards of face fabric needed: 2.5 yards

Yards of lining needed: 2.5 yards. The repeat doesn't have to be calculated for the lining. The cut length is 76 in. ÷ 36 in. = 2.11 yd.. Round up to 2.5 yards for ordering.

Example 4—Balloon Shade

You have created a country French look for your client's kitchen that includes an inside-mounted, lined balloon shade at the sink window (Figure 11.28). The treatment will be 36 inches wide × 30 inches long, and the fabric is 54 inches wide with an 18-inch repeat.

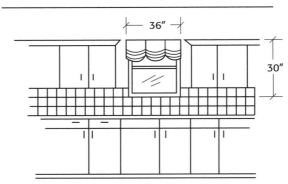

Figure 11.28 Example 4—Balloon shade.

Basic Balloon Shade:

Step 1: Calculate widths.

Finished width of shade:	36	in.
Multiply for fullness (2.5 to 3 times):	× 3	fullness
Total:	108	in.
Add 6 inches for side hem	+ 6	in.
Total cut width:	114	in.
Divide by fabric width:	÷ 54	in.
Total widths needed:	2.11	widths
Round up to whole number:	3	full widths

Note: In an actual situation, the interior designer may decide that the fullness can be reduced a little so that 2 widths are used instead of 3. Two widths equals 108 inches. With 2½ times fullness, the total cut width, including side hems, is 96 inches instead of 114 inches. By keeping this to 2 widths, the fullness is more than 2½ but a little less than 3. This is a decision the designer will make. For these exercise and practice lessons, don't make the judgment call—just follow the numbers to make sure you can follow the process. Once you have a little experience, you will easily be able to make these decisions.

Step 2: Determine cut length.

Finished length of shade:	30	in.
Add 20 to 30 inches for poufy bottom look:	+ 30	in.
Add 10 inches for hem and board allowance:	+ 10	in.
Total cut length:	70	in.

If necessary, calculate for repeat in the length at this point. Normally a repeat doesn't affect the width. If there is no repeat, proceed to Step 3.

Total cut length from above:	70	in.
Divide cut length by length of repeat:	÷ 18	in.
Resulting number is the number of repeats:	3.89	repeats
Round up to whole number:	4	full repeats
Multiply repeats by the length of the repeat	× 18	in.
Adjusted cut length (ACL) in inches:	72	in.

Step 3: Determine yardage.

Cut length or adjusted cut length from Step 2:	72	in.
Multiply by number of widths:	× 3	widths
Total:	216	in.
Divide by 36 to convert inches to yards:	÷ 36	in.
Total yards:	6	yd.
Round up to nearest ½ yard:	**6**	**yd. to be ordered**

Widths of fabric needed: 3 widths

Cut or adjusted cut length: 72 inches adjusted cut length

Face yards required: 6 yards

Yards of lining required: 2 yards. 70 in. cut length × 3 widths = 210 in. ÷ 36 in. = 5.83 yd. Round up to 6 yards.

Manual Worksheets

Cornice and Lambrequin Worksheet

Step 1: Determine widths.

Finished width of treatment:		_____	in.
Add right return:	+	_____	in.
Add left return:	+	_____	in.
Add 6 inches for upholstering:	+	6	in.
Total:		_____	**in.**
Divide by fabric width:	÷	_____	in.
Total widths needed:		_____	**widths**
Round up to whole number:		_____	**full widths**

Step 2: Determine cut length.

Finished length of treatment:		_____	in.
Add 6 inches for upholstering:	+	6	in.
Total cut length:		_____	**in.**

Note: For a shaped bottom edge or lambrequin, take the longest point of the length. Usually 2 widths are needed for the length of the lambrequin legs. Calculate any widths beyond what is needed for the legs at the shorter length.

If necessary:

Finished length of treatment:		_____	in.
Add 6 inches for upholstering:	+	6	in.
Total cut length:		_____	**in.**

Step 3: Calculate for repeat.

If there is no repeat, proceed to Step 4. Normally a repeat doesn't affect the width.

Total cut length from Step 2:		_____	in.
Divide by length of repeat:	÷	_____	in.
Number of repeats:		_____	**repeats**
Round up to whole number:		_____	**full repeats**
Multiply repeats by the length of the repeat:	×	_____	in.
Adjusted cut length (ACL):		_____	**in.**

For lambrequins with more than 2 widths, repeat Step 3 for the different lengths involved.

Step 4: Determine yardage.

Cut length or adjusted cut length:		_____	in.
Multiply by number of widths:	×	_____	widths
Total:		_____	**in.**
Divide by 36 to convert inches to yards:	÷	36	in.
Total yards:		_____	**yd.**
Round up to nearest ½ yard:		_____	**yd.**

This step may have to be repeated for a lambrequin with more than 2 widths.

For self-welt, add 1 to 1.5 yards:	+	_____	yd.
Total:		_____	**yd. to be ordered**

Gathered Valance Worksheet

Step 1: Determine total width dimension requiring fullness.

Flat measure of treatment:	_____	in.
Add right return : +	_____	in.
Add left return : +	_____	in.
Total width:	_____	**in.**

Note: If this is the first window treatment layer, the return is 3 inches; if it is the second, it is 6 to 6.5 inches; if it is the third, it is 9 to 10 inches.

Step 2: Determine widths.

Total width from Step 1:	_____	in.
Multiply for fullness (× 2.5 or 3): ×	_____	fullness
Total:	_____	**in.**
Add 6 inches for side hems: +	6	in.
Total:	_____	**in.**
Divide by width of fabric: ÷	_____	in.
Total widths of fabric:	_____	**widths**
Round up to whole number:	_____	**full widths**

Step 3: Determine cut length.

Finished length:	_____	in.
Add for seam allowances (this number may vary): +	2	in.
Add bottom hem (1.5 in. for shirt-tail hem; 4 in. for double 2-in. hem): +	_____	in.

Add for rod pocket and/or header (if applicable):

Add rod pocket size with take-up allowance: +	_____	in.
Add header height: +	_____	in.
Total cut length:	_____	**in.**

If the fabric has a repeat:

Take cut length:	_____	in.
Divide by length of repeat: ÷	_____	in.
Total:	_____	**repeats**
Round up to whole number:	_____	**full repeats**
Multiply by the length of repeat: ×	_____	in.
Adjusted cut length (ACL):	_____	**in.**

Step 4: Determine yardage.

Take cut length or ACL from Step 3:	_____	in.
Multiply by total widths from Step 2: ×	_____	widths
Total:	_____	**in.**
Divide by 36 to convert inches to yards: ÷	36	in.
Total yards:	_____	**yd.**
Round up to nearest ½ yard:	_____	**yd. to be ordered**

To find yardage for lining: Multiply CL × W = total inches, divide by 36 inches to find yards, round up or stay at the nearest yard or ½ yard.

Tabbed Valance Worksheet

Step 1: Determine widths for valance.

Flat measure of treatment:	_____	in.
Multiply for fullness (× 1.5 or 2): ×	_____	fullness
Total:	_____	**in.**
Add return size × 2 for right and left returns: +	_____	in.

Note: If this is the first window treatment layer, the return is 3 inches; if it is the second, it is 6 to 6.5 inches; if it is the third, it is 9 to 10 inches.

Add 6 inches for side hems: +	6	in.
Total:	_____	**in.**
Divide by width of fabric: ÷	_____	in.
Total widths of fabric:	_____	**widths**
Round up to whole number:	_____	**full widths**

Step 2: Determine widths for tabs.

Width of tab × 2:	_____	in.
Add 1 inch for seam allowance: +	1	in.
Total cut tab width:	_____	**in.**
Width of fabric:	_____	in.
Divide by cut tab width: ÷	_____	in.
Total tabs per width:	_____	**tabs**
Round down to nearest whole number:	_____	**tabs per width**
Number of tabs desired for treatment:	_____	tabs
Divide by tabs available per width: ÷	_____	tabs
Total widths:	_____	**widths**
Round up to whole number:	_____	**full widths**

Step 3: Determine cut length for valance.

Finished length of valance not including tabs:	_____	in.
Add for seam allowances (this number may vary): +	2	in.
Add bottom hem (1.5 in. for shirt-tail hem; 4 in. for double 2-in. hem): +	_____	in.
Total cut length:	_____	**in.**

If the fabric has a repeat:

Take cut length:	_____	in.
Divide by length of repeat: ÷	_____	in.
Total:	_____	**repeats**
Round up to whole number:	_____	**full repeats**
Multiply by the length of repeat: ×	_____	in.
Adjusted cut length (ACL):	_____	**in.**

Step 4: Determine cut length for tabs.

Use Table 11.7 on page 194 to find tab length:	_____	in.
Add 2 inches seam allowance: +	2	in.
Total:	_____	**in.**

Usually the repeat is ignored for tabs; however, if it is important, calculate for repeat as shown above.

Step 5: Calculate yardage.

Cut length or ACL from Step 3:		in.
Multiply by total widths from Step 1: ×		widths
Total A:		**in.**
Cut length or ACL from Step 4:		in.
Multiply by Total widths from Step 2: ×		widths
Total B:		**in.**
Total A:		in.
Add Total B: +		in.
Total:		**in.**
Divide by 36 to convert inches to yards: ÷	36	in.
Total yards:		**yd.**
Round up to nearest ½ yard:		**yd. to be ordered**

Step 6: Calculate lining for treatments.

Cut length from Step 3:		in.
Multiply by total widths from Step 3: ×		widths
Total:		**in.**
Divide by 36 to convert inches to yards: ÷	36	in.
Total yards:		**yd.**
Round up to nearest ½ yard:		**yd. to be ordered for lining**

Pulled-Up Valance Worksheet

Step 1: Determine total width dimension requiring fullness.

Flat measure of treatment:		in.
Multiply for fullness (× 1.5 or 2): ×	2	fullness
Total:		**in.**
Add return size × 2 for right and left returns: +		in.

Note: If this is the first window treatment layer, the return is 3 inches; if it is the second, it is 6 to 6.5 inches; if it is the third, it is 9 to 10 inches.

Add 6 inches for side hems: +	6	in.
Total:		**in.**
Divide by width of fabric: ÷		in.
Total widths of fabric:		**widths**
Round up to whole number:		**full widths**

Step 2: Determine cut length.

Finished length:		in.
Add for seam allowances (this number may vary): +	2	in.
Total cut length:		**in.**

If the fabric has a repeat:

Take cut length:		in.
Divide by length of repeat:		in.
Total:		**repeats**
Round up to whole number:		**full repeats**
Multiply by the length of repeat: ×		in.
Adjusted cut length (ACL):		**in.**

continued

Step 3: Determine yardage.

Take cut length or ACL from Step 2:	_____	in.
Multiply by total widths from Step 1: ×	_____	widths
Total:	_____	**in.**
Divide by 36 to convert inches to yards: ÷	36	in.
Total yards:	_____	**yd.**
Round up to nearest ½ yard:	_____	**yd. to be ordered**

Step 4: Determine yardage for lining.

The lining of pulled-up valances will show. Recommend using contrast lining for lining.

Finished length:	_____	in.
Add for seam allowances (this number may vary): +	2	in.
Total cut length:	_____	**in.**
Multiply by total widths from Step 1: ×	_____	widths
Total:	_____	**in.**
Divide by 36 to convert inches to yards: ÷	36	in.
Total yards:	_____	**yd.**
Round up to nearest ½ yard:	_____	**yd. to be ordered for lining**

Yardage for Tabs:

If tabs will be used to pull up the valance over a rod, calculate yardage for tabs.

Step A: Determine widths for tabs.

Width of tab × 2:	_____	in.
Add 1 inch for seam allowance: +	1	in.
Total cut tab width:	_____	**in.**
Width of fabric:	_____	in.
Divide cut tab width: ÷	_____	in.
Total tabs:	_____	**tabs**
Round down to nearest whole number:	_____	**tabs per width**
Number of tabs desired for treatment:	_____	tabs
Divide by tabs available per width: ÷	_____	tabs
Total widths:	_____	**widths**
Round up to whole number:	_____	**full widths**

Step B: Determine cut length for tabs.

Use Table 11.7 on page 194 to find tab length:	_____	in.
Add 2 inches seam allowance: +	2	in.
Total cut tab length:	_____	**in.**

Step C: Calculate yardage for tabs.

Cut length from Step B:	_____	in.
Multiply by total widths from Step A: ×	_____	widths
Total:	_____	**in.**
Divide by 36 to convert inches to yards: ÷	36	in.
Total yards:	_____	**yd.**
Round up to nearest ½ yard:	_____	**yd. to be ordered**

Swags, Cascades, and Jabots Worksheet

Swags

Step 1: Determine number of swags,

Total width of treatment:		_____	in.
Divide by 30 inches:	÷	____30____	in.
Number of swags:		_____	**swags**
Round up or down to whole number:		_____	**total number of swags**

Step 2: Determine yardage for swags.

Total number of swags:		_____	swags
Multiply by 1.5 to 2 yards:	×	____1.5____	yd.
Total yardage for swags:		_____	**yd. to order**

Note: This same amount will be needed for lining.

Cascades

Step 1: Determine widths.

Commonly, 1 width of fabric is needed per cascade:		_____	width
Multiply by number of cascades (normally 2 per window) :	×	_____	cascade
Total number of widths necessary for treatment:		_____	**widths**

Step 2: Determine cut length.

Finished length of cascade:		_____	in.
Add 4 inches for hems and placement:	+	____4____	in.
Total cut length of cascade:		_____	**in.**

If there is a repeat, factor for the repeat. If lining is solid, calculate from the cut length.

Take cut length:		_____	in.
Divide by length of repeat:	÷	_____	in.
Number of repeats:		_____	**repeats**
Round up to whole number:		_____	**full repeats**
Multiply by the length of the repeat:	×	_____	in.
Adjusted cut length (ACL):		_____	**in.**

Step 3: Determine yardage.

Cut length or adjusted cut length from Step 2:		_____	in.
Multiply by widths from Step 1:	×	_____	widths
Total:		_____	**in.**
Divide by 36 to convert inches to yards:	÷	____36____	in.
Total yards:		_____	**yd.**
Round up to nearest ½ yard:		_____	**yd. to order**

Jabots

Step 1: Determine widths.

Determine total area per jabot to be covered:		_____	in.
Multiply for fullness (× 2.5 or 3):	×	____3____	fullness
Total:		_____	**in.**
Divide by width of fabric:	÷	_____	in.
Total widths:		_____	**widths**
Round up to whole number:		_____	**full widths**
Multiply by total number of jabots used:	×	_____	jabots
Total widths:		_____	**widths**

Step 2: Determine cut length in exactly the same manner as for cascades.

Step 3: Combine Steps 1 and 2 in exactly the same manner as for cascades.

This same amount needs to be ordered for the back of the jabot, since the back of the jabot shows to the front.

Roman/Hobbled Shade Worksheet

Basic Flat Roman Shade

Step 1: Calculate cut width.

> **Note:** Unlike most other treatments, shades have a cut width.

Finished width of shade:	_____	in.
Add 6 inches for side hem: +	6	in.
Total cut width:	_____	**in.**

Step 2: Determine widths.

Cut width from Step 1:	_____	in.
Divide by fabric width: ÷	_____	in.
Total widths needed:	_____	**widths**
Round up to whole number:	_____	**full widths**

Step 3: Determine cut length.

Finish length of shade:	_____	in.
Add 10 inches for hem and board allowance: +	10	in.
Total cut length:	_____	**in.**

If necessary, calculate for repeat in the length at this point. Normally a repeat doesn't affect the width. If there is no repeat, skip to Step 4.

Total cut length from Step 3:	_____	in.
Divide by length of repeat: ÷	_____	in.
Number of repeats:	_____	**repeats**
Round up to whole number:	_____	**full repeats**
Multiply repeats by the length of the repeat: ×	_____	in.
Adjusted cut length:	_____	**in.**

Step 4: Determine yardage.

Cut length or adjusted cut length:	_____	in.
Multiply by number of widths: ×	_____	widths
Total:	_____	**in.**
Divide by 36 to convert inches to yards: ÷	36	in.
Total yards:	_____	**yd.**
Round up to nearest ½ yard:	_____	**yd. to be ordered**

Hobbled Roman (has fullness to the length)

Modified Step 3 for Hobbled Roman

Finish length of shade:	_____	in.
Multiply for fullness (× 2): ×	2	fullness
Total:	_____	**in.**
Add 10 inches for hem and board allowance: +	10	in.
Total cut length:	_____	**in.**

If necessary, calculate for repeat in the length. Continue regular calculations from this point.

Balloon and Austrian Shades Worksheet

Basic Balloon Shade

Step 1: Calculate widths.

Finished width of shade:		_____	in.
If outside mounted, add return size × 2 for right and left returns:	+	_____	in.
Total:		_____	**in.**
Multiply for fullness (× 2.5 or 3):	×	3	fullness
Total:		_____	**in.**
Add 6 inches for side hem:	+	6	in.
Total:		_____	**in.**
Divide by fabric width:	÷	_____	in.
Total widths needed:		_____	**widths**
Round up to whole number:		_____	**full widths**

Step 2: Determine cut length.

Finish length of shade:		_____	in.
Add 20 to 30 inches for poufy bottom look:	+	30	in.
Add 10 inches for hem and board allowance:	+	10	in.
Total cut length:		_____	**in.**

If necessary, calculate for repeat in the length at this point. Normally a repeat doesn't affect the width. If there is no repeat, skip to Step 3.

Total cut length from above:		_____	in.
Divide by length of repeat:	÷	_____	in.
Number of repeats:		_____	**repeats**
Round up to whole number:		_____	**full repeats**
Multiply repeats by the length of the repeat:	×	_____	in.
Adjusted cut length (ACL) in inches:		_____	**in.**

Step 3: Determine yardage.

Cut length or adjusted cut length:		_____	in.
Multiply by number of widths:	×	_____	widths
Total:		_____	**in.**
Divide by 36 to convert inches to yards:	÷	36	in.
Total yards:		_____	**yd.**
Round up to nearest ½ yard:		_____	**yd. to be ordered**

Austrian Shade (has fullness to width and length)

Modified Step 2 for Austrian Shade

Finished length of shade:		_____	in.
Multiply for fullness (× 2.5 or 3):	×	3	fullness
Total:		_____	**in.**
Add 10 inches for hem and board allowance:	+	10	in.
Total cut length:		_____	**in.**

If necessary, calculate for repeat in the length and continue regular calculations in Step 3. Note that the amount of fabric in an Austrian can make it heavy to operate.

Mock Roman/Hobbled Shade Worksheet

Step 1: Calculate cut width

Note: Unlike most other treatments, shades have a cut width.

Finished width of shade:		in.
Add 6 inches for side hem: +	6	in.
Total cut width:		**in.**

Step 2: Determine widths.

Cut width from Step 1:		in.
Divide by fabric width: ÷		in.
Total widths needed:		**widths**
Round up to whole number:		**full widths**

Step 3: Determine cut length.

Finished length of mock shade:		in.
Multiply for fullness for mock bottom: ×	2	fullness
Total:		**in.**
Add 10 inches for hem and board allowance: +	10	in.
Total cut length:		**in.**

If necessary, calculate for repeat in the length at this point. Normally a repeat doesn't affect the width. If there is no repeat, skip to Step 4.

Total cut length:		in.
Divide by length of repeat: ÷		in.
Number of repeats:		**repeats**
Round up to whole number:		**full repeats**
Multiply repeats by the length of the repeat: ×		in.
Adjusted cut length (ACL):		**in.**

Step 4: Determine yardage.

Cut length or adjusted cut length:		in.
Multiply by number of widths: ×		widths
Total:		**in.**
Divide by 36 to convert inches to yards: ÷	36	in.
Total yards:		**yd.**
Round up to nearest ½ yard:		**yd. to be ordered**

Practice Lessons: Top Treatments and Window Shades

BASIC

Cornice

You are specifying a cornice to go above draperies in a women's shelter. The finished width of the cornice needs to be 68 inches (4 inches wider than the traversing drapery underneath) with 6-inch returns and 1 yard self-cording. The overall length of the cornice is 18 inches (Figure 11.29). The fabric is 54 inches wide with a 15-inch repeat.

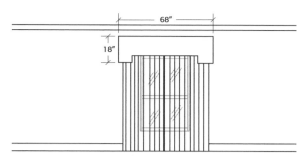

Figure 11.29 Practice lesson: Basic—Cornice.

1. How many widths of fabric are needed?
2. What is the adjusted cut length?
3. How many feet will the workroom charge you to make this?
4. How many yards of fabric must be ordered?

Gathered Valance

A gathered and lined valance is being specified for a kitchen sink window (Figure 11.30). The finished width is 42 inches with a 3-inch return; the finished length is 16. The treatment has a 1½-inch header, 3 times fullness, and a double 2-inch hem and will be installed on a 2½-inch flat rod. The fabric is 54 inches wide with an 8-inch repeat. Refer to Table 11.2 on page 173 for Rod Pocket Allowance.

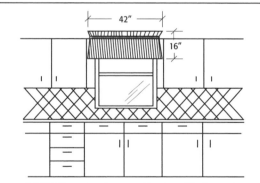

Figure 11.30 Practice lesson: Basic—Gathered valance.

1. How many widths of fabric will be used?
2. What is the adjusted cut length?
3. How many yards of face fabric must be ordered?
4. How many yards of lining must be ordered?

Roman Shade

To coordinate with the great room window treatments and to provide privacy, a lined Roman shade will be made for the door to the deck (Figure 11.31). The finished dimensions for the shade are 27 inches × 83 inches. The 54-inch-wide fabric has a distinctive pattern with a 27-inch repeat.

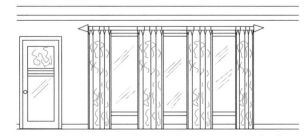

Figure 11.31 Practice lesson: Basic—Roman shade.

1. How many square inches and how many square feet are in this treatment?
2. What is the adjusted cut length?
3. How many yards of face fabric must be ordered?
4. How many yards of lining must be ordered?

INTERMEDIATE

Lambrequin

Your client wants to use a lambrequin treatment in his office (Figure 11.32). The overall treatment is 88 inches wide and 96 inches tall with 3-inch returns. The legs and the face of the lambrequin are 15 inches. The fabric is 54 inches wide and plain. One and one-half yards of contrast cording will be used on the interior frame of the lambrequin as well as on the top face and returns.

1. What is the overall perimeter in feet of the treatment?
2. How many widths of fabric will be used?
3. What is the cut length?
4. How many yards of fabric must be ordered?

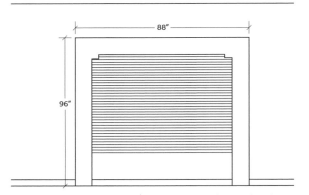

Figure 11.32 Practice lesson: Intermediate—lambrequin.

Tabbed Valance

A tabbed valance will be used in a family room (Figure 11.33). The treatment is 120 inches wide and 16 inches long before the tabs, and has 6-inch returns. It will be lined, have a 1½ times fullness and a double 2-inch hem. The tabs will be ½-inch wide and spaced every 6 inches on the 2-inch-diameter rod. The fabric is 54 inches wide with a 24-inch repeat. Use Table 11.7 to determine tab length.

1. How many tabs are required and how much fabric is needed for the tabs?
2. How many widths of fabric are needed?
3. What is the adjusted cut length of the valance portion?
4. How many yards, including the tabs, must be ordered for the face fabric?
5. How many yards of lining must be ordered?

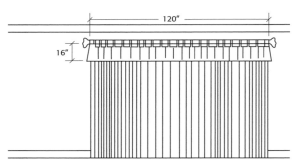

Figure 11.33 Practice lesson: Intermediate—Tabbed valance.

Rod	Tab Length for Workroom
¾-in. curtain rod	4 in.
1-in. round pole	5 in.
1⅜-in. round pole	6 in.
2-in. round pole	8 in.
3-in. round pole	11 in.

Radius of pole × pi (3.14) + 1½ in. to 2 in. equals tab length. An additional 2 inches will be added to this amount for the raw tab length to be sewn into window treatment.

Table 11.7 Recommended Tab Lengths

Mock Hobbled Shade

Lined mock hobbled shades will be used in the breakfast area of a continuing care unit to provide a tailored softness (Figure 11.34). There are a total of 8 windows. The finished width will be 43 inches, and the finished length will be 18 inches. Do not calculate for returns. The fabric is 54 inches wide with a 6-inch repeat.

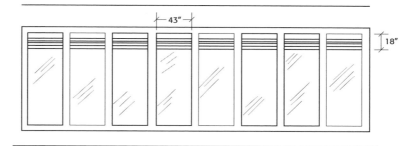

Figure 11.34 Practice lesson: Intermediate—Mock hobbled shade.

1. What is the adjusted cut length of the fabric?
2. How many square feet are in each mock shade?

3. How many total yards for the face fabric must be ordered for the 8 windows?
4. How many total yards must be ordered for the lining?

Balloon Shade

A lined balloon shade will be used on two windows in a young girl's room (Figure 11.35). The finished dimensions of the shade are 34½ inches wide by 56 inches long. It will be stapled to a 1-inch × 4-inch board, with 3½-inch returns. The fabric is 54 inches wide with a 9-inch repeat.

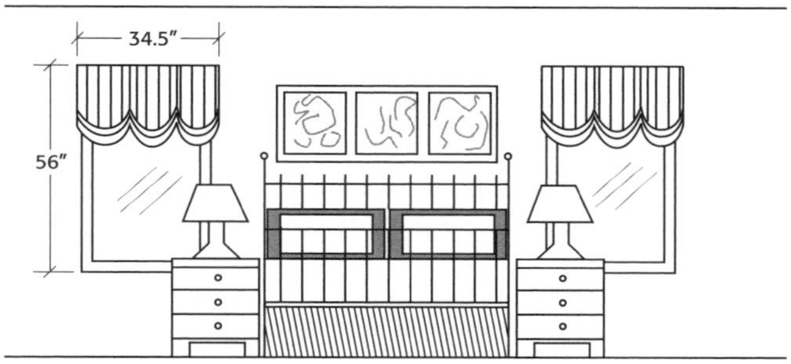

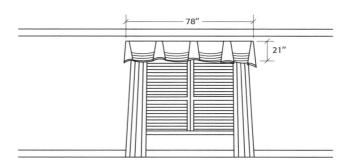

Figure 11.35 Intermediate—Balloon shade.

1. How many widths of fabric per window are needed?
2. What is the adjusted cut length?
3. How many square inches of the finished treatment per window are needed?

4. How many yards of face fabric must be ordered for the two windows?
5. How many yards of lining must be ordered for the two windows?

ADVANCED
Pulled-Up Valance

You have specified a pulled-up valance in the reception area of a lawyer's office (Figure 11.36). The treatment is stapled to a board 78 inches wide by 21 inches long with 3½-inch returns and 2 times fullness. The fabric is 54 inches wide with 27-inch repeat.

1. How many widths of fabric will be used?
2. What is the adjusted cut length?
3. How many yards of face fabric are needed?
4. How many yards of lining are needed?

Figure 11.36 Practice lesson: Advanced—Pulled-up valance.

Swags and Cascades

To create a more formal look, you are using swags and cascades attached to a 1-inch × 6-inch board in the dining room of a model home (Figure 11.37). The treatment is 80 inches wide with 60-inch-long cascades. The face fabric of the swag and the cascades is 54 inches wide with a 24-inch repeat. The lining for the cascade is 54 inches wide and plain.

1. How many swags will be used?
2. How much fabric is needed for the swags?
3. How much fabric is needed for the face of the cascades?
4. How much fabric must be ordered for the face of the swags and the cascades?
5. How much lining must be ordered for the swags?
6. How much lining must be ordered for the cascades?

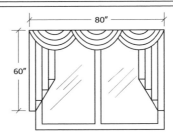

Figure 11.37 Practice lesson: Advanced—Swags and cascades.

Austrian Shade

Your client has a retreat area for herself that is full of light with four windows. You have specified inside-mounted, unlined Austrian shades at her windows (Figure 11.38). Each window is 42 inches wide by 72 inches long. The sheer fabric is 48 inches wide with no repeat.

1. How many widths of fabric are needed per window?
2. What is the cut length?
3. How many square inches per finished shade are needed?
4. How many yards of fabric must be ordered for the four windows?

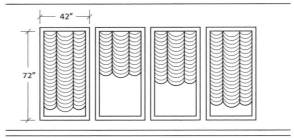

Figure 11.38 Practice lesson: Advanced— Austrian shade.

Pricing for Basic Gathered Valance

Use the scenario, labor, and fabric quantity found for the Basic Gathered Valance practice lesson and the prices that follow to calculate pricing for your client. The shade is being made by a local workroom and will be picked up when finished. The lining is purchased from your workroom and doesn't have any additional shipping costs.

Fabric—$48.00/yard

Fabric shipping—$12.00 total

Lining—$8.00/yard

Hardware—$18.00

Hardware shipping—$10.00 total

Labor—$58.00 per width

Installation—$36.00. The minimum installation charge is $80.

1. What is the subtotal for materials?
2. What is the subtotal for labor and installation?
3. What is the overall price for these two windows?

Pricing for Basic Roman Shade

Use the scenario, labor, and fabric quantity found for the Basic Roman Shade practice lesson and the prices that follow to calculate pricing for your client. The shade is being made by a local workroom and will be picked up when finished. The lining is purchased from your workroom and doesn't have any additional shipping costs.

Fabric—$94.00/yard

Fabric shipping—$16.00 total

Lining—$8.00/yard

Hardware—There is no additional hardware to order, as the workroom supplies all hardware needed, which is included in the labor price.

Labor—$20.00 per square foot

Installation—$18.00. The minimum installation charge is $80; however, more treatments are being installed in the home which will surpass the minimum charge. The exact installation charge can be calculated for this treatment.

1. What is the subtotal for materials?
2. What is the subtotal for labor and installation?
3. What is the overall price for these two windows?

Pricing for Advanced Swags and Cascades

Use the scenario, labor, and fabric quantity found for the Advanced Swags and Cascades practice lesson and the prices that follow to calculate pricing for your client. These are being made by a local workroom and will be picked up when they are finished. The lining is purchased from your workroom and doesn't have any additional shipping costs.

Face fabric for swags and cascades—$82.00/yard

Face fabric shipping—$24.00 total

Cascade lining—$36.00/yard

Cascade lining shipping—$15

Lining—$8.00/yard

Hardware—This is a boarded treatment and the board is included in the price the workroom quotes.

Labor—$75.00 per swag; $60.00 per cascade

Installation—$145.00

1. What is the subtotal for materials?
2. What is the subtotal for labor and installation?
3. What is the overall price for these two windows?

References

Neal, M. *Custom Draperies in Interior Design*. Norwalk, CT: Appleton & Lange, 1982.

Von Tobel, J. *The Design Directory of Window Treatments*. Layton, UT: Gibbs Smith Publisher, 2007.

Chapter 12 | Hard Window Treatments

Hard window treatments are sometimes referred to as alternative window treatments, alternative to fabric or soft treatments. This includes such things as horizontal and vertical blinds, pleated and cellular shades, window shadings, and shutters. These products provide a simple way to achieve privacy, light control, and/or insulative properties without a lot of bulk. Today, many homeowners and business owners install hard window treatments before they consider the fabric treatments that provide style, color, and acoustical properties. Soft and hard window treatments complement each other.

Companies such as Hunter Douglas, Graber, Levolor, and Bali supply these types of products and are well known to the public, although there are many smaller companies that also make and sell hard window treatments. Each manufacturer has specifications and price charts for its products. Before specifying the product, be sure to read the information the manufacturer provides. The intent of this chapter is to provide a basic understanding of these products.

Chapter Outline

Terminology

Types of Hard Window Treatments
  Blinds—Horizontal and Vertical
  Shades—Pleated, Cellular, Woven
  Wood/Grass, and Roll-Up
  Shutters

Sizes and Packaging

Cost Factors

Calculations

Step-by-Step Example

Reference

Terminology

Allowance The amount in inches taken as a deduction to allow for clearance at the top or bottom or at the sides of window treatments that will allow them to function without dragging on the sides of the window.

Clearance The portion of a window treatment that is airspace: behind, beside, above, below, and in front of it.

Headrail The horizontal piece at the top of a hard window treatment that contains all the controls for the treatment. The raising and tilting mechanisms are stored in the headrail as well as the ends of the cords that are threaded through the treatment that allow it to be raised and lowered. Sometimes, as in the case of some shades, the treatment will roll up into the headrail.

IB Abbreviation for "inside brackets." When you are specifying a treatment that is an inside mount, IB tells the manufacturer to take deductions off the overall width so that it will operate smoothly within the window frame and to provide the appropriate brackets.

Louvers The slats used in shutters. The majority of louvers are horizontal, but they may also be angled for specialty windows.

OB Abbreviation for "outside brackets." When you are specifying a treatment that is an outside mount, OB tells the manufacturer not to take any deductions and to provide the appropriate brackets.

Projection The measurement from the wall out into the room. This is different from

clearance, since the projection goes to the most forward point and the clearance stops at the back of the rod or treatment.

Sill Horizontal piece of wood that is the bottom of the window.

Slat The horizontal piece in a blind or shade that is able to be tilted to minimize or maximize views.

Stack Area covered by a window treatment when the treatment is opened. Stack will vary greatly depending on the hard window product used.

Vane The vertical piece in a vertical blind that opens and closes and tilts.

Types of Hard Window Treatments

Window treatments can be categorized as (1) blinds—horizontal and vertical; (2) shades—pleated, cellular, and roll-up, and (3) shutters.

Blinds—Horizontal and Vertical

Horizontal blinds are commonly made of metal, plastic, or wood or wood products (Figure 12.1). The horizontal component, called a slat, can be as narrow as ½ inch or as wide as 3 inches. Commercially, plastic and metal horizontal blinds have been popular, whereas residentially, wood and wood products have been most popular. When horizontal blinds are specified for doors, they can be ordered with hold-down brackets for the bottom of the blind to keep it from swinging when the door is opened and closed. When pulled up, there is a considerable amount of stack from the top of the treatment.

Vertical blinds are commonly made of plastic, metal, or fabric (Figure 12.2). There are a few companies that fabricate wood vertical blinds. The slat in this product is the vertical component and is usually 3½ inches wide. Slats can hang freely with weighted hems, or the fabric can be inserted into a plastic vane. They can be specified as a one-way or a split draw and are most commonly used residentially on sliding doors. They have been popular in commercial/contract buildings,

Figure 12.1 Two-inch wood blinds installed as inside mount in the windows. (Courtesy of Hunter Douglas)

Figure 12.2 Vertical blinds. (Courtesy of Hunter Douglas)

where they are used for windows and sliding or patio doors. Just as with a drapery, there is a stack when they are opened that must be considered in the overall width.

Shades—Pleated, Cellular, Woven Wood/Grass, and Roll-Up

Pleated shades are made from a single layer of fabric that has a permanent 1-inch horizontal pleat, creating a "Z" profile (Figure 12.3). They can be specified to lower from the top (top down) instead of or in addition to the normal rise from the bottom. When pulled all the way up, because these shades are constructed from lightweight fabric, there is very little stack.

Cellular shades are similar to pleated shades but are made with at least two layers of fabric that create a hexagonal "cell" pattern in profile (Figure 12.4). Many of the options available for the pleated shade are also available for the cellular shade; however, cellular shades can often be made wider and longer. When they are drawn up, they have minimal stack.

Woven wood/grass shades are made of natural materials and rise like a Roman shade (Figure 12.5). They have a significant amount of stack. Most can be lined for privacy or, if there is room, a second pleated shade installed behind them for privacy. They can become very heavy if specified for a wide window.

Roll–up shades roll up to the top, often into a headrail (Figure 12.6). These can be simple roller shades or more elaborate shades with horizontal fabric slats stabilized between sheer material to the front and

Figure 12.3 Pleated shades installed as an inside mount. (Courtesy of Hunter Douglas)

Figure 12.5 Woven wood shades with valance. (Courtesy of Hunter Douglas)

Figure 12.4 Duette cellular shades from Hunter Douglas. (Courtesy of Hunter Douglas)

Figure 12.6 Roller shade. (Courtesy of Hunter Douglas)

Figure 12.7 Hunter Douglas Pirouette window shades—more elaborate roll-up shades that roll up into the headrail. (Courtesy of Hunter Douglas)

back of the shade (Figure 12.7). The headrail size varies depending on the length of the shade and the amount of fabric that must be rolled into it.

Shutters

Shutters are made of wood, wood products, or vinyl (Figure 12.8). The most commonly used shutters have louvers set into a framed panel. Many framework options are available for shutters, and they vary slightly with each manufacturer. The louvers can be as narrow as 1 inch to as wide as 4 inches. Other types of panels include shirred panels, where fabric is gathered and installed into the opening; raised panels, which look like a raised-panel cabinet door; and vertical louvers, whereby the louvers run vertically instead of horizontally.

Figure 12.8 Shutters installed with specialty cutout for doors. (Courtesy of Hunter Douglas)

Sizes and Packaging

Custom items are made to specifications within ⅛ inch and packaged from as few as one item to a box to as many as will safely ship in a box. Depending on the product and material, minimum and maximum widths and heights can be made. Hard treatments can be measured for mounting inside or outside the frame (inside mount, also called inside brackets or IB, or outside mount, also called outside brackets or OB). Placement depends on client preference and on the actual construction of the window frame. Some windows don't have enough clearance on the frame for a screw to be drilled in to support the treatment for an inside mount. For an outside-mount vertical blind, it is advisable to add a minimum of 6 inches to 7 inches to the glass measurement to allow for privacy when the blind is in a closed position.

When measuring for inside-mount treatments like blinds and shades, always measure three places across (top, middle, and bottom) and at least two places down (each side). (See Figure 12.9). Windows are manmade and therefore subject to error. Buildings will also settle and shift, making a dimension

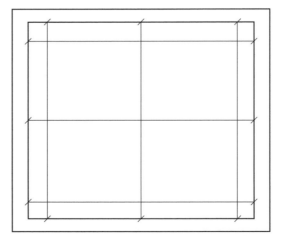

Figure 12.9 When measuring windows, make it a practice to measure horizontally at the top, the bottom, and the middle to find the narrowest dimension for the width of the treatment. When measuring vertically, measure at both ends and use the longest measurement for the length. Shown are suggestions for inside-mount measurements. Outside-mount measurements will depend on where you choose to mount the treatment.

Pricing

MODERN PRECIOUS METALS® ALUMINUM BLINDS

Product price only, not including freight, state/local taxes, measuring and installation, and other services associated with a custom installation.

MODERN PRECIOUS METALS®
A5 **1" Décor® Blinds** ➤ Duotone and Solid Colors .008 Gauge Slats

WIDTH TO:	12"	24"	28"	32"	36"	40"	44"	48"	52"	57"	62"	67"	72"	82"	92"	102"	112"	122"	132"	144"
42"	$102	85	94	101	110	121	131	138	146	167	176	189	198	226	246	282	344	371	398	418
48"	111	94	103	107	124	133	141	154	162	186	196	209	221	246	273	309	376	405	432	456
54"	120	103	108	120	133	143	155	164	175	197	215	226	241	272	297	335	404	436	463	492
60"	128	107	120	128	141	155	166	172	191	216	227	244	261	292	322	365	434	470	500	529
66"	133	117	128	138	155	166	176	193	201	228	246	262	280	312	346	390	462	500	534	566
72"	140	125	135	144	162	176	191	201	218	246	264	280	297	336	368	417	492	534	569	604
78"	145	133	143	155	170	188	200	218	233	262	280	297	318	358	395	443	523	564	604	643
84"	156	139	154	164	185	197	217	228	246	280	295	318	336	381	418	470	552	600	640	677
90"	161	147	160	170	195	212	227	244	261	293	312	335	356	401	443	497	581	628	674	717
96"	167	155	168	184	201	223	241	257	273	311	329	353	374	424	466	525	612	663	706	753
102"	175	162	176	191	216	233	250	271	289	324	349	368	394	447	495	551	640	695	743	788
108"	182	169	185	199	223	244	264	283	304	337	365	388	413	466	521	580	670	727	777	825
114"	188	176	195	209	233	255	276	295	318	356	387	408	433	490	540	607	698	758	812	866
120"	194	185	199	218	244	265	287	311	331	369	398	424	451	512	564	635	729	790	844	900
126"	201	195	211	227	255	279	301	322	346	387	414	443	471	532	589	660	758	821	879	938

Note: Blind prices in the 12" width column include a surcharge for narrow blinds.

MODERN PRECIOUS METALS
A6 **1" Décor Blinds** ➤ Brushed, Matte™, Metallic™, Opalescence, Pearlescent and SoftWeave® Finishes .008 Gauge Slats

WIDTH TO:	12"	24"	28"	32"	36"	40"	44"	48"	52"	57"	62"	67"	72"	82"	92"	102"	112"	122"	132"	144"
42"	$111	94	101	110	123	132	143	153	162	187	195	207	221	248	272	311	376	405	432	457
48"	120	101	113	120	137	144	156	166	177	201	217	228	243	272	301	338	410	443	470	497
54"	127	113	122	130	144	159	169	183	192	218	234	248	264	295	328	368	440	477	507	538
60"	136	120	130	140	156	169	185	194	211	235	249	269	285	321	354	400	476	513	547	580
66"	145	128	140	151	169	185	195	212	223	254	270	287	307	343	381	429	506	549	584	618
72"	152	138	150	160	179	193	211	223	240	270	290	308	328	368	406	458	538	584	620	658
78"	158	144	159	169	191	206	223	240	255	287	308	328	349	393	434	489	571	618	658	701
84"	167	154	166	183	200	217	235	251	271	307	328	349	368	417	460	519	604	655	697	742
90"	175	162	175	189	215	233	248	283	285	322	343	368	391	442	487	549	633	690	737	784
96"	182	169	186	199	223	244	264	293	301	339	363	388	413	464	514	578	669	725	773	824
102"	190	179	193	211	235	257	275	295	319	357	386	406	433	491	543	606	700	759	814	865
108"	196	187	201	221	246	269	290	312	333	370	400	427	455	514	572	636	734	794	875	906
114"	204	195	215	228	257	280	306	328	349	391	418	449	477	539	594	668	764	833	889	946
120"	212	201	221	240	269	292	318	339	365	406	436	464	495	560	620	697	798	866	928	986
126"	218	215	232	248	280	307	329	356	381	425	456	487	521	586	649	726	833	900	964	1028

Note: Blind prices in the 12" width column include a surcharge for narrow blinds.

Lifting System Upgrade Surcharges (Available with traditional routed blinds only. Add surcharge to base price.)

WIDTH TO:	24"	30"	36"	42"	48"	54"	60"	66"	72"	84"	100"
LITERISE® HEIGHT TO 66"	$58	58	58	61	61	61	61	70	70	70	70
LITERISE HEIGHT OVER 66"	61	61	61	75	75	75	75	86	86	86	101

Note: The LiteRise system is not available with cut-outs, multiple blinds on one headrail or perforated finishes.

Design Options Surcharges (Add surcharge to base price of blind.)

			For Further Info See Page
MULTI-COLOR BLINDS:	FIRST ADDED COLOR	Add $20	MPM-14
	EACH ADDITIONAL COLOR	Add $10	
CUT-OUTS:	SIDE CUT-OUT 5" OR LESS	Add $12 per side	MPM-23
	SIDE CUT-OUT 5⅛" OR MORE	Add $31 per side	
	CENTER CUT-OUT	Add $20	
	MULTIPLE BLINDS ON ONE HEADRAIL	Add $40; price each blind individually and add together for total unit price	MPM-14

MPM-6 Go to the **online Reference Guide** at my.hunterdouglas.com for the most up-to-date information. Effective 4/3/12

Figure 12.10 Hunter Douglas price chart for 1-inch décor metal blinds. (Courtesy of Hunter Douglas)

---

that was the same in all places when it was built shift ¼ inch to ½ inch. Sometimes these variants can be as much as 1 inch. Use narrowest-width and longest-length measurements to allow the treatment to clear the window when the user is raising or lowering it and to allow the treatment to fully close. Specify as inside brackets or inside mount, and let the manufacturer take the necessary allowances from the actual measurements.

When you are measuring for an outside mount, which can include blinds, shades, shutters, and so on, you must take the exact measurement of the space the treatment is to cover. It is important to take two measurements on width and two measurements on length. There are no additional allowances taken from the actual measurements, and it is specified as outside mount or outside brackets.

Cost Factors

Hard window treatments are the simplest product to specify and price for windows. Cost factors include the product, shipping, and installation. Options such as motorization may add cost to the product. Pricing becomes slightly more complicated when you are pricing specialty shaped windows, such as arches and angular windows, but the process has been simplified by the manufacturers. Be sure to read the specifications provided in price sheets.

Calculations

For most residential pricing, you can simply read the manufacturer's pricing chart to calculate the retail price (Figure 12.10), usually available on its website.

INSIGHT FROM THE FIELD

❝Designers who do their own measures often forget some of the details, such as specifying returns on horizontal blind valances that extend beyond the window frame. When I measure for blinds, I am taking not only the dimensions for the window, but also the other little details that can be missed when you aren't used to looking for them.❞

Wayne Daugherty, *owner and installer with WD Installations in Kansas City, Missouri*

If enough square footage of the same specified product is ordered, you can often obtain special pricing from the manufacturer. These square footage quantities are likely to be met in large commercial jobs. Contact your product representative to determine if the product you are specifying fits into this category.

Residential installation pricing for shades and blinds is calculated by the piece up to a certain width and length. Shutters are often priced by the square foot with additional pricing for various options. As with draperies and top treatments, there are additional charges for installations above a specific height designated by the installer and for motorized products, as well as for trip charges involved in measuring and creating templates. Commercial installation pricing is calculated either in the same manner as residential or by the square foot when there is sufficient quantity.

A good idea is to record dimensions on a table in order to keep track of not only measurements, but the full specifications (Table 12.1). Costs of the material, shipping, and installation can also be recorded here. The more organized the designer is with specifications and pricing, the less chance there is for mistakes.

Hard Window Treatment Schedule												
Client: Phone #s: Address:								Workroom: Installer:				
Room/Window: **Finished Dimensions:**												
Rooms	**Qty.**	**OB or IB**	**Size** **Width × Length**	**Mfr./Vendor**	**Style**	**Color**	**Cost Per**	**Subtotal**	**Est. Ship.**	**Total**	**PO**
Install A											
Install B											
Install C											
									Overall Cost		
Additional Information:												

Table 12.1 Hard Window Treatment Schedule

Step-by-Step Example

Using Figure 12.10, price a window that measures 34½ inches × 70¼ inches IB, using a solid-color 1-inch décor blind.

Using Chart A5 in the figure, move across the "WIDTH TO" horizontal line to 36 inches, since 34½ inches is larger than 32 inches. Move down the "HEIGHT TO" vertical line to 72 inches, since 70¼ inches is larger than 66 inches. Where the two lines meet is the suggested retail price, which is $162.00.

Your client wants to cover four windows this size, and needs to know the total price, including

	Quantity	Price Per	Total
Mini blinds	4	$162.00	$648
Installation	4	Minimum	$60
Total Installed Price			**$708**

Table 12.2 Retail pricing for Four 1-Inch Mini Blinds

installation, of these four windows in a solid-color, 1-inch décor blind. The minimum installation price is $60 and includes four shades. See Table 12.2.

Reference

Hunter Douglas. Designing Windows 2: *1*, 2007.

Chapter 13 | Pillows and Accent Table Coverings

Throw pillows and accent table coverings are used commercially and residentially in conversation areas as well as in bedrooms. The majority of table coverings are found in cafes, restaurants, and other places where small round tables are set for people to eat. While it is common that linens come from a linen supply company, there are times when the interior designer will provide these.

Chapter Outline

Terminology

Banding Flat strips of fabric usually sewn at or near the edge of a pillow, table topper, or table round that are used to create a contrast and accent. Banding is normally created from fabric cut on the bias.

Flange Flat strip of folded fabric sewn to and added beyond the edge of a pillow, table topper, or table round.

Fringe Decorative trim created and manufactured from threads and other materials finished at one end and loose at the other end, creating a fringed effect. Sold by the yard, fringe is sewn into the edge seam of pillows, table toppers, and table rounds. See Figure 13.1.

Cording Decorative trim created and twisted from threads and other materials into round cord. Sold by the yard and ½ yard, cording usually has a fabric lip that allows it to be sewn into the edge seam of pillows, table toppers, and table rounds. See Figure 13.2.

Lumbar pillow Rectangular-shaped pillow that can be used decoratively and to provide support for the lumbar area of the spine. Sizes include 12 inches × 20 inches and 16 inches × 24 inches, among others.

Pillow face A side of a pillow. The majority of pillows have two sides—that is, two pillow faces. A cube pillow has six pillow faces. Knowing the number of faces is important when you are calculating yardage.

Seam Where two pieces of fabric are sewn together. When the fabric has a pattern, the

A.   B.

Figure 13.1 There are many different types of fringes that can be specified. This is an example of a brush fringe (A) and a tassel fringe (B). The seamed part of the brush fringe is hidden in the seam of the product to which it's attached. In the case of this tassel fringe, it is meant to be sewn to the top of the product, since the entire piece is decorative. (A–B: Robert Allen Design)

Figure 13.2 This decorative cord has a lip that can be sewn into a seam. Decorative cords can come without a lip, so when specifying, make sure the correct cord is ordered depending on how it will be attached to the product. (F. Schumacher Company)

pattern must be matched at the seam. Pillows and table coverings should never have a seam down the center unless it is an intentional part of the design.

Table form A functional table that is intended to be covered. Residentially, this is sometimes known as a decorator table.

Table round The round cloth that covers tables and table forms.

Table topper A piece of fabric that covers the top of a table and hangs down at least several inches on the side. It is not meant to go to the floor like a table round and is normally seen on top of a table round.

Welt cord A trim created by cutting fabric on the bias and sewing it around a stiff cord, leaving a lip. This lip is then sewn into the edge seam of pillows, table toppers, and table rounds. Self-welt is made of the same fabric as the item being created.

Types of Pillows and Accent Table Coverings

Throw pillows and accent table coverings can help emphasize a theme or just pull color and pattern to a different level in the room. They can be made in nearly any size and in an endless selection of fabrics. Throw pillows are used to add color, pattern, and style to upholstery. Pillows on furniture can either be used behind the back to provide support, such as in the case of a lumbar pillow, or to minimize the seat depth to make the furniture fit the person sitting on it. Other pillows are made purely for aesthetic purposes and aren't made to be functional and even may be uncomfortable to lean against, as in the case of pillows with rhinestone or shell embellishments. The pillows can have self-welt, cord, brush fringe, tassel fringe, and many other types of trim at the seam to add to the style and décor. Common pillow filling, include polyester batting and feather.

Accent table coverings are commonly table rounds and table toppers, which are layered to create interest. Just as with throw pillows, sizes, fabrics, and trims are limitless. Most table coverings that interior designers specify and work with are table rounds made to cover table forms that have no aesthetic appeal. As the name table round implies, these are round cloths that drape over the form. Normally these forms require a minimum of two widths of fabric, which means there will be a seam. Just as with bedding, the seam shouldn't be located in the center of the cloth. There will always be a width of fabric in the center with seams flanking on each side (Figure 13.3).

Table toppers and runners are used to enhance the design scheme (Figure 13.4). Table toppers are layered over table rounds and can be round or square. Runners are sometimes used on dressers, buffets, dining tables, and sofa tables. Because these items are smaller than the round, not taking as much fabric, it is common to see sheer fabric, more expensive fabric, brighter fabric, or strongly patterned fabric used here. And like the throw pillows, all types of trims are used on them.

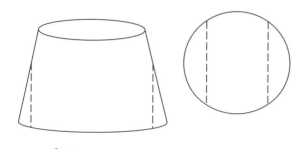

— — — Seam

Figure 13.3 Table rounds and table toppers, just like bedspreads, should not have a seam down the center. If there are two widths (or any even number), one width will go down the center and the other width will be cut in half and sewn to the sides of the center width.

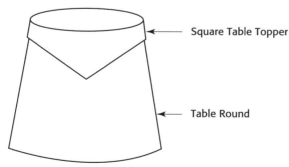

Square Table Topper

Table Round

Figure 13.4 A minimum of an additional 4 inches are required beyond the table size for the table topper to waterfall over the sides and lie appropriately. It is common for the table topper to be in a pattern while the table round is in a solid, or vice versa. Because there is less fabric required, a table topper is a great way to use a more expensive fabric to pull the look through the room.

Sizes and Packaging

Throw pillows and accent table coverings can be made in nearly every conceivable size and shape. In conversation areas, common sizes of throw pillows on furniture are 16 inches × 16 inches, 18 inches × 18 inches, 20 inches × 20 inches, 22 inches x 22 inches, 12 inches × 20 inches, and 16 inches × 20 inches. Floor pillows start at 24 inches × 24 inches and go up from there. Accent table covering sizes are dictated by the size of the table upon which they will be used. The table form can be customized to the size needed.

As stated in previous chapters, fabric ordered from the manufacturers is ordered by the full and the ½ yard. Most manufacturers require that a minimum of 1 to 2 yards be ordered. The majority of fabric used in interiors today is approximately 54 inches wide. However, some fabrics, due to the nature of the weaving, may be 48 inches or even 36 inches wide. Pillow forms do not hold any limitations because they can be customized to the size desired.

Cost Factors

Pillows and accent table coverings can have three to five costs that must be considered in calculations (Table 13.1). Materials include fabric, possibly more than one, possibly accent trim, shipping costs of

Material	Labor
Fabric	Basic labor
Freight/shipping	Additional labor beyond basic*
Fabric #2*	
Freight/shipping*	
Trim*	
Freight/shipping*	
Pillow form or table form**	
Freight/shipping*	
*If applicable. **Sometimes the workroom will supply the pillow and table forms, in which case the cost comes on the workroom invoice.	

Table 13.1 Cost Components for Throw Pillows and Accent Table Coverings

these items, and the pillow form or table form. Labor includes the basic labor to construct, plus additional costs for special designs. Labor costs usually depend on the size of the pillow or table covering. Pillow and accent table coverings schedules allow all specifications and costs to be pulled together in one place (Tables 13.2 and 13.3).

Round table forms can be built to any size required. These are sometimes built by the drapery installer, the drapery workroom, or the upholsterer. These tables are sturdy, often utilizing four legs. A cheap table form, using three legs, can be purchased from large discount places, but it might not be very sturdy.

Calculations

Calculating labor and materials for these items is relatively easy, even though it requires some thought and sometimes geometry. Geometry is used when you are calculating how much trim needs to be ordered at the bottom of a table round. Remember pi for determining circumference? You will be using it for these calculations.

Throw Pillows

To calculate yardage for throw pillows, you must consider horizontal and vertical repeats (Figure 13.5). The majority of pillows are 16 to 24 inches square. This size allows more than one pillow face to be cut from the width of 48-inch-wide or 54-inch-wide fabric if the horizontal repeat allows.

First, determine the size of the finished pillow and add a total of 2 inches for hems. Divide this number by the size of the horizontal repeat to determine full repeats from the width of the fabric. If this number includes a fraction, round up to the next whole number and

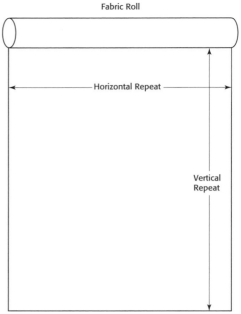

Fabric Roll

Horizontal Repeat

Vertical Repeat

Figure 13.5 Vertical repeats will always affect the amount of yardage required. Horizontal repeats affect how much fabric is required for pillows, since a pillow is a smaller item and it is possible to get more than one pillow face from a width.

multiply by the size of the repeat. This is the cut width or adjusted cut width in the case of a repeat. Divide the fabric width by the cut/adjusted cut width. If this is a fraction, round down. This is how many pillow faces can be cut from one width of fabric.

Next, determine the length of each cut. Take the length of the finished pillow and add a total of 2 inches to be used in hems. Divide this number by the size of the vertical repeat and round up to the next whole number. Multiply this by the size of the repeat to determine the adjusted cut length for the pillow.

Determine how many pillow faces are required. Sometimes a very expensive fabric is used on one side of a pillow. However, if both sides of a pillow are the same and two pillows are specified, 4 pillow faces are needed. Divide the number of pillow faces by the number of cuts per width. If this number is a fraction, round up to the next whole number. This is the total number of widths required. Multiply this number by the cut length/adjusted cut length. This is how much fabric is needed for the pillows. This

Throw Pillow Schedule

Client:
Phone #s:
Address:
Room:

Finished Dimension	Mfr./Vendor	Pattern	Color	Width	Repeat	Qty.	Cost Per	Subtotal	Est. Ship.	Total	PO
Fabric											
Trim											
Form											
Labor											
									Total		

Finished Dimension	Mfr./Vendor	Pattern	Color	Width	Repeat	Qty.	Cost Per	Subtotal	Est. Ship.	Total	PO
Fabric											
Trim											
Form											
Labor											
									Total		

Size	Mfr./Vendor	Pattern	Color	Width	Repeat	Qty.	Cost Per	Subtotal	Est. Ship.	Total	PO
Fabric											
Trim											
Form											
Labor											
									Total		

Additional Information:

Table 13.2 Throw Pillow Schedule

Client:

Phone #s:

Address:

Room:

Table Round	Finished Dimension	Mfr./Vendor	Pattern	Color	Width	Repeat	Qty.	Cost Per	Subtotal	Est. Ship.	Total	PO
Fabric												
Trim												
Form												
Labor												
										Total		

Table Topper	Finished Dimension	Mfr./Vendor	Pattern	Color	Width	Repeat	Qty.	Cost Per	Subtotal	Est. Ship.	Total	PO
Fabric												
Trim												
Form												
Labor												
										Total		

Table Runner	Size	Mfr./Vendor	Pattern	Color	Width	Repeat	Qty.	Cost Per	Subtotal	Est. Ship.	Total	PO
Fabric												
Trim												
Form												
Labor												
										Total		

Additional Information:

Table 13.3 Accent Table Coverings Schedule

number is divided by 36 inches and rounded up to the nearest ½ yard or full yard, since fabric must be ordered in these increments.

If the pillows are to be self-corded, you must allow for extra fabric to make the cording. The cording is usually cut on the bias. Discuss with your workroom to determine the total yardage needed for cording, although at least ½ yard must be allowed for self-cording. Normally, 1½ yards of fabric can accommodate two self-corded pillows up to 20 or 22 inches, with repeats of up to 27 inches.

Table Rounds

The finished size of the table round is determined by adding the height of the table twice to the diameter. A total of 4 inches is added to this for hems. Because this is a round cloth, this dimension is the cut width and cut length. Divide the cut width by the fabric width and round up to a whole number. This is the number of widths needed. Horizontal repeats usually don't affect yardage.

If there is a vertical repeat, yardage must be calculated by taking the cut length and dividing by the repeat. Round this number up to a whole number and multiply by the repeat to find the adjusted cut length. A drop match pattern will affect yardage because it will add 1½ times the vertical repeat to the adjusted cut length, but the majority of fabrics have straight matches. Multiply the number of widths by the cut length/adjusted cut length and divide by 36 inches, rounding up to the nearest ½ yard or full yard to determine how much fabric must be ordered.

When contrast cording or trim is used along the bottom of a table round, you must find the circumference to determine yardage for this item. To find circumference, take the diameter of the cloth (not the table), multiply by π (3.14), and then divide by 36 inches, rounding up to the nearest ½ yard or full yard for premade trim. One-inch jumbo self-cording takes a 5-inch cut of fabric. To determine yardage for this, divide the circumference by the width of fabric. Round up to determine full widths. Multiply this by the cut needed for trim. Finally, divide by 36 inches for yardage.

Table Toppers

Table toppers are squares of fabric thrown over the top of a table. It is preferable for the sides to hang over each side by at least 4 inches. Sometimes the topper may have cording or fringe around the perimeter and/or a decorative tassel at each point. Once the overall size of the square has been determined, 2 inches will be added for hems. Residentially, table toppers normally take no more than one width of fabric, since these tables are usually narrower than those used commercially. However, if you are calculating toppers for larger tables used in commercial applications, you might need multiple widths. Even if there is not a seam, the table topper yardage should be factored by the full repeat to allow the workroom flexibility with pattern placement. Some interior designers will add an additional repeat to the amount required for this purpose.

If there is a fringe or cording used on the topper, find the perimeter by adding all sides in inches together. Divide by 36 inches, rounding up to the nearest ½ or full yard to determine how much must be ordered. If tassels are used, it is important to make sure the tassels don't drag the ground. Utilizing geometry, $a^2 + b^2 = c^2$, take the length of the side and multiply it by itself. This will give you the numbers for a^2 and b^2. Adding these numbers together results in c^2, which is the diagonal line across the square. Use the square root function on the calculator to "un-square" the dimension to determine the actual diagonal length. To this dimension, add the length of the tassel twice (two sides) to discover the total length across the table with the tassels.

Step-by-Step Examples

Example 1—Throw Pillow

You have specified four 20-inch throw pillows with brush fringe for your client's two sofas. The fabric is 54 inches wide with a 27-inch vertical and horizontal repeat.

Step 1: Determine cut width of pillow.

Width of pillow:	20	in.
Add 2 inches for hems:	+ 2	in.
Total cut width:	22	in.

If there is a horizontal repeat, determine adjusted cut width.

Total cut width from Step 1:	22	in.
Divide by horizontal repeat of fabric:	÷ 27	in.
Total:	.81	repeats
Round up to whole number:	1	full repeat
Multiply by horizontal repeat:	× 27	in.
Total adjusted cut width:	27	in.

Step 2: Determine number of cuts from width of fabric.

Width of fabric:	54	in.
Divide by cut width or adjusted cut width from Step 1:	÷ 27	in.
Total pillow face cuts per width of fabric:	2	cuts
Round down to nearest whole number:	2	total cuts from width

Step 3: Determine cut length of pillow.

Length of pillow form:	20	in.
Add 2 inches for hems:	+ 2	in.
Total cut length:	22	in.

If there is a vertical repeat, determine adjusted cut length:

Total cut length from above:	22	in.
Divide by vertical repeat:	÷ 27	in.
Total:	.81	repeats
Round up to whole number:	1	full repeat
Multiply by vertical repeat:	× 27	in.
Total adjusted cut length:	27	in.

Step 4: Determine number of widths/cuts.

Number of pillows:	4	pillows
Multiply by number of pillow faces:	× 2	pillow faces
Total:	8	total pillow faces

Note: If the front and back of the pillow are the same, this requires 2 faces per pillow.

Divide by cuts per width from Step 2:	÷ 2	cuts
Total:	4	widths
Round up to whole number:	4	full widths

Step 5: Determine yardage to order.

Cut length or adjusted cut length:	27	in.
Multiply by number of widths from Step 4:	× 4	widths
Total:	108	in.
Divide by 36 to convert inches to yards:	÷ 36	in.
Total yards:	3	yd.
Round up to nearest ½ yard:	**3**	**yd. to be ordered**

To determine amount of brush fringe:

Add all sides together (20 + 20 + 20 + 20):	80	in.
Add 2 inches for start and stop of trim:	+ 2	in.
Total:	82	in.
Multiply by quantity of items/products:	× 4	quantity
Total:	328	in.
Divide by 36 to convert inches to yards:	÷ 36	in.
Total:	9.11	yd.
Round up to nearest ½ yard:	**9.5**	**yd. to be ordered**

Example 2—Table Round

A 30-inch-diameter 28-inch-tall form table is being made to go between two chairs in a hotel lobby. The fabric is 54 inches wide with a 27-inch repeat. Decorative cording will be sewn at the bottom.

Step 1: Determine finished width and length.

Diameter of table:	30	in.
Add drop to floor:	+ 28	in.
Add second drop to floor (2 sides):	+ 28	in.
Total finished diameter of tablecloth:	86	in. finished width and length

Step 2: Determine cut width and cut length.

Finished diameter of tablecloth:	86	in.
Add for hems (2 in. each side):	+ 4	in.
Total cut width and total cut length:	90	in.

If there is a repeat in the length, calculate for the repeat; if not, proceed to Step 3. Normally a repeat doesn't affect the width.

Cut length from above:	90	in.
Divide by length of repeat:	÷ 27	in.
Number of repeats:	3.33	repeats
Round up to whole number:	4	full repeats
Multiply by length of the repeat:	× 27	in.
Adjusted cut length (ACL):	108	in.

Step 3: Determine widths.

Cut width from Step 2:	90	in.
Divide by fabric width:	÷ 54	in.
Total widths needed:	1.67	widths
Round up to whole number:	2	full widths

Step 4: Determine yardage.

Cut length or adjusted cut length:	108	in.
Multiply by number of widths:	× 2	in.
Total:	216	in.
Divide by 36 to convert inches to yards:	÷ 36	in.
Total yards:	6	yd.
Round up to nearest ½ yard:	**6**	**yd. to be ordered**

Step 5: Determine circumference for cording.

Total diameter from Step 1:	86	in.
Multiply by π (3.14):	× 3.14	π
Total circumference of hem:	270.04	in.
Add 2 inches for start and stop of trim:	+ 2	in.
Total:	272.04	in.
Divide by 36 to convert inches to yards:	÷ 36	in.
Total yards:	7.56	yd.
Round up to nearest ½ yard:	**8**	**yd. to be ordered**

Example 3—Table Topper

A square table topper will be made for the table above with a 5-inch drop over the sides. The fabric is 54 inches wide with an 18-inch repeat.

Step 1: Determine side dimension.

Diameter of table:	30	in.
Add length of drop over side (at least 4 in.):	+ 5	in.
Add drop again to account for both sides:	+ 5	in.
Total finished dimension per side of topper:	40	in.

Step 2: Determine cut width and cut or adjusted cut length.

Finished dimension from Step 1:	40	in.
Add 1 inch to each side for hems:	+ 2	in.
Cut width and cut length:	42	in.

If there is a repeat in the length, calculate for the repeat; if not, proceed to Step 3.

Total cut length from above:	42	in.
Divide by length of repeat:	÷ 18	in.
Number of repeats:	2.33	repeats
Round up to whole number:	3	full repeats
Multiply by length of the repeat:	× 18	in.
Adjusted cut length (ACL):	54	in.

Step 3: Determine widths.

Cut width from Step 2 (before repeat):	42	in.
Divide by fabric width:	÷ 54	in.
Total widths needed:	.78	width
Round up to whole number:	1	full width

Step 4: Determine yardage.

Cut length or adjusted cut length:	54	in.
Multiply by number of widths:	× 1	in.
Total:	54	in.
Divide by 36 to convert inches to yards:	÷ 36	in.
Total yards:	1.5	yd.
Round up to nearest ½ yard:	**1.5**	**yd. to be ordered**

Manual Worksheets

Throw Pillow Worksheet

Step 1: Determine cut width of pillow.

Width of pillow:	_____	in.
Add 2 inches for hems:	+ _____2_____	in.
Total cut width:	_____	**in.**

If there is a horizontal repeat, determine adjusted cut width.

Total cut width from above:	_____	in.
Divide by horizontal repeat of fabric:	÷ _____	in.
Total:	_____	repeats
Round up to whole number:	_____	full repeats
Multiply by horizontal repeat:	× _____	in.
Total adjusted cut width:	_____	**in.**

Step 2: Determine number of cuts from width of fabric.

Width of fabric:	_____	in.
Divide by cut width or adjusted cut width from Step 1:	÷ _____	in.
Total pillow face cuts per width:	_____	cuts
Round down to nearest whole number:	_____	total cuts per width

Step 3: Determine cut length of pillow.

Length of pillow:	_____	in.
Add 2 inches for hems:	+ _____2_____	in.
Total cut length:	_____	**in.**

If there is a vertical repeat, determine adjusted cut length.

Total cut length from above:	_____	in.
Divide by vertical repeat:	÷ _____	in.
Number of repeats:	_____	repeats
Round up to whole number:	_____	full repeats
Multiply by the length of the vertical repeat:	× _____	in.
Adjusted cut length (ACL):	_____	**in.**

Step 4: Determine number of widths.

Number of pillows:	_____	pillows
Multiply by number of pillow faces:	× _____	pillow faces
Total number of pillow faces:	_____	total pillow faces

Note: If the front and back of the pillow are the same, this requires 2 faces per pillow.

Divide by cuts per width from Step 2:	÷ _____	cuts
Total:	_____	**widths**
Round up to whole number:	_____	**full widths**

Step 5: Determine yardage to order.

Cut length or adjusted cut length from Step 3:	_____	in.
Multiply by number of widths from Step 4:	× _____	widths
Total inches:	_____	**in.**
Divide by 36 to convert inches to yards:	÷ _____36_____	in.
Total yards:	_____	**yd.**
Round up to nearest ½ yard:	_____	**yd. to be ordered**

Table Round Worksheet

Step 1: Determine finished width and length.

Diameter of table:	_____	in.
Add drop to floor:	+ _____	in.
Add second drop to floor (2 sides):	+ _____	in.
Total finished diameter to tablecloth:	_____	**in. finished width and length**

Step 2: Determine cut width and length.

Finished diameter of tablecloth:	_____	in.
Add for hems (2 inches each side):	+ 4	in.
Total cut width and length:	_____	**in.**

Note: When calculating an oval cloth, you must calculate the width and length separately.

If there is a repeat in the length, calculate for the repeat; if not, proceed to Step 3. Normally a repeat doesn't affect the width.

Total cut length from above:	_____	in.
Divide by length of repeat:	÷ _____	in.
Number of repeats:	_____	**repeats**
Round up to whole number:	_____	**full repeats**
Multiply this number by the length of the repeat:	× _____	in.
Adjusted cut length (ACL):	_____	**in.**

Step 3: Determine widths.

Cut width from Step 2:	_____	in.
Divide by fabric width:	÷ _____	in.
Total widths needed:	_____	**widths**
Round up to whole number:	_____	**full widths**

Step 4: Determine yardage.

Cut length or adjusted cut length from Step 2:	_____	in.
Multiply by number of widths:	× _____	widths
Total inches:	_____	**in.**
Divide by 36 to convert inches to yards:	÷ 36	in.
Total yards:	_____	**yd.**
Round up to nearest ½ yard:	_____	**yd. to be ordered**

Step 5: Determine circumference for cording or fringe, if applicable.

Total finished diameter from Step 1:	_____	in.
Multiply by π (3.14):	× 3.14	π
Total circumference of hem:	_____	**in.**
Add 2 inches for start and stop of trim:	+ 2	in.
Total inches:	_____	**in.**
Divide by 36 to convert inches to yards:	÷ 36	in.
Total yards:	_____	**yd.**
Round up to nearest ½ yard:	_____	**yd. to be ordered**

Table Topper Worksheet

Step 1: Determine side dimension.

Diameter or length of one side of table:	_____	in.
Add length of drop over edge (at least 4 in.): +	_____	in.
Add drop again to account for both sides: +	_____	in.
Total finished length per side of topper:	_____	**in. finished width and length**

Step 2: Determine cut width and cut or adjusted cut length.

Finished dimension from Step 1:	_____	in.
Add 1 inch each side for hems: +	2	in.
This is the cut width and cut length:	_____	**in.**

If there is a repeat in the length, calculate for the repeat; if not, proceed to Step 3.

Cut length from above: ÷	_____	in.
Divide by length of repeat: ÷	_____	in.
Resulting number is the number of repeats:	_____	**repeats**
Round up to whole number:	_____	**full repeats**
Multiply by the length of the repeat: ×	_____	in.
Adjusted cut length (ACL):	_____	**in.**

Step 3: Determine widths.

Cut width from Step 2:	_____	in.
Divide by fabric width: ÷	_____	in.
Total widths needed:	_____	**widths**
Round up to whole number:	_____	**full widths**

Step 4: Determine yardage.

Cut length or adjusted cut length from Step 2:	_____	in.
Multiply by number of widths: ×	_____	widths
Total inches:	_____	**in.**
Divide by 36 to convert inches to yards: ÷	36	in.
Total yards:	_____	**yd.**
Round up to nearest ½ yard:	_____	**yd. to be ordered**

Note: To determine the diagonal distance across a square topper to see how long the points fall over the side, use $a^2 + b^2 = c^2$. This is important to know when you are adding tassels on the ends of square toppers, to ensure the tassels don't drag on the floor.

Step A: Determine Side A^2.

Side A:	_____	in.
Multiply by Side A: ×	_____	in.
Total Side A^2:	_____	**in.**

Step B: Determine Side B^2.

Side B:	_____	in.
Multiply by Side B: ×	_____	in.
Total Side B^2:	_____	**in.**

Step C: Determine the diagonal distance (C).

Total from Step A:	_____	in.
Add total from Step B: +	_____	in.
Equals C^2:	_____	**in.**
Use the square root (√) function on the calculator to find the root of C^2:	_____	in.

This is the diagonal distance of the topper in inches.

Fringe and Cording Worksheet

Step 1: Determine finished perimeter.

Finished dimension side A:	_____	in.
Add finished dimension side B:	+ _____	in.
Add finished dimension side C:	+ _____	in.
Add finished dimension side D:	+ _____	in.
Total finished perimeter:	_____	**in.**

Step 2: Determine yardage.

Total from Step 1:	_____	in.
Add 2 inches for start and stop of trim:	+ _____2_____	in.
Total:	_____	**in.**
Multiply by quantity of items/products:	× _____	quantity
Total inches:	_____	**in.**
Divide by 36 to convert inches to yards:	÷ _____36_____	in.
Total yards:	_____	**yd.**
Round up to nearest ½ yard:	_____	**yd. to be ordered**

For round shapes: determine circumference:

Step 1: Determine diameter.

Diameter of table:	_____	in.
Add drop to floor:	+ _____	in.
Add second drop to floor (2 sides):	+ _____	in.
Total finished diameter to tablecloth:	_____	**in.**

Step 2: Determine yardage.

Total finished diameter from Step 1:	_____	in.
Multiply by π (3.14):	× _____3.14_____	π
Total circumference of hem:	_____	**in.**
Add 2 inches for start and stop of trim:	+ _____2_____	in.
Total inches:	_____	**in.**
Divide by 36 to convert inches to yards:	÷ _____36_____	in.
Total yards:	_____	**yd.**
Round up to nearest ½ yard:	_____	**yd. to be ordered**

Practice Lessons—Pillows and Accent Table Coverings

BASIC

Throw Pillows

You are creating two 18-inch throw pillows for your client's sofa. The fabric is 54 inches wide and has no repeat. Decorative cording (sold by the yard and ½ yard) will be used at the seams of the pillows.

1. How many pillow faces can be cut from a width of fabric?
2. What is the cut length of the pillows?
3. How many yards must be ordered for the pillows?
4. How many yards must be ordered for the decorative cording?

Table Round

A table round will be made for your client's table form in the bedroom. It is 26 inches diameter and 25 inches tall. The fabric is 54 inches wide and has no repeat.

1. What is the finished diameter of the table round?
2. How many widths of fabric are required?
3. How many yards must be ordered?

Table Topper

A square table topper will be made for the preceding 26-inch table round with a 6-inch drop on all sides. This topper will be made from a fabric matching the bedskirt. The fabric is 54 inches wide with an 18-inch repeat.

1. What is the finished measurement for the topper?
2. How many widths of fabric are required?
3. How many yards must be ordered?

INTERMEDIATE

Throw Pillows

You are working on a clubhouse and will provide four 20-inch throw pillows for the two large leather sofas. The fabric is 54 inches wide and has a 10.8-inch horizontal repeat and a 10-inch vertical repeat. The pillows will have a decorative tassel fringe.

1. How many pillow faces can be cut from a width?
2. What is the adjusted cut length?
3. How many yards of fabric must be ordered?
4. How many yards must be ordered for the decorative tassel fringe?

Table Round

A new boutique store is opening in the historic main street area of town. The owners need four table rounds made for their display tables and want decorative cording at the bottom. The tables are 28 inches diameter and 30 inches tall. The fabric is 54 inches wide with a 24-inch repeat.

1. What is the finished diameter of the table round?
2. What is the adjusted cut length of the fabric?
3. What is the finished circumference of the table?
4. How many total yards of fabric must be ordered for the four tables?
5. How many total yards must be ordered for the decorative cording?

Table Topper

The boutique wants square table toppers for the four 28-inch-diameter table rounds. There will be an 8-inch drop on all sides. The fabric is 54 inches wide with a 2-inch horizontal and vertical repeat.

1. What is the finished measurement for the topper?
2. What is the adjusted cut length?
3. How many total yards must be ordered?

ADVANCED
Throw Pillows

You are updating a hotel's lounging area with distinctively patterned pillows for its upholstery. There will be three 22-inch pillows (Pillow A) in a 54-inch-wide solid fabric. There will be five 20-inch pillows (Pillow B) in a fabric 54 inches wide with a 27-inch horizontal and 27-inch vertical repeat. Pillow A will be trimmed in decorative cording. Pillow B will be trimmed in a decorative fringe.

1. How many pillow faces can be cut from a width of fabric for Pillow A? Pillow B?
2. What is the adjusted cut length of pillow B?
3. How many yards must be ordered for Pillow A? Pillow B?
4. How many yards must be ordered for the decorative cording for Pillow A? How many yards must be ordered for the decorative fringe for Pillow B?

Table Round

One of your clients wants you to provide table rounds with square table toppers for her guests to sit at for a special event she is hosting at her home. She needs eight table rounds for tables that are 60 inches diameter and 30 inches tall. The fabric is 54 inches wide with a 21-inch vertical repeat.

1. What is the finished diameter of the table round?
2. How many widths are needed per table?
3. How many total yards must be ordered for the eight tables?

Table Topper

Eight square table toppers for the preceding 60-inch-diameter table will hang 10 inches over each side. She wants a decorative cording around the edge of the toppers. The fabric is 54 inches wide with a 4-inch repeat.

1. What is the finished measurement for the topper?
2. What is the adjusted cut length?
3. How many widths of fabric are needed per table?
4. What is the diagonal measurement from one corner to another? Will it touch the ground?
5. How many total yards fabric must be ordered?
6. How many total yards decorative cording must be ordered?

Pricing for Advanced Throw Pillows

Use the fabric quantity found for the Advanced Throw Pillows practice lesson and the prices that follow to calculate pricing for your client. Your local workroom will make the pillows, and you will pick them up.

Fabric A—$48.00/yard

Shipping Fabric A—$12.00

Fabric B—$108.00/yard

Shipping Fabric B—$18.00

Trim A (decorative cording)—$30.00/yard

Trim B (decorative fringe)—$45.00/yard

Shipping for all trim (from same manufacturer)—$15.00

Pillow A: Labor and form—$76 each pillow

Pillow B: Labor and form—$70.00 each pillow

1. What is the total price for Pillows A?
2. What is the total price for Pillows B?
3. What is the total price for all pillows?

Pricing for Advanced Table Round

Use the fabric quantity found for the Advanced Table Round practice lesson and the prices that follow to calculate pricing for your client. These are being made by a local workroom and will be picked up when they are finished.

Fabric—$18.00/yard (reflects extra discount for large quantity)

Fabric shipping—$85.00

Table round labor—$175.00 each

1. What is the total price for all eight table rounds?

Pricing for Advanced Table Topper

Use the fabric quantity found for the Advanced Table Topper practice lesson and the prices that follow to calculate pricing for your client. These are being made by a local workroom and will be picked up when they are finished.

Fabric—$26.00/yard (reflects extra discount for large quantity)

Fabric shipping—$55.00

Trim: Decorative cording—$12.00/yard (reflects extra discount for large quantity)

Trim shipping—$35.00

Table topper labor—$90.00 each

1. What is the total price for all eight table toppers?

References

Jennifer Allred. Personal communication. August to December, 2012.

Jenee Coleman. Personal communication. October to December 2012.

Chapter 14 | Bedding: Spreads, Coverlets, Duvets, Bedskirts, Shams

From a hotel bed to a child's bed, the bed can be dressed as simply or elaborately as desired. In the hospitality field, businesses are trying to create an experience for their guests. This is usually a sense of luxury, comfort, and pampering. Residentially, some people want to re-create that luxurious feeling they experience in hotels and spas. Others just want one covering that looks good in their room, goes to the floor, and covers their sleeping pillows. After designing the look for the client's purpose, the designer calculates materials and costs to determine the overall price.

Chapter Outline

Terminology

Types of Bedding

Sizes

Cost Factors

Calculations

Step-by-Step Examples
Example 1—Coverlet
Example 2—Duvet Cover
Example 3—Bedscarf
Example 3—Bedskirt
Example 4—Sham with Flange

Manual Worksheets
Bedspread and Coverlet Worksheet
Duvet Cover Worksheet
Bedskirt Worksheet
Bedscarf Worksheet
Pillow Worksheet
Flange and Ruffle Worksheet

Practice Lessons: Bedding
Basic
Bedspread
Bedscarf
Intermediate
Coverlet
Gathered Bedskirt
Advanced
Duvet Cover
Bedskirt with Relaxed Pleat
Sham with Ruffles
Pricing for Intermediate Coverlet
Pricing for Intermediate Gathered Bedskirt

References

Terminology

Bedscarf Narrow, rectangular piece of fabric, sometimes quilted, that is placed at the foot of a bed (Figure 14.1).

Figure 14.1 Bedscarf at foot of bed. (iStockphoto / © darrenwise)

Bedskirt Fabric covering placed on top of the box spring that hangs to the floor (Figure 14.2). Depending on the type of bed, a bedskirt can be held in place with fabric decking over the box spring, with Velcro on the inside of a wood frame, or by other means.

Figure14.2 Bedskirt showing pleat and banding around the white decking. (Courtesy of Diana Allison)

Bedspread A top layer bedcovering that goes to the floor (Figure 14.3). It can be tailored; otherwise, it will naturally create a "bell" at the corners. Options for the top of the bedspread include pillow tucks or reverse shams. When the bedspread is made without a pillow tuck or reverse sham, separate pillow shams are normally used to cover pillows.

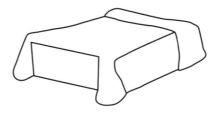

Bedspread

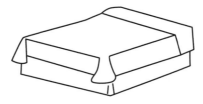

Coverlet

Figure 14.3 Bedspreads fall all the way to the floor from the top of the mattress. Coverlets fall several inches below the mattress and box spring seam. Both of these examples are a throw style and show the belling of the corners that occurs with this popular style.

Coverlet A top layer bedcovering that is usually made to fall 2 inches to 3 inches past the mattress and box spring "seam" (see Figure 14.3). Many times a bedskirt/duster is used to "finish" or hide the space under the bed. Like a bedspread, this can be made with or without a pillow tuck or reverse sham. When the coverlet is made without a pillow tuck or reverse sham, separate pillow shams are normally used to cover pillows.

Comforter Another type of top-layer bedcovering that is usually quilted and reversible with bulky filling that provides warmth. Normally, they aren't long enough to cover the length and drop of the bed like a bedspread or coverlet will (Figure 14.4).

Figure 14.4 Down comforter. (Creative Commons)

Decking The top part of a bedskirt/duster that goes between the mattress and box spring. The decorative sides of the bedskirt/duster are sewn to this. Some interior designers will have the face fabric of the bedskirt sewn as a 4-inch to 6-inch banding around the decking so that if the bedskirt shifts, the decorative fabric is still seen (see Figure 14.2).

Drop Vertical dimension of bedding from the top of the mattress toward the floor. The important dimensions include the drop to the mattress and box spring seam and the drop to the floor.

Duster See *bedskirt*.

Duvet Either a top bedcovering or secondary layer that is commonly filled with down and feathers or other material that creates warmth. Today duvets are often channel- or box-quilted between high-count cotton fabric, which keeps the feathers or other material in place. Duvets are sometimes referred to as comforters, though usually a duvet has a separate duvet cover, whereas a comforter is a single piece (see Figure 14.4).

Duvet cover An "envelope" of fabric, usually decorative, that fits around a duvet (Figure 14.5). It is like a large pillowcase for the duvet. Covers can be made of washable fabrics so that they can be thrown into the washing machine. A cover made from decorative sheets can be less expensive and also does not have the seams that a cover made from narrower fabric widths will.

Figure 14.5 Duvet cover with comforter already inside. (© BUILT Images / Alamy)

Pillow shams A decorative covering for bed pillows (Figure 14.6). They can be reversible, removable, or permanent.

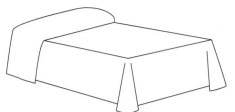

Figure 14.6 Pillow shams for the sleeping pillows. (Courtesy of Diana Allison)

Pillow tuck Extra material at the head of a bedspread or coverlet that allows pillows to be placed under the bedcovering (Figure 14.7). The bedcovering can then be tucked a little under the pillows.

Figure 14.7 Pillow tucks use an additional 20 to 24 inches of fabric so that as the bed is made, some extra fabric is slightly tucked under the pillow before the bedding goes over the pillow.

Reverse sham In contrast to the pillow tuck, extra material in a bedspread or coverlet that is sewn at the top of the bedcovering. The pillows are placed on the bedcovering, and the reverse sham is then folded over them from the top (Figure 14.8).

Seamed at Head of Bedspread or Coverlet And Pulled Over Pillow

Figure 14.8 Reverse shams use approximately 20 inches to 24 inches of additional fabric. The fabric is sewn to the head of the bed in order for the pattern to show as it is pulled forward over the pillows.

Types of Bedding

The number of bedding items required depends on how simple or elaborate the desired look is. Someone wanting a very simple look may opt for a bedspread with a pillow tuck, since it goes to the floor and covers both the mattress and box spring (Figure 14.9). Others may want a very layered yet tailored look that consists of coverlet, bedskirt, pillow shams, and throw pillows (Figure 14.10).

Figure 14.10 Layering of bedding is popular because it looks welcoming and inviting. This shows a duvet cover, two Euro shams, four king shams, a lumbar pillow, several decorative pillows, and a bedscarf. (© Oleksiy Maksymenko / Alamy)

Figure 14.9 Bedspread, throw style, showing the belling that occurs at the foot of the bed with this popular style. (Courtesy of Diana Allison)

No matter how simple the look, you want to hide the mattress and box spring. Because bedspreads go to the floor, they will do this. If there is no pillow tuck, decorative shams are required for the pillows. Many hotels use bedspreads to simplify housekeeping. Coverlets will cover the mattress and extend past the mattress and box spring seam by several inches. Some beds have side rails and footboards. It is possible to specify a longer drop for the coverlet so that nothing else is required to hide the box spring.

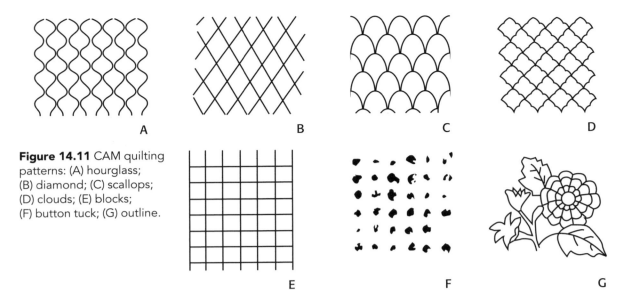

Figure 14.11 CAM quilting patterns: (A) hourglass; (B) diamond; (C) scallops; (D) clouds; (E) blocks; (F) button tuck; (G) outline.

Bedspreads and coverlets are quilted. There are numerous quilting patterns; some are computer-aided machine (CAM) patterns and some are hand-guided patterns (Figure 14.11). Many quilt companies publish yardage estimates based on certain drops. These are starting points. Understanding how the fabric must be calculated allows you as the interior designer to do very accurate calculations on-site if necessary.

The quilt pattern has a direct relationship to how much fabric must be allowed for take-up by the quilting. A tightly quilted vermicelli pattern uses more fabric than does a 6-inch channel quilt. A hand-guided quilt pattern literally has someone guiding the quilting machine around the actual fabric pattern, and the quilt take-up will depend on how intricate the quilt pattern becomes.

There are also varying thicknesses of batting. Many interior designers will specify an 8-ounce quilt fill. Four-ounce quilt fill is very lightweight, and a 12-ounce quilt fill can be very heavy. It is important to consider the strength of your client when specifying the type of bedcovering and weight of fill. Someone without a lot of upper body strength may have a hard time making a bed with a bedspread utilizing 12-ounce fill. Even an 8-ounce fill can be heavy and difficult to maneuver for a bedspread on a king-size bed.

Usually when a coverlet is used, a bedskirt of some kind is used to cover the space between the top of the box spring and the floor. Bedskirts can be gathered (dust ruffles) or pleated. The pleats can be spaced evenly along the sides, approximately every 10 feet or one pleat to each long side and at the corners at the foot of the bed (Figure 14.12).

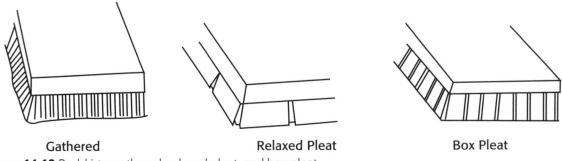

Gathered   Relaxed Pleat   Box Pleat

Figure 14.12 Bedskirts: gathered, relaxed pleat, and box pleat.

Normally comforters and duvets are used in addition to the bedspread or coverlet and folded toward the end of the bed. Hotels often have a comforter or duvet on the bed in this manner. However, comforters and duvets can be custom -made to the measurements that will fully cover the mattress and box spring seam. It is possible to add flanges or ruffles to the sides of a commercially purchased duvet cover to extend the length and width (Figure 14.13). A queen-size bed can use a king-size comforter, since it is usually big enough to cover the bed. It is also possible to purchase extra-long comforters, since it is usually the length that is too short. Bedscarves have become popular recently. These consist of a hemmed, sometimes reversible, long and narrow piece of fabric that can be laid across the foot of the bed. The hotel industry often uses bedscarves to add an accent to the bed.

After the bed has been covered, you then determine if pillow shams and throw pillows will be used. Many people like the look of numerous pillows even though they will sleep on only one or two (Figure 14.14). Decorative pillow shams can be removable if your client wants to put the sleeping pillows in the shams. Often clients will place their sleeping pillows behind permanent decorative shams. Sham edges can be ruffled, flanged, and corded. They can be made to the size of bed pillows or as a European (Euro) size, which is approximately 24 inches × 24 inches. When layering, some designers will start with three Euro shams along the back of a king- or queen-size bed and put two king-size pillow shams in front of those. The quantity of pillows is really dependent on your client. An appropriate number of additional throw pillows are necessary. One throw pillow for a twin bed is appropriate, but for a king bed, it is out of scale. In general, one to two throw pillows create an appropriate balance for a twin bed, two to three for a full-size bed, three to five for a queen, and five to seven for a king. Of course, some clients will want more than what is recommended. By varying sizes and shapes, this can easily be done. The only limit will be the client's budget.

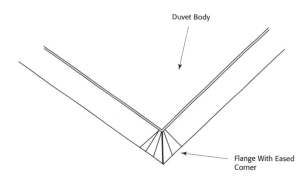

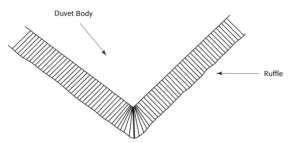

Figure 14.13 Flanges and ruffles are sometimes used when it is necessary to extend the size of the duvet cover past the actual size of the comforter. Ruffles are usually 2½ to 3 times full, depending on fabric weight. When flanges are used, they tend to look better if they are slightly padded, and they will lie better at the corners if there are several tucks made.

Figure 14.14 King-size pillow shams behind five throw pillows. (Courtesy of Diana Allison)

Sizes

Today, mattresses and pillows have become standardized; however, if your client has an antique bed, the mattress may have been custom-made for the bed and will deviate from the norm (Table 14.1). Pillows can also be custom-made. The mattress sizes must be confirmed by a field measure of the bed. Before measuring, always be sure the client has the quantity of blankets and anything else that will be on the bed when the spread or coverlet is on it. Make sure the client isn't planning on buying a new mattress and box spring within a couple of months. Both of these things will change the dimensions taken for the workroom. Take the dimension of the width (side to side), the length (top to bottom), and the drop to the seam and the drop to the floor (Figure 14.15). Do this for both the mattress and box spring.

Cost Factors

Factors that impact the cost of bedding are fabric, trim, form, shipping, and labor. Because bedding can have so many different components, it is important to have some way to keep track of material specifications and costs and labor costs (Table 14.2).

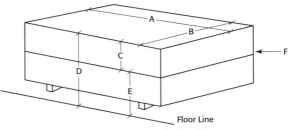

Figure 14.15 When measuring for bedding, measure the following: (A) length; (B) width; (C) drop of mattress; (D) top of mattress to the floor; and (E) top of box spring to the floor. (F) shows the seam of the mattress and box spring.

A schedule can be created that not only keeps track of specifications and costs but also ordering information. Several computer programs specifically for bedding are available. An Excel spreadsheet can be formatted to keep track of the information and to calculate running totals of the product.

When specifying pillow shams, throw pillows, and duvet covers, you must also consider that the pillow forms and duvets may need to be purchased if the client doesn't already have them. This will add a cost to the item. Some interior designers will ask their clients to find and buy forms, while others have their own sources for these items and will supply them. Shipping is one item that designers sometimes forget to include. For instance, suppose the fabric ships to a company that will make the bedspread. After the bedspread has been made, it must be shipped to your location. There will be a shipping charge from the fabric company for the fabric shipped to the bedspread fabricator. There is also a shipping charge from the bedspread fabricator for shipping the fabric to you. Be sure to allow for these costs because they will quickly eat away your profit.

Depending on the location of the interior design firm, there may be no workrooms or just a few workrooms that can quilt bedspreads and coverlets. Local and national workrooms that can make pillow shams, bedskirts, bedscarves, and duvet covers are more numerous, since these items generally aren't

Mattresses	Size
Crib	28 in. × 52 in.
Twin	39 in. × 75 in.
Twin Extra Long	39 in. × 80 in.
Full	54 in. × 75 in.
Full Extra Long	54 in. × 80 in.
Queen	60 in. × 80 in.
King	76 in. × 80 in.
	78 in. × 80 in.
California King	72 in. × 84 in.
Pillows	
Standard	20 in. × 26 in.
Queen	20 in. × 30 in.
King	20 in. × 36 in.

Table 14.1 Mattress and Pillow Sizes

Bedding Schedule

Client:

Phone #s:

Address:

Room:

	Mfr./Vendor	Pattern	Color	Width	Repeat	Qty.	Cost Per	Subtotal	Est. Ship.	Total	PO
Bedspread/ Coverlet/Duvet — Finished Dimension											
Fabric											
Form (if applicable)											
Labor											
Bedskirt — Finished Dimension											
Fabric											
Labor											
Shams — Size											
Fabric											
Form											
Labor											
Dec. Pillows — Size											
Fabric											
Form											
Labor											
Bedscarf — Size											
Fabric											
Labor											
Additional Information:										**Overall Cost**	

Table 14.2 Bedding Cost Worksheet

quilted. When you are selecting a workroom, quality of workmanship, options available, turnaround time, speed of communication, and pricing are important to consider. It is important for the workroom to unroll the fabric and inspect it before they cut it. Make sure the workroom doesn't expect you to do this, because it is difficult for you to do this without the appropriate equipment and space. Sometimes there are up-charges if you don't use fabric that the manufacturer of the product sells. Be sure to network with interior design colleagues and fabric showrooms to find names of workrooms.

Calculations

Calculations for bedding involve calculating widths and finding the cut length in order to find yardage.

Bedspreads and Coverlets

Bedcoverings should never have a seam at the center (Figure 14.16). If only two widths of fabric are used, the second width is cut in half and sewn to each side

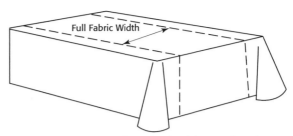

Figure 14.16 A sign of quality bedding is that there is a full width in the center of the bedding. You never want a seam in the middle of the bed.

of the center width. Most beds will need 2 to 3 widths of fabric.

In the preparations for calculating yardage, take the dimensions of the bed; if you are measuring for a bedspread, subtract ¼ inch to ½ inch from the drop so that the bedspread won't touch the floor. Determine whether you will use banding around the decking. Determine what type of quilting pattern and fill weight will be used.

The steps are as follows:

Step 1: Determine finished width and cut width.

Width of bed:	_____	in.
Add drop:	+ _____	in.
Add second drop (there are sides to a bed):	+ _____	in.

The drop used on the worksheet must already have ¼ inch to ½ inch deducted from the actual drop if the bedspread/coverlet is not to drag on the floor.

Total finished width:	_____	in.
Add hems (2 in. each side):	+ 4	in. (2 sides)
Total:	_____	in.
Add quilting allowance (10 to 15 percent):	× _____	(multiply by 1.10 to 1.15)

Depending on how tight the quilt pattern is and how thick the fill weight, 10 percent to 15 percent quilting allowance must be added in. A 4-ounce channel quilt pattern may take up 10 percent, while an 8-ounce vermicelli quilt pattern may take up 15 percent. When you are new to estimating coverlets and bedspreads, allow the full 15 percent.

Total cut width:	_____	in.

Step 2: Determine number of widths to use.

Cut width from Step 1:	_____	in.
Divide by width of fabric:	÷ _____	in.
Total widths:	_____	widths
Round up to whole number:	_____	full widths

Fabric must be ordered by full widths even if the full width isn't used. Be sure to ask for any leftover fabric to be returned to you.

Step 3: Determine finished length and cut length.

Length of bed:	_____	in.
Add drop:	+ _____	in.
Add pillow tuck if applicable (24 in. is plenty):	+ 24	in.

Note: A pillow tuck isn't necessary if pillow shams are planned.

Total finished length:	_____	in.
Add hems (2 in. each end):	+ 4	in. (2 ends)
Total:	_____	in.
Add quilting allowance (10 to 15 percent):	× _____	(multiply by 1.10 to 1.15)

The quilting allowance must be calculated for the length as well as the width, since it will take up in both directions.

Total cut length before repeat:	_____	in.

If the fabric has a repeat:

Take cut length from above:	_____	in.
Divide by length of repeat:	÷ _____	in.
Total number of repeats:	_____	repeats
Round up to whole number:	_____	full repeats

In order for the pattern to match when it is sewn, full repeats must be calculated. In practice, some interior designers will add one additional repeat to the final yardage total so they can to determine where the repeat will begin on the product.

Multiply by length of repeat:	× _____	in.
Adjusted cut length (ACL):	_____	in.

Step 4: Determine yardage to order.

Cut length or ACL from Step 3:	_____	in.
Multiply by total number of widths from Step 2:	× _____	widths
Total inches:	_____	in.
Divide by 36 to convert inches to yards:	÷ 36	in.
Total yards:	_____	yd.
Round up to nearest ½ yard:	_____	**yd. to be ordered**

Fabric must be ordered in ½-yard increments. There are a few companies that vary from this, so be sure to ask.

Duvet Cover

Duvet covers are a little different from bedspreads and coverlets because they take their size from the duvet/comforter they will cover. Table 14.3 shows generic comforter sizes; however, these sizes can vary greatly depending on which company the comforter or duvet is purchased from. Some companies make extra-long and oversized styles. The overall size of the duvet/comforter bedcovering can be larger than the actual duvet/comforter because of cording, flanges, or ruffles added to the outside edge to extend the dimension. If adding a flange, consider padding it lightly so that it has the padded look of the overall

Twin	68 in. × 86 in.
Full	86 in. × 86 in.
Queen	86 in. × 86 in.
King	100 in. × 90 in.
There are many different variations of these sizes. Look at different companies to find specific sizes available.	

Table 14.3 Generic Comforter Sizes

duvet. Ties or snaps can be sewn to the inside foot corners of the duvet cover, with corresponding ties or tabs sewn to the foot corners of the duvet/comforter. This will take a minimal amount of fabric and can be made from lining or scraps.

Step 1: Determine cut width.

Width of duvet/comforter:	_____	in.
Add seam allowance:	+ 2	in.
Total cut width:	_____	in.

Step 2: Determine total widths.

Cut width from Step 1:	_____	in.
Divide by width of fabric:	÷ _____	in.
Total widths:	_____	widths

If the duvet is self-lined, multiply by 2. Don't forget to calculate for fabric on the back side if it has a repeat.

Round up to whole number:	_____	total widths

Step 3: Determine length.

Length of duvet/comforter:	_____	in.
Add for closure:	+ 6	in.

The closure may be buttons, Velcro, or fabric ties. Check with workroom for amount needed for closure.

Add seam allowance:	+ 2	in.
Total cut length before repeat:	_____	in.

If the fabric has a repeat:

Take cut length:	_____	in.
Divide by length of repeat:	÷ _____	in.
Total number of repeats:	_____	repeats
Round up to whole number:	_____	full repeats
Multiply by length of repeat:	× _____	in.
Adjusted cut length (ACL):	_____	in.

Step 4: Determine yardage to order.

Cut length or ACL from Step 3:	_____	in.
Multiply by total number of widths from Step 2:	× _____	widths
Total inches:	_____	in.
Divide by 36 to convert inches to yards:	÷ 36	in.
Total yards:	_____	yd.
Round up to nearest ½ yard:	_____	**yd. to be ordered**

Bedskirt

There are many variations to bedskirts. Ruffled and box-pleated bedskirts usually have a 2½ to 3 times fullness factor. A bedskirt that has only four or five pleats will not need a fullness factor, but the pleats must be factored into the overall width. The variation will occur in Step 2 of the worksheet. The bedskirt decking also takes fabric. While a full-sized flat sheet can be used for king decking and a twin-sized flat sheet can be used for decking for the other mattress sizes, many times your workroom uses lining that you stock with them. Table 14.4 shows yardage totals needed for bedskirt decking for standard-sized beds.

	Yardage*
Twin	2½ yards
Full	2½ yard
Queen	3½ yards seamed horizontally or 4½ yards seamed vertically
King	4½ yards
Based on 54 in. wide fabric.	

Table 14.4 Bedskirt Deck Yardage Chart

Step 1: Determine perimeter of bedskirt.

Width of box spring:	_____	in.
Add length of box spring:	+ _____	in.
Second length of box spring:	+ _____	in.
Total perimeter of skirt:	_____	in.

Step 2: Determine total widths.

For gathered and box pleated bedskirt:

Total perimeter from Step 1:	_____	in.
Multiply for fullness:	× 2.5	fullness

Note: Depending on the fabric and desired look, this could be more or less fullness.

Total:	_____	in.
Divide by width of fabric:	÷ _____	in.
Widths of fabric:	_____	widths
Round up to whole number:	_____	total widths needed

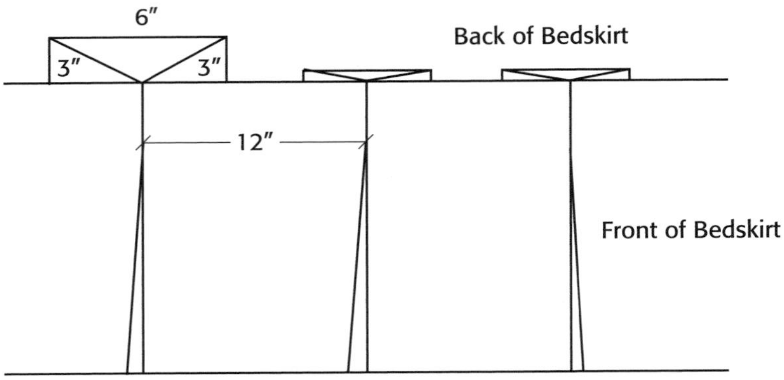

6"

3" **3"**

Back of Bedskirt

⊢—— 12" ——⊣

Front of Bedskirt

Figure 14.17 "Pleat" depth refers to how far back the fabric goes behind the pleat. Fabric behind the pleat will extend from the pleat in both directions the same amount of inches. If the pleat depth is 3 inches, multiply 3 inches × 4 sides to the pleat = 12 inches. Twelve inches is necessary to cover a 3-inch pleat. Often box-pleated bedskirts take the same amount of fabric as gathered bedskirts.

3" × 4" = 12"

12" Fabric needed for 3" pleat

For relaxed pleat bedskirt:

Depth of pleat: _____ in.

The depth of the pleat is how far back you want the pleat to be from the pleat opening. It is common for interior designers to use a 2-inch to 4-inch pleat depth.

Multiply by 4: × 4 _____

To understand how much fabric is actually used, multiply the desired pleat depth by 4 to allow for both sides of pleat (Figure 14.17). If there is to be a space between the edges of the pleat, you must add this dimension to the total after multiplying by 4.

Total fabric per pleat: _____ in.
Multiply by number of pleats: × _____ pleats

In this case, count how many pleats will be used. It is common with this style to have one pleat in the center of each side and at each foot corner. This is a total of 5 pleats.

Total: _____ in.
Add total perimeter from Step 1: + _____ in.
Total: _____ in.
Divide by width of fabric: ÷ _____ in.
Widths of fabric: _____ widths
Round up to whole number: _____ total widths needed

Step 3: Determine length.

Drop from box spring to floor: _____ in.

The drop used on the worksheet must already have ¼ inch to ½ inch deducted from the actual drop if the bedskirt is not to drag on the floor.

Add top hem: + 2 _____ in.
Top banding, if used (6 in.): + _____ in.

Note: The banding is sewn to the decking and lies horizontally on top of the box spring. This keeps the color of the decking from showing if the bedskirt shifts. If using a banding around the decking, add an additional 6 inches. This will actually be cut from the length of fabric, as the banding is created and then sewn to the decking before the skirt is sewn to it.

Add bottom hem: + _____ in.

- For shirt-tail hem add 1.5 inches.
- For double 2-inch hem add 4 inches.

Total cut length: _____ in.

If the fabric has a repeat:

Take cut length from above: _____ in.

Divide by length of repeat: ÷ _____ in.

Total number of repeats: _____ repeats

Round up to whole number: _____ full repeats

Multiply by the length of repeat: × _____ in.

Adjusted cut length (ACL): _____ in.

Step 4: Determine yardage to order.

Take length from Step 3: _____ in.

Multiply by widths from Step 2: × _____ widths

Total: _____ in.

Divide by 36 to convert inches to yards: ÷ 36 in.

Total yards: _____ yd.

Round up to nearest ½ yard: _____ **yd. needed to order**

INSIGHT FROM THE FIELD

❝The original purpose of a duvet was to cover the comforter and be taken off to wash. Today duvets are folded at the end of the bed to provide a luxurious look. A larger 4-foot-wide bed scarf, folded over, can give the same look as a folded duvet, but without the cost of a full duvet. Since less fabric is used this can be a way to save money or potentially to use more flashy, expensive fabric without breaking the budget.❞

Dan Edinger, *Project Manager at Ethan Allen in Austin, Texas*

Bedscarf

Bedscarves lie along the bottom width of the bed. The two most common sizes are 21 inches long to 26 inches long. Sometimes they are doubled so that they can be folded at the bottom. The scarf is usually the width of the bed plus a 12-inch drop to each side (a total of 24 inches). Since these are custom-made, they can be constructed to any dimension desired. Sometimes these are quilted. This will add more expense and take up a little more fabric because of the quilting.

Step 1: Determine finished width and cut width of bedscarf.

Width of bed:	_____	in.
Add drop:	+ _____	in.
Add second drop:	+ _____	in.
Total finished width:	_____	in.
Add hems/seam allowance:	+ 2	in.
Total cut width:	_____	in.

Step 2: Determine number of widths to use.

Cut width from Step 1:	_____	in.
Divide by width of fabric:	÷ _____	in.
Total widths:	_____	widths
Round up to whole number:	_____	full widths
Multiply by number of scarf sides:	× _____	scarves/scarf sides
Total number of widths:	_____	widths

Step 3: Determine finished length and cut length.

Finished length of bedscarf (commonly 21 to 26 in.):	_____	in.
Add hems/seam allowance:	+ 2	in.
Total cut length:	_____	in.

If the fabric has a vertical repeat:

Take cut length from above:	_____	in.
Divide by length of repeat:	÷ _____	in.
Total number of repeats:	_____	repeats
Round up to whole number:	_____	full repeats
Multiply by length of repeat:	× _____	in.
Adjusted cut length (ACL):	_____	in.

Step 4: Determine yardage to order.

Cut length or adjusted cut length from Step 3:	_____	in.
Multiply by total number of widths from Step 2:	× _____	widths
Total inches:	_____	in.
Divide by 36 to convert inches to yards:	÷ 36	in.
Total yards:	_____	yd.
Round up to nearest ½ yard:	_____	**yd. needed to order**

Shams

Shams are calculated in the exact same way as throw pillows. Usually a whole width is needed per sham. Shams are often finished with cording, ruffles, or flanges. Additional fabric will need to be calculated for this.

Step 1: Determine cut width of pillow.

Width of pillow:		in.
Add 2 inches for seam allowance:	+ 2	in.
Total cut width:		in.

If there is a horizontal repeat, determine adjusted cut width:

Total cut width from Step 1:		in.
Divide by horizontal repeat of fabric:	÷	in.
Total number of repeats:		repeats
Round up to whole number:		full repeats
Multiply by horizontal repeat:	×	in.
Total adjusted cut width:		in.

Step 2: Determine number of cuts from width of fabric.

Width of fabric:		in.
Divide by total from Step 1:	÷	in.
Total number of cuts or sides:		cuts or sides
Round down to nearest whole number:		total cuts/sides per width

Step 3: Determine cut length of pillow.

Length of pillow:		in.
Add 2 inches for seam allowance:	+ 2	in.
Total cut length:		in.

If there is a vertical repeat, determine adjusted cut length:

Total from Step 3:		in.
Divide by vertical repeat:	÷	in.
Total number of repeats:		repeats
Round up to whole number:		full repeats
Multiply by vertical repeat:	×	in.
Total adjusted cut length (ACL):		in.

Step 4: Determine number of widths.

Number of pillows:		pillows
Multiply by number of sides (pillow faces):	×	sides

Note: If the front and back of the pillow are the same, this requires 2 faces per pillow.

Total number of pillow faces:		pillow faces
Divide by cuts per width:	÷	cuts per width
Total number of widths:		widths
Round up to whole number:		full widths

Step 5: Determine yardage to order.

Cut length or adjusted cut length from Step 3:		in.
Multiply by number of widths from Step 4:	×	widths
Total:		in.
Divide by 36 to convert inches to yards:	÷ 36	in.
Total yards:		yd.
Round up to nearest ½ yard:		**yd. needed to order**

Flanges and Ruffles

Flanges and ruffles are commonly added to the edges of pillows and duvet covers. Sometimes flanges are padded lightly with batting so they maintain a shape. The length of the flange or ruffle is doubled because the fabric creates the finished back side (Figure 14.18). The perimeter may include three sides as in the case of a duvet cover, or it may include four sides as found in a pillow sham.

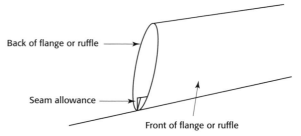

Figure 14.18 Since the back of a flange or ruffle is seen, the face fabric wraps to the back of the flange or ruffle.

Step 1: Determine perimeter.

Finished dimension side A:	_____	in.
Add finished dimension side B:	+ _____	in.
Add finished dimension side C:	+ _____	in.
Add finished dimension side D:	+ _____	in.

Note: If this is being calculated for a duvet cover, there will be only three sides to consider.

Total perimeter:	_____	in.

Step 2: Determine number of widths.

A. Flange

Total from Step 1:	_____	in.
Add 4 inches for each corner:	+ _____	in.

As the flange comes around the corner, slight tucks need to be made so that it lies properly. If the flange is to be more tailored, it may be sewn with a miter at the corners. When the corners are mitered, 2 inches will be needed per corner. This is something to discuss with your workroom.

Total:	_____	in.
Multiply by quantity of items/products:	× _____	quantity
Total:	_____	in.
Divide by fabric width:	÷ _____	in.
Total widths:	_____	widths
Round up to whole number:	_____	full widths

B. Ruffle

Total from Step 1:	_____	in.
Multiply for fullness (2 to 3 times):	× _____	fullness
Total:	_____	in.
Multiply by quantity of items/products:	× _____	quantity
Total:	_____	in.
Divide by fabric width:	÷ _____	in.
Total widths:	_____	widths
Round up to whole number:	_____	full widths

Step 3: Determine length.

Length of flange or ruffle:	×	2	in.

The back of the flange or the ruffle requires fabric.

Add 2 inches for seam allowance:	+	2	in.
Total cut length:			in.

If there is a vertical repeat, determine adjusted cut length:

Total cut length:			in.
Divide by vertical repeat:	÷		in.
Total number of repeats:			repeats
Round up to whole number:			full repeats
Multiply by vertical repeat:	×		in.
Total adjusted cut length (ACL):			in.

Step 4: Determine yardage to order.

Cut length or adjusted cut length from Step 3:			in.
Multiply by number of widths from Step 2:	×		widths
Total:			in.
Divide by 36 to convert inches to yards:	÷	36	in.
Total yards:			yd.
Round up to nearest ½ yard:			yd. needed to order

Step-by-Step Examples

Example 1—Coverlet

Your client wants a coverlet made for the queen sleigh bed in her guest room (Figure 14.19). She prefers a pillow tuck and an 8-ounce fill weight for a 6-inch block quilt pattern. The specifications are as follows:

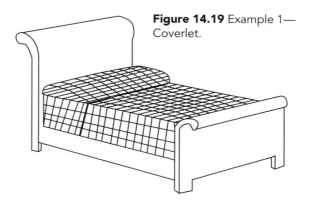

Figure 14.19 Example 1—Coverlet.

- 54-inch-wide fabric with 18-inch pattern repeat
- Bed—60 inches wide × 79¾ inches long
- 16-inch drop will be used
- 10 percent quilting allowance

Step 1: Determine finished width and cut width.

Width of bed:		60	in.
Add drop:	+	16	in.
Add second drop:	+	16	in.
Total finished width:		92	in.
Add hems (2 in. each side):	+	4	in. (2 sides)
Total:		96	in.
Add quilting allowance (10 to 15 percent):	×	1.10	(multiply by 1.10 to 1.15)
Total cut width:		105.6	in.

Step 2: Determine number of widths to use.

Cut width from Step 1:	105.6	in.
Divide by width of fabric:	÷ 54	in.
Total widths:	1.96	widths
Round up to whole number:	2	full widths

Step 3: Determine finished length and cut length.

Length of bed:	79.75	in.
Add drop:	+ 16	in.
Add pillow tuck if applicable (24 in. is plenty):	+ 24	in.
Total finished length:	119.75	in.
Add hems (2 in. each end):	+ 4	in.
Total:	123.75	in.
Add quilting allowance (10 to 15 percent)	× 1.10	(multiply by 1.10 to 1.15)
Total cut length before repeat:	136.13	in.

If the fabric has a repeat:

Take cut length from Step 3:	136.13	in.
Divide by length of repeat:	÷ 18	in.
Total number of repeats:	7.56	repeats
Round up to whole number:	8	full repeats
Multiply by length of repeat	× 18	in.
New adjusted cut length (ACL):	144	in.

Step 4: Determine yardage to order.

Adjusted cut length from Step 3:	144	in.
Multiply by total number of widths from Step 2:	× 2	widths
Total inches:	288	in.
Divide by 36 to convert inches to yards:	÷ 36	in.
Total yards:	8	yd. needed to order

Finished dimension of the coverlet: 92 inches × 119.75 inches

Widths required: 2 widths

Adjusted cut length of each width: 144 inches adjusted cut length

Yards to be ordered: 8 yards

Example 2—Duvet Cover

A duvet cover is needed for a down comforter to "finish" the desired look for the master bedroom bed (Figure 14.20). The cover will be reversible and will use two different fabrics. The specifications are as follows:

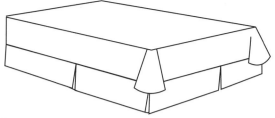

Figure 14.20 Example 2—Duvet cover.

- Fabric A is 54 inches wide with a 6-inch repeat
- Fabric B is 54 inches wide with a 27-inch repeat
- Queen-sized comforter—92 inches wide × 98 inches long

Step 1: Determine cut width.

Width of duvet/comforter:	92	in.
Add seam allowance:	+ 2	in.
Total cut width:	94	in.

Step 2: Determine total widths.

Cut width from Step 1:	94	in.
Divide by width of fabric:	÷ 54	in.
Total widths:	1.7	widths
Round up to whole number:	2	full widths

Step 3: Determine length.

Length of duvet/comforter:	98	in.
Add for closure:	+ 6	in.
Add seam allowance:	+ 2	in.
Total cut length before repeat:	106	in.

If the fabric has a repeat: Fabric A

Take cut length:	106	in.
Divide by length of repeat:	÷ 6	in.
Total number of repeats:	17.67	repeats
Round up to whole number:	18	full repeats
Multiply by length of repeat:	× 6	in.
Adjusted cut length (ACL):	108	in.

Step 4: Determine yardage to order.

Cut or adjusted length from Step 3:	108	in.
Multiply by total number of widths from Step 2:	× 2	widths
Total inches:	216	in.
Divide by 36 to convert inches to yards:	÷ 36	in.
Total yards:	6	yd.

If the fabric has a repeat: **Fabric B**

Take cut length:	106	in.
Divide by length of repeat:	÷ 27	in.
Total number of repeats:	3.93	repeats
Round up to whole number:	4	full repeats
Multiply by length of repeat:	× 27	in.
Adjusted cut length (ACL):	108	in.

Step 4: Determine yardage to order.

Cut or adjusted length from Step 3:	108	in.
Multiply by total number of widths from Step 2:	× 2	widths
Total inches:	216	in.
Divide by 36 to convert inches to yards:	÷ 36	in.
Total yards:	6	**yd. to be ordered**

Widths needed per side: 2 widths

Adjusted cut length for both Fabric A and B: 108 inches. Do not count on the adjusted cut length of two different fabrics with different repeats being the same. It can happen, but it does not always happen.

Yards to be ordered: Fabrics A and B: 6 yards each.

Example 3—Bedscarf

Your client wants to add a self-lined bedscarf for the end of her king-sized bed (Figure 14.21). The specifications are as follows:

Figure 14.21 Example 3—Bedscarf.

- Fabric is 54-inch-wide stripe with no vertical repeat.
- Bed—80 inches wide.
- Drop—15 inches.
- Scarf width—25 inches.

Step 1: Determine finished width and cut width of bedscarf.

Width of bed:	80	in.
Add drop:	+ 15	in.
Add second drop:	+ 15	in.
Total finished width:	110	in.
Add hems/seam allowance:	+ 2	in.
Total cut width:	112	in.

Step 2: Determine number of widths to use.

Cut width from Step 1:		112	in.
Divide by width of fabric:	÷	54	in.
Total widths:		2.07	widths
Round up to whole number:		3	full widths
Multiply by number of scarf sides:	×	2	scarves/scarf sides
Total number of widths:		6	widths

Step 3: Determine finished length and cut length.

Length of bedscarf (commonly 21 to 26 in.):		25	in.
Add hems/seam allowance:	+	2	in.
Total cut length:		27	in.

There is no vertical repeat:

Step 4: Determine yardage to order.

Cut length or adjusted cut length from Step 3:		27	in.
Multiply by total number of widths from Step 2:	×	6	widths
Total inches:		162	in.
Divide by 36 to convert inches to yards:	÷	36	in.
Total yards:		4.5	yd.
Round up to nearest ½ yard:		**4.5**	**yd. needed to order**

Finished width of the scarf: 110 inches

Cut length of the scarf: 27 inches

Yards to be ordered: 4.5 yards

Example 4—Sham with Flange

Two queen-sized shams with flanges will be made to coordinate with the coverlet from Example 1 (Figure 14.22). The fabric is the same as the coverlet. The specifications are as follows:

- Fabric—54 inches with an 18-inch pattern repeat
- Pillows—20 inches deep × 30 inches wide
- Flange—3 inches

Figure 14.22 Example 4—Sham with flange.

Calculate pillow sham:

Step 1: Determine cut width of pillow.

Width of pillow:		30	in.
Add 2 inches for seam allowance:	+	2	in.
Total cut width:		32	in.

If there is a horizontal repeat, determine adjusted cut width.

There is no horizontal repeat.

Step 2: Determine number of cuts from width of fabric.

Width of fabric:	54	in.
Divide by total from Step 1:	÷ 32	in.
Total number of cuts per width:	1.69	cuts per width
Round down to nearest whole number:	1	total cut per width

Step 3: Determine cut length of pillow.

Length of pillow:	20	in.
Add 2 inches for seam allowance:	+ 2	in.
Total cut length:	22	in.

If there is a vertical repeat, determine adjusted cut length:

Total from Step 3:	22	in.
Divide by vertical repeat:	÷ 18	in.
Total number of repeats:	1.22	repeats
Round up to whole number:	2	full repeats
Multiply by vertical repeat:	× 18	in.
Total adjusted cut length (ACL):	36	in.

Step 4: Determine number of widths.

Number of pillows:	2	pillows
Multiply by number of sides (pillow faces):	× 2	sides
Total number of pillow faces:	4	pillow faces
Divide by cuts per width or adjusted cuts per width:	÷ 1	cuts per width
Total widths:	4	widths

Step 5. Calculate yardage to order.

Cut length or adjusted cut length from Step 3:	36	in.
Multiply by number of widths from Step 4:	× 4	widths
Total:	144	in.
Divide by 36 to convert inches to yards:	÷ 36	in.
Total yards:	4	**yd. to be ordered**

Calculate flange:

Step 1: Determine perimeter.

Finished dimension side A:	20	in.
Add finished dimension side B:	+ 20	in.
Add finished dimension side C:	+ 30	in.
Add finished dimension side D:	+ 30	in.
Total perimeter:	100	in.

Step 2: Determine widths.

Flange

Total from Step 1:	100	in.
Add 4 inches for each corner (4 corners × 4):	+ 16	in.
Total:	116	in.
Multiply by quantity of items/products:	× 2	shams
Total:	232	in.
Divide by fabric width:	÷ 54	in.
Total widths:	4.3	widths
Round up to whole number:	5	full widths

Step 3: Determine length.

Length of flange or ruffle × 2 (3 in. × 2):	6	in.

The back of the flange of the ruffle requires fabric.

Add 2 inches for seam allowance:	+ 2	in.
Total cut length:	8	in.

If there is a vertical repeat, determine adjusted cut length:

Total cut length:	8	in.
Divide by vertical repeat:	÷ 18	in.
Total number of repeats:	.44	repeats
Round up to whole number:	1	full repeats
Multiply by vertical repeat:	× 18	in.
Total adjusted cut length (ACL):	18	in.

Step 4: Calculate yardage to order.

Cut length or adjusted cut length from Step 3:	18	in.
Multiply by number of widths from Step 2:	× 5	widths
Total:	90	in.
Divide by 36 to convert inches to yards:	÷ 36	in.
Total yards:	**2.5**	**yd. to be ordered**

Pillow faces from one width: 1 side per width

Adjusted cut length of pillow face: 36 inches

Widths required for flange: 5 widths

Adjusted cut length of flange: 18 inches

Yards needed for the pillow sham including flange: 2½ yards

Manual Worksheets

Bedspread and Coverlet Worksheet

Step 1: Determine finished width and cut width.

Width of bed:	_____	in.
Add drop: +	_____	in.

Note: The drop used in the calculation must already have ¼ inch to ½ inch deducted from the actual drop if the bedspread/coverlet is not to drag on the ground.

Add second drop: +	_____	in.
Total finished width:	_____	in.
Add hems (2 in. each side): +	4	in. (2 sides)
Total:	_____	in.
Add quilting allowance (10 to 15 percent): ×	_____	(multiply by 1.10 to 1.15)
Total cut width:	_____	in.

Step 2: Determine number of widths to use.

Cut width from Step 1:	_____	in.
Divide by width of fabric: ÷	_____	in.
Total widths:	_____	widths
Round up to whole number:	_____	full widths

Step 3: Determine finished length and cut length.

Length of bed:	_____	in.
Add drop: +	_____	in.
Add pillow tuck if applicable (24 in. is plenty): +	24	in.
Total finished length:	_____	in.
Add hems (2 in. each end): +	4	in.
Total:	_____	in.
Add quilting allowance (10 to 15 percent): ×	_____	(multiply by 1.10 to 1.15)
Total cut length before repeat:	_____	in.

If the fabric has a repeat:

Take cut length from above:	_____	in.
Divide by length of repeat: ÷	_____	in.
Total:	_____	repeats
Round up to whole number:	_____	full repeats
Multiply by length of repeat: ×	_____	in.
Adjusted cut length (ACL):	_____	in.

Step 4: Determine yardage to order.

Cut length or adjusted cut length (ACL) from Step 3:	_____	in.
Multiply by total number of widths from Step 2: ×	_____	widths
Total inches:	_____	in.
Divide by 36 to convert inches to yards: ÷	36	in.
Total yards:	_____	yd.
Round up to nearest ½ yard:	_____	yd. needed to order

Duvet Cover Worksheet

Step 1: Determine cut width.

Width of duvet/comforter:		in.
Add seam allowance: +	2	in.
Total cut width:		**in.**

Step 2: Determine total widths.

Cut width from Step 1:		in.
Divide by width of fabric: ÷		in.
Widths:		**widths**
For same fabric both sides, multiply by 2: ×	2	sides
Total widths:		**widths**
Round up to whole number:		**full widths**

Step 3: Determine length.

Length of duvet/comforter:		in.
Add for closure: +	6	in.
Add seam allowance: +	2	in.
Total cut length before repeat:		**in.**

If the fabric has a repeat:

Take cut length from above:		in.
Divide by length of repeat: ÷		in.
Total number of repeats:		**repeats**
Round up to whole number:		**full repeats**
Multiply by length of repeat: ×		in.
Adjusted cut length (ACL):		**in.**

Step 4: Determine yardage to order.

Cut length or adjusted cut length (ACL) from Step 3:		in.
Multiply by total number of widths from Step 2: ×		widths
Total inches:		**in.**
Divide by 36 to convert inches to yards: ÷	36	in.
Total yards:		**yd.**
Round up to nearest ½ yard:		**yd. needed to order**

Note: Sometimes the duvet must cover more area than the comforter allows. In these instances, flanges (possibly padded) and ruffles can be added to the sides.

Bedskirt Worksheet

Step 1: Find perimeter of bedskirt.

Width of box spring:	_____	in.
Add length of box spring: +	_____	in.
Second length of box spring: +	_____	in.
Total perimeter of skirt:	_____	**in.**

Step 2: Determine total widths.

For gathered and box-pleated bedskirt:

Total perimeter from Step 1:	_____	in.
Multiply for fullness: ×	2.5	fullness

Note: Depending on the fabric and style, this could be more or less fullness.

Total:	_____	**in.**
Divide by width of fabric: ÷	_____	in.
Total widths of fabric:	_____	**widths**
Round up to whole number:	_____	**full widths**

For relaxed pleat bedskirt:

Depth of pleat:	_____	in.
Multiply by 4: ×	4	in.
Total needed for pleat:	_____	**in.**
Multiply by number of pleats: ×	_____	pleats
Total:	_____	**in.**
Add total perimeter from Step 1: +	_____	in.
Total:	_____	**in.**
Divide by width of fabric: ÷	_____	in.
Total widths of fabric:	_____	**widths**
Round up to whole number:	_____	**full widths**

Step 3: Determine cut length.

Drop from box spring to floor:	_____	in.
Add top hem: +	2	in.
Optional top banding (6 in.): +	_____	in.
Add bottom hem: +	_____	in.

- For shirt-tail hem, add 1.5 inches.
- For double 2-inch hem, add 4 inches.

Total cut length:	_____	**in.**

If the fabric has a repeat:

Take cut length from above:	_____	in.
Divide by length of repeat: ÷	_____	in.
Total number of repeats:	_____	**repeats**
Round up to whole number:	_____	**full repeats**
Multiply by the length of repeat: ×	_____	in.
Adjusted cut length (ACL):	_____	**in.**

Step 4: Determine yardage to order.

Cut length or adjusted cut length (ACL) from Step 3:	_____	in.
Multiply by widths from Step 2: ×	_____	widths
Total inches:	_____	**in.**
Divide by 36 to convert inches to yards: ÷	36	in.
Total yards:	_____	**yd.**
Round up to nearest ½ yard:	_____	**yd. needed to order**

Bedscarf Worksheet

Step 1: Determine finished width and cut width of bedscarf.

Width of bed:	_____	in.
Add drop: +	_____	in.
Add second drop: +	_____	in.
Total finished width:	_____	**in.**
Add hems/seam allowance: +	2	in.
Total cut width:	_____	**in.**

Step 2: Determine number of widths to use.

Cut width from Step 1:	_____	in.
Divide by width of fabric: ÷	_____	in.
Total widths:	_____	**widths**
Round up to whole number:	_____	**full widths**
Multiply by number of scarf sides: ×	_____	scarves/scarf sides
Total number of widths:	_____	**widths**

Step 3: Determine finished length and cut length.

Finished length of bedscarf (commonly 21 to 26 in.):	_____	in.
Add hems/seam allowance: +	2	in.
Total cut length:	_____	**in.**

If the fabric has a vertical repeat:

Take cut length from above:	_____	in.
Divide by length of repeat: ÷	_____	in.
Total number of repeats:	_____	**repeats**
Round up to whole number:	_____	**full repeats**
Multiply by length of repeat: ×	_____	in.
Adjusted cut length (ACL):	_____	**in.**

Step 4: Determine yardage to order.

Cut length or adjusted cut length (ACL) from Step 3:	_____	in.
Multiply by total number of widths from Step 2: ×	_____	widths
Total inches:	_____	**in.**
Divide by 36 to convert inches to yards: ÷	36	in.
Total yards:	_____	**yd.**
Round up to nearest ½ yard:	_____	**yd. needed to order**

Sham Worksheet

Step 1: Determine cut width of pillow.

Width of pillow:	_____	in.
Add 2 inches for seam allowance: +	2	in.
Total cut width:	_____	**in.**

If there is a horizontal repeat, determine adjusted cut width:

Total cut width from Step 1:	_____	in.
Divide by horizontal repeat of fabric: ÷	_____	in.
Total number of repeats:	_____	**repeats**
Round up to whole number:	_____	**full repeats**
Multiply by horizontal repeat ×	_____	in.
Total adjusted cut width:	_____	**in.**

Step 2: Determine number of cuts from width of fabric.

Width of fabric:	_____	in.
Divide by total cut width or adjusted cut width from Step 1: ÷	_____	in.
Total number of cuts or sides:	_____	**cuts or sides**
Round down to nearest whole number:	_____	**total cuts/sides per width**

Step 3: Determine cut length of pillow.

Length of pillow	_____	in.
Add 2 inches for seam allowance +	2	in.
Total cut length:	_____	**in.**

If there is a vertical repeat, determine adjusted cut length:

Total cut length from above:	_____	in.
Divide by vertical repeat: ÷	_____	in.
Total number of repeats:	_____	**repeats**
Round up to whole number:	_____	**full repeats**
Multiply by vertical repeat: ×	_____	in.
Total adjusted cut length (ACL):	_____	**in.**

Step 4: Determine number of widths.

Number of pillows:	_____	pillows
Multiply by number of pillow faces: ×	_____	pillow faces
Total:	_____	**pillow faces**

Note: If the front and back of the pillow are the same, this requires 2 faces per pillow.

Divide by cuts per width: ÷	_____	cuts per width
Total widths needed:	_____	**widths**
Round up to nearest whole number:	_____	**full widths**

Step 5: Determine yardage to order.

Cut length or ACL from Step 3:	_____	in.
Multiply by number of widths from Step 4: ×	_____	widths
Total:	_____	**in.**
Divide by 36 to convert inches to yards: ÷	36	in.
Total yards:	_____	**yd.**
Round up to nearest ½ yard:	_____	**yd. needed to order**

Flange and Ruffle Worksheet

Step 1: Determine perimeter

Finished dimension side A:	_____	in.
Add finished dimension side B: +	_____	in.
Add finished dimension side C: +	_____	in.
Add finished dimension side D: +	_____	in. (if applicable)
Total finished perimeter:	_____	**in.**

Step 2: Determine number of widths.

Flange:

Total finished perimeter from Step 1:	_____	in.
Add 4 inches for each corner: +	_____	in.
Total:	_____	**in.**
Multiply by quantity of items/products: ×	_____	quantity
Total:	_____	**in.**
Divide by fabric width: ÷	_____	in.
Total widths:	_____	**widths**
Round up to whole number:	_____	**full widths**

Ruffle:

Total finished perimeter from Step 1:	_____	in.
Multiply for fullness (× 2 to 3): ×	_____	fullness
Total:	_____	**in.**
Multiply by quantity of items/products: ×	_____	quantity
Total:	_____	**in.**
Divide by fabric width: ÷	_____	in.
Total widths:	_____	**widths**
Round up to whole number:	_____	**full widths**

Step 3: Determine length.

Length of flange or ruffle: ×	2	in.
Add 2 inches for seam allowance: +	2	in.
Total cut length:	_____	**in.**

If there is a vertical repeat, determine adjusted cut length:

Total cut length from above:	_____	in.
Divide by vertical repeat: ÷	_____	in.
Total number of repeats:	_____	**repeats**
Round up to whole number:	_____	**full repeats**
Multiply by vertical repeat: ×	_____	in.
Total adjusted cut length (ACL):	_____	**in.**

Step 4: Determine yardage to order.

Cut length or ACL from Step 3:	_____	in.
Multiply by number of widths from Step 2: ×	_____	widths
Total inches:	_____	**in.**
Divide by 36 to convert inches to yards: ÷	36	in.
Total yards:	_____	**yd.**
Round up to nearest ½ yard:	_____	**yd. needed to order**

Practice Lessons: Bedding

BASIC
Bedspread

You are making a quilted bedspread with a pillow tuck for a client's queen-sized bed. It has an 8-ounce fill with an outline quilt pattern (Figure 14.23). The specifications are as follows:

- Fabric—54 inches wide with a 27-inch repeat
- Bed—60 inches wide × 80 inches long
- Drop—24 inches after allowance
- Quilting allowance—15 percent

1. Draw a seaming diagram
2. What is the cut width?
3. How many widths are needed?

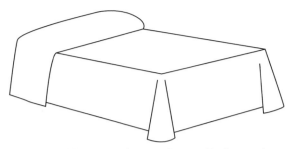

Figure 14.23 Practice lesson: Basic—Bedspread.

4. What is the adjusted cut length?
5. How many yards must be ordered?

Bedscarf

You will make a reversible bedscarf for the foot of the previous bed (Figure 14.24). The specifications are as follows:

- Fabric—54 inches wide with no repeat
- Scarf—24 inches wide
- Bed—60 inches wide
- Drop—12 inches

1. What is the finished width?
2. What is the cut length?
3. How many yards must be ordered?

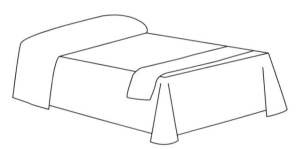

Figure 14.24 Practice lesson: Basic—Bedscarf.

INTERMEDIATE
Coverlet

Your client wants a quilted coverlet for a king-size bed (Figure 14.25). There is no pillow tuck. It is an outline quilt pattern with 8-ounce fill. The specifications are as follows:

- Fabric—54 inches wide with a 21-inch repeat
- Bed—75½ inches wide × 79½ inches long
- Drop—17 inches
- Quilting allowance—15 percent

1. How many widths of fabric are used?
2. Draw a seaming diagram.

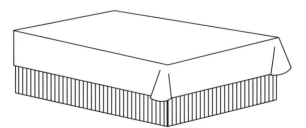

Figure 14.25 Practice lesson: Intermediate—Coverlet.

3. What is the adjusted cut length?
4. How many yards must be ordered?

Gathered Bedskirt

It is decided that a gathered bedskirt will be used for the king-size bed in the previous practice lesson (Figure 14.26). Banding will be used around the decking. The specifications are as follows:

- Fabric—54-inch-wide floral with a 15-inch repeat.
- Box spring—75 inches wide × 79¼ inches long.
- Drop—15 inches after allowance.
- Hem—Double 2 inch
- 2½ times fullness will be used.

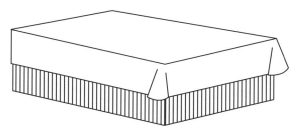

Figure 14.26 Practice lesson: Intermediate— Gathered bedskirt.

1. How many widths will be used?
2. What is the adjusted cut length?
3. How many yards must be ordered?
4. How many yards must be ordered for the decking (refer to Table 14.4)?

ADVANCED
Duvet Cover

You are making a reversible duvet cover in the same fabric on both sides for a teenage girl's bedroom (Figure 14.27). Make sure the duvet cover is long enough to extend past the mattress and box spring seam by 3 inches. Otherwise you need to attach a flange. The specifications are as follows:

- Fabric is 54-inch-wide floral with 30-inch repeat
- Down comforter—92 inches × 98 inches
- Bed—60 inches × 80 inches
- Drop to seam—12 inches

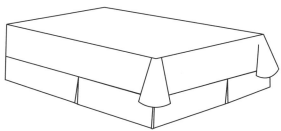

Figure 14.27 Practice lesson: Advanced—Duvet cover.

1. Does the comforter extend past the seam by 3 inches?
2. How many total widths are needed?
3. What is the adjusted cut length?
4. How many yards must be ordered?

Bedskirt with Relaxed Pleat

A bedskirt with a relaxed pleat will be made for the queen-size bed in the previous practice lesson (Figure 14.28). A banding will be used around the deck to disguise any shifting by the bedskirt. Specifications are as follows:

- Fabric—54 inches wide with 4-inch repeat
- Box spring—59½ inches wide × 79½ inches long
- Drop—14 inches after allowance
- Hem—Double 2 inch
- Number of pleats—5 pleats
- Pleat depth—3 inches

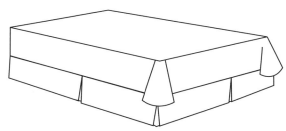

Figure 14.28 Practice lesson: Advanced—Bedskirt with relaxed pleat.

1. How many inches are required per pleat?
2. How many widths of fabric are required?
3. What is the adjusted cut length?
4. How many yards of fabric must be ordered for the bedskirt?
5. How many yards of fabric must be ordered for the decking (refer to Table 14.4)?

Sham with Ruffles

Two queen-sized pillow shams will be made for the teenager's bed (Figure 14.29). The main pillow fabric is solid, and the ruffle matches the bedskirt. The specifications are as follows:

- Fabric A—Pillow body, 54 inches wide, no pattern
- Fabric B—Ruffle, 54 inches wide with a 4-inch repeat
- Pillows—30 inches wide × 20 inches long
- Ruffle—3 inches wide, 2½ times fullness

1. How many pillow faces can be obtained from one width of fabric?
2. What is the cut length of the pillow body?
3. How many widths of fabric are needed for the ruffle for the 2 shams?
4. What is the adjusted cut length of the ruffle?
5. How many yards of fabric are to be ordered for Fabric A pillow body? For Fabric B ruffle?

Pricing for Intermediate Coverlet

Use the fabric quantity found for the intermediate coverlet practice lesson and the prices that follow to calculate pricing for your client. The coverlet is made in another state and will be shipped to your business.

Fabric—$62.00/yard

Fabric shipping—$22.00

Labor charge—$400.00

Coverlet shipping—$38.00

1. What is the price you will quote to your client?

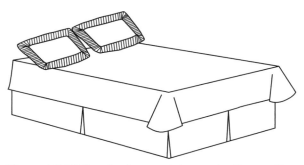

Figure 14.29 Practice lesson: Advanced—Sham with ruffles.

Pricing for Intermediate Gathered Bedskirt

Use the fabric quantity found for the intermediate gathered bedskirt practice lesson and the prices that follow to calculate pricing for your client. The gathered bedskirt is made locally, and you will pick it up from your workroom. The decking for the bedskirt is included in the price from the workroom.

Fabric—$36.00/yard

Fabric shipping—$22.00

Labor charge—$175.00

1. What is the price you will quote to your client?

References

The Company Store website. Accessed December 10, 2012. http://www.thecompanystore.com.

Designer's Express. *Custom Bedding and Upholstery Catalog 1995.*

Kasmir Fabric. *Kasmir Fabric Custom Expressions Book 2012.*

Chapter 15 | New Upholstery

Chapter Outline

Terminology

COL Stands for "customer's own leather." Upholstery manufacturers sometimes have a selection of leathers to choose from for certain frames they make. When none of the manufacturer's leathers are used and another selection is sent to them, this is referred to as COL.

COM Stands for "customer's own material." Upholstery manufacturers usually have a selection of fabrics to choose from for their frames. When none of the manufacturer's fabrics are used and another selection is sent to them, this is referred to as COM.

Cushion The loose backs and loose seats of upholstery. Cushion construction varies from manufacturer to manufacturer, and even within one manufacturer, there will be several selections of cushions based on seating comfort. Most seat cushions start with a foam core or a spring coil that is wrapped with other materials before being encased in the fabric covering. Back cushions are often filled with batting or feathers.

Flaws Holes, heavy slubs, misweaves, or misprints in fabrics that make it unacceptable to use. The fabric must be inspected for flaws before cutting. This fabric must be sent back to the manufacturer for replacement before it is cut.

Frame The basic structure of upholstery that creates the style of the piece. It is padded, wrapped, and upholstered. Most frames are made of wood. In some upholstered pieces, some of the frame is exposed and finished.

Pattern repeat Lengthwise or crosswise measurement of one design motif to where that same pattern is again repeated.

Straight match Repeat matches straight across.

Drop match or half drop Repeat is staggered so that only every other width matches along the same horizontal line. The match runs diagonally (see Figure 3.2 in Chapter 3, "Wallpaper," for an example).

Railroaded fabric The vertical pattern of regular rolled fabric runs up the bolt. The vertical pattern of a railroaded fabric runs side to side, selvage to selvage. A vertical stripe will run horizontally, like railroad tracks, when the fabric is made railroaded (Figure 15.1). Railroaded fabric is ideal for upholstery because it will allow anything over 54 inches wide to be seamless along the back.

Selvage Edge of fabric formed on the loom when the fabric is woven. It is frequently woven tighter than fabric body.

Welt Cording used to finished edges of upholstery, cushions, and pillows. While the majority of upholstered furniture is welted using the same fabric all over (self-welting), it is possible to specify contrast welt when a different material is selected than what is used on the main body of the frame.

Width Single width of fabric sometimes referred to as a cut. Most upholstery fabric is 54 inches wide. Other less common widths of fabric are 36 inches, 45 inches, 48 inches, 60 inches. It is important to check the width of fabric used.

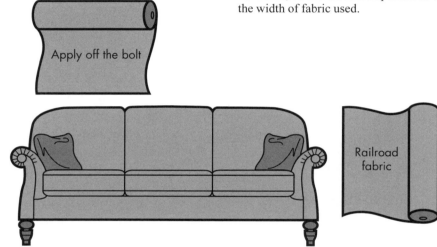

Apply off the bolt

Railroad fabric

Figure 15.1 Railroaded fabric allows a sofa to be upholstered without a seam to the back. With railroaded fabric, the pattern runs selvage to selvage. Regular, non-railroaded fabric runs up the bolt. (Source: Godsey, L. *Interior Design Materials and Specifications*. New York: Fairchild Publications, 2008.)

New Upholstery

New upholstered furniture is generally ordered when clients need seating or desire new styles and fabrics. They may not have existing furniture to use or existing furniture that they want to use. Sometimes the furniture can be found already made in the interior designer's inventory or on a showroom floor, but usually items are ordered customized for the client from a manufacturer. There is a research phase with your client that involves getting a sense of the type of furniture that will best fit the client and the space.

The designer's inventory and furniture showrooms can be used for a client to get a sense of the quality and feel of the furniture line.

The time frame for ordering a piece of new furniture, dependent on availability of the fabric, is usually 8 to 12 weeks before shipping. Shipping can add 1 to 2 weeks to this time frame. Some quality furniture lines have been able to move their production time up to 4 to 6 weeks. Since clients' project time frames will vary, it is important to learn the production times of the furniture lines.

Furniture companies often offer a selection of fabrics to be applied to their frames. It is possible to send fabric yardage to the manufacturer to use on their frames if none of their fabrics are workable for the client. These fabrics are priced by grade levels. Grade levels have nothing to do with the durability of the fabric, but everything to do with the expense and waste involved because of repeat. Two fabrics that cost the same will be priced at different grade levels if one is solid and one has a repeat. If the interior designer is sending the manufacturer his or her own fabric yardage, this is referred to as COM (customer's own material).

If the client wants to use leather, keep in mind that not every frame will accommodate this material. Again, the manufacturer will supply a selection of leather hides to choose from. It is possible to send the manufacturer COL (customer's own leather); however, this isn't sent as yardage, since leather is actually the hide of an animal. Leather hides can range from 50 to 55 square feet and are sold by the square foot in full hides and sometimes half hides. Refer to the leather supplier for the actual square footage amounts for leather hides, since they can vary greatly. Normally, full hides must be purchased. This means that if 75 square feet of leather are needed, 2 full hides, or 110 square feet of leather, must be purchased. There are a few instances whereby the leather supplier will offer ½ hide. It is very important

to be in close communication with the furniture manufacturer if COL or COM is being considered, as the manufacturer will require more yardage or square feet depending on the width of fabric, length/width of repeat, or size of hide.

The manufacturer's representative will be invaluable as you learn the furniture line. The manufacturer's price list is a gold mine of information. In the pages of the price list can be found details of the furniture and cushion construction, options for bases and arms, options for cushions and pillows, various sofa lengths available, COM yardage charts, other options, and the price, depending on the fabric grade (Figure 15.2 on the next page). For COM or COL, the price list includes a page that the designer can fill in with the project specifications, attach a sample or photo of the material, and mail to the manufacturer (Figure 15.3 on the next page). Usually multiple copies are made of this page before it is filled in so that it can be used for other jobs.

Note that while some furniture manufacturers are making the transition to computerize the process, allowing the interior designer to order online, many have not computerized to that extent. Some manufacturers give the designer access to a computer program that will digitally cover the style in the fabric selected so long as the fabric is one of their own selections. This can be invaluable to help the client visualize the piece of furniture in the fabric selected.

Cost Factors

New upholstery can be as simple or complex as needed for the client. A furniture schedule, such as Table 15.1 on page 261, is helpful for the designer to keep track of all the various components. If the fabric selected is the manufacturer's fabric and there are no other modifications, costs include the cost of the furniture piece, the cost of shipping, and costs for receiving and delivering the piece of furniture, even if your company has its own warehouse and

Pearson

Retail Price List

	2323-30	2324-20
	85" Sofa	86" Sofa
Standard Cushion	Loose (F6)	Loose (F6)
Standard Back	Loose (F7)	Loose (F7)
Standard Skirt	n/a	n/a
Skirt Length (inches)	n/a	n/a
Exposed Wood - Finish	Maple - 102	Maple - 102
Cubic Feet	87	96
Weight	200	220
Yards 54" Plain	20	20 3/4
Standard Throw Pillows	(2)20"KEW	(2)20"KEW

Price by Grade

21 (COM)	5475	5754
22-23	5600	5879
24-25 (COL)	5780	6059
26-27	6002	6281
28-29	6224	6503
30-31	6488	6767
32-33	6765	7044
34-35	7057	7336
36-37	7390	7669
38-39	7723	8002
40-41	8097	8376
42-43	8486	8765
44-45	8888	9167
46-47	9332	9611
48-49	9776	10055
50-51	10262	10541
52-53	10761	11040
54-55	11275	11554
56-57	11830	12109
58-59	12385	12664
91 - Leather	8148	9675
92 - Leather	8748	10575
93 - Leather	9348	11475
94 - Leather	9948	12375

Custom Options

Cushions:

F-1 Foam/Fiber	No Charge	No Charge
F-2 Spring/Down	150	150
F-3 25/75 Down	450	450
F-6 Spring/Comfortdown	Standard	Standard
F-9 Spring/Fiber	No Charge	No Charge
F-10 Foam/Comfortdown	No Charge	No Charge
F-16 Comfort Plush	n/a	No Charge

Backs:

F-3 25/75 Down	225	210
F-7 All Comfortdown	Standard	Standard
F-14 Foam/Fiber	No Charge	No Charge

Miscellaneous:

Finishes - Premium	60	60
Finishes - Custom Special	90	90
Optional Skirts	n/a	n/a
Contrast Welt - Fabric	90	90
Casters	n/a	n/a
Swivel	n/a	n/a

Trims:

DC, VC	285	360
FC,LC,EC,SC,PC	420	540
VF	405	390
DF, FF, EF,SF,PF	615	810
LF	1095	1050
VT	n/a	150
BR, WT,EB,PT	n/a	n/a
DTS	n/a	n/a
DB	n/a	n/a
Brass Nails - *small, touching*	240	180
Brass Nails - *large, spaced*	480	360
Brass Nails - *large, touching*	600	450
Brass Nails - *square, touching*	480	360

Figure 15.2 This is part of a Pearson Upholstery price list. Most upholstery price lists will show a thumbnail of the furniture piece, pricing of the piece by fabric grade, dimensions, yardage needed, standard features, upgrades, and add-ons. (© Pearson Company)

Pearson   COM INFORMATION

Please copy this page and send the following information to ensure its proper application to: Pearson Company, 1420 Progress Avenue, High Point, NC 27260

Name: _____

Tag For: _____ Purchase Order Number: _____

Frame style number to which fabric is to be applied: _____

Name of fabric supplier: _____

Fabric name and color: _____

COM country of origin: _____ Price per yard _____

Signature: _____

This information is necessary to comply with NAFTA regulations, and applies to shipments to Canada and Mexico only.

Note: In the absence of specific instructions, Pearson Company reserves the right to use its best judgement concerning the application of your COM. Do not assume that the fabric application is obvious.

Circle the sketch to indicate if pattern will be applied "up the bolt" or "railroad":

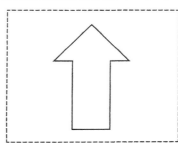

UP THE BOLT   RAILROAD

Special Instructions (e.g. "apply stripe vertically" or "center on the large medallion"): _____
_____
_____
_____

Important: Attach a swatch of the fabric below, indicating the face side and top:

Figure 15.3 COM information sheets are sent to manufacturers when a COM or COL material is used. It gives specific information identifying the material and the specifications regarding the size of fabric and repeat and the direction the pattern will be placed on the furniture. (© Pearson Company)

delivery truck (Table 15.2 on page 262). When a COM or COL is used, additional costs of the material and shipping material to the manufacturer must be included (see Table 15.2).

In addition, there are minimum freight charges to consider. Keep in mind that it can cost the same amount to ship one ottoman as it does a sofa. Large orders that fill over a certain percentage of the truck can affect the rates. The freight rates also vary depending on how the merchandise is packaged. Your ability to successfully make a claim for freight damage may be affected by the chosen method of packaging the merchandise. The more expensive,

Furniture Schedule

Client:

Phone #s:

Address:

Room	Key	Item	Qty.	Mfr./ Vendor	Finish	Fabric														Furn. Cost	Furn. Est. Ship.	Furn. Subtotal (include fabric)	Overall Total	Furn. PO
						Mfr.	Pattern	Color	**Additional COM Information**														
									Width	Repeat	Yds.	Cost Per	Ydg. Cost	Est. Ship.	Subtotal	Fabric PO					

Table 15.1 Furniture Schedule

Using Manufacturer's Fabric/Leather	Using COM/COL
Furniture piece	Furniture piece
Upgrades for cushions/style	Fabric/leather cost
Add-ons for trim, etc.	Shipping material to furniture manufacturer
Shipping from manufacturer to interior designer	Upgrades for cushions/style
Receiving and inspection of furniture	Add-ons for trim, etc.
Delivery of furniture from interior designer to client	Shipping from manufacturer to interior designer
	Receiving and inspection of furniture
	Delivery of furniture from interior designer to client

Table 15.2 New Upholstery Costs

high-end goods will have a lower percentage of shipping costs compared to furniture piece cost. The less expensive, lower-end goods will have a higher percentage of shipping costs compared to furniture piece cost. Shipping runs as high as 40 to 50 percent on lower-priced goods. Because petroleum prices have skyrocketed in recent years, some companies will also add an additional gas surcharge to the shipping costs.

Independent designers will need to arrange and pay for the merchandise to be received at a local warehouse unless they have a space where semi-trucks can deliver. Most trucking companies will not deliver to a residential area. Truck drivers are responsible only for getting the freight to the back of their truck and ready to unload. They are not responsible for unloading it and moving it to the appropriate area. The items will need to be unpacked, inspected, and prepared for delivery. All of these processes add to the cost that the designer must cover when he or she is selling an item to a client.

Delivery to the client's home or office is an additional cost. Some delivery firms charge a flat rate for delivery within a certain geographic region. Others charge a rate for each piece being delivered into the client's home or office.

Calculations

Calculations for new upholstery begin with the manufacturer's price list. When the fabric is the manufacturer's fabric, find the style number of the piece of furniture and follow the grid to the fabric grade level. If there are upgrades to the cushion or add-ons such as contrast throw pillows, trim, and so on, these charges are added to the base price of the furniture. Depending on how the company you work for charges for items, shipping/freight charges may be charged to the client or absorbed by the firm.

When the material is a COM or COL, go to the price list to find the style number, and follow the grid to find the yardage required. This amount will be for a 54-inch-wide fabric with no repeat. Each manufacturer will have a chart showing how much fabric it requires if the fabric is narrower than 54 inches and if there is a repeat (Figure 15.4). These amounts will vary from manufacturer to manufacturer, so be sure to follow the specific manufacturer's request for estimating yardage. Confirm this yardage amount by calling the manufacturer.

Sometimes manufacturers group fabrics in the price list. In Figure 15.5 four fabric grades are grouped together. A fabric grade #37 will be the same price as fabric grade #38 for this manufacturer. At the bottom of the grade levels is a grade riser. A riser is used to calculate the price of furniture for grades above the last one listed. For each grade above the last shown,

Fabric Width	Plain Fabric	2"-14" Repeat	15"-26" Repeat	27"-36" Repeat
54		10%	15%	20%
50	10%	20%	25%	30%
45	35%	45%	50%	55%
36	45%	55%	60%	65%

Figure 15.4 COM chart from Artistic Frame. This shows the amount of fabric added because of fabric width and repeat. Each manufacturer will have its own charts with slightly varying amounts. Use the chart provided by the manufacturer from which furniture is ordered.

Item #	1357-82 Darcie Sofa	1357-32 Darcie Lounge Chair	1357-00 Darcie Ottoman	1358-184 Nancy Sofa	1358-36 Nancy Lounge Chair	1359-36 Sandy Chair
Fabric/Leather Pricing						
COM/Muslin/Grade 6	4770	2535	1170	4470	2535	2535
COL/Grade 10	5370	2835	1290	5070	2775	2685
Grade 14	5970	3135	1410	5670	3015	2835
Grade 18	6570	3435	1530	6270	3255	2985
Grade 22	7170	3735	1650	6870	3495	3135
Grade 26	7770	4035	1770	7470	3735	3285
Grade 30	8370	4335	1890	8070	3975	3435
Grade 34	8970	4635	2010	8670	4215	3585
Grade 38	9570	4935	2130	9270	4455	3735
Grade 42	10170	5235	2250	9870	4695	3885
Grade 46	10770	5535	2370	10470	4935	4035
Grade 50	11370	5835	2490	11070	5175	4185
Grade Riser	600	300	120	600	240	150
Decorative Additions						
Decorative Trims: Page 10	Chart	Chart	Chart	Chart	Chart	Chart
Contrast Welt: Page 11	Chart	Chart	Chart	Chart	Chart	Chart
Finish Options: Page 5						
Wood Species	Maple	Maple	Maple	Maple	Maple	Maple
Standard	Specify	Specify	Specify	Specify	Specify	Specify
SW Lacquer	PLUS 150	PLUS 150	PLUS 150	PLUS 150	PLUS 150	PLUS 150
SW Rubbed Glaze	PLUS 150	PLUS 150	PLUS 150	PLUS 150	PLUS 150	PLUS 150
SW Time Honored	PLUS 225	PLUS 75	PLUS 225	PLUS 225	PLUS 225	PLUS 75
Rustic Barn	N/A	N/A	N/A	N/A	N/A	N/A
Striping	PLUS 45	PLUS 45	N/A	PLUS 60	PLUS 60	PLUS 45
Decorative Nails: Page 6						
Standard Fabric	Standard	Standard	Standard	PLUS 300	PLUS 210	PLUS 210
Standard Leather	Standard	Standard	Standard	Specify	Specify	Specify
Premium	PLUS 240	PLUS 120	PLUS 60	PLUS 240	PLUS 120	PLUS 120
Nail Pattern	N/A	N/A	N/A	N/A	N/A	N/A
Slipcover: Page 13	Chart 7	Chart 4	Chart 1	Chart 6	Chart 3	Chart 2
General Information						
COM/COL: Page 9						
54" Plain COM	21	9	4 Yds.	21	10	6
Leather Sq. Ft.	365	170	55 Ft.	310	165	95
Leather/Fabric Combo	170 Ft./11 Yds.	105 Ft./5 Yds.	N/A	150 Ft./11 Yds.	105 Ft./5 Yds.	40 Ft./3 Yds.
Dimension & Weight:						
Outside(W" D" H")	82" 39" 39"	32" 39" 39"	29" 23" 19"	84" 40" 39"	36" 39" 39"	36" 35" 39"
Inside(W" D" H")	72" 21" 18"	22" 18" 18"	N/A	72" 22" 19"	23" 21" 19"	19" 22" 20"
Seat Height	21"	21"	N/A	20"	20"	20"
Arm Height	25"	25"	N/A	25"	25"	21"
Specifications:	Welted	Welted	Welted	Welted	Welted	Tight St/Tufted Bk
Shipping Weight	150	60	30	150	65	45
Matching Ottoman/	N/A	1357-00	N/A	N/A	N/A	N/A
Storage Ottoman	N/A	N/A	N/A	N/A	N/A	N/A
Construction						
Cushions:						
Spring Down/Blend Down	Standard	Standard	N/A	Standard	Standard	N/A
Feathersoft/Blend Down	Opt/Specify	Opt/Specify	N/A	Opt/Specify	Opt/Specify	N/A
Perma Crown/Fiber	LESS 235	LESS 75	N/A	LESS 150	LESS 75	N/A
Deluxe Down	Call Factory	Call Factory	N/A	Call Factory	Call Factory	N/A
Throw Pillows	2-20"	1-13"X24"	N/A	2-20"	N/A	N/A
Base Treatment: Page 4						
Skirt/Plinth/Fixed Leg/Opt. Leg	Fixed Leg	Fixed Leg	Fixed Leg	Fixed Leg	Fixed Leg	Turned/Tapered
Swivel Base	N/A	N/A	N/A	N/A	N/A	N/A
Swivel Rocker	N/A	N/A	N/A	N/A	N/A	N/A
Swivel Glider	N/A	N/A	N/A	N/A	N/A	N/A
Notes						

Figure 15.5 This is one page from Stanford Furniture's retail price list. (© Stanford Furniture Corporation)

a certain dollar amount will be added. In Figure 15.5, the last grade shown is #50 for $11,370. For each grade over #50, $600 will be added. If fabric grade #53 is used, $600 will be multiplied by 3 (53 − 50 = 3) and $1,800 will be added to $11,370, making a sofa in grade #53 retail at $13,170.

If this is a COL, multiply the yardage amount by 18 to find the number of square feet for leather. While 1 yard of 54-inch fabric equals 13.5 square feet, a 30 percent plus waste allowance must be factored in. While this is helpful when you are quickly

Pearson
Retail Price List

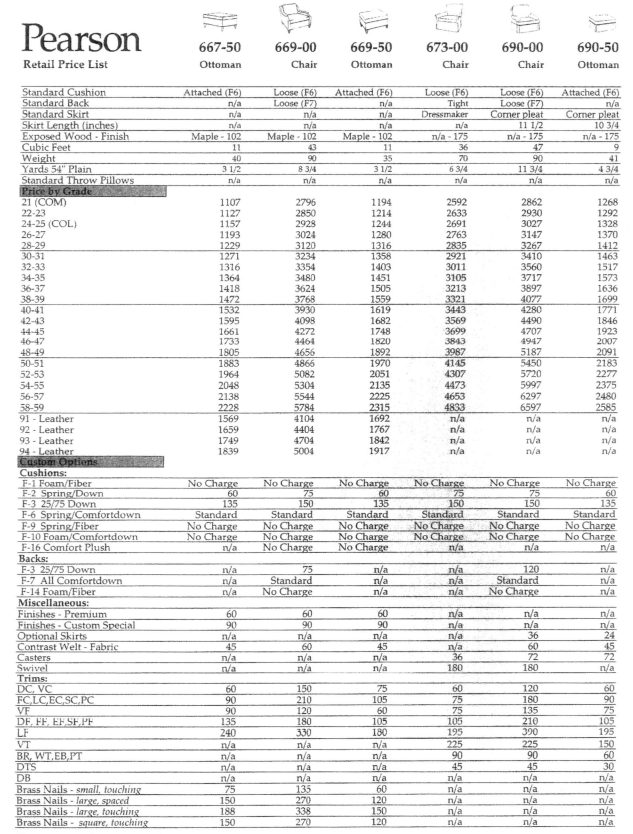

	667-50 Ottoman	669-00 Chair	669-50 Ottoman	673-00 Chair	690-00 Chair	690-50 Ottoman
Standard Cushion	Attached (F6)	Loose (F6)	Attached (F6)	Loose (F6)	Loose (F6)	Attached (F6)
Standard Back	n/a	Loose (F7)	n/a	Tight	Loose (F7)	n/a
Standard Skirt	n/a	n/a	n/a	Dressmaker	Corner pleat	Corner pleat
Skirt Length (inches)	n/a	n/a	n/a	n/a	11 1/2	10 3/4
Exposed Wood - Finish	Maple - 102	Maple - 102	Maple - 102	n/a - 175	n/a - 175	n/a - 175
Cubic Feet	11	43	11	36	47	9
Weight	40	90	35	70	90	41
Yards 54" Plain	3 1/2	8 3/4	3 1/2	6 3/4	11 3/4	4 3/4
Standard Throw Pillows	n/a	n/a	n/a	n/a	n/a	n/a
Price by Grade						
21 (COM)	1107	2796	1194	2592	2862	1268
22-23	1127	2850	1214	2633	2930	1292
24-25 (COL)	1157	2928	1244	2691	3027	1328
26-27	1193	3024	1280	2763	3147	1370
28-29	1229	3120	1316	2835	3267	1412
30-31	1271	3234	1358	2921	3410	1463
32-33	1316	3354	1403	3011	3560	1517
34-35	1364	3480	1451	3105	3717	1573
36-37	1418	3624	1505	3213	3897	1636
38-39	1472	3768	1559	3321	4077	1699
40-41	1532	3930	1619	3443	4280	1771
42-43	1595	4098	1682	3569	4490	1846
44-45	1661	4272	1748	3699	4707	1923
46-47	1733	4464	1820	3843	4947	2007
48-49	1805	4656	1892	3987	5187	2091
50-51	1883	4866	1970	4145	5450	2183
52-53	1964	5082	2051	4307	5720	2277
54-55	2048	5304	2135	4473	5997	2375
56-57	2138	5544	2225	4653	6297	2480
58-59	2228	5784	2315	4833	6597	2585
91 - Leather	1569	4104	1692	n/a	n/a	n/a
92 - Leather	1659	4404	1767	n/a	n/a	n/a
93 - Leather	1749	4704	1842	n/a	n/a	n/a
94 - Leather	1839	5004	1917	n/a	n/a	n/a
Custom Options						
Cushions:						
F-1 Foam/Fiber	No Charge	No Charge	No Charge	No Charge	No Charge	No Charge
F-2 Spring/Down	60	75	60	75	75	60
F-3 25/75 Down	135	150	135	150	150	135
F-6 Spring/Comfortdown	Standard	Standard	Standard	Standard	Standard	Standard
F-9 Spring/Fiber	No Charge	No Charge	No Charge	No Charge	No Charge	No Charge
F-10 Foam/Comfortdown	No Charge	No Charge	No Charge	No Charge	No Charge	No Charge
F-16 Comfort Plush	n/a	No Charge	No Charge	n/a	n/a	n/a
Backs:						
F-3 25/75 Down	n/a	75	n/a	n/a	120	n/a
F-7 All Comfortdown	n/a	Standard	n/a	n/a	Standard	n/a
F-14 Foam/Fiber	n/a	No Charge	n/a	n/a	No Charge	n/a
Miscellaneous:						
Finishes - Premium	60	60	60	n/a	n/a	n/a
Finishes - Custom Special	90	90	90	n/a	n/a	n/a
Optional Skirts	n/a	n/a	n/a	n/a	36	24
Contrast Welt - Fabric	45	60	45	n/a	60	45
Casters	n/a	n/a	n/a	36	72	72
Swivel	n/a	n/a	n/a	180	180	n/a
Trims:						
DC, VC	60	150	75	60	120	60
FC,LC,EC,SC,PC	90	210	105	75	180	90
VF	90	120	60	75	135	75
DF, FF, EF,SF,PF	135	180	105	105	210	105
LF	240	330	180	195	390	195
VT	n/a	n/a	n/a	225	225	150
BR, WT,EB,PT	n/a	n/a	n/a	90	90	60
DTS	n/a	n/a	n/a	45	45	30
DB	n/a	n/a	n/a	n/a	n/a	n/a
Brass Nails - *small, touching*	75	135	60	n/a	n/a	n/a
Brass Nails - *large, spaced*	150	270	120	n/a	n/a	n/a
Brass Nails - *large, touching*	188	338	150	n/a	n/a	n/a
Brass Nails - *square, touching*	150	270	120	n/a	n/a	n/a

Figure 15.6 This is a page from Pearson Upholstery's retail price list. (© Pearson Company)

estimating, you must call the manufacturer to confirm how many square feet it needs. A few manufacturers, such as the one in Figure 15.5, will show the number of square feet needed for leather and square feet and yards needed when you are using a combination of fabric and leather.

Step-by-Step Examples

Example 1—Upholstery Using Manufacturer's Fabric

You are specifying a Stanford Sofa, Darcie #1357-82 for your client. The fabric chosen is a grade 43, and there are no upgrades or add-ons. Using the price list in Figure 15.5, what is the retail price of this sofa?

Answer: The Darcie sofa #1357-82 is the first sofa in the price list in Figure 5.5. Following the column down, grade 43 is found between grades 42 and 46. Since grade 43 is greater than grade 42, the price shown at grade 46 is used. This sofa retails at $10,770.

Example 2—Upholstery Using COM

You are specifying a Pearson chair #669-00 to be upholstered in another manufacturer's fabric. The fabric retails at $87 per yard and is 54 inches wide with a 25¼-inch repeat.

1. Using Figure 15.6, what is the retail price of the chair in COM from Pearson?
2. Using Figures 15.6 and 15.7 on page 266, how much fabric must be ordered, and what is the total price of the fabric without shipping?
3. What is the total retail price of the chair including the fabric?

Answer:
1. When looking at Figure 15.6 and the column under chair 669-00, COM grade is found beside grade 21. The retail price of the chair before fabric is $2796.
2. Using Figure 15.6, the column under chair #669-00 shows 8¾ yards of 54-inch plain fabric. Go to Figure 15.7 and find the column heading "With repeat of 15 inches to 29 inches." Follow the column under 54 inches to where it intersects

with the row for 9 yards 54 inches plain. You must round up to 9, since there is not a row showing 8¾. At this intersection it shows that 11¾ yards are required. Since yardage is ordered by the full or ½ yard, this amount is rounded up to 12 yards, and 12 yards must be ordered. Multiply 12 yards × $87 = $1,044. The fabric yardage will retail for $1,044.

3. Chair: $2,796
   Fabric: + $1,044
   $3,840 retail for the chair in the fabric specified

Example 3—Upholstery Using COM with Upgrades and Add-Ons

Using the chair from Example 2, a Spring/Down seat with the All Comfortdown back will be used. A custom premium finish will also be used with a DC trim.

1. How much will the cushion upgrade, seat and back, retail?
2. How more will is the premium finish and the DC trim cosy?
3. What is the total retail price of the chair in the COM and with these upgrades and add-ons?

Answer:
1. The Spring/Down will add $75.00. There is no additional charge for the All Comfortdown. The total upgrade for cushions is $75.00.
2. The premium finish adds $60, and the DC trim adds $150. $60 + $150 = $210 for finish and trim add-ons.
3. The total retail price of the chair is:
   Chair with COM: $3,840.00
   Cushion upgrade: + $75.00
   Finish and trim add-on: + $210.00
   Total retail for chair: $4,125.00

Example 4—Upholstery Using COL

Using the sofa from Example 1, leather is being specified. This leather comes as 55 square feet per hide and retails at $32.00 per square foot.

1. Using Figure 15.5, how many square feet are required for the sofa?

2. Since leather must be ordered by the whole hide, how many hides and how many square feet of leather must be ordered?

3. How much is the sofa in COL including the leather?

Answer:

1. Figure 15.5 shows that 365 square feet of leather are required.

2. 365 sq. ft. ÷ 55 sq. ft. per hide = 6.6 hides.

3. Since leather must be ordered by the full hide, round up to 7 full hides that must be ordered.
7 full hides × 55 sq. ft. per hide = 385 sq. ft.

4. To calculate for the cost of the leather:
385 sq. ft. × \$32/sq. ft. = \$12,320 leather retail

Sofa COL price from
Figure 15.5:   + \$5,370 COL/grade 10
Total price for sofa
in leather: \$17,690

COM Yardage Chart

Yards 54" Plain	With Repeat Of 1" to 5"			With Repeat Of 6" to 14"			With Repeat Of 15" to 29"			With Repeat Of 30" to 36"		
	54"	53"-46"	45"-36"	54"	53"-46"	45"-36"	54"	53"-46"	45"-36"	54"	53"-46"	45"-36"
2.00	2.25	2.75	3.00	2.50	3.00	3.25	2.75	3.25	3.50	3.00	3.75	4.00
2.50	2.75	3.25	3.75	3.00	3.75	4.00	3.25	4.00	4.50	3.75	4.50	4.75
3.00	3.50	4.00	4.50	3.75	4.50	4.75	4.00	5.00	5.50	4.50	5.50	5.75
3.50	4.00	4.75	5.25	4.50	5.25	5.75	4.75	5.75	6.50	51/4	6.50	6.75
4.00	4.50	5.25	6.00	5.00	6.00	6.50	5.25	6.50	7.25	5.50	7.25	7.75
4.50	5.00	5.75	6.75	5.50	6.75	7.25	6.00	7.25	8.00	6.50	8.00	8.50
5.00	5.50	6.50	7.50	6.00	7.25	8.00	6.50	8.00	9.00	7.00	9.25	9.75
5.50	6.25	7.00	8.00	6.75	8.25	9.00	7.25	9.00	10.00	7.75	10.25	10.75
6.00	6.75	7.50	8.25	7.25	9.00	9.75	8.00	9.50	10.75	8.75	11.00	11.75
6.50	7.25	8.00	9.00	8.00	9.50	10.50	8.50	10.50	11.75	9.00	12.00	12.75
7.00	7.75	8.50	9.50	8.50	10.25	11.25	9.25	11.25	12.50	9.75	12.75	13.50
7.50	8.25	9.00	10.25	9.00	11.00	12.00	9.75	12.00	13.50	10.25	13.75	14.50
8.00	9.00	9.50	10.75	9.75	11.75	13.00	10.50	13.00	14.50	10.75	14.50	15.50
8.50	9.50	10.25	11.50	10.25	12.50	13.75	11.25	13.75	15.25	11.75	15.75	16.75
9.00	10.00	10.75	12.25	11.00	13.25	14.50	11.75	14.50	16.25	12.50	16.50	17.50
9.50	10.50	11.50	13.00	11.50	14.00	15.25	12.50	15.25	17.00	13.50	17.50	18.75
10.00	11.00	12.00	13.50	12.00	14.50	16.00	13.00	16.00	18.00	14.25	18.25	19.50
10.50	11.75	12.75	14.25	12.75	15.25	16.75	13.75	17.00	19.00	15.00	19.25	20.75
11.00	12.25	13.25	15.00	13.25	16.25	17.75	14.50	17.75	20.00	15.50	20.25	21.75
11.50	12.75	13.75	15.50	14.00	16.75	18.50	15.00	18.50	21.00	16.25	21.25	22.75
12.00	13.25	14.50	16.25	14.50	17.50	19.25	15.75	19.25	21.75	16.75	22.00	23.50
12.50	13.75	15.00	17.00	15.00	18.25	20.00	16.25	20.00	22.50	17.50	23.00	24.75
13.00	14.50	15.75	17.75	15.75	19.00	20.75	17.00	20.75	23.25	18.25	23.75	25.50
13.50	15.00	16.25	18.50	16.25	19.75	21.75	17.75	21.50	24.25	19.00	24.75	26.50
14.00	15.50	16.75	19.00	17.00	20.50	22.50	18.25	22.25	25.00	19.75	25.75	27.50
14.50	16.00	17.50	19.75	17.50	21.25	23.25	19.00	23.25	26.00	20.50	26.75	28.50
15.00	16.50	18.00	20.25	18.00	21.75	24.00	19.50	24.00	27.00	21.00	27.50	29.25
15.50	17.25	18.75	21.00	18.75	22.75	25.00	20.25	24.75	27.75	21.75	28.50	30.25
16.00	17.75	19.50	21.75	19.25	23.50	25.75	21.00	25.50	28.75	22.50	29.50	31.50
16.50	18.25	20.00	22.50	20.00	24.00	26.50	21.50	26.50	29.75	23.25	30.25	32.25
17.00	18.75	20.75	23.25	20.50	25.00	27.50	22.25	27.25	30.50	24.00	31.25	33.25
17.50	19.25	21.25	23.75	21.00	25.50	28.00	22.75	28.00	31.50	24.75	32.00	34.25
18.00	20.00	22.00	24.50	21.75	26.25	28.75	23.50	29.00	32.50	25.25	33.00	35.00
18.50	20.50	22.75	25.25	22.25	27.00	29.50	24.25	29.50	33.25	26.00	33.75	36.00
19.00	21.00	23.25	26.00	23.00	27.50	30.25	24.75	30.50	34.25	26.75	34.75	37.00
19.50	21.50	24.00	26.75	23.50	28.50	31.25	25.50	31.25	35.00	27.25	35.75	38.25
20.00	22.00	24.50	27.25	24.00	29.00	32.00	26.00	32.00	36.00	28.00	36.50	39.00
20.50	22.75	25.25	28.00	24.75	29.75	32.75	26.75	33.00	37.00	29.00	37.50	40.00
21.00	23.25	26.00	28.75	25.25	30.50	33.50	27.50	33.50	37.75	29.75	38.50	41.25
21.50	23.75	26.50	29.50	26.00	31.25	34.50	28.00	34.50	38.75	30.25	39.50	42.25
22.00	24.25	27.25	30.25	26.50	32.00	35.25	28.75	35.25	39.50	31.00	40.25	43.00
22.50	24.75	27.75	30.75	27.00	32.75	36.00	29.25	36.00	40.50	31.75	41.25	44.00
23.00	25.50	28.50	31.50	27.75	33.50	36.75	30.00	36.75	41.25	32.25	42.25	45.25
23.50	26.00	29.25	32.25	28.25	34.25	37.50	30.75	37.50	42.25	33.00	43.00	46.00
24.00	26.50	29.75	32.75	29.00	35.00	38.50	31.25	38.50	43.25	33.75	44.00	46.75
24.50	27.00	30.50	33.50	29.50	35.75	39.25	32.00	39.25	44.00	34.50	44.75	47.75
25.00	27.50	31.00	34.25	30.00	36.25	40.00	32.50	40.00	45.00	35.00	45.75	48.75

Figure 15.7 Pearson COM chart for sofas and chairs. (Pearson)

Practice Lessons: New Upholstery

BASIC

Use Figure 15.2. Pearson sofa #2323-30 is ideal for your client's law office. The fabric selected is a Pearson fabric grade 37. You are upgrading the cushion to an F-2 Spring/Down and using brass nails that are small and touching.

1. What is the base retail price of the sofa before upgrades and add-ons?
2. How much does the F-2 cushion add?
3. How much do the brass nails add?
4. What is the total retail price of the sofa?

INTERMEDIATE

Use Figure 15.6 and 15.7. You are specifying two Pearson chairs #690-00 and one Pearson ottoman #690-50 for your client's family room. The fabric selected is Vervain, which is $118.00 per yard and 54 inches wide with a 12-inch repeat. You are upgrading the seat cushion to an F-2 Spring/Down on all the pieces and adding a swivel mechanism to the chairs.

1. What is the base retail price for (a) the two chairs, (b) the ottoman, and (c) the total of all three pieces?
2. What does the seat cushion upgrade and the swivel base add to this price?
3. (a) How much fabric must be ordered for these three pieces? (b) How much will the fabric retail for?
4. What is the total retail price for these three pieces including fabric, upgrade, and add-ons?

ADVANCED

Use Figure 15.5. Stanford's 1368-184 Nancy sofa is being specified for a hearth room. A COM and COL fabric/leather combination will be used. The fabric is Schumacher, which retails for $76.00 per yard and is a 54-inch plain fabric. The leather is from Edelman and comes in 55-square-foot hides, retailing at $26.00 per square foot.

1. What is the base price of the sofa? Since it is a COM/COL combination, price it as a COL.
2. How many yards of fabric and how many square feet of leather does Stanford require?
3. How many hides and square feet of leather must be ordered?
4. What is the total for fabric and leather?
5. What is the total retail price for this sofa including fabric and leather?

References

Artistic Frame. Artistic Frame Price List, 2006.
Godsey, L. *Interior Design Materials and Specifications.* New York: Fairchild Publications, 2008.

Chapter 16 | Reupholstered and Slipcovered Furniture

Reupholstery and slipcovers involve working with an existing piece of upholstered furniture. Sometimes this furniture has been passed down in the family or purchased at a consignment store or yard sale—or even found discarded beside the road. While reupholstering is a permanent way of changing the look of upholstered furniture by attaching fabric to the frame, slipcovers are temporary and give the client opportunities for changing the look easily. Whether to reupholster or have slipcovers made, or both, depends on the client and his or her situation.

Chapter Outline

Terminology

Reupholstered and Slipcovered Furniture
    Reupholstery
    Slipcovers

Cost Factors
    Reupholstery
    Slipcovers

Calculations
    Reupholstery
    Slipcovers

Step-by-Step Examples
    Example 1—Reupholstery
    Example 2—Slipcover
    Example 3—Reupholstery
    Example 4—Leather Reupholstery

Manual Worksheets
    Reupholstery and Slipcover Worksheet
    Fabric Yardage Conversion to Leather Hides
    Worksheet

Practice Lessons: Reupholstered and Slipcovered Furniture
    Basic
        Reupholstered Chair
        Slipcovered Chair
    Intermediate
        Reupholstered Sofa
        Slipcovered Loveseat
    Advanced
        Reupholstered Sofa
        Slipcovered Sofa and Loveseat
        Pricing for Intermediate Reupholstered Sofa

References

Terminology

Arm covers Fabric coverings made for the arms of upholstered furniture in order to protect them from soil and wear.

Cushion The loose backs and loose seats of upholstery are commonly referred to as cushions. Most seat cushions start with a foam core or a spring coil that is wrapped with other materials before being encased in the fabric covering. Back cushions are often filled with batting or feathers.

Flaws Holes, heavy slubs, misweaves, or misprints in fabrics that make them unacceptable to use. The fabric must be inspected for flaws before it is cut. The flawed fabric must be sent back to the manufacturer for replacement before it is cut.

Frame The basic structure of upholstery that creates the style of the piece. It is padded, wrapped, and upholstered. Most frames are made of wood.

Pattern repeat Lengthwise or crosswise measurement of one design motif to where that same pattern is again repeated.

    Straight match Repeat matches straight across.

    Drop match or half drop Repeat is staggered so that every other width matches along the same line. The match runs diagonally (see Figure 3.2 on page 22 for an example).

Railroaded fabric The vertical pattern of regular rolled fabric runs up the bolt. The vertical pattern of a railroaded fabric runs side to side, selvage to selvage. A vertical stripe will run horizontally, like railroad tracks, when the fabric is railroaded (see Figure 15.1 on page 258). Railroaded fabric is ideal for upholstery because it will allow anything over 54 inches wide to be seamless along the back.

Selvage The edge of fabric formed on the loom when the fabric is woven. It is frequently woven tighter than the fabric body.

Slipcover A fabric covering for upholstered furniture that is not attached to the frame and that can be removed and changed seasonally or as desired. Specially made slipcovers can sometimes make it difficult to tell that the furniture isn't upholstered.

Welt Cording used to finish edges of upholstery, cushions, and pillows. While the majority of upholstered furniture is welted using the same fabric all over (self-welting), you can specify a contrasting welt by selecting a different material than what is used on the main body of the frame.

Width A single width of fabric, sometimes referred to as a *cut*. Most upholstery fabric is 54 inches wide. Other less common widths of fabric are 36 inches, 45 inches, 48 inches, and 60 inches. It is important to check the width of the fabric used.

Reupholstered and Slipcovered Furniture

Reupholstery

There are many reasons clients reupholster instead of buying new or using a slipcover, such as:

- The fabric is worn out.
- The furniture is good quality.
- The furniture has a unique or unusual size or style.
- The client has an emotional attachment to the furniture.
- The client is environmentally conscious.
- The fabric selected is too heavy for a slipcover.
- The client does not want a slipcover.

Materials—fabrics, leathers, and trim—are normally ordered by the interior designer and delivered to the upholsterer with a work order that includes a description of the furniture to be reupholstered and the fabric to be used and details of the work to be done. Reupholstering will save money over buying the same quality of new furniture in the same fabric being considered. If comparisons are made based on only the money to be spent between reupholstering or buying new furniture of a lesser quality, reupholstery may not cost less. In terms of delivery, it may not be faster than new furniture either, depending on several factors:

- Number of upholstery jobs workroom already has in queue
- Complexity of the work and speed of upholsterer
- Delays with fabric or trim
- Holidays
- Workroom vacations

It is not uncommon for an upholstery workroom to close for several weeks during the summer and at the end of December. The interior designer should anticipate that the workroom will be backed up close to holidays. If possible, the designer should allow a two- to three-month lead time for the upholsterer to ensure that the client will have the furniture for his or her special occasion.

Slipcovers

Slipcovers are removable covers made to fit the upholstery. They aren't tacked to the frame, and they aren't permanent. Good slipcovers are tailored to the piece, and it is sometimes hard to tell that the piece isn't upholstered. Cheap slipcovers utilize elastic and gathered corners, and it is easy to tell that the piece isn't upholstered. There are several reasons to use slipcovers:

- The client wants to change the look of the room seasonally or easily
- Furniture is in good condition; it just doesn't go with the new look.
- The client wants to protect the original fabric from kids and pets. (Don't use plastic!)
- The client wants to save money (although this does not always save money over reupholstering).

Slipcovers can be made by upholsterers, but there are also workrooms that specialize in slipcovers. The same time frame issues that upholstery workrooms encounter are the same issues that slipcover workrooms encounter. Keep in mind that a heavy fabric, such as chenille, can't be used for a slipcover because there is too much fabric in the seams with the heavier fabric and it won't lie on the furniture smoothly.

Cost Factors

It is important to keep track of all specifications and costs of reupholstering and/or slipcovering. A furniture schedule, such as that shown in Table 16.1, can be used effectively to do this. When pricing furniture to be reupholstered or slipcovered, you need to consider two types of costs: labor costs and material costs (Table 16.1).

Reupholstery

For reupholstery, labor charges include basic labor, repairs and tightening of the frame, restyling of the frame, retying coils, and foam and Dacron wrap or Spring/Down for the cushions. Some upholsterers include arm covers and throw pillows in their labor charges, and some charge separately for these. Depending on the region of the country and the standards in that area, the upholsterer may charge for going to the home to give the estimate. The upholsterer may also charge for picking up and delivering the piece of furniture. All of these items are included in the invoice from the upholsterer.

Reupholstery		Slipcover	
Labor Costs	**Material Costs**	**Labor Costs**	**Material Costs**
Base labor	Fabric/leather	Base labor	Fabric
New cushions and wrap	Shipping of fabric/leather	Labor add-ons, such as trims	Shipping of fabric
Tightening/repair of frame	Trim	Measure/estimate charges, if applicable	Trim
Retying of coils	Shipping of trim	Delivery charges, if applicable	Shipping of trim
Arm covers			
Throw pillows			
Redesign of frame			
Measure/estimate charges, if applicable			
Delivery charges, if applicable			

Table 16.1 Reupholstery and Slipcover Costs

Materials usually provided by the interior designer include fabric/leather and any contrast trim. There will be shipping charges for these items. If the interior designer has to take these materials to the workroom, the designer will incur indirect charges for time and gas.

A few upholsterers charge by the yard, but most upholsterers charge by the piece. Anything extra, such as arm covers, foam, wrap, and repairs and retying springs or restyling the piece, will cost more. Always have the upholsterer look at the furniture in order to give a labor quote and yardage amount. This is much easier today because photos can be taken on cell phones and e-mailed along with the dimensions to the upholsterer. Beware of fabric charts for estimating fabric, since most of the commercial fabric charts available today were created in the mid-20th century. They do not reflect current sizes of furniture and therefore do not reflect appropriate yardage amounts. Table 16.2 has been created through research of several different furniture manufacturers, discussion with upholstery workrooms, and personal experience. This is intended to suggest possible yardage using 54-inch-wide fabric that has no repeat and is only to be used for estimations. More yards are necessary for fabric that is less than 54 inches wide and has a repeat.

When giving an estimate to the client, always make sure that the client knows that this is what you anticipate the cost to be, but when the fabric is removed, the upholsterer may find something unexpected and the price could go up. Be sure to include on any estimate/quote the length of time for which the estimate/quote will be good. If the client is quoted and six months later the client decides to go ahead with the order, you will need to check with the fabric manufacturer and the upholsterer to make sure the original price is still good. Most cushion fillings are petroleum products—if oil prices take an upward surge, anything made of petroleum will also go up. Labor costs are usually constant for a number of years. Fabric prices have increases every six months to one year, and fabric patterns are discontinued without notice.

Slipcovers

For slipcovers, labor costs include the base labor to make the slipcovers and any add-ons for contrast trim or other decorative details. Depending on the region of the country and the standards in that area, the slipcover workroom may charge for estimates, pickup, and/or delivery. Some slipcover workrooms leave the furniture in the client's home, doing the cutting and fitting in the home. Some workrooms will also provide new cushions and stuffing for seat and back cushions if requested. The time frame for making slipcovers will vary depending on fabric availability, number of jobs in queue, and the speed of the workroom.

The fabric that is provided by the interior designer must be light- to medium-light-weight. Leather and heavy-weight fabric create too much bulk at the seams and are unsuitable for slipcovers. There will be shipping charges for fabric.

Once you have determined all the specifics and the fabric has been ordered, you must create a work order for the workroom (Table 16.3). Important information to include on the work order are your company, workroom, and client information, date,

Furniture Item		Dimensions Width × Depth × Height	Suggested Yardage
1. Dining room chair removable seat—Side chair		21 in. w × 22 in. d	¾ yd. per chair
2. Dining room chair removable seat—Arm chair		24 in. w × 24 in. d	1 yd. per chair
3. Ottoman with tall exposed leg		21 in. w × 18 in. d × 17 in. h	2½ yd.
4. Larger ottoman with tall exposed leg		28 in. w × 21 in. d × 19 in. h	3 yd.
5. Ottoman with short exposed leg		28 in. w × 21 in. d × 19 in. h	3½ yd.
6. Ottoman with skirt		28 in. w × 21 in. d × 18 in. h	4½ yd.
7. Wood frame dining chair with seat and back		25 in. w × 26 in. d × 38 in. h	2½ yd.
8. Fully upholstered dining chair		24 in. w × 26 in. d × 40 in. h	4 yd.
9. Martha Washington chair		27 in. w × 30 in. d × 42 in. h	4 yd.
10. Gooseneck chair		26 in. w × 29 in. d × 43 in. h	4 yd.

Table 16.2 Yardage Chart for Furniture (yardages include self-cording) *continued*

11. French accent chair		26 in. w × 29 in. d × 37 in. h	3½ yd.
12. Wing chair		33 in. w × 33 in. d × 43 in. h	8 yd.
13. French lounge chair		30 in. w × 38 in. d × 40 in. h	6 yd.
14. Tight-back club chair		31 in. w × 37 in. d × 32 in. h	8 yd.
15. Loose-back club chair		32 in. w × 35 in. d × 33 in. h	9 yd.
16. Tuxedo sofa		88 in. w × 40 in. d × 35 in. h	19 yd.
17. Tuxedo loveseat		64 in. w × 40 in. d × 35 in. h	17 yd.
18. Loose cushion sofa		88 in. w × 37 in. d × 36 in. h	20 yd.
19. Loose cushion loveseat		64 in. w × 37 in. d × 36 in. h	18 yd.
20. Tight-back sofa, no skirt—taller legs		86 in. w × 33 in. d × 35 in. h	16 yd.
21. Tight-back loveseat, no skirt—taller legs		60 in. w × 33 in. d × 35 in. h	13½ yd.

Table 16.2 *continued*

Re-Upholstery/Slipcover Work Order

P.O. #:

Date:	
Designer:	
Phone:	

Upholstery Workroom		Client	
Address		Address	
E-mail		E-mail	
Phone		Phone	
Fax		Phone	

Special Instructions (i.e., contrast fabrics, retying, repairing, restyling):

Fabric Information

Furniture Item	Fabric Company	Fabric Pattern	Fabric Color	Fabric Width	Pattern Repeat	Railroaded? Y or N	Yards	Placement on Furn.
1.								
2.								
3.								
4.								
5.								

Furniture Information

Skirt/ Base Style	Arm Style	Seat and Back Cushion Style and Filling	Throw Pillows?	Arm Covers?

Table 16.3 Work Order for Reupholstering or Slipcovering

and purchase order associated with the work order. If you have the estimated cost from the workroom, it can also be written in the special instruction area of the work order. The special instruction area is used to designate additional items that need to be done to the piece, such as repair of frame, retying of coils, restyling of frame, and any special information regarding fabrics being used, especially if there are contrast fabrics.

The rest of the work order will be filled in showing piece of furniture, fabric information, and furniture information. The fabric information includes the fabric company; fabric pattern and color; fabric width and pattern repeat; whether the fabric is railroaded; whether it is to be used for the entire piece, the body, cording, or just the seats and backs; and finally the number of yards of fabric you are giving the workroom. The furniture information includes what type of skirt or base and arm style, the seat and back cushion style and filling, and whether the workroom will make throw pillows and arm covers. Some workrooms provide other services, such as fabric protection, so make sure to note them somewhere on the work order you create. It is common for designers to make drawings and diagrams for the upholsterer.

Calculations

Reupholstery

Interior designers usually follow upholstery yardage charts when estimating fabric for furniture. As previously mentioned, be sure that the upholstery chart you use is current. The yardage chart in Table 16.2 is current for today's styles and sizes. These fabric yardage charts are figured for 54-inch-wide plain fabric (fabric with no repeat). When fabric is narrower than this or has a repeat, additional yardage is necessary so there is enough material to cover the piece of furniture.

There is an order of operations when you are determining how much yardage is necessary. The first

Fabric Width	Additional Fabric Required
54 in.	0
50/52 in.	10%
48 in.	15%
45 in.	20%
36 in.	50%

Table 16.4 Calculating Fabric of Narrower Width

step is to check the width of the fabric. If the fabric is narrower, yardage must be added before considering the repeat (Table 16.4). The next thing is to check the fabric repeat and to make adjustments accordingly (Table 16.5).

For example, the fabric you have selected to reupholster a chair like Chair #15 from Table 16.2 is 50 inches wide with a 25-inch repeat. Table 16.2 shows that it takes 9 yards of 54-inch-wide plain fabric. To calculate yardage, factor for the narrowness first and then factor for the repeat.

Table 16.4 shows that 10 percent more fabric is needed for the narrowness. Because of the narrowness of the fabric, 9 yards × 1.1 = 9.9 yards. Table 16.5 shows that 20 percent more fabric is needed for the repeat. Take this number and multiply it by the additional percentage: 9.9 yards × 1.2 = 11.88 yards. Because fabric must be ordered by the full or ½ yard, this amount is rounded up to 12 yards.

Leather is different from fabric in that it comes from an animal and does not come 54 inches wide to be sold in yards (Figure 16.1). Leather is normally sold

Vertical Repeat	Additional Fabric Required
0–2¾ in.	5%
3–14¾ in.	10%
15–19¾ in.	15%
20–27¾ in.	20%
28–36¾ in.	35%

Table 16.5 Calculating Fabric with Fabric Vertical Repeat

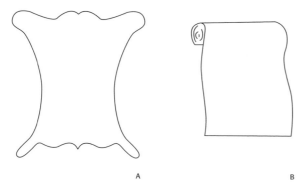

Figure 16.1 (A) Hide of leather; (B) roll of fabric.

Item	Additional Yardage
Chair or ottoman	1 yd.
Loveseat	2 yd.
Sofa (3 seat)	3 yd.
Sofa (4 seat)	4 yd.

Table 16.6 Slipcover Yardage Allowance

by the whole hide, and depending on the type of animal, the size of the hide will vary. A whole cow hide may have approximately 55 square feet. You must convert furniture yardage to square feet in order to determine how many hides are needed. There is also waste involved with leather. Using a 30 percent waste factor, 1 yard of 54-inch-wide fabric will equal 18 square feet of leather.

From the previous example of Chair #15 from Table 16.2, 9 yards × 18 square feet = 162 square feet. 162 square feet ÷ 55 square feet per hide = 2.95 hides. Whole hides must be ordered, so 2.95 is rounded up to 3 hides. Since pricing is still done by the square feet, 3 hides × 55 square feet = 165 square feet. The charge for the leather will be based on 165 square feet. Normally, the number of square feet required and the number that must be ordered are not so close to each other. Be sure to be in contact with your leather supplier, since square feet on each hide can vary and the supplier may be able to pull several hides together that get closer to your total needed square footage.

Slipcovers

While labor costs for slipcovers are usually less than for reupholstering, since the fabric isn't tacked and tailored to the frame in a slipcover, more fabric is usually required than that for reupholstering. As a rule of thumb, 1 yard is added per seat, although this can certainly vary with each workroom (Table 16.6). This means that for a one-person chair or ottoman, 1 more yard is added than what is required to reupholster. If a loveseat is a two-person piece, as expected, it will take 2 additional yards. A sofa for three people takes 3 additional yards, and a longer sofa for four people will take 4 additional yards. Some furniture manufacturers understand the potential add-on sale and offer slipcovers for the new upholstered furniture being ordered.

To calculate for yardage, you must first calculate as if the piece of furniture were being reupholstered before adding the additional amounts of fabric required. From the previous example, using Chair #15 in 50-inch-wide fabric with a 25-inch repeat for a slipcover, the upholstery calculations show that it takes a total of 12 yards. Since the chair is a single seat, 1 more yard will be added to the 12 yards for slipcovering. 12 yard + 1 yards = 13 yards for slipcovering.

Step-by-Step Examples

Example 1—Reupholstery

Your client's sofa looks like sofa #18 in Table 16.2. The fabric you have chosen is plain and 48 inches wide. According to the yardage chart from Table 16.2, the sofa requires 20 yards for 54-inch plain fabric. According to Table 16.4 the sofa will require 15 percent more fabric because of its narrowness.

Step 1: Check upholstery yardage chart.

Yardage required:	20	yd.

Step 2: Calculate for fabric narrower than 54 inches.

Multiply by percentage from Allowance Chart:	× 1.15	narrowness allowance
Total:	23	yd.
Round up to nearest ½ yard:	**23**	**yd. to be ordered**

There is no repeat to consider, so 23 yards is the amount of fabric to order for this sofa.

Example 2—Slipcover

Another client has a sofa similar to Sofa #16 and wants a slipcover made for it. The fabric chosen has a 25-inch repeat and is 54 inches wide. According to the yardage chart in Table 16.2 the sofa requires 19 yards of plain, 54-inch-wide fabric. According to Table 16.5, 20 percent more fabric is required for the repeat. Since the sofa can easily seat 3 people, 3 additional yards must be added.

Step 1: Determine yardage.

Yardage required from Upholstery Yardage Chart:	19	yd.

Step 2: Calculate for fabric narrower than 54 inches.

Fabric is not narrower than 54 inches, so use base yardage.

Total:	19	yd.

If fabric has a repeat, continue to Step 3.

Step 3: Calculate for fabric with repeat.

Total from Step 1 or Step 2:	19	yd.
Multiply by percentage from Allowance Chart:	× 1.2	repeat allowance
Total:	22.8	yd.
Round up to nearest ½ yard:	**23**	**yd. to be ordered**

For slipcover:

Total yards to be ordered from above:	23	yd.
Add 1 yard per seat:	+ 3	yd.
Total yards:	**26**	**yd. to be ordered**

Example 3—Reupholstery

The client with the sofa from Example 2 has decided that she wants to reupholster it, and you have chosen a fabric that has a 27-inch repeat and is 48 inches wide. It is necessary to factor for the narrow width first and then to calculate for the repeat. According to Table 16.2 this sofa takes 19 yards in a plain, 54-inch-wide fabric.

Table 16.4 shows that 15 percent additional fabric is needed because of the narrowness of the fabric. Table 16.5 shows that 20 percent additional fabric is needed for the repeat.

Step 1: Determine yardage.

Yardage required from Upholstery Yardage Chart:	19 yd.

Step 2: Calculate for fabric narrower than 54 inches.

Multiply by percentage from Allowance Chart:	× 1.15	narrowness allowance
Total:	21.85 yd.	
Round up to nearest ½ yard:	22 yd. to be ordered	

If fabric has a repeat, continue to Step 3.

Step 3: Calculate for fabric with repeat.

Total from Step 1 or Step 2:	22 yd.	
Multiply by percentage from Allowance Chart:	× 1.2	repeat allowance
Total:	26.4 yd.	
Round up to nearest ½ yard:	**26.5 yd. to be ordered**	

Example 4—Leather Reupholstery

You will be upholstering a sofa similar to sofa #18 from Table 16.2. Leather has been specified. This sofa requires 20 yards of plain, 54-inch-wide fabric. There are 55 square feet in each hide.

Step 1: Determine base square feet.

Yardage required from Upholstery Yardage Chart:	20	yd.
Multiply by leather allowance:	× 18	sq. ft.
Total:	360	sq. ft.

Step 2: Calculate number of hides.

Total from Step 1:	360	sq. ft.
Divide by square feet per hide:	÷ 55	sq. ft.
Total:	6.55	hides
Round up to nearest whole number:	**7**	**hides to be ordered**

Step 3: Calculate square feet to charge.

Total from Step 2:	7	hides
Multiply by square feet per hide:	× 55	sq. ft.
Total:	**385**	**sq. ft. to be charged**

Manual Worksheets

Reupholstery and Slipcover Worksheet

Step 1: Determine yardage.

Yardage required from Upholstery Yardage Chart: _____ yd.

If fabric is 54 inches wide or wider and has no repeat, use yardage as shown on Upholstery Yardage Chart. Otherwise, follow steps as necessary below.

Step 2: Calculate for fabric narrower than 54 inches.

Multiply by percentage from Allowance Chart: × _____ narrowness allowance

Total: _____ **yd.**

Round up to nearest ½ yard: _____ **yd. to be ordered**

If fabric has a repeat, continue to Step 3.

Step 3: Calculate for fabric with repeat.

Total from Step 1 or Step 2: _____ yd.

Multiply by percentage from Allowance Chart: × _____ repeat allowance

Total: _____ **yd.**

Round up to nearest ½ yard: _____ **yd. to be ordered**

For slipcover:

Total yards to be ordered: _____ yd.

Add 1 yard per seat: + _____ yd.

Total yards: _____ **yd. to be ordered**

Fabric Yardage Conversion to Leather Hides Worksheet

Step 1: Determine base square feet.

Yardage required from Upholstery Yardage Chart: _____ yd.

Multiply by leather allowance: × _____18_____ sq. ft.

Total: _____ **sq. ft.**

Step 2: Calculate number of hides.

Total from Step 1: _____ sq. ft.

Divide by square feet per hide: ÷ _____ sq. ft.

Total: _____ **hides**

Round up to whole number: _____ **hides to be ordered**

Step 3: Calculate square feet to charge.

Total from Step 2: _____ total hides

Multiply by square feet per hide: × _____ sq. ft.

Total: _____ **sq. ft. to be charged**

Practice Lessons: Reupholstered and Slipcovered Furniture

BASIC

Reupholstered Chair

Your client has a wing chair similar to #12 in Table 16.2. The fabric selected is 54 inches wide with an 18-inch repeat.

1. What is the base yardage required from the chart?
2. What is the total yardage that must be ordered?

Slipcovered Chair

For this same wing chair similar to #12, your client wants to be able to slipcover it for the summer months to create a lighter look. The fabric selected is a white and blue stripe that is 48 inches wide and has no vertical repeat.

1. What percentage must be added because of the narrowness of the fabric?
2. How many yards must be ordered for the slipcover?

INTERMEDIATE

Reupholstered Sofa

A doctor's reception room has a sofa similar to #20 in Table 16.2. You have specified a 50-inch-wide fabric with a 30-inch repeat.

1. What is the base yardage needed from Table 16.2?
2. What percentage must be added because of the narrowness of the fabric?
3. What percentage must be added because of the repeat?
4. How much fabric will be ordered for the sofa?

Slipcovered Loveseat

The doctor has a loveseat in her personal office similar to #17 in Table 16.2. You have found a fabric she loves that is 54 inches wide with a 4-inch repeat.

1. What percentage must be added because of the repeat?
2. How much fabric will be ordered for the loveseat?

ADVANCED

Reupholstered Sofa

You will be reupholstering a sofa like #18 in Table 16.2 in leather. The leather specified is from the company Cowco, pattern 3818, color red, and there are 55 square feet in a hide. Instead of a skirt, it will be an upholstered base with a wedge foot. The arm style is a Lawson style, and the seat and back cushions are to be remade as they are but with new high-density foam cushions wrapped in Dacron.

1. What is the base yardage according to Table 16.2?
2. What is the minimum amount of square footage required?
3. How many hides are needed?
4. How many square feet of leather will your client be charged?

Slipcovered Sofa and Loveseat

Your client has a sofa and loveseat in the living room, similar to #16 and #17 in Table 16.2, that are in good shape but the fabric is dated. You have determined that a slipcover will be appropriate and have found a fabric that is 54 inches wide with a 21-inch repeat.

1. What is the base fabric needed for (a) the sofa and (b) the loveseat?
2. What percentage is added because of the repeat?
3. How many yards must be ordered for the (a) sofa and (b) the loveseat?
4. What is the total yardage amount to order?

Pricing for Intermediate Reupholstered Sofa

Use the fabric quantity found for the Intermediate Reupholstered Sofa practice lesson and the prices listed below to calculate pricing for your client. This sofa will need new cushions and the springs will need to be retied. The workroom will charge for pickup and delivery.

Fabric—$78.00/yard

Shipping—$34.00 total

Base labor—$1,050.00

New cushions and wrap—$250.00

Retie spring labor—$300.00

Pickup and delivery—$70.00

1. What is the price of the fabric and shipping?
2. What is the total for labor: base labor, new cushions and wrap, retying coils, and pickup and delivery?
3. What is the total price for reupholstering this sofa?

References

DeLeon, Albert. Personal communication. December 18, 2012.

Ketteman, Marilyn. Personal communications. August to December 2012.

Epilogue | The Sales Process

The sales process begins from the moment you meet your client. Some would even say that it begins before you meet your client, because you must have knowledge about what you are doing and a confident attitude that shows you can bring something of value to the project. A large industry has been built on showing how to sell. I highly recommend buying books or audio files and attending seminars on this subject. The purpose of this epilogue is to explain what happens after the client is given a quote and after the client decides to proceed.

Let's remember what has occurred so far. You've gained a client, assessed the client's needs and wants, and specified products. Then you estimated or priced specific items. Your client wants to move forward with this project. Now what? Depending on the company you work for, there may be some variations to the following process.

For some of the products you have priced, you can feel confident enough to write a contract and obtain your client's signature along with the appropriate deposit amount to begin the project. Some of the products will require the installer or subcontractor to confirm the price. However, now the client is aware of the price or the price range, and basically the job is sold, just awaiting final pricing. This ensures that your installers and subcontractors aren't wasting their time or your client's time.

Whenever the final amount for the project is confirmed, a contract is written, a signature obtained, and a deposit received. It is not uncommon for deposits to be 50 percent, 75 percent, or, in some cases, 100 percent of the total quoted. Each company will have its own parameters for writing the contract and recording the deposit. Once this is done, materials must be ordered, work orders must be written, and any necessary construction drawings must be created. Fundamental to this process is being organized and keeping track of everything so that you know what is occurring with the project at any point. Devising a system for this will keep aspects of the project from falling into a crack that will cause delays and cost money.

There are companies who still handwrite purchase orders. There are also companies whose purchase orders are generated when the sales order is input into the computer. Normally manufacturers will send an acknowledgement of the order. It is crucial to review the acknowledgement to make sure the order is exactly as you want it and that it is shipping to the correct address. With some products, such as hard window treatments, time is of the essence in order to catch any errors. Errors can happen and do happen at every level of a project. Take every opportunity to minimize errors.

Work orders and construction drawings must be written for those doing the labor and construction aspects of the project. Clear written instructions are crucial, and diagrams or photos can be very helpful in conveying expectations. Timing can sometimes be tricky when multiple workrooms and subcontractors are involved in the same project. As products arrive for the components of the job, vendor invoices arrive as well. Coordination of various workrooms and installers enables a project to be completed and billed efficiently so that the company's cash flow is kept fluid.

Many interior designers are either present for the full installation or make an appearance during the installation or shortly after. This is a good business practice for your client to see you involved at the final stage. It also allows you, as the interior designer, to answer the client's questions and to handle situations that may not go exactly as planned.

Once the installation is finished, there is a review of the work completed. This occurs with all projects, but the process is more formalized in very large and commercial projects. This process begins with a walkthrough. During the walkthrough a punch list is created, showing any work or final details that need to be finished. From this punch list, additional work orders may have to be generated to finish the job. Once this job is complete, the balance for the product is due. Some companies have a policy of billing the client. For smaller jobs, it is common for the interior designer or another company-designated person to actually collect the balance due at the time it is received.

Finally, be sure not only to tell the client thank you but to also follow up with a thank-you card. Yes, a handwritten card. The client entrusted you and your firm to do the work it needed. A handwritten thank-you card stands out because you took time to do this. These cards don't take a lot of time to write, but they can help to differentiate you from others in this profession. At the very least, e-mail a thank-you note. It can be very effective to do both.

While this book will not have made you an expert on each subject, I hope it has given you some insight and useful worksheets to help you as you become the expert. In this industry, time is your friend. Your knowledge grows exponentially each month and each year you are a practicing interior designer. Keep putting one foot in front of the other and soon you will be the seasoned interior designer able to help the new kid.

Appendix A: Practice Lesson Answer Key

Chapter 2: Paint

BASIC

1. 1 gallon of paint

Step 1: Find perimeter of room in feet (e.g., 65.3 ft.).
Remember to convert inches to feet by dividing by 12 inches.

Wall A:	3	ft.
Wall B:	+ 3	ft.
Wall C:	+ 7	ft.
Wall D:	+ 7	ft.
Total perimeter:	**20**	**ft.**

Step 2: Find square footage of area to be covered.

Total from Step 1:	20	ft.
Multiply by height:	× 9	ft.
(This may not be full height of wall.)		
Total square feet:	**180**	**sq. ft.**

Step 3: Determine deductions.

Width of opening or cabinets:	2.5	ft.
Multiply by height of opening/cabinets:	× 7	ft.
Total square feet:	**17.5**	**sq. ft.**

Step 4: Determine square footage of paint needed.

Take total square feet from Step 2:	180	sq. ft.
Subtract total from Step 3:	− 17.5	sq. ft.
Total square feet needed for 1 coat of paint:	**162.5**	**sq. ft.**
Multiply by anticipated coats of paint:	× 1	coat
Total square feet of paint needed:	**162.5**	**sq. ft.**

Step 5: Determine gallons of paint needed.

Take total from Step 4:	162.5	sq. ft.
Divide by square feet of coverage/gallon:	÷ 350	sq. ft.
Total gallons of paint needed:	**.46**	**gallon**
Round up to whole number:	**1**	**gallon of paint needed to purchase**

INTERMEDIATE

1. 2 gallons of paint for light-colored walls
2. 4 gallons of paint for dark-colored walls
3. 2 gallons of primer

Step 1: Find perimeter of room in feet (e.g., 65.3 ft.).

Wall A:	14	ft.
Wall B:	+ 14	ft.
Wall C:	+ 22	ft.
Wall D:	+ 22	ft.
Total perimeter:	**72**	**ft.**

Step 2: Find square footage of area to be covered.

Total from Step 1:	72	ft.
Multiply by height:	× 9	ft.
Total square feet:	**648**	**sq. ft.**

Step 3: Determine deductions.

Door width:	3	ft.
(36 in. ÷ 12 in. = 3 ft.)		
Height:	× 7	ft.
Total:	**21**	**sq. ft.**
Number of doors:	× 2	doors
Total:	**42**	**sq. ft.**
Window width:	3.67	ft.
(44 in. ÷ 12 in. = 3.67 ft.)		
Height:	× 5.5	ft.
(66 in. ÷ 12 in. = 5.5 ft.)		
Total:	**20.19**	**sq. ft.**
Number of windows:	× 2	windows
Total:	**40.38**	**sq. ft.**

Add all deductions together:

Doors:	42	sq. ft.
Windows:	+ 40.38	sq. ft.
Total deductions:	**82.38**	**sq. ft.**

Step 4: Determine square footage of paint needed.

Take total square feet from Step 2:	648	sq. ft.
Subtract total from Step 3:	− 82.38	sq. ft.
Total square feet needed for 1 coat of paint:	**565.62**	**sq. ft.**
Multiply by anticipated coats of paint:	× 2	coats
Total square feet of paint needed:	**1131.24**	**sq. ft.**

Step 5A: Determine gallons of paint for light-colored walls.

Take total from Step 4 for 1 coat:	565.62	sq. ft.
Divide by square feet of coverage per gallon:	÷ 350	sq. ft.
Total gallons of paint needed:	**1.62**	**gallons**
Round up to whole number:	**2**	**gallons of paint needed to purchase**

Step 5B: Determine gallons of paint for dark-colored walls.

Take total from Step 4 for 2 coats:	1131.24	sq. ft.
Divide by square feet of coverage per gallon:	÷ 350	sq. ft.
Total gallons of paint needed:	**3.23**	**gallons**
Round up to whole number:	**4**	**gallons of paint needed to purchase**

The total needed for primer is the same total found for light-colored walls in Step 5A:

Gallons of primer needed:	**2**	**gallons of primer needed to purchase**

ADVANCED

1. 1 gallon of paint below the chair rail for the medium-colored paint
2. 2 gallons of paint above the chair rail for the dark-colored paint
3. $161.96 for materials before sales tax
4. $1661.96 total cost of this job

Below the Chair Rail:

Step 1: Find perimeter of room below the chair rail in feet (e.g., 65.3 ft.).

Wall A:	14	ft.
Wall B:	+ 14	ft.
Wall C:	+ 14	ft.
Wall D:	+ 14	ft.
Total perimeter:	**56**	**ft.**

Step 2: Find square footage of area to be covered.

Total from Step 1:	56	ft.
Multiply by height:	× 3	ft.
(This may not be full height of wall.)		
Total square feet:	**168**	**sq. ft.**

Step 3: Determine deductions.

Cased opening width:	8	ft. wide
Height:	× 3	ft. tall
(below chair rail is only 3 ft.)		
Total:	**24**	**sq. ft.**
	× 2	openings
Total:	**48**	**sq. ft.**
Window width:	6	ft. wide
(72 in. ÷ 12 in. = 6 ft.)		
Height:	× 3	ft. tall

(66 in. tall windows hung at 68 in. that are then trimmed will have no wall for paint.)

Total:	**18**	**sq. ft.**

Add all deductions together:		
Cased openings:	48	sq. ft.
Window:	+ 18	sq. ft.
Total deductions:	**66**	**sq. ft.**

Step 4: Determine square footage of paint needed.

Take total square feet from Step 2:	168	sq. ft.
Subtract total from Step 3:	− 66	sq. ft.
Total square feet needed for 1 coat of paint:	**102**	**sq. ft.**
Multiply by anticipated coats of paint:	× 2	coats
Total square feet of paint needed:	**204**	**sq. ft.**

Step 5: Determine gallons of paint needed.

Take total from Step 4:	204	sq. ft.
Divide by square feet of coverage per gallon:	÷ 350	sq. ft.
Total gallons of paint needed:	**.58**	**gallon**
Round up to whole number:	**1**	**gallon of paint needed to purchase**

Above the Chair Rail:

Step 1: Find perimeter of room above chair rail in feet (e.g., 65.3 ft.).

Wall A:	14	ft.
Wall B:	+ 14	ft.
Wall C:	+ 14	ft.
Wall D:	+ 14	ft.
Total perimeter:	**56**	**ft.**

Step 2: Find square footage of area to be covered.

Total from Step 1:	56	ft.
Multiply by height:	× 6	ft.
(9-ft. ceiling – 3-ft. chair rail)		
Total square feet:	**336**	**sq. ft.**

Step 3: Determine deductions.

Cased opening width:	8	ft.
Height:	× 4	ft. tall
(7 ft. tall – 3 ft. chair rail = 4 ft.; above chair rail is only 4 ft.)		
Total:	**32**	**sq. ft.**
Number of openings:	× 2	openings
Total:	**64**	**sq. ft.**
Window width:	6	ft.
Height:	× 3.67	ft.
(Windows standardly hung at 6.67 ft. [68 in.] – 3 ft. chair rail = 3.67 ft.)		
Total:	**22.02**	**sq. ft.**

Add all deductions together:

Cased openings:	64	sq. ft.
Windows:	+ 22.02	sq. ft.
Total deductions:	**86.02**	**sq. ft.**

Step 4: Determine square footage of paint needed.

Take total square feet from Step 2:	336	sq. ft.
Subtract total from Step 3:	– 86.02	sq. ft.
Total square feet needed for 1 coat of paint:	**249.98**	**sq. ft.**
Multiply by anticipated coats of paint:	× 2	coats
Total square feet of paint needed:	**499.96**	**sq. ft.**

Step 5: Determine gallons of paint needed.

Take total from Step 4:	499.96	sq. ft.
Divide by square feet of coverage per gallon:	÷ 350	sq. ft.
Total gallons of paint needed:	**1.43**	**gallons**
Round up to whole number:	**2**	**gallons of paint needed to purchase**

Pricing:

Below chair rail: eggshell paint at $39.99 per gallon × 1 gallon:		$39.99
Above chair rail: eggshell paint at $47.99 per gallon × 2 gallons:	+	$95.98
Primer: $25.99 per gallon × 1 gallon:	+	$25.99
Material price:		**$161.96**
As quoted by painting contractor:		
Labor price:	+	**$1500.00**
Total price for painting:		**$1661.96** plus tax

Chapter 3: Wallcoverings

BASIC

1. 20-foot perimeter
2. 0 deduction. Door is smaller than 41 inches.
3. 8 s/r to be ordered.

Step 1: Find perimeter of room in feet (e.g., 65.3 ft.).

Wall A:		3	ft.
Wall B:	+	3	ft.
Wall C:	+	7	ft.
Wall D:	+	7	ft.
Total perimeter:		**20**	**ft.**

Step 2: Find height of area.

Height of area to be wallpapered in feet:		9	ft.

The wallpaper has a repeat:

Take the height of area to be wallpapered in feet:		9	ft.
Divide by length of the repeat, in feet:	÷	1.25	ft.

(15 in. ÷ 12 in. = 1.25 ft.)

Total number of repeats:		**7.2**	**repeats**
Round up to whole number:		**8**	**full repeats**
Multiply by length of the repeat:	×	1.25	ft.
New adjusted height:		**10**	**ft.**

Step 3: Determine base square feet of area.

Height, adjusted or otherwise, from Step 2:		10	ft.
Multiply by total perimeter from Step 1:	×	20	ft.
Total square feet:		**200**	**sq. ft.**

Step 4: Determine deductions.

Because you only deduct openings or cabinets 41 inches wide and over, there are no deductions.

Step 5: Calculate adjusted square feet.

Take total square feet from Step 3:		200	sq. ft.
Subtract total square feet of openings from Step 4:	−	0	sq. ft.
Total adjusted square feet of wallpaper:		**200**	**sq. ft.**

Step 6: Calculate number of rolls to be ordered.

Adjusted square feet of wallpaper from Step 5:		200	sq. ft.
Divide by square feet of single roll of wallpaper:	÷	26.5	sq. ft.
Total number of single rolls:		**7.55**	**s/r**
Round up to nearest even whole number:		**8**	**total single rolls**

Most wallpaper sold today is packaged in double-roll bolts.

INTERMEDIATE

1. 72-foot perimeter
2. 10.5-foot adjusted cut length
3. 40.37 square feet deduction
4. 24 s/r
5. 24 s/r × $45.95 = $1,102.80 retail
6. 24 s/r × $1.00 s/h per s/r = $24.00 shipping & handling
7.

24 s/r × $30.00 per s/r:	$720	
24 s/r × $5.00 per s/r:	+ $120	
	$840	**labor**

8.

Wallpaper material:	$1,102.80
Shipping & handling:	+ 24.00
Labor:	+ 840.00
Total:	**$1,966.80**

Step 1: Find perimeter of room in feet (e.g., 65.3 ft.).

Wall A:		14	ft.
Wall B:	+	14	ft.
Wall C:	+	22	ft.
Wall D:	+	22	ft.
Total perimeter:		**72**	**ft.**

Step 2: Find height of area.

Height of area to be wallpapered in feet:		9	ft.

The wallpaper has a repeat:

Take the height of the area to be wallpapered:		9	ft.
Divide by the length of the repeat in feet:	÷	1.75	ft.

(21 in. ÷ 12 in. = 1.75 ft.)

Total number of repeats:		**5.14**	**repeats**
Round up to whole number:		**6**	**full repeats**
Multiply by length of the repeat:	×	1.75	ft.
New adjusted height:		**10.5**	**ft.**

Step 3: Determine base square feet of area.

Height, adjusted or otherwise,
from Step 2: _____10.5_____ ft.
Multiply by total perimeter
from Step 1: × _____72_____ ft.
Total square feet: **756** sq. ft.

Step 4: Determine deductions.

Only deduct openings or cabinets 41 in. wide and over.
Width of deduction in feet
(e.g., 4 ft. for 48 in.): _____7.34_____ ft.
No deduction for door, since door is under 41 in.
Windows: 44 in. by 66 in. Convert to feet by dividing each
number by 12 in.:

44 in. ÷ 12 in. = 3.6666 ft., round up to 3.67 ft. wide
66 in. ÷ 12 in. = 5.5 ft. height

Total width: 3.67 ft. × 2 = 7.34 ft.
Multiply by height of
deduction in feet: × _____5.5_____ ft.
**Total square feet of
deduction:** **40.37** sq. ft.

Step 5: Calculate adjusted square feet.

Take total square feet
from Step 3: _____756_____ sq. ft.
Subtract total square feet of
openings from Step 4: _____40.37_____ sq. ft.
**Total adjusted square feet
of wallpaper:** **715.63** sq. ft.

Step 6: Calculate number of rolls to be ordered.

Adjusted square feet of
wallpaper from Step 5: _____715.63_____ sq. ft.
Divide by square feet of
single roll of wallpaper: ÷ _____30_____ sq. ft.
Total number of single rolls: **23.85** s/r
**Round up to nearest even
whole number:** **24** total single rolls
Most wallpaper sold today is packaged in double-roll bolts.

1. 135.5 ft.
2. 11.12 ft.
3. 1506.76 sq. ft.
4. 112 yards
5. 112 yards × $18.95 = $2122.40

Step 1: Find perimeter of room in feet (e.g., 65.3 ft.).

Wall A: _____19.5_____ ft.
Wall B: + _____15_____ ft.
Wall C: + _____13_____ ft.
Wall D: + _____15_____ ft.
Wall E: + _____19.5_____ ft.
Wall F: + _____4.5_____ ft.
Wall G: + _____4.5_____ ft.
Wall H: + _____4.5_____ ft.
Wall I: + _____10_____ ft.
Wall J: + _____10_____ ft.
Wall K: + _____10_____ ft.
Wall L: + _____10_____ ft.
Total perimeter: **135.5** ft.

Step 2: Find height of area.

Height of area to be
wallpapered in feet: _____9_____ ft.

The wallpaper has a repeat:
Take the height of the area
to be wallpapered: _____9_____ ft.
Divide by the length of the
repeat in feet: ÷ _____1.71_____ ft.
(20.5 in. ÷ 12 in. = 1.71 ft.)
Total number of repeats: **5.26** repeats
Round up to whole number: **6** full repeats
Multiply by length of the
repeat: × _____1.71_____ ft.
New adjusted height: **10.26** ft.

For a drop match repeat:
If drop match, add ½ the
length of the repeat: + _____.86_____ ft.
(1.71 ft. ÷ 2 = .86 ft.)
**New total height for paper
with drop match:** **11.12** ft.

Step 3: Determine base square feet of area.

Height, adjusted or otherwise,
from Step 2: _____11.12_____ ft.
Multiply by total perimeter
from Step 1: × _____135.5_____ ft.
Total square feet: **1506.76** sq. ft.

Step 4: Determine deductions.
Only deduct openings or cabinets 108 in. wide and over.
Therefore, no deductions.

Step 5: Calculate adjusted square feet.
Take total square feet from
Step 3:   1506.76   sq. ft.
Subtract total square feet of
openings from Step 4:   –   0   sq. ft.
**Total adjusted square feet
of wallpaper:**   1506.76   sq. ft.

Step 6: Calculate number of rolls to be ordered.
Adjusted square feet of
wallpaper from Step 5:   1506.76 sq. ft.
Divide by square feet of
single roll of wallpaper: ÷   13.5   sq. ft.

- 27–28 in. wide—American-sized roll is 30 square feet per single roll.
- 20–22 in. wide—European/metric-sized roll is 26.5 square feet per single roll.
- 54 in. wide—Commercial roll has approximately 13.5 square feet per yard.

**Total number of single rolls
(or yards):**   111.61 yards

If this is a decimal, round up to nearest even whole number, since most wallpaper sold today is packaged in double-roll bolts. If this is yardage, round up to the nearest full yard.

                                          112   total yards

Chapter 4: Other Wall Materials

BASIC

Wall Tile

1. 42 square feet base tile
2. 46.2 square feet tile needed, including waste allowance
3. 4 boxes/cartons totaling 50 square feet of tile
4. 2
5. 10

Field Tile:

Step 1: Calculate base square footage of space.

Take width of area in feet: _____6_____ ft.
(There are two walls that are 3 feet each. Add both walls together: 3 ft. + 3 ft. = 6-ft. width.)
Multiply by height of area
in feet: × _____7_____ ft.
Total base square footage: _____42_____ sq. ft.

Step 2: Calculate additional materials for waste allowance.

For wall tile laid straight:
Take square footage from
Step 1: _____42_____ sq. ft.
Multiply by 10 percent to
allow for waste: × ___1.10___ waste allowance
Total square footage needed: ___46.2___ sq. ft.

Tile material is sold by the full box/carton, so proceed to Step 3 to determine amount needed.

Step 3: Calculate number of full boxes/cartons to be ordered.

Take square footage needed
from Step 2: _____46.2_____ sq. ft.
Divide by square footage
per box/carton: ÷ ___12.5___ sq. ft.
Total boxes/cartons needed: _____3.7_____ boxes/cartons
Round up to whole number: _____4_____ full boxes/
cartons to order

Step 4: Calculate square feet in boxes/cartons ordered to calculate pricing to client for material.

Take number of boxes/cartons
from Step 3: _____4_____ boxes/cartons
Multiply by square feet
per box/carton: × ___12.5___ sq. ft.
Total square footage ordered: _____50_____ sq. ft.

Out Corners:

When calculating for out corners, keep in mind that there are two exposed corners, resulting in two out corners.

Bullnose:

Step 1: Calculate total length of accent or trim needed.

Add length of trim needed: _____7_____ ft.
Add additional lengths: + _____3_____ ft.
Add additional lengths: + _____3_____ ft.
Add additional lengths: + _____7_____ ft.
**Total length needed for
accent or trim:** _____20_____ ft.

Step 2: Deduct for openings. If this step is not needed, skip to Step 3.

This step is not necessary for this scenario.

Step 3: Calculate total number of pieces of trim to be ordered.

Take total from Step 1 or
Step 2: _____20_____ ft.
Divide by length of
accent/trim piece: ÷ _____.5_____ ft.
(6-inch tile divided by 12 inches = .5 feet.)

Total pieces needed: _____10_____ pieces
Round up to whole number: _____10_____ full pieces

Since this bullnose is sold by the piece, calculations for material can stop at this point.

Paneling

1. 39.6 feet
2. 5 panels
3. 160 square feet

Step 1: Find perimeter of room in feet (e.g., 65.3 ft.).

Wall A:		12	ft.
Wall B:	+	12	ft.
Wall C:	+	12	ft.
Total perimeter:		**36**	**ft.**

Step 2: Calculate additional materials for waste allowance:

Total from Step 1:		36	ft.
Multiply by 10 percent to allow for waste:	×	1.10	waste allowance
Total perimeter needed:		**39.6**	**ft.**

Step 3: Calculate total number of panels to be ordered.

Take total from Step 2:		39.6	ft.
Divide by width of panel:	÷	8	ft.
Total:		**4.95**	**panels**
Round up to whole number:		**5**	**full panels**

Items are sold by the square foot, so continue to Step 4.

Step 4: Calculate square feet in panels ordered to calculate pricing to client for material.

Take number of panels from Step 3:		5	panels
Multiply by square feet per panel:	×	32	sq. ft.
Total square footage ordered:		**160**	**sq. ft.**

INTERMEDIATE

Wall Tile

1. 30 square feet base tile
2. 34.5 square feet with allowance for diagonal placement
3. 2 cartons should be ordered; 36 square feet
4. 7 bullnose pieces should be ordered

Field Tile:

Step 1: Calculate base square footage of space.

Take width of area in feet:		20	ft.

(Because the height is the same, the two walls can be added together: 10 ft. + 10 ft. = 20 ft.)

Multiply by height of area in feet:	×	1.5	ft.
Total base square footage:		**30**	**sq. ft.**

Step 2: Calculate additional materials for waste allowance.

For wall tile laid diagonally and staggered:

Take square footage from Step 1:		30	sq. ft.
Multiply by 15 percent to allow for waste:	×	1.15	waste allowance
Total square footage needed:		**34.5**	**sq. ft.**

Tile material is sold by the full box/carton, so proceed to Step 3 to determine amount needed.

Step 3: Calculate number of full boxes/cartons to be ordered.

Take square footage needed from Step 2:		34.5	sq. ft.
Divide by square footage per box/carton:	÷	18	sq. ft.
Total boxes/cartons needed:		**1.92**	**boxes/cartons**
Round up to whole number:		**2**	**full boxes/ cartons to order**

Step 4: Calculate square feet in boxes/cartons ordered to calculate pricing to client for material.

Take number of boxes/cartons from Step 3:		2	boxes/cartons
Multiply by square feet per box/carton:	×	18	sq. ft.
Total square footage ordered:		**36**	**sq. ft.**

Bullnose:

The only place to calculate for bullnose is on each side of the wall tile and 2 inches from each side of the window.

Step 1: Calculate total length of accent or trim needed.

Add length of trim needed: _____1.5_____ ft.

Add additional lengths: + _____1.5_____ ft.

Add additional lengths: + _____.33_____ ft.

(2 inches are needed for each side of sink.
2 in. + 2 in. = 4 in., divided by 12 in. = .33 ft.)

**Total length needed for
accent or trim:** _____3.33_____ ft.

Step 2: Deduct for openings. If this step is not needed, skip to Step 3.

This step is not necessary for this scenario.

Step 3: Calculate total number of pieces of trim to be ordered.

Take total from Step 1 or Step 2: _____3.33_____ ft.

Divide by length of
accent/trim piece: ÷ _____.5_____ ft.

Total pieces of trim needed: _____6.66_____ pieces

Round up to whole number: _____7_____ full pieces

Since this bullnose is sold by the piece, calculations for material can stop at this point.

Paneling

1. 66 feet
2. 17 panels
3. 544 square feet
4. 60 feet of crown molding; 5 pieces. This total is an exact total. In practice, it will probably take another piece. If it is possible to order a 6-foot or 8-foot piece of the same crown molding, that will create the cushion needed for installing.
5. 60 feet of baseboard; 5 pieces

Paneling:

Step 1: Find perimeter of room in feet (e.g., 65.3 ft.).

Wall A: _____12_____ ft.

Wall B: + _____12_____ ft.

Wall C: + _____18_____ ft.

Wall D: + _____18_____ ft.

Total perimeter _____60_____ ft.

Step 2: Calculate additional materials for waste allowance:

Total from Step 1: _____60_____ ft.

Multiply by 10 percent to
allow for waste: × _____1.10_____ waste allowance

Total perimeter needed: _____66_____ ft.

Step 3: Calculate total number of panels to be ordered.

Take total from Step 2: _____66_____ ft.

Divide by width of panel: ÷ _____4_____ ft.

Total: _____16.5_____ panels

Round up to whole number: _____17_____ full panels

Items are sold by the square foot, so continue to Step 4.

Step 4: Calculate square feet in panels ordered to calculate pricing to client for material.

Take number of panels from
Step 3: _____17_____ panels

Multiply by square feet
per panel: × _____32_____ sq. ft.

Total square footage ordered: _____544_____ sq. ft.

Crown Molding:

Step 1: Calculate total length of accent or trim needed.

Add length of trim needed: _____12_____ ft.

Add additional lengths: + _____12_____ ft.

Add additional lengths: + _____18_____ ft.

Add additional lengths: + _____18_____ ft.

**Total length needed for
accent or trim:** _____60_____ ft.

Step 2: Deduct for openings. If this step is not needed, skip to Step 3.

There are no deductions for crown molding.

Step 3: Calculate total number of pieces of trim to be ordered.

Take total from Step 1 or
Step 2: _____60_____ ft.

Divide by length of
accent/trim piece: ÷ _____12_____ ft.

Total pieces of trim needed: _____5_____ pieces

Round up to whole number: _____5_____ full pieces

Items are sold by the foot, so continue to Step 4.

Step 4: Calculate total length to be ordered.

Take total from Step 3: _____5_____ pieces

Multiply by actual length of
pieces: × _____12_____ ft.

Total feet actually ordered: _____60_____ ft.

Baseboard:

You can start with the 60 feet from Step 1 of the crown molding and then take deductions for the doors. The window does not interfere with the baseboard.

Step 1: Calculate total length of accent or trim needed.

Add length of trim needed:	12	ft.
Add additional lengths:	+ 12	ft.
Add additional lengths:	+ 18	ft.
Add additional lengths:	+ 18	ft.
Total length needed for accent or trim:	**60**	**ft.**

Step 2: Deduct for openings. If this step is not needed, skip to Step 3.

Total length from Step 1:	60	ft.
Subtract opening:	– 3	ft.
Continue to subtract as needed:	– 3	ft.

Note: The two doors could also have been added together on one line.

Total adjusted length:	**54**	**ft.**

Step 3: Calculate total number of pieces of trim to be ordered.

Take total from Step 1 or Step 2:	54	ft.
Divide by length of accent/trim piece:	÷ 12	ft.
Total pieces of trim needed:	**4.5**	**pieces**
Round up to whole number:	**5**	**full pieces**

Step 4: Calculate total length to be ordered.

Take total from Step 3:	5	pieces
Multiply by actual length of pieces:	× 12	ft.
Total feet actually ordered:	**60**	**ft.**

ADVANCED

Wall Tile

1. 98 square feet base
2. 107.8 square feet with waste allowance
3. 9 cartons ordered; 120.6 square feet
4. 2 corner bullnose
5. 14 pieces of bullnose
6. 20 pieces of accent liner

Field Tile:

Step 1: Calculate base square footage of space.

Take width of area in feet:	14	ft.

Note: Add the widths of all the walls together, since they will have the same height.

Multiply by height of area in feet:	× 7	ft.
Total base square footage:	**98**	**sq. ft.**

Step 2: Calculate additional materials for waste allowance.

For wall tile laid straight:

Take square footage from Step 1:	98	sq. ft.
Multiply by 10 percent to allow for waste:	× 1.10	waste allowance
Total square footage needed:	**107.8**	**sq. ft.**

Tile material is sold by the full box/carton, so proceed to Step 3 to determine amount needed.

Step 3: Calculate number of full boxes/cartons to be ordered.

Take square footage needed from Step 2:	107.8	sq. ft.
Divide by square footage per box/carton:	÷ 13.4	sq. ft.
Total boxes/cartons needed:	**8.04**	**boxes/cartons**
Round up to full number:	**9**	**full boxes/ cartons to order**

Step 4: Calculate square feet in boxes/cartons ordered to calculate pricing to client for material.

Take number of boxes/cartons from Step 3:	9	boxes/cartons
Multiply by square feet per box/carton:	× 13.4	sq. ft.
Total square footage ordered:	**120.6**	**sq. ft.**

Corner Bullnose:

Because the corner bullnose is considered, there are 2 out corners so only 2 corner bullnoses necessary.

Bullnose:

Step 1: Calculate total length of accent or trim needed.

Add length of trim needed:	7	ft.
Add additional lengths:	+ 7	ft.
Add additional lengths:	+ 14	ft.
Total length needed for accent or trim:	**28**	**ft.**

Step 2: Deduct for openings. If this step is not needed, skip to Step 3.

This step is not needed for this tile application.

Step 3: Calculate total number of pieces of trim to be ordered.

Take total from Step 1 or Step 2:	28	ft.
Divide by length of accent/trim piece:	÷ .5	ft.
Total pieces of trim needed:	**56**	**pieces**
Round up to whole number:	**56**	**full pieces**

Since this bullnose is sold by the piece, calculations for material can stop at this point.

Accent Liner:

Step 1: Calculate total length of accent or trim needed.

Add length of trim needed:	4	ft.
Add additional lengths:	+ 4	ft.
Add additional lengths:	+ 6	ft.
Total length needed for accent or trim:	**14**	**ft.**

Step 2: Deduct for openings. If this step is not needed, skip to Step 3.

This step is not needed for this tile application.

Step 3: Calculate total number of pieces of trim to be ordered.

Take total from Step 1 or Step 2:	14	ft.
Divide by length of accent/trim piece:	÷ .71	ft.
(8.5 in. ÷ 12 in. = .708333. Round up to .71 feet.)		
Total pieces of trim needed:	**19.72**	**pieces**
Round up to whole number:	**20**	**full pieces**

Since this trim is sold by the piece, calculations for material can stop at this point.

Paneling

1. 88 feet
2. 88 panels
3. 704 square feet
4. 60 feet of plate rail; 6 pieces
5. 80 feet of baseboard; 8 pieces

Main Paneling:

Step 1: Find perimeter of room in feet (e.g., 65.3 ft.).

Wall A:	24	ft.
Wall B:	+ 24	ft.
Wall C:	+ 16	ft.
Wall D:	+ 16	ft.
Total perimeter:	**80**	**ft.**

Step 2: Calculate additional materials for waste allowance:

Total from Step 1:	80	ft.
Multiply by 10 percent to allow for waste:	× 1.10	waste allowance
Total perimeter needed:	**88**	**ft.**

Step 3: Calculate total number of panels to be ordered.

Take total from Step 5:	88	ft.
Divide by width of panel:	÷ 1	ft.
Total:	**88**	**panels**
Round up to whole number:	**88**	**full panels**

Items are sold by the square foot, so continue to Step 4.

Step 4: Calculate square feet in panels ordered to calculate pricing to client for material.

Take number of panels from Step 3:	88	panels
Multiply by square feet per panel:	× 8	sq. ft.
Total square footage ordered:	**704**	**sq. ft.**

Plate Rail:

Step 1: Calculate total length of accent or trim needed.

Add length of trim needed:	16	ft.
Add additional lengths:	+ 16	ft.
Add additional lengths:	+ 24	ft.
Add additional lengths:	+ 24	ft.
Total length needed for accent or trim:	**80**	**ft.**

Step 2: Deduct for openings. If this step is not needed, skip to Step 3.

Total length from Step 1:	80	ft.
Subtract opening:	− 14	ft.
Continue to subtract as needed:	− 9	ft.

(There are three 3-foot openings: 3 ft. × 3 ft. = 9 ft.)

Total adjusted length: 57 ft.

Step 3: Calculate total number of pieces of trim to be ordered.

Take total from Step 1 or Step 2:	57	ft.
Divide by length of accent/trim piece:	÷ 10	ft.
Equals pieces of trim needed:	**5.7**	**pieces**
Round up to whole number:	**6**	**full pieces**

Items are sold by the foot, so continue to Step 4.

Step 4: Calculate total length to be ordered.

Take total from Step 3:	6	pieces
Multiply by actual length of pieces:	× 10	ft.
Total feet actually ordered:	**60**	**ft.**

Baseboard:

Step 1: Calculate total length of accent or trim needed.

Add length of trim needed:	16	ft.
Add additional lengths:	+ 16	ft.
Add additional lengths:	+ 24	ft.
Add additional lengths:	+ 24	ft.
Total length needed for accent or trim:	**80**	**ft.**

Step 2: Deduct for openings. If this step is not needed, skip to Step 3.

The only deduction will be for the door, which interrupts the baseboard.

Total length from Step 1:	80	ft.
Subtract opening:	− 3	ft.
Total adjusted length:	**77**	**ft.**

Step 3: Calculate total number of pieces of trim to be ordered.

Take total from Step 1 or Step 2:	77	ft.
Divide by length of accent/trim piece:	÷ 10	ft.
Total pieces of trim needed:	**7.7**	**pieces**
Round up to whole number:	**8**	**full pieces**

Step 4: Calculate total length to be ordered.

Take total from Step 3:	8	pieces
Multiply by actual length of pieces:	× 10	ft.
Total feet actually ordered:	**80**	**ft.**

Pricing of Wall Tile

1. $641.41
2. $2150.60
3. $2792.01

Note: It will help if you organize more complicated pricing into a schedule or worksheet.

Master Bathroom Shower			
Client:	**Address:**		
	Quantity	Price	Total
Material Wall tile	120.6 sq. ft.	$3.15/sq. ft.	$379.89
Trim pieces Bullnose	56 pieces	$1.86 each	$104.16
Out corners bullnose	2 pieces	$3.98 each	$7.96
Accent liner	20 pieces	$7.47 each	$149.40
		Material Total	**$641.41**
Installation Wall tile	120.6 sq. ft.	$15.00/sq. ft.	$1809.00
All bullnose (including out corner)	56 bullnose × .5 ft. (6 in.) = 28 ft. 2 out corners × .25 ft. (3 in.) = .5 ft. Total running ft. = 28.5 ft.	$8.00/running ft.	$228.00
Accent liner	8.5 in. ÷ 12 in. = .71 ft. 20 pieces × .71 ft. = 14.2 running ft.	$8.00/running ft.	$113.60
Mastic and grout			Included
Sealant			n/a
Shipping			n/a
		Labor Total	**$2150.60**
		Total Price of Project (Materials + Labor)	**$2792.01**

Advanced—Pricing for Wall Tile

Chapter 5: Suspended Ceilings

BASIC

Decorative Ceiling

1. 384 square feet base
2. 422.4 square feet with waste allowance
3. 106 ceiling tiles to be ordered

Step 1: Calculate base square footage of space.
For odd-shaped rooms, divide room into geometric shapes and calculate for each space.

Take width of room in feet:	24	ft.
Multiply by length of room in feet:	× 16	ft.
Total base square footage of space:	**384**	**sq. ft.**

Step 2: Calculate additional materials for waste allowance.

Take square footage from Step 1:	384	sq. ft.
Multiply by 10 percent to allow for waste:	× 1.10	waste allowance
Total square footage needed:	**422.4**	**sq. ft.**

Step 3: Calculate number of ceiling tiles to be ordered.

Take square footage needed from Step 2:	422.4	sq. ft.
Divide by square footage of individual tiles:	÷ 4	sq. ft.
(2 ft. × 2 ft. = 4 sq. ft.)		
Total tiles needed:	**105.6**	**tiles**
Round up to full number:	**106**	**tiles to order**

INTERMEDIATE

Suspended Ceiling

1. 1440 square feet base
2. 1584 square feet with waste allowance
3. 198 ceiling tiles to be ordered

Step 1: Calculate base square footage of space.
For odd-shaped rooms, divide room into geometric shapes and calculate for each space.

Take width of room in feet:	48	ft.
Multiply by length of room in feet:	× 30	ft.
Total base square footage of space:	**1440**	**sq. ft.**

Step 2: Calculate additional materials for waste allowance.

Take square footage from Step 1:	1440	sq. ft.
Multiply by 10 percent to allow for waste:	× 1.10	waste allowance
Total square footage needed:	**1584**	**sq. ft.**

Step 3: Calculate number of ceiling tiles to be ordered.

Take square footage needed from Step 2:	1584	sq. ft.
Divide by square footage of individual tiles:	÷ 8	sq. ft.
(2 ft. × 4 ft. = 8 sq. ft.)		
Total tiles needed:	**198**	**tiles**
Round up to full number:	**198**	**tiles to order**

ADVANCED
Suspended and Decorative Ceilings
1. 360 square feet base
2. 396 square feet with waste allowance
3. 99 ceiling tiles to order
4. 520 square feet base
5. 572 square feet with waste allowance
6. 143 ceiling tiles to order

Suspended Ceiling:

Step 1: Calculate base square footage of space for the suspended ceiling.

Space #1—Take width of room in feet:	8	ft.
Multiply by length of room in feet:	× 10	ft.
Total base square footage of space:	80	sq. ft. #1
Space #2—Take width of room in feet:	20	ft.
Multiply by length of room in feet:	× 14	ft.
Total base square footage of space:	280	sq. ft. #2
Add all spaces together:	80	sq. ft. #1
	+ 280	sq. ft. #2
Total Step 1:	360	sq. ft.

Step 2: Calculate additional materials for waste allowance.

Take square footage from Step 1:	360	sq. ft.
Multiply by 10 percent to allow for waste:	× 1.10	waste allowance
Total square footage needed:	396	sq. ft.

Step 3: Calculate number of ceiling tiles to be ordered.

Take square footage needed from Step 2:	396	sq. ft.
Divide by square footage of individual tiles: (2 ft. × 2 ft. = 4 sq. ft.)	÷ 4	sq. ft.
Total tiles needed:	99	tiles
Round up to full number:	99	tiles to order

Tin Ceiling:

Step 1: Calculate base square footage for the decorative tin ceiling

Space #1—Take width of room in feet:	12	ft.
Multiply by length of room in feet:	× 10	ft.
Total base square footage of space #1:	120	sq. ft. #1
Space #2—Take width of room in feet:	20	ft.
Multiply by length of room in feet:	× 20	ft.
Total base square footage of space:	400	sq. ft. #2
Add all spaces together:	120	sq. ft. #1
	+ 400	sq. ft. #2
Total Step 1:	520	sq. ft.

Step 2: Calculate additional materials for waste allowance.

Take square footage from Step 1:	520	sq. ft.
Multiply by 10 percent to allow for waste:	× 1.10	waste allowance
Total square footage needed:	572	sq. ft.

Step 3: Calculate number of ceiling tiles to be ordered.

Take square footage needed from Step 2:	572	sq. ft.
Divide by square footage of individual tiles: (2 ft. × 2 ft. = 4 sq. ft.)	÷ 4	sq. ft.
Total tiles needed:	143	tiles
Round up to full number:	143	tiles to order

Pricing
1. $2607.60
2. $3377.60

106 ceiling tiles × $24.00 per tile = $2544.00

106 ceiling tiles × $0.60 per tile = $63.60 (This surpasses the $10.00 minimum shipping charge.)

$2544.00 for ceiling tiles + $63.60 for shipping = $2607.60

Materials $2607.60 + Installation $770 = $3377.60

Chapter 6: Plank and Tile Flooring

BASIC

Plank Flooring

1. 180 square feet   2. 198 square feet   3. 198 square feet

Step 1: Calculate base square footage of space.

Take width of room in feet:	12	ft.
Multiply by length of room in feet:	× 15	ft.
Base square footage of space:	**180**	**sq. ft.**

Step 2: Calculate additional materials for waste allowance.

For tile or plank flooring laid straight:

Take square footage from Step 1:	180	sq. ft.
Multiply by 10 percent to allow for waste:	× 1.10	waste allowance
Total square footage needed:	**198**	**sq. ft.**

Tile Flooring

1. 80 square feet   2. 88 square feet   3. 88.92 square feet

Step 1: Calculate base square footage of space.

Take width of room in feet:	10	ft.
Multiply by length of room in feet:	× 8	ft.
Base square footage of space:	**80**	**sq. ft.**

Step 2: Calculate additional materials for waste allowance.

For tile or plank flooring laid straight:

Take square footage from Step 1:	80	sq. ft.
Multiply by 10 percent to allow for waste:	× 1.10	waste allowance
Total square footage needed:	**88**	**sq. ft.**

Since tile is 15 in. × 15 in. (1.25 ft. × 1.25 ft.), each tile is 1.56 sq. ft. To find the actual amount to order, 88 sq. ft divided by 1.56 sq. ft. = 56.41 tiles. Round up to full tiles = 57 tiles × 1.56 sq. ft. = 88.92 sq. ft. ordered.

INTERMEDIATE

Plank Flooring

1. 719 square feet
2. 790.9 square feet
3. 804.10 square feet
4. 34 cartons
5. 25.5 feet
6. 30 feet

Step 1: Calculate base square footage of space.

For odd-shaped rooms, divide room into geometric shapes and calculate for each space. In this scenario, the overall square feet of the larger rectangle is first calculated. Then the triangular areas that aren't included are subtracted.

Take width of room in feet:	40	ft.
Multiply by length of room in feet:	× 20	ft.
Base square footage of space:	**800**	**sq. ft.**

Next, calculate the triangular areas not part of that rectangle to subtract.

Base of triangular space:	9	ft. width
Multiply by height of triangular space:	× 9	ft. height
Total:	**81**	**sq. ft.**
Divide by 2 to find the amount not included:	÷ 2	
Total to be deducted:	**40.5**	**sq. ft.**

In this scenario there are two "clipped" or angled corners. Therefore, the square footage found is multiplied by 2.

	× 2	corners
Final total to be deducted:	81	sq. ft.
Base square footage:	800	sq. ft.
Subtract corner deductions:	− 81	sq. ft.
Total base square footage:	**719**	**sq. ft.**

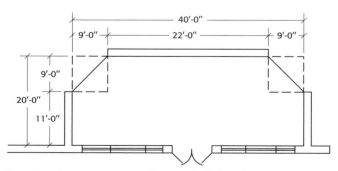

Practice Answer: Intermediate—Plank flooring.

Step 2: Calculate additional materials for waste allowance.

For tile or plank flooring laid straight.

Take square footage from Step 1: ___719___ sq. ft.

Multiply by 10 percent to
allow for waste: × __1.10__ waste allowance

Total square footage needed: __790.9__ sq. ft.

Hard flooring material is sold by the full box/carton, so proceed to Step 3 to determine amount needed.

Step 3: Calculate number of full boxes/cartons to be ordered.

Take square footage needed
from Step 2: __790.9__ sq. ft.

Divide by square footage
per box/carton: ÷ __23.65__ sq. ft.

Total boxes/cartons needed: __33.4__ boxes/cartons

Round up to whole number: __34__ boxes/cartons to order

Step 4: Calculate square feet in boxes/cartons ordered to calculate pricing to client for material.

Take number of boxes from
Step 3: __34__ boxes/cartons

Multiply by square feet
per box/carton: × __23.65__ sq. ft.

Total square footage ordered: __804.1__ sq. ft.

Flooring Transition:

Step 1: Calculate total length of transition needed.

Add widths of flooring change: __12.75__ ft.

Continue to add additional
widths: + __12.75__ ft.

**Total length needed for
transition: __25.5__ ft.**

Step 2: Calculate total number of pieces of transition to be ordered.

Take total from Step 1: __25.5__ ft.

Divide by length of transition
piece: ÷ __6__ ft.

Pieces of transition needed: __4.25__ pieces

Round up to whole number: __5__ full pieces

Step 3: Calculate total length of transition to be ordered.

Take total from Step 2: __5__ pieces

Multiply by actual length
of pieces: × __6__ ft. per piece

Total feet actually ordered: __30__ ft.

Tile Flooring

1. 418 square feet   4. 27 cartons
2. 480.7 square feet   5. 29 feet
3. 486 square feet   6. 32.5 feet

Step 1: Calculate base square footage of space.

Take width of room in feet: __22__ ft.

Multiply by length of room
in feet: × __19__ ft.

Base square footage of space: __418__ sq. ft.

Step 2: Calculate additional materials for waste allowance.

For tile and plank flooring laid diagonally and tile flooring staggered:

Take square footage from
Step 1: __418__ sq. ft.

Multiply by 15 percent to
allow for waste: × __1.15__ waste allowance

Total square footage needed: __480.7__ sq. ft.

Hard flooring material is sold by the full box/carton, so proceed to Step 3 to determine amount needed.

Step 3: Calculate number of full boxes/cartons to be ordered.

Take square footage needed
from Step 2: __480.7__ sq. ft.

Divide by square footage
per box/carton: ÷ __18__ sq. ft.

Total boxes/cartons needed: __26.71__ boxes/cartons

Round up to full number: __27__ boxes/cartons to order

Step 4: Calculate square feet in boxes/cartons ordered to calculate pricing to client for material.

Take number of boxes from
Step 3: __27__ boxes/cartons

Multiply by square feet
per box/carton: × __18__ sq. ft.

Total square footage ordered: __486__ sq. ft.

Flooring Transition:

Step 1: Calculate total length of transition needed.

Add widths of flooring change:	20	ft.
Continue to add additional widths:	+ 9	ft.
Total length needed for transition:	**29**	**ft.**

Step 2: Calculate total number of pieces of transition to be ordered.

Take total from Step 1:	29	ft.
Divide by length of transition piece:	÷ 6.5	ft.
Pieces of transition needed:	**4.46**	**pieces**
Round up to whole number:	**5**	**full pieces**

Step 3: Calculate total length of transition to be ordered.

Take total from Step 2:	5	pieces
Multiply by actual length of pieces:	6.5	ft.
Total feet actually ordered:	**32.5**	**ft.**

ADVANCED
Plank Flooring

1. 210 square feet
2. 262.5 square feet
3. 274.34 square feet
4. 11 cartons
5. 33 feet
6. 39 feet; 6 pieces

Step 1: Calculate base square footage of space.

For odd-shaped rooms, divide room into geometric shapes and calculate for each space.

Take width of room in feet:	7	ft.
Multiply by length of room in feet:	× 22	ft.
Total #1 base square footage of space:	**154**	**sq. ft. #1**
Take width of room in feet:	14	ft.
Multiply by length of room in feet:	× 4	ft.
Total #2 base square footage of space:	**56**	**sq. ft. #2**
Total #1:	154	sq. ft.
Total #2:	+ 56	sq. ft.
Base square footage:	**210**	**sq. ft.**

Step 2: Calculate additional materials for waste allowance.

For hard flooring laid in a herringbone pattern:

Take square footage from Step 1:	210	sq. ft.
Multiply by 25 percent to allow for waste:	× 1.25	waste allowance
Total square footage needed:	**262.5**	**sq. ft.**

Hard flooring material is sold by the full box/carton, so proceed to Step 3 to determine amount needed.

Step 3: Calculate number of full boxes/cartons to be ordered.

Take square footage needed from Step 2:	262.5	sq. ft.
Divide by square footage per box/carton:	÷ 24.94	sq. ft.
Total boxes/cartons needed:	**10.53**	**boxes/cartons**
Round up to full number:	**11**	**boxes/cartons to order**

Step 4: Calculate square feet in boxes/cartons ordered to calculate pricing to client for material.

Take number of boxes from Step 3:	11	boxes/cartons:
Multiply by square feet per box/carton:	× 24.94	sq. ft.
Total square footage ordered:	**274.34**	**sq. ft.**

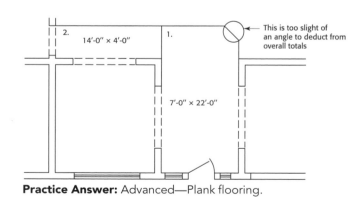

Practice Answer: Advanced—Plank flooring.

Flooring Transition:

Step 1: Calculate total length of transition needed.

Add widths of flooring change: _____12_____ ft.

Continue to add additional
widths: +___12___ ft.

Continue to add additional
widths: +___9___ ft.

**Total length needed for
transition:** _____33_____ ft.

**Step 2: Calculate total number of pieces of transition to
be ordered.**

Take total from Step 1: _____33_____ ft.

Divide by length of
transition piece: ÷___6.5___ ft.

Pieces of transition needed: ___5.08___ **pieces**

Round up to whole number: ___6___ **full pieces**

Step 3: Calculate total length of transition to be ordered.

Take total from Step 2: _____6_____ pieces

Multiply by actual length
of pieces: ×___6.5___ ft. per piece

Total feet actually ordered: _____39_____ **ft.**

Pricing for Plank Flooring

1. $1421.66
2. $350.88
3. $2887.50
4. $4660.04

Plank Hickory Floorcovering					
	Quantity	**Price**	**Subtotal**	**Shipping**	**Total**
Flooring	274.34 sq. ft.	$ 4.30/sq. ft.	$1179.66	11 boxes × $22.00 = $242	$1421.66
Transition pieces	6 pieces	$55.98 each	$ 335.88	$15.00	$350.88
Installation	262.5 sq. ft.	$11.00/sq. ft.	$2887.50	N/A	$2887.50
				Total	$4660.04

Price of Hickory Flooring

BASIC

Resilient Tile

1. 182 square feet
2. 200.2 square feet
3. 6 full boxes/cartons; 216 square feet

Step 1: Draw diagram of room and take room dimensions.

Step 2: Calculate base square footage of space.

Take width of room in feet:	14	ft.
Multiply by length of room in feet:	× 13	ft.
Base square footage of space:	**182**	**sq. ft.**

Step 3: Calculate additional material for waste allowance.

Take square footage from Step 2:	182	sq. ft.
Multiply by 10 percent to allow for waste:	× 1.1	waste allowance
Total square footage needed:	**200.2**	**sq. ft.**

Step 4: Calculate additional materials for replacement allowance.

The tiles will not have a replacement allowance, so this step is skipped.

Step 5: Calculate number of full boxes/cartons to be ordered.

Take square footage needed from Step 3 or 4:	200.2	sq. ft.
Divide by square feet per box/carton:	÷ 36	sq. ft.
Total boxes/cartons needed:	**5.56**	**boxes/cartons**
Round up to whole number:	**6**	**full boxes/ cartons to order**

Step 6: Calculate actual square feet in boxes/cartons ordered.

Take number of boxes from Step 5:	6	boxes/cartons
Multiply by square feet per box/carton:	× 36	sq. ft.
Total square footage ordered:	**216**	**sq. ft.**

Note in the example that the client will be charged for 216 square feet of material. Depending on industry standards in the region where you work, labor may be charged at 200.2 square feet or at 216 square feet.

Sheet Goods

1. 14.5 feet
2. 19.33 square yards
3. 138.6 square feet

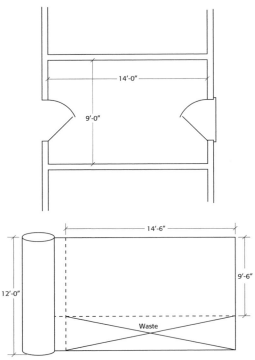

Practice Answer: Basic—Sheet goods.

Step 1: Draw diagram of room and take room dimensions.

Do not use inches. Convert everything to feet. A dimension 13 feet 8 inches converted to feet will be 13.67 feet.

Step 2: Determine width with allowance.

Take width of room in feet (e.g., 15.5 feet):	9	ft.
Add 6 inches (.5 feet):	+ .5	ft.
Total cut width:	**9.5**	**ft.**

Step 3: Determine number of cuts based on material width.

Take cut width from Step 2:	9.5	ft.
Divide by width of material:	÷ 12	ft.

(4-foot rubber; 6-foot vinyl; 6.58-foot linoleum/Marmoleum, or 12-foot vinyl width)

Total:	**.79**	**cut**
Round up to whole number:	**1**	**cut**

Step 4: Determine cut length.

Take length of room in feet
(e.g., 9.25 feet): _____14_____ ft.
Add 6 inches (.5 feet): +_____.5_____ ft.
Total length of cuts: **__14.5__** **ft.**

Step 5: Determine length to order.

Take total from Step 3: _____1_____ cut
Multiply by the total
from Step 4: ×__14.5__ ft.
**Total length of material
to be ordered:** **__14.5__** **ft.**

Step 6: Determine square feet and square yards.

Take length of material from
Step 5: __14.5__ ft.
Multiply by width of material: ×__12__ ft.
(4-ft., 6-ft., 6.58-ft., or 12-ft.width)
Total square feet: **__174__** **sq. ft.**
Divide by 9 to convert to
square yards: ÷__9__
Total square yards needed: **__19.3333__** **sq. yd.**
**Round to two numbers to
right of decimal point:** **__19.33__** **sq. yd. to order**

Underlayment:

Step 1: Determine base square footage of room.

Take exact width of room: _____14_____ ft.
Multiply by exact length
of room: ×_____9_____ ft.
Base square feet of room: **__126__** **sq. ft.**

Step 2: Determine square footage of underlayment needed.

Take total from Step 1: __126__ sq. ft.
Multiply by 1.10 to allow
for waste: ×__1.1__ waste allowance
Total for underlayment: **__138.6__** **sq. ft.**
**Round to two numbers to
right of decimal point:** **__138.60__** **sq. ft. to order**

Broadloom Carpet

1. Toward the entry
2. 18.5 feet
3. 24.67 square yards

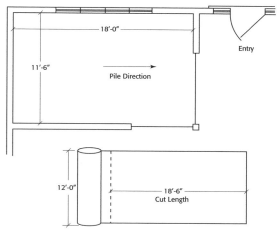

Practice Answer: Basic—Broadloom carpet.

Step 1: Draw diagram of room and take room dimensions.

Step 2: Determine carpet direction in room.

Decide which way the carpet will run. The length dimension of the room is determined by the direction the carpet will come off the roll. The width dimension of the room is the other dimension.

Step 3: Determine overall width with allowance.

Take width of room in feet
(e.g., 15.5 ft.): __11.5__ ft.
Add 6 inches (.5 ft.): +__.5__ ft.
Total cut width: **__12__** **ft.**

Step 4: Determine whether fill is necessary.

Take cut width from Step 3: __12__ ft.
Subtract width of carpet
in feet: −__12__ ft.
(12-ft., 13.17-ft., or 15-ft. width)
Total: **__0__** **ft.**

This number is not greater than 0, so no fill is needed.

Step 5: Determine fill width.

Since there is no fill, this step is skipped.

Step 6: Determine length of first cut.

Take length of room in feet (e.g., 9.25 ft.):	18	ft.
Add 6 inches (.5 feet):	+ .5	ft.
Total length of first cut:	**18.5**	**ft.**

Step 7: Determine fill length.

Since there is no fill, this step is skipped.

Step 8: Determine total length to be ordered.

Take length of first cut from Step 6:	18.5	ft.
Add length of second cut from Step 7:	+ 0	ft.

If more rooms with same carpet, continue to add as many lengths as needed.

Total length of carpet to be ordered:	**18.5**	**ft.**

Step 9: Determine square feet and square yards.

Take length of carpet from Step 8:	18.5	ft.
Multiply by width of carpet:	× 12	ft.
Total square feet:	**222**	**sq. ft.**
Divide by 9 to convert to square yards:	÷ 9	sq. ft.
Total square yards of carpet:	**24.67**	**sq. yd.**

Carpeted Stairs

1. 24 inches
2. 5 cuts
3. 3 pieces
4. 10 feet

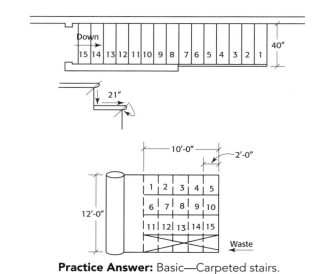

Practice Answer: Basic—Carpeted stairs.

Step 1: Determine cut width.

Measure width of stair in inches:	40	in.
Add 3 inches cut allowance:	+ 3	in.
Total cut width:	**43**	**in.**
Convert to feet:	÷ 12	in.
Total cut width in feet:	**3.58**	**ft.**

Step 2: Determine number of cuts from carpet width.

Take width of carpet in feet:	12	ft.
Divide by total from Step 1:	÷ 3.58	ft.
Total:	**3.35**	**cuts**
Round down to nearest whole number:	**3**	**vertical cuts from carpet width**

This tells you how many full strips will come out of a 12-foot-wide piece of carpet.

Step 3: Determine total number of cuts for carpet length.

Take total number of treads:	15	treads
Divide by total from Step 2:	÷ 3	cuts
Total:	**5**	**cuts**
Round up to whole number:	**5**	**total carpet cuts needed**

Step 4: Determine length of cuts.

Take length of stair cut (riser + tread + around nose):	21	in.
Add 3 inches cut allowance:	+ 3	in.
Total:	**24**	**in.**
Convert to feet:	÷ 12	in.
Total:	**2**	**ft.**

Step 5: Determine total length of carpet.

Take total from Step 3:	5	cuts
Multiply by total from Step 4:	× 2	ft.
Total length of carpet needed:	**10**	**ft.**

Step 6: Determine square feet and square yards.

Take length of carpet from Step 5:	10	ft.
Multiply by width of carpet:	× 12	ft.
Total square feet:	**120**	**sq. ft.**
Divide by 9 to convert to square yards:	÷ 9	sq. ft.
Total square yards of carpet:	**13.33**	**sq. yd. to order**

INTERMEDIATE

Resilient Tile

1. 468 sq. ft.
2. 617.76 sq. ft.
3. 13 boxes/cartons; 624 sq. ft.

Step 1: Draw diagram of room and take room dimensions.

Step 2: Calculate base square footage of space.

Take width of room in feet:	26	ft.
Multiply by length of room in feet:	× 18	ft.
Base square footage of space:	**468**	**sq. ft.**

Step 3: Calculate additional material for waste allowance.

Take square footage from Step 2:	468	sq. ft.
Multiply by 10 percent to allow for waste:	× 1.1	waste allowance
Total square footage needed:	**514.8**	**sq. ft.**

Step 4: Calculate additional materials for replacement allowance.

Take square footage from Step 2:	514.8	sq. ft.
Multiply by 20 percent to allow for replacement:	× 1.20	replacement allowance
Total square footage needed:	**617.76**	**sq. ft.**

Step 5: Calculate number of full boxes/cartons to be ordered

Take square footage needed from Step 3 or 4:	617.76	sq. ft.
Divide by square feet per box/carton:	÷ 48	sq. ft.
Total boxes/cartons needed:	**12.87**	**boxes/cartons**
Round up to whole number:	**13**	**full boxes/ cartons to order**

Step 6: Calculate actual square feet in boxes/cartons ordered.

Take number of boxes from Step 5:	13	boxes/cartons
Multiply by square feet per box/carton:	× 48	sq. ft.
Total square footage ordered:	**624**	**sq. ft.**

Note in this example that the client will be charged for 624 square feet of material. Labor should be charged on the 514.8 square feet that are ordered for installation.

Sheet Goods

1. Parallel to sink; 2 seams   2. 33 ft.   3. 24.13 sq. yd.

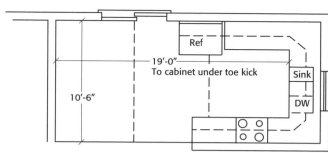

Practice Answer: Intermediate—Sheet goods.

When considering the direction to run the Marmoleum, you must first calculate the seam placement. It is not desirable to have a seam perpendicular to the sink in that traffic area. It is possible in this space to run the seams parallel to the sink wall. This works at the sliding door because the seam is to the right of the open side of the door.

Step 1: Draw diagram of room and take room dimensions.

Step 2: Determine width with allowance.

Take width of room in feet (e.g., 15.5 ft.):	19	ft.
Add 6 inches (.5 feet):	+ .5	ft.
Total:	**19.5**	**ft.**

Step 3: Determine number of cuts based on material width.

Take total from Step 2:	19.5	ft.
Divide by width of material: (79 in. ÷ 12 in. = 6.58 ft.)	÷ 6.58	ft.
Total:	**2.96**	**cuts**
Round up to whole number:	**3**	**cuts**

Step 4: Determine cut length.

Take length of room in feet (e.g., 9.25 ft.):	10.5	ft.
Add 6 inches (.5 feet):	+ .5	ft.
Total length of cuts:	**11**	**ft.**

Step 5: Determine length to order.

Take total from Step 3:	3	cuts
Multiply by the total from Step 4:	× 11	ft.
Total length of material to be ordered:	**33**	**ft.**

Step 6: Determine square feet and square yards.

Take length of material from Step 5:	33	ft.
Multiply by width of material:	× 6.58	ft.
Total (square feet):	**217.14**	**sq. ft.**
Divide by 9 to convert to square yards:	÷ 9	sq. ft.
Total square yards needed:	**24.1266**	**sq. yd.**
Round to two numbers to right of decimal point:	**24.13**	**sq. yd.**

Broadloom Carpet

1. Toward the hall, since carpet must run in the same direction as the hall
2. 31 feet
3. 41.33 square yards

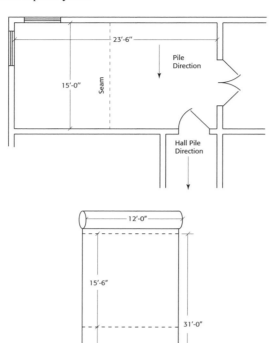

Practice Answer: Intermediate—Broadloom carpet.

Step 1: Draw diagram of room and take room dimensions.

Step 2: Determine carpet direction in room.
Decide which way the carpet will run. The length dimension of the room is determined by the direction the carpet will come off the roll. The width dimension of the room is the other dimension.

Step 3: Determine overall width with allowance.

Take width of room in feet (e.g., 15.5 ft.):	23.5	ft.
Add 6 inches (.5 feet):	+ .5	ft.
Total:	**24**	ft.

Step 4: Determine whether fill is necessary.

Take cut width from Step 3:	24	ft.
Subtract width of carpet in feet:	− 12	ft.
Total:	**12**	ft.

This is a positive number (greater than 0), so determine seam placement and possible fill.

Step 5: Determine fill width.

Take width of carpet in feet:	12	ft.
Divide by total from Step 4:	÷ 12	ft.
Total:	**1**	cuts
Round down to nearest whole number:	**1**	**full piece from carpet width**

This tells you how many full strips will come out of a 12-foot-wide piece of carpet.

Step 6: Determine length of first cut.

Take length of room in feet (e.g., 9.25 ft.):	15	ft.
Add 6 inches (.5 ft.):	+ .5	ft.
Total length of first cut:	**15.5**	ft.

Step 7: Determine fill length.

Take length of room in feet + 6 inches (.5 feet):	15.5	ft.
Divide by total from Step 5:	÷ 1	full piece from carpet width
Total length of second cut:	**15.5**	ft.

Step 8: Determine total length to be ordered.

Take length of first cut from Step 6:	15.5	ft.
Add length of second cut from Step 7:	+ 15.5	ft.

If more rooms with same carpet, continue to add as many lengths as needed.

Total length of carpet to be ordered:	**31**	ft.

Step 9: Determine square feet and square yards.

Take length of carpet from Step 8:	31	ft.
Multiply by width of carpet:	× 12	ft.
Total square feet (sq. ft.):	**372**	sq. ft.
Divide by 9 to convert to square yards:	÷ 9	sq. ft.
Total square yards of carpet:	**41.33**	sq. yd. to order

Carpeted Stairs

1. 1.96 feet
2. 6
3. The first five steps get 2 cuts per carpet width; the next nine steps get 3 cuts per carpet width.

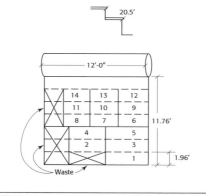

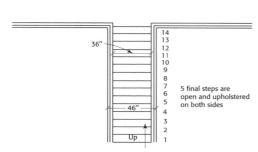

Practice Answer: Intermediate—Carpeted stairs.

Step 1A: Determine cut width for top nine steps.

Measure width of stair in inches:	36	in.
Add 3 inches cut allowance:	+ 3	in.
Total:	**39**	**in.**
Convert to feet:	÷ 12	in.
Total in feet:	**3.25**	**ft.**

The stair widths will change from the top of the run to the bottom. Write down the width measurements and how many treads this affects.

Step 1B: Determine cut width for first five steps.

First five steps are wider and are upholstered on both sides.

Measure width of stair in inches: _____52_____ in.

Both sides are upholstered, so add 3 inches each side, a total of 6 inches, to the width.

	+ 6	in.
Add 3 inches cut allowance:	+ 3	in.
Total:	**55**	**in.**
Convert to feet:	÷ 12	in.
Total in feet:	**4.58**	**ft.**

Step 2A: Determine number of cuts from carpet width for top nine steps.

Take width of carpet in feet:	12	ft.
Divide by total from Step 1A:	÷ 3.25	ft.
Total:	**3.69**	**cuts**
Round down to nearest whole number:	**3**	**vertical cuts from carpet width**

Step 2B: Determine number of cuts from carpet width for first five steps.

Take width of carpet in feet:	12	ft.
Divide by total from Step 1B:	÷ 4.58	ft.
Total:	**2.62**	**cuts**
Round down to nearest whole number:	**2**	**vertical cuts from carpet width**

Step 3A: Determine total number of cuts for top nine steps.

Take total number of treads:	9	treads
Divide by total from Step 2A:	÷ 3	cuts
Total:	**3**	**cuts**
Round up to whole number:	**3**	**total carpet cuts needed**

Step 3B: Determine total number of cuts for first five steps.

Take total number of treads:	5	treads
Divide by total from Step 2B:	÷ 2	cuts
Total:	**2.5**	**cuts**
Round up to whole number:	**3**	**total carpet cuts needed**

Add totals from Step 3A and Step 3B for total carpet cuts:	**6**	**total carpet cuts**

Step 4: Determine length of cuts.

Take length of stair cut (riser + tread + around nose):	20.5	in.
Add 3 inches:	+ 3	in.
Total:	**23.5**	**in.**
Convert to feet:	÷ 12	in.
Total:	**1.96**	**ft.**

Step 5: Determine total length of carpet.

Take total from Step 3:	6	cuts
Multiply by total from Step 4:	× 1.96	ft.
Total length of carpet needed:	**11.76**	**ft.**

Step 6: Determine square feet and square yards.

Take length of carpet from Step 5:	11.76	ft.
Multiply by width of carpet:	× 12	ft.
Total square feet:	**141.12**	**sq. ft.**
Divide by 9 to convert to square yards:	÷ 9	sq. ft.
Total square yards of carpet:	**15.68**	**sq. yd. to order**

ADVANCED

Resilient Tile

1. 522.75 base square feet
2. 690.04 total square feet
3. 17 boxes; 728.28 square feet

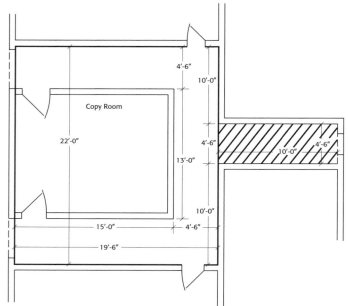

Practice Answer: Advanced—Resilient tiles.

Step 1: Draw diagram of room and take room dimensions.

Consider this space as two different rectangles. For a quick estimate, ignore the walls around the copy room and calculate the large area first and then calculate the small hallway. You will add them both together to get the total base square footage of the space.

Step 2A: Calculate base square footage of first space.

Take width of room in feet:	19.5	ft.
Multiply by length of room in feet:	× 24.5	ft.
Total base square footage of first space:	**477.75**	**sq. ft.**

Step 2B: Calculate base square footage of second space.

Take width of room in feet:	4.5	ft.
Multiply by length of room in feet:	× 10	ft.
Total base square footage of second space:	**45**	**sq. ft.**

Add totals from Step 2A and Step 2B together to get the total base square footage:	**522.75**	**sq. ft.**

Step 3: Calculate additional material for waste allowance.

Take square footage from Step 2:	522.75	sq. ft.
Multiply by 10 percent to allow for waste:	× 1.1	waste allowance
Total square footage needed:	**575.03**	**sq. ft.**

Step 4: Calculate additional materials for replacement allowance.

Take square footage from Step 2:	575.03	sq. ft.
Multiply by 20 percent to allow for replacement:	× 1.2	replacement allowance
Total square footage needed:	**690.04**	**sq. ft.**

Step 5: Calculate number of full boxes/cartons to be ordered.

Take square footage needed from Step 3 or 4:	690.04	sq. ft.
Divide by square feet per box/carton:	÷ 42.84	sq. ft.
Total boxes/cartons needed:	**16.11**	**boxes/cartons**
Round up to whole number:	**17**	**full boxes/cartons to order**

Step 6: Calculate actual square feet in boxes/cartons ordered.

Take number of boxes/cartons from Step 5:	17	boxes/cartons
Multiply by square feet per box/carton:	× 42.84	sq. ft.
Total square footage ordered:	**728.28**	**sq. ft.**

Sheet Goods

There are two different ways of calculating this material in this room. This will be shown as Sheet Goods A and Sheet Goods B.

Sheet Goods A:

1. 5 seams   2. 87 ft.   3. 38.67 sq. yd.

Step 1: Draw diagram of room and take room dimensions.

Step 2: Determine width with allowance.

Take width of room in feet (e.g., 15.5 ft.):	22	ft.
Add 6 inches (.5 ft.):	+ .5	ft.
Total:	**22.5**	**ft.**

Step 3: Determine number of cuts based on material width.

Take total from Step 2:	22.5	ft.
Divide by width of material:	÷ 4	ft.
Total:	**5.63**	**cuts**
Round up to whole number:	**6**	**cuts**

Step 4: Determine cut length.

Take length of room in feet (e.g., 9.25 ft.):	14	ft.
Add 6 inches (.5 ft.):	+ .5	ft.
Total length of cuts:	**14.5**	**ft.**

Step 5: Determine length to order.

Take total from Step 3:	6	cuts
Multiply by the total from Step 4:	× 14.5	ft.
Total length of material to be ordered:	**87**	**ft.**

Step 6: Determine square feet and square yards.

Take length of material from Step 5:	87	ft.
Multiply by width of material:	× 4	ft.
Total square feet:	**348**	**sq. ft.**
Divide by 9 to convert to square yards:	÷ 9	sq. ft.
Total square yards needed:	**38.6666**	**sq. yd.**
Round to two numbers to right of decimal point:	**38.67**	**sq. yd.**

Sheet Goods B:

1. 3 seams   2. 90 ft.   3. 40 sq. yd.

Step 1: Draw diagram of room and take room dimensions.

Step 2: Determine width with allowance.

Take width of room in feet (e.g., 15.5 ft.):	14	ft.
Add 6 inches (.5 ft.):	+ .5	ft.
Total:	**14.5**	**ft.**

Step 3: Determine number of cuts based on material width.

Take total from Step 2:	14.5	ft.
Divide by width of material:	÷ 4	ft.
Total:	**3.63**	**cuts**
Round up to whole number:	**4**	**cuts**

Step 4: Determine cut length.

Take length of room in feet (e.g., 9.25 ft.):	22	ft.
Add 6 inches (.5 ft.):	+ .5	ft.
Total length of cuts:	**22.5**	**ft.**

Step 5: Determine length to order.

Take total from Step 3:	4	cuts
Multiply by the total from Step 4:	× 22.5	ft.
Total length of material to be ordered:	**90**	**ft.**

Step 6: Determine square feet and square yards.

Take length of material from Step 5:	90	ft.
Multiply by width of material:.	× 4	ft.
Total square feet:	**360**	**sq. ft.**
Divide by 9 to convert to square yards:	÷ 9	sq. ft.
Total square yards needed:	**40**	**sq. yd.**
Round to two numbers to right of decimal point:	**40**	**sq. yd..**

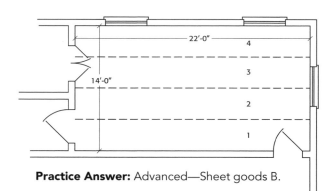

Practice Answer: Advanced—Sheet goods A.

Practice Answer: Advanced—Sheet goods B.

Broadloom Carpet

1. Toward the opening
2. 3 fill pieces
3. 8.83 feet
4. 35.33 feet
5. 47.11 square feet

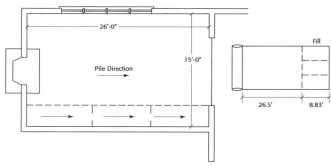

Practice Answer: Advanced—Broadloom carpet.

Step 1: Draw diagram of room and take room dimensions.

Step 2: Determine carpet direction in room.
Decide which way the carpet will run.

Step 3: Determine overall width with allowance.

Take width of room in feet (e.g., 15.5 ft.):	15	ft.
Add 6 inches (.5 ft.):	+ .5	ft.
Total cut width:	**15.5**	**ft.**

Step 4: Determine whether fill is necessary.

Take cut width from Step 3:	15.5	ft.
Subtract width of carpet in feet:	− 12	ft.
Total:	**3.5**	**ft.**

This is a positive number (greater than 0), so you have to determine seam placement and possible fill.

Step 5: Determine fill width.

Take width of carpet in feet:	12	ft.
Divide by total from Step 4:	÷ 3.5	ft.
Total:	**3.43**	**cuts**
Round down to nearest whole number:	**3**	**full pieces from carpet width**

This tells you how many full strips will come out of a 12-foot-wide piece of carpet.

Step 6: Determine length of first cut.

Take length of room in feet (e.g., 9.25 ft.):	26	ft.
Add 6 inches (.5 ft.):	+ .5	ft.
Total length of the first cut:	**26.5**	**ft.**

Step 7: Determine fill length.

Take length of room in feet + 6 inches (.5 feet):	26.5	ft.
Divide by total from Step 5:	÷ 3	full pieces from carpet width
Total for the second cut:	**8.83**	**ft.**

Step 8: Determine total length to be ordered.

Take length of first cut from Step 6:	26.5	ft.
Add length of second cut from Step 7:	+ 8.83	ft.
Total length of carpet to be ordered:	**35.33**	**ft.**

Step 9: Determine square feet and square yards.

Take length of carpet from Step 8:	35.33	ft.
Multiply by width of carpet:	× 12	ft.
Total square feet:	**423.96**	**sq. ft.**
Divide by 9 to convert to square yards:	÷ 9	sq. ft.
Total square yards of carpet:	**47.11**	**sq. yd.**

Pricing Broadloom Carpet

1. $2061.70 for all materials
2. $768.10 for all labor
3. $2829.80 total
4. $60.07 per sq. yd.

Broadloom Carpet for Living Room			
	Quantity	**Price**	**Total**
Carpet	47.11 sq. yd.	$38.49/sq. yd.	$1813.26
Freight/Shipping	47.11 sq. yd. (47.11 × $.85 = 40.04)	$0.85/sq. yd. $60 minimum	$60.00
Pad	47.11 sq. yd.	$4.00/sq. yd.	$188.44
Transition Pieces	n/a		n/a
		Materials Subtotal	$2061.70
Installation	47.11 sq. yd.	$12.00/sq. yd.	$565.32
Take-Up	47.11 sq. yd.	$2.50/sq. yd.	$117.78
Haul-Off	1	$85.00	$85.00
		Labor Subtotal	$768.10
		TOTAL	**$2829.80**

To calculate per square yard price:

$2829.80 ÷ 47.11 sq. yd. = $60.07

This will not give the same original when multiplied back because of rounding of the numbers.

$60.07 × 47.11 sq. yd. = $2829.90

Advanced—Pricing for Advanced Broadloom Carpet Practice Lesson

Chapter 8: Area Rugs

BASIC

1. 11 square yards for carpet
2. 2 feet × 8 feet 3 inches of waste
3. 36 feet binding
4. 80 square feet of backing

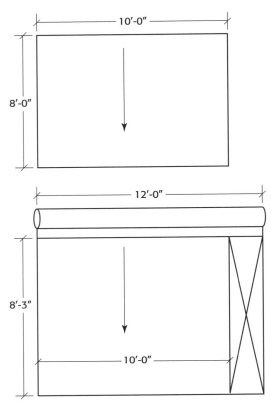

Practice Answer: Basic.

Labor:

Step 1: Draw diagram of area rug and determine finished size of total rug (including size of borders, if applicable).

Step 2: Find the perimeter of the area rug for binding.
Add length of all sides together:

Side 1:	10	ft.
Side 2:	+ 10	ft.
Side 3:	+ 8	ft.
Side 4:	+ 8	ft.

Total perimeter of area rug for binding: 36 ft.

Steps 3 and 4: Find perimeters of first and second seams.
Since this area rug is one piece (not bordered), the steps for seaming are not required.

Step 5: Calculate for backing.

Take overall width of area rug:	8	ft.
Multiply by overall length of area rug:	× 10	ft.

Total square feet of area rug for backing: 80 sq. ft.

Materials:

Use diagram from labor calculations.

Steps 1 and 2: Determine yardage needed for outer and inner borders.
Since this area rug is one piece (not bordered), skip to Step 3.

Step 3: Determine yardage needed for field (length and width can be found under labor calculations).

Take shortest side of field + .25 ft. (3 in.) for total length:	8.25	ft.
Multiply by width of carpet (normally 12 ft.):	× 12	ft.
Total square feet:	99	sq. ft.
Divide by 9 to convert to square yards: ÷	9	sq. ft.

Total square yards to be ordered for field: 11 sq. yd.

Step 4: Calculate for area rug pad.
There is no area rug pad used, so Step 4 is skipped.

INTERMEDIATE

1. 10 square yards for border
2. 11.67 square yards for field
3. 50 feet for binding
4. 40 feet for seaming
5. 154 square feet for backing
6. 18.67 square yards for pad

Labor:

Step 1: Draw diagram of area rug and determine finished size of total rug (including size of borders, if applicable).

Step 2: Find the perimeter of the area rug for binding.
Add length of all sides together:

Side 1:	14	ft.
Side 2:	+ 14	ft.
Side 3:	+ 11	ft.
Side 4:	+ 11	ft.

Total perimeter of area rug for binding: 50 ft.

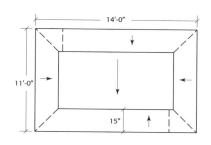

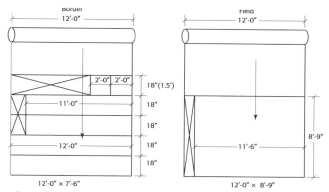

Practice Answer: Intermediate.

Step 1: Determine yardage needed for outer border.

Add length of border in feet + .25 ft. (3 in.):

Top:	1.5	ft.
Bottom:	+ 1.5	ft.
Side:	+ 1.5	ft.
Side:	+ 1.5	ft.

One side of the area rug is wider than 12 feet, so fill width must be determined.

14 ft. wide area rug – 12 ft. wide carpet = 2 ft. needed for fill pieces. Two pieces are needed, one for the top and one for the bottom. 2 ft. × 2 pieces = 4 ft. The 4-foot-wide piece needed for the fill can come from 1 fill cut.

Fill:	+ 1.5	ft.
Total length of carpet needed for outer border:	**7.5**	**ft.**
Multiply by width of carpet (normally 12 ft.):	× 12	ft.
Total square feet:	**90**	**sq. ft.**
Divide by 9 to convert to square yards:	÷ 9	sq. ft.
Total square yards to be ordered for outer border:	**10**	**sq. yd.**

Step 2: Determine yardage needed for inner border.

Area rug does not have an inner border, so we skip to Step 3.

Step 3: Determine yardage needed for field (length and width can be found under labor calculations).

Take shortest side of field + .25 ft. (3 in.) for total length:	8.75	ft.
Multiply by width of carpet in feet (normally 12 ft.):	× 12	ft.
Total square feet:	**105**	**sq. ft.**
Divide by 9 to convert to square yards:	÷ 9	sq. ft.
Total square yards to be ordered for field:	**11.67**	**sq. yd.**

Step 4: Calculate for area rug pad.

Take dimension that is 12 feet wide or less. Round up to 12 feet:	12	ft.
Multiply by other dimension of area rug:	× 14	ft.
Total square feet of pad:	**168**	**sq. ft.**
Divide by 9 to convert to square yards:	÷ 9	sq. ft.
Total square yards of pad:	**18.67**	**sq. yd.**

Step 3: Find perimeter of first seam.

Total width of area rug:	14	ft.
Subtract exact size of top border:	– 1.25	ft.
Subtract exact size of bottom border:	– 1.25	ft.
Subtotal A—width of field:	**11.5**	**ft.**
Total length of area rug:	11	ft.
Subtract exact size of right side border:	– 1.25	ft.
Subtract exact size of left side border:	– 1.25	ft.
Subtotal B— length of field:	**8.5**	**ft.**
Take Subtotal A:	11.5	ft.
Add to Subtotal B:	+ 8.5	ft.
Total:	**20**	**ft.**
	× 2	
Total perimeter for seaming first seam:	**40**	**ft.**

Step 4: Find perimeter of second seam.

There is only one border and one seam. Skip to Step 5.

Step 5: Calculate for backing.

Take overall width of area rug:	14	ft.
Multiply by overall length of area rug:	× 11	ft.
Total square feet of area rug for backing:	**154**	**sq. ft.**

Materials:

Use diagram from labor calculations.

ADVANCED

1. 9 square yards for field
2. 6.67 square yards for outer border
3. 2.67 square yards for inner border
4. 41 feet for binding
5. 33 feet + 31 feet = 64 feet for seaming
6. 103.5 square feet for backing
7. 12 square yards for pad

Labor:

Step 1: Draw diagram of area rug and determine finished size of total rug (including size of borders, if applicable).

Step 2: Find the perimeter of the area rug for binding.

Add length of all sides together:

Side 1:		11.5	ft.
Side 2:	+	11.5	ft.
Side 3:	+	9	ft.
Side 4:	+	9	ft.
Total perimeter of area rug for binding:		**41**	**ft.**

Step 3: Find perimeter of first seam.

Total width of area rug:	11.5	ft.
Subtract exact size of top border:	– 1	ft.
Subtract exact size of bottom border:	– 1	ft.
Subtotal A—width of inner border:	**9.5**	**ft.**
Total length of area rug:	9	ft.
Subtract exact size of right side border:	– 1	ft.
Subtract exact size of left side border:	– 1	ft.
Subtotal B—length of inner border:	**7**	**ft.**
Take Subtotal A:	9.5	ft.
Add to Subtotal B:	+ 7	ft.
Total:	**16.5**	**ft.**
	× 2	
Total perimeter for seaming first seam:	**33**	**ft.**

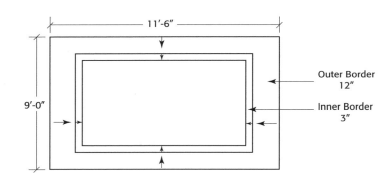

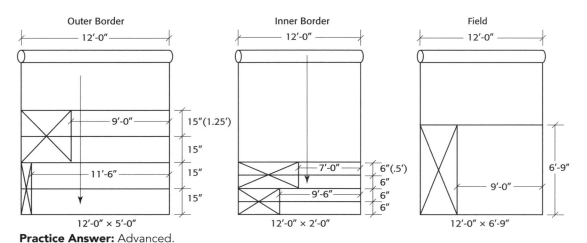

Practice Answer: Advanced.

Step 4: Find perimeter of second seam.

Take Subtotal A—width of inner border:	9.5	ft.
Subtract exact size of top border:	− .25	ft.
Subtract exact size of bottom border:	− .25	ft.
Subtotal C—width of field:	**9**	**ft.**
Take Subtotal B—length of inner border:	7	ft.
Subtract exact size of top border:	− .25	ft.
Subtract exact size of bottom border:	− .25	ft.
Subtotal D—length of field:	**6.5**	**ft.**
Take Subtotal C:	9	ft.
Add to Subtotal D:	+ 6.5	ft.
Total:	**15.5**	**ft.**
	× 2	
Total perimeter for seaming second seam:	**31**	**ft.**

Step 5: Calculate for backing.

Take overall width of area rug:	11.5	ft.
Multiply by overall length of area rug:	× 9	ft.
Total square feet of area rug for backing:	**103.5**	**sq. ft.**

Materials:

Use diagram from labor calculations.

Step 1: Determine yardage needed for outer border.

Add length of border in feet + .25 ft. (3 in.):

Top:	1.25	ft.
Bottom:	+ 1.25	ft.
Side:	+ 1.25	ft.
Side:	+ 1.25	ft.
Total length of carpet needed for outer border:	**5**	**ft.**
Multiply by width of carpet (normally 12 ft.):	× 12	ft.
Total square feet:	**60**	**sq. ft.**
Divide by 9 to convert to square yards:	÷ 9	sq. ft.
Total square yards to be ordered for outer border:	**6.67**	**sq. yd.**

Step 2: Determine yardage needed for inner border.

Add length of inner border in feet + .25 ft. (3 in.):

Top:	.5	ft.
Bottom:	+ .5	ft.

Since 6.5 feet is more than 6 feet, 2 pieces must be used:

Side:	+ .5	ft.
Side:	+ .5	ft.
Total length of carpet needed for inner border:	**2**	**ft.**
Multiply by width of carpet (normally 12 ft.):	× 12	ft.
Total square feet:	**24**	**sq. ft.**
Divide by 9 to convert to square yards:	÷ 9	sq. ft.
Total square yards to be ordered for inner border:	**2.67**	**sq. yd.**

Step 3: Determine yardage needed for field (length and width can be found under labor calculations).

Take shortest side of field + .25 ft. (3 in.) for total length:	6.75	ft.
Multiply by width of carpet (normally 12 ft.):	× 12	ft.
Total square feet:	**81**	**sq. ft.**
Divide by 9 to convert to square yards:	÷ 9	sq. ft.
Total of square yards to be ordered for field:	**9**	**sq. yd.**

Step 4: Calculate for area rug pad.

Take dimension that is 12 feet wide or less. Round up to 12 feet:	12	ft.
Multiply by other dimension of area rug:	× 9	ft.
Total square feet of pad:	**108**	**sq. ft.**
Divide by 9 to convert to square yards:	÷ 9	sq. ft.
Total square yards of pad:	**12**	**sq. yd.**

Pricing of Two-Piece Area Rug

1. $1093.95 for materials
2. $539.50 for labor
3. $1633.45 total for materials and labor

Material				Labor			
	Quantity	Price	Total		Quantity	Price	Total
Carpet—Border	10 sq. yd.	$33.69/sq. yd.	$336.90	Binding	50 ft.	$2.00/l.f.	$100.00
Freight/shipping*	1	$60	$60.00	Seaming	40 ft.	$3.00/l.f.	$120.00
Carpet—Field	11.67 sq. yd.	$40.99/sq. yd.	$478.35	Backing	154 sq. ft.	$1.75/sq. ft.	$269.50
Freight/shipping*	1	$60	$60.00	Delivery	1	$50	$50.00
Pad	18.67 sq. yd.	$8.50/sq. yd.	$158.70				
Materials Subtotal			**$1093.95**			**Labor Subtotal**	**$539.50**
Total for Area Rug $1633.45							

*Freight and shipping for each carpet do not meet the minimum amount when calculating square yardage × shipping allowance. For border: 10 sq. yd. × $0.85 = $8.50. For field: 11.67 × $0.85 = $9.92 The minimum amount of $60 each carpet is then charged.

l.f. = Lineal feet

sq. ft. = square feet

sq. yd. = square yards

Advanced—Pricing for Intermediate Two-Piece Area Rug

Chapter 9: Countertops and Cabinetry

BASIC

Laminate Countertop

1. 2.5 feet
2. 9 feet
3. 36 inches wide × 120 inches long
4. 30 square feet

Step 1: Determine width of slabs or sheets to be used.

Width of slab or sheet being used
in feet: 3   ft.

Divide by depth of counter
in feet: ÷   2.5   ft.

(Cabinet depth is 24 in. + 1-in. front overhang
+ 4-in. backsplash + 1-in. depth = 30 in.
30 in. ÷ 12 = 2.5 ft.)

**Total number of counter cuts
possible from slab/sheet:**   **1.2**   cuts

Round down to whole number: **1**   cuts per
                                                         slab/sheet

Step 2: Determine length of slab/sheet to be used.

Length A of counter to
counter/wall in feet: 9   ft.

There is no overhang.

Divide by length of slab/sheet
being used in feet: ÷   10   ft.

A 10-foot-long sheet is closer to and exceeds the 9-foot-long
counter. Eight-foot sheets are too short.

Total: .9   slab/sheet

**Round up to whole
number—Total A:**   1   slab/sheet

There is only one counter to consider.

Step 3: Determine total number of slabs/sheets needed.

From Step 2: Total A: 1   slab/sheet
Total: **1**   **slab/sheet**
Divide by total from Step 1:   ÷   1   cuts per slab/sheet
Total: **1**   **slab/sheet**

Step 4: Find square feet of material.

Width of slab or sheet being
used in feet: 3   ft.
Multiply by slab/sheet length: ×   10   ft.
Total: **30**   **sq. ft.**
Multiply by total from Step 3:   ×   1   slab/sheet
Total square footage priced: **30**   **sq. ft.**

INTERMEDIATE

Tile Countertop

1. 13 square feet of tile
2. 15 pieces of counter edge
3. 11 pieces of accent trim

Step 1: Calculate base square footage of space.

Take depth of counter in feet: 1.58   ft.
(18 in. + 1-in. front overhang = 19 in. ÷ 12 in. = 1.58 ft.)

Multiply by length of counter
in feet: ×   7   ft.
Base square footage of space: **11.06**   **sq. ft.**

**Step 2: Calculate additional materials for waste
allowance.**

For tile laid straight:
Take square footage from Step 1:   11.06   sq. ft.
Multiply by 10 percent to
allow for waste: ×   1.10   waste allowance
Total square footage needed: **12.17**   **sq. ft.**

Step 3: Calculate square feet to be ordered:

Total from Step 2:   12.17   sq. ft.
Divide by tile unit
(width × length):   ÷   1   sq. ft.
(12 in. × 12 in. tile sheets = 1 ft. × 1 ft. = 1 sq. ft.)

Total tiles: **12.17**   **tiles**
Round up to whole number: **13**   **full tiles**
Multiply by the tile unit: ×   1   sq. ft.
Total square feet ordered: **13**   **sq. ft.**

For Counter Edge:

**Step 1: Calculate total length of counter edge, accent, or
trim needed.**

Add length of trim needed: 7   ft.
Add additional lengths: +   1.58   ft.

1.58 is the depth found earlier by adding the cabinet depth
to the overhang. This is needed on only the one side that is
exposed.

**Total length needed for
accent or trim:**   **8.58**   **ft.**

Step 2: Calculate total number of pieces of trim to be ordered.

Take total from Step 1:   8.58   ft.

Divide by length of trim
piece: ÷ .67   ft.
(Trim is 8 inches wide. 8 in. ÷ 12 in. = .666 ft.;
round up to .67 ft.)

Pieces of trim needed: 12.81   pieces
Round up to whole number: **13**   **full pieces to order**
Add 2 to allow for breakage: +   2   breakage allowance
Total: **15**   **total**

For Counter Backsplash:

Step 1: Calculate total length of counter edge, accent, or trim needed.

Depending on the different trims (including edge and accent) needed, this process may need to be done several times.

Add length of trim needed: 1.58   ft.

This is for the side against the wall.

Add additional lengths: +   7   ft.
**Total length needed for
accent or trim:**   **8.58**   **ft.**

Step 2: Calculate total number of pieces of trim to be ordered.

Take total from Step 1:   8.58   ft.

Divide by length of trim
piece: ÷ 1   ft.
(12-in.-wide trim ÷ 12 in. = 1 ft.)

Pieces of trim needed: **8.58**   **pieces**
Round up to whole number: **9**   **full pieces to order**
Add 2 to allow for breakage: +   2   breakage allowance
Total: **11**   **total**

ADVANCED
Granite Countertop
1. 25 inches   2. 1 slab   3. 57.75 square feet
Step 1: Determine width of slabs or sheets to be used.
Width of slab or sheet being
used in feet: 5.5   ft.
(66-in.-wide slab ÷ 12 in. = 5.5 ft.)

Divide by depth of counter
in feet: ÷ 2.08   ft.
(Cabinet depth is 24 in. + 1-in. overhang
= 25 in. ÷ 12 in. = 2.08 ft.)

**Total number of counter cuts
possible from slab/sheet:**   **2.64**   **cuts**
**Round down to nearest
whole number:**   **2**   **cuts per slab/sheet**

Since the backsplash is the same material, to see if this can be obtained from the slab, add 6 inches to the counter depth before dividing into the slab:

5.5 ft. ÷ 2.58 ft. = 2.13 cuts; round down to 2 cuts per slab/sheet. There is enough width to calculate for the backsplash from the same slab.

Step 2: Determine length of slabs to be used.
Length A of counter to wall
in feet: 10   ft.
Divide by length of slab/sheet
being used in feet: ÷ 10.5   ft.
(126 in. ÷ 12 in. = 10.5 ft.)

Total: **.95**   **slab/sheet**
**Round up to whole
number—Total A:**   **1**   **slab/sheet**

Length B of counter to wall
in feet: 10   ft.
Divide by length of slab/sheet
being used in feet: ÷ 10.5   ft.
Total: **.95**   **slab/sheet**
**Round up to whole
number—Total B:**   **1**   **slab/sheet**

Step 3: Determine total number of slabs/sheets needed.
Add Total A from Step 2:   1   slab/sheet
Add Total B from Step 2:   +   1   slab/sheet
Total: **2**   **slabs/sheets**
Divide by total from Step 1:   ÷   2   cuts per slab/sheet
Total: **1**   **slab/sheet**

Step 4: Find square feet of material.
Width of slab or sheet being
used in feet: 5.5   ft.
Multiply by slab/sheet length: × 10.5   ft.
Total: **57.75**   **sq. ft.**
Multiply by total from Step 3: ×   1   slab/sheet
Total square footage priced: **57.75**   **sq. ft.**

Pricing for Advanced Granite Countertop
1. $6319.00

Granite Countertop			
	Quantity	Price	Total
Granite and installation	57.75 sq. ft.	$96.00/sq. ft.	$5544.00
Cutouts	2	$75.00 each	$150.00
Ogee edge charge		$625.00	$625.00
		Total	$6319.00

Advanced—Pricing for Advanced Granite Countertop

Chapter 10: Curtains and Draperies

BASIC
Gathered Curtains

1. 3 widths
2. 4 widths
3. 65.75 inches
4. 5.5 yards
5. 5.5 yards

Step 1: Calculate finished width of treatment.

Flat measure of treatment:	36	in.
Right return:	+ 3	in.
Left return:	+ 3	in.
Total finished width to be gathered:	**42**	**in.**

Step 2: Calculate the number of widths of fabric

Total from Step 1:	42	in.
Multiply for fullness:	× 2.5	fullness
Total fullness:	**105**	**in.**
Add 6 inches for side hems:	+ 6	in.
Total:	111	in.
Divide by width of fabric:	÷ 48	in.
Cuts/widths of fabric:	**2.31**	**widths**
Round up to whole number:	**3**	**full widths**

Step 3: Calculate length of each width.

Finished length:	56	in.
Add for seam allowance:	+ 2	in.
Add bottom hem (double 2-in. hem):	+ 4	in.
Add rod pocket with take-up allowance (see Table 11.2):	+ 1.75	in.
Add header height:	+ 2	in.
Total cut length (CL):	**65.75**	**in.**

There is no repeat, so we skip to Step 4.

Step 4: Combine Steps 2 and 3.

Cut length or ACL from Step 3:	65.75	in.
Multiply by total widths from Step 2:	× 3	widths
Total:	**197.25**	**in.**
Divide by 36 to convert inches to yards:	÷ 36	in.
Total yards:	**5.48**	**yd.**
Round up to nearest ½ yard:	**5.5**	**yd. to be ordered**

Lining: Because there is no repeat, lining is same as decorative face fabric.

Stationary Side Panels

1. 12-inch minimum measurement
2. 2 widths
3. 2 widths
4. 112 inches
5. 6.5 yards
6. 6 yards

Step 1: Calculate flat measure of stationary side panels.

Take trim-to-trim measure of window:	66	in.
Multiply by 25 percent:	× .25	
Total:	**16.5**	**in.**
Divide by 2 to determine width per side:	÷ 2	sides
Total flat measure each side of window:	**8.25**	**in.**
If less than 12 inches, round up to 12 inches:	**12**	**in.**

Step 2: Calculate the number of widths of fabric.

Desired flat measure of side panel:	12	in.
Multiply for fullness:	× 2.5	fullness
Total fullness:	**30**	**in.**
Add 6 inches for side hems:	+ 6	in.
Add depth of return:	+ 4	in.
Total:	**40**	**in.**
Multiply by number of side panels desired:	× 2	side panels
Total:	**80**	**in.**
Divide by width of fabric:	÷ 54	in.
Number of widths of fabric:	**1.48**	**widths**
Round up to whole number:	**2**	**full widths**

Step 3: Calculate length of each cut (width).

Finished length (FL) of drapery:	89	in.
Add 18 inches for hems and heading:	+ 18	in.
Cut length (CL):	**107**	**in.**

There is a repeat, so continue with the following calculation.

Take cut length:	107	in.
Divide by length of repeat:	÷ 16	in.
Total number of repeats:	**6.69**	**repeats**
Round up to whole number:	**7**	**full repeats**
Multiply by length of repeat:	× 16	in.
Adjusted cut length (ACL):	**112**	**in.**

Step 4: Combine Steps 2 and 3.

Cut length or ACL from Step 3:	112	in.
Multiply by number of cuts (widths) from Step 2:	× 2	widths
Total length of fabric required:	**224**	**in.**
Divide by 36 to convert inches to yards:	÷ 36	in.
Resulting yardage:	**6.22**	**yd.**
Round up to nearest ½ yard:	**6.5**	**yd. to order**

Lining: 107 in. CL × 2 W = 214 in. ÷ 36 in. = 5.94 yd. Round up to 6 yards to order.

Traversing, Pleated Draperies

1. 57.5 inches
2. 4 widths
3. 4 widths
4. 89 inches
5. 107 inches
6. 12 yards

Step 1: Calculate flat measure of treatment.

Take trim-to-trim measure of window:	50	in.
Multiply to allow for stack (15 percent to 33 percent):	× 1.15	(1.15 to 1.33)
Total flat measure (FM) of treatment:	**57.5**	**in.**

Step 2: Calculate the number of widths (cuts) of fabric.

Total from Step 1:	57.5	in.
Multiply for fullness:	× 3	fullness
Total fullness:	**172.5**	**in.**
Add 20 in. for overlaps and returns for center draw:	+ 20	in.
Total:	**192.5**	**in.**
Divide by width of fabric:	÷ 54	in.
Cuts/ widths of fabric:	**3.56**	**widths**
Round up to whole number:	**4**	**full widths**

Step 3: Calculate length of each cut (width).

Finished length (FL) of drapery (84 inches + 5 inches):	89	in.

(To calculate finished length, add dimensions for trim to floor to inches above trim to install.)

Add 18 inches for hems and heading:	+ 18	in.
Cut length (CL):	**107**	**in.**

There is no repeat, so we skip to Step 4.

Step 4: Combine Steps 2 and 3.

Cut length or ACL from Step 3:	107	in.
Multiply by number of cuts (widths) from Step 2:	× 4	widths
Total length of fabric required:	**428**	**in.**
Divide by 36 to convert inches to yards:	÷ 36	in.
Resulting yardage:	**11.89**	**yd.**
Round up to nearest ½ yard:	**12**	**yd.**

Lining: There is no lining.

INTERMEDIATE
Gathered Curtains

1. 44 inches
2. 3 widths
3. 4 widths
4. 90 inches
5. 114 inches
6. 19 yards
7. 19 yards

Step 1: Calculate finished width of treatment.

Flat measure of treatment (42 in. + 1 in. + 1 in.):	44	in.
Right return:	+ 3	in.
Left return:	+ 3	in.
Total finished width to be gathered:	**50**	**in.**

Step 2: Calculate the number of widths (cuts) of fabric.

Total from Step 1:	50	in.
Multiply for fullness:	× 3	fullness
Total fullness:	**150**	**in.**
Add 6 inches for side hems:	+ 6	in.
Total:	**156**	**in.**
Divide by width of fabric:	÷ 54	in.
Cuts/widths of fabric:	**2.89**	**widths**
Round up to whole number:	**3**	**full widths**

Step 3: Calculate length of each cut (width).

Finished length (84 in. + 6 in.):	90	in.
Add for seam allowances:	+ 2	in.
Add bottom hem (double 4-inch):	+ 8	in.
Add rod pocket with take-up allowance (see Table 11.2):	+ 6.5	in.
Add header height:	+ 2	in.
Total cut length (CL):	**108.5**	**in.**

There is a repeat, so continue with the following calculation.

Take cut length:	108.5	in.
Divide by length of repeat:	÷ 19	in.
Number of repeats:	**5.71**	**repeats**
Round up to whole number:	**6**	**full repeats**
Multiply by length of repeat:	× 19	in.
Adjusted cut length (ACL):	**114**	**in.**

Step 4: Combine Steps 2 and 3.

Cut length or ACL from Step 3:	114	in.
Multiply by total widths from Step 2:	× 3	widths
Total:	**342**	**in.**
Divide by 36 to convert inches to yards:	÷ 36	in.
Total yards:	**9.5**	**yd.**
9.5 yd. × 2 windows:	**19**	**total yd. ordered**

Lining: 108.5 in. CL × 3 W = 325.5 in. ÷ 36 in. = 9.04 yd. × 2 windows = 18.08 yd. Round up to 18.5 yards to order.

Stationary Side Panels

1. 12 inches
2. 4 panels
3. 4 widths
4. 4 widths
5. 101 inches
6. 135 inches
7. 15 yards
8. 13.5 yards

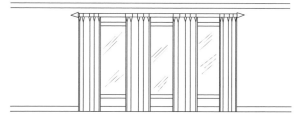

Practice Answer Intermediate—Stationary side panels.

Step 1: Calculate flat measure of stationary side panels.

Take trim-to-trim measure of window:	30	in.
Multiply by 25 percent:	× .25	
Total:	**7.5**	**in.**
Divide by 2 to determine width per side:	÷ 2	sides
Total flat measure each side of window:	**3.75**	**in.**
If less than 12 inches, round up to 12 inches:	**12**	**in.**

Step 2: Calculate the number of widths (cuts) of fabric.

Desired flat measure of side panel:	12	in.
Multiply by fullness factor (2.5 or 3):	× 3	fullness
Total fullness:	**36**	**in.**
Add 6 inches for side hems:	+ 6	in.
Add depth of return:	+ 4	in.
Total:	**46**	**in.**
Multiply by number of side panels desired:	× 4	side panels
Total:	**184**	**in.**
Divide by width of fabric (normally 48 or 54 in.):	÷ 54	inches.
Number of widths of fabric:	**3.4**	**widths**
Round up to whole number:	**4**	**full widths**

Step 3: Calculate length of each cut (width).

Finished length (FL) of drapery (96 inches + 5 inches):	101	in.

To find finished length, add dimensions for trim to floor to inches above trim to install.

Add 18 inches for hems and heading:	+ 18	in.
Cut length (CL):	**119**	**in.**

There is a repeat, so continue with the following calculation.

Take cut length:	119	in.
Divide by length of repeat:	÷ 27	in.
Number of repeats:	**4.41**	**repeats**
Round up to whole number:	**5**	**full repeats**
Multiply by length of repeat:	× 27	in.
Adjusted cut length (ACL):	**135**	**in.**

Step 4: Combine Steps 2 and 3.

Cut length or ACL from Step 3:	135	in.
Multiply by number of cuts (widths) from Step 2:	× 4	widths
Total length of fabric required:	**540**	**in.**
Divide by 36 to convert inches to yards:	÷ 36	in.
Resulting yardage:	**15**	**yd.**

Lining: 119 in. CL × 4 W = 476 in. ÷ 36 in. = 13.22 yd. Round up to 13.5 yards to order.

Traversing, Pleated Draperies

1. 105 inches
2. 10 inches
3. 7 widths
4. 7 widths
5. 87 inches
6. 108 inches
7. 21 yards
8. 20.5 yards

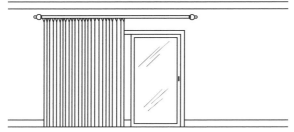

Practice Answer Intermediate—Traversing, pleated draperies.

Step 1: Calculate flat measure of treatment.

Take trim-to-trim measure of window:	84	in.
Multiply to allow for stack (15 percent to 33 percent):	× 1.25	(1.15 to 1.33)
Total flat measure (FM) of treatment:	**105**	**in.**

Step 2: Calculate the number of widths (cuts) of fabric.

Total from Step 1:	105	in.
Multiply for fullness:	× 3	fullness
Total fullness:	**315**	**in.**
Add 10 inches for one-way draw:	+ 10	in.
Total:	**325**	**in.**
Divide by width of fabric:	÷ 54	inches
Cuts/widths of fabric:	**6.02**	**widths**
Round up to whole number:	**7**	**full widths**

Step 3: Calculate length of each cut (width).

Finished length (FL) of drapery:	87	in.
Add 18 inches for hems and heading:	+ 18	in.
Cut length (CL):	**105**	**in.**

There is a repeat, so continue with the following calculation.

Take cut length:	105	in.
Divide by length of repeat:	÷ 18	in.
Number of repeats:	**5.8**	**repeats**
Round up to whole number:	**6**	**full repeats**
Multiply by length of repeat:	× 18	in.
Adjusted cut length (ACL):	**108**	**in.**

Step 4: Combine Steps 2 and 3.

Cut length or ACL from Step 3:	108	in.
Multiply by number of cuts (widths) from Step 2:	× 7	widths
Total length of fabric required:	**756**	**in.**
Divide by 36 to convert inches to yards:	÷ 36	in.
Resulting yardage:	**21**	**yd.**

Lining: 105 in. CL × 7 W = 735 in. ÷ 36 in. = 20.42 yd. Round up to 20.5 yards.

ADVANCED
Gathered Curtains

1. 26 inches
2. 28 inches
3. 2 widths
4. 2 widths
5. 76 inches
6. 85.5 inches
7. 10 yards

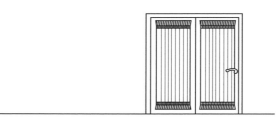

Practice Answer Advanced—Gathered curtains (sash curtains).

Step 1: Calculate finished width of treatment.

Flat measure of treatment (24 in. + 1 in. = 1 in.):	26	in.

To find flat measure, add dimensions of trim-to-trim to placement either side of trim:

Right return:	+ 1	in.
Left return:	+ 1	in.
Total finished width to be gathered:	**28**	**in.**

Step 2: Calculate the number of widths (cuts) of fabric.

Total from Step 1:	28	in.
Multiply for fullness:	× 3	fullness
Total:	**84**	**in.**
Add 6 inches for side hems:	+ 6	in.
Total:	**90**	**in.**
Divide by width of fabric:	÷ 54	in.
Cuts/widths of fabric:	**1.67**	**widths**
Round up to whole number:	**2**	**full widths**

Step 3: Calculate length of each cut (width).
Finished length
(72 in. + 1 in. + 1 in. + 1 in. + 1 in.):   76   in.

To find finished length, add dimensions for trim-to-trim to inches for rod pocket and heading.

There are rod pockets top and bottom and headings top and bottom, so the following numbers will be doubled.

Add for seam allowances:
2 inches × 2:   +   4   in.
Add bottom hem: + n/a   in.
Add rod pocket and take-up
allowance (1.75 in. × 2):   + 3.5   in.
Add header height (1 in. × 2):   +   2   in.
Total cut length (CL):   **85.5** **in.**

There is no repeat, so we skip to Step 4.

Step 4: Combine Steps 2 and 3.
Cut length or ACL from Step 3:   85.5   in.
Multiply by total widths
from Step 2:   ×   2   widths
Total fabric required: **171** **in.**
Divide by 36 to convert
inches to yards: ÷ 36   in.
Total yards: **4.75** **yd.**
4.75 yd × 2 curtains: **9.50** **yd. to be**
                                                 ordered

Lining: There is no lining.

Seamless, Traversing Draperies and Traversing, Pleated Draperies

1. 126.5 inches
2. 137.5 inches
3. 9 widths
4. 10 widths
5. 10 widths
6. 87 inches
7. 89 inches
8. 126 inches
9. 31.5 yards
10. 27 yards
11. 11.5 yards

Seamless, Traversing Draperies:

Step 1: Calculate length of each cut (width).
Finished length (FL) of drapery
(84 in. + 3 in.):   87   in.

To find finished length, add dimensions for trim to floor to inches above trim to install.

Add 18 inches for hems
and heading: + 18   in.

(18 inches allows for double 6-inch hem; if narrower or wider hem, this number will change.)

Cut length (CL):   **105** **in.**

There is no repeat, so we proceed to Step 2.

Step 2: Determine if selected fabric will railroad.
Fabric width of 118 inches is less than cut length 105 inches.

Step 3: Calculate flat measure of treatment.
Take trim-to-trim measure
of window: 110   in.
Multiply to allow for stack
(15 to 33 percent):   × 1.15   (1.15 to 1.33)
**Total flat measure (FM)
of treatment:**   **126.5** **in.**

Step 4: Calculate yardage.
Total from Step 1:   126.5 in.
Multiply for fullness: ×   3   fullness
Total fullness: **379.5** **in.**

Add 20 inches for overlaps and
returns for center draw: + 20   in.
Total of fabric in inches: 399.5 in.
Divide by 36 to convert
inches to yards: ÷ 36   in.
Resulting yardage: **11.1** **yd.**
Round up to nearest ½ yard: **11.5** **yd.**

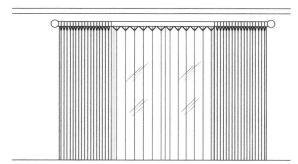

Practice Answer Advanced—Traversing, pleated draperies.

Step 5: Calculate number of labor widths of fabric the workroom will charge.

Total of fabric in inches:	399.5	in.
Divide by 48 inches to find labor widths:	÷ 48	in.
Widths of fabric:	**8.3**	**widths**
Round up to the nearest even whole number:	**10**	**labor widths**

Traversing, Pleated Draperies:

Step 1: Calculate flat measure of treatment.

Take trim-to-trim measure of window:	110	in.
Multiply to allow for stack (15 percent to 33 percent):	× 1.25	(1.15 to 1.33)
Total flat measure (FM) of treatment:	**137.5**	**in.**

Step 2: Calculate the number of widths (cuts) of fabric.

Total from Step 1:	137.5	in.
Multiply for fullness:	× 3	fullness
Total fullness:	**412.5**	**in.**
Add 20 inches for overlaps and returns for center draw:	+ 20	in.

This allows for 3-inch to 4-inch returns. If returns are deeper, add additional beyond allowed + 5 in.

Allowed for returns: 4 in. + 4 in. = 8 in.
Actual returns: 6.5 + 6.5 = 13 in.

13 in. − 8 in.:	5	in. additional.
Total:	**437.5**	**in.**
Divide by width of fabric:	÷ 54	in.
Cuts/ widths of fabric:	**8.1**	**widths**
Round up to whole number:	**9**	**full widths**

Step 3: Calculate length of each cut (width).

Finished length (FL) of drapery (84 inches + 5 inches):	89	in.

To find finished length, add dimensions for trim to floor to inches above trim to install.

Add 18 inches for hems and heading:	+ 18	in.
Cut length (CL):	**107**	**in.**

There is a repeat, so continue with the following calculation.

Take cut length:	107	in.
Divide by length of repeat:	÷ 21	in.
Number of repeats:	**5.1**	**repeats**
Round up to whole number:	**6**	**full repeats**
Multiply by length of repeat:	× 21	in.
Adjusted cut length (ACL):	**126**	**in.**

Step 4: Combine Steps 2 and 3.

Cut length or ACL from Step 3:	126	in.
Multiply by number of cuts (widths) from Step 2:	× 9	widths
Total length of fabric required:	**1134**	**in.**
Divide by 36 to convert inches to yards:	÷ 36	in.
Resulting yardage:	**31.5**	**yd.**

Lining: 107 in. CL × 9 W = 963 in. ÷ 36 in. = 26.75 yd. Round up to 27 yards.

Pricing for Intermediate Gathered Curtains
1. $1198.00
2. $634.00
3. $1832.00

Materials											
	Mfr./ Vendor	Pattern	Color/ Finish	Width	Repeat	Qty.	Cost Per	Sub-total	Est. Ship.	Total	PO
Fabric				54 in.	19 in.	19 yd.	$36	$684	$27	$711	
Lining						19 yd.	$8	$152	n/a	$152	
Hdwr.						2	$150	$300	$35	$335	
Rod											
Brackets											
Supports											
Finials											
Batons											
							Subtotal for Materials			**$1198**	

Labor & Installation										
Labor						Qty	Cost Per	Sub-total	Est. Ship	Total	WO
	4 widths per window × 2 windows					8	$58/w	$464		$464	
Install						2	$85 each	$170		$170	
						Subtotal for Labor & Installation				**$634**	

	Overall Total	**$1832**

Diagram:

Advanced—Pricing for Intermediate Gathered Curtains

Pricing for Intermediate Traversing, Pleated Draperies

1. $1864.00
2. $550.00
3. $2414.00

Materials											
	Mfr./ Vendor	Pattern	Color/ Finish	Width	Repeat	Qty.	Cost Per	Sub-total	Est. Ship.	Total	PO
Fabric						21 yd.	$62	$1302	$27	$1329	
Lining						20.5 yd.	$8	$164	n/a	$164	
Hdwr.						1	$325	$325	$46	$371	
Rod											
Brackets											
Supports											
Finials											
Batons											
							Subtotal for Materials			$1864	

Labor & Installation											
Labor						Qty	Cost Per	Sub-total	Est. Ship	Total	WO
						7 w	$60/w	$420		$420	
Install						1	$130	$130		$130	
							Subtotal for Labor & Installation			$550	
							Overall Total			$2414	

Diagram:

Advanced—Pricing for Intermediate Traversing, Pleated Draperies

Chapter 11: Top Treatments and Window Shades

BASIC

Cornice

1. 2 widths
2. 30 inches adjusted cut length
3. 68 in. + 6 in. return + 6 in. return = 80 in. ÷ 12 in. = 6.67 ft. Most workrooms will round up to 7 ft.
4. 3 yards

Step 1: Determine widths.

Finished width of treatment:	68	in.
Right return:	+ 6	in.
Left return:	+ 6	in.
Add 6 inches for upholstering:	+ 6	in.
Total:	**86**	**in.**
Divide by fabric width:	÷ 54	in.
Total widths needed:	**1.59**	**widths**
Round up to whole number:	**2**	**full widths**

Step 2: Determine cut length.

Finished length of treatment:	18	in.
Add 6 inches for upholstering:	+ 6	in.
Total cut length:	**24**	**in.**

Step 3: Calculate for repeat.

Total cut length from Step 2:	24	in.
Divide by length of repeat:	÷ 15	in.
Number of repeats:	**1.6**	**repeats**
Round up to whole number:	**2**	**full repeats**
Multiply by length of repeat:	× 15	in.
Adjusted cut length (ACL):	**30**	**in.**

Step 4: Determine yardage.

Cut length or adjusted cut length:	30	in.
Multiply by number of widths:	× 2	widths
Total:	**60**	**in.**
Divide by 36 to convert inches to yards:	÷ 36	in.
Total yards:	**1.67**	**yd.**
Round up to nearest ½ yard:	**2**	**yd.**
For self-welt, add 1 to 1.5 yards:	+ 1	yd.
Total:	**3**	**yd. to be ordered**

Gathered Valance

1. 3 widths
2. 32 inches adjusted cut length
3. 3 yards face fabric
4. 2½ yards lining. CL 27.5 in. × 3 W = 82.5 in. divide by 36 in. = 2.29 yds. Round up to 2.5 yards.

Step 1: Determine total width dimension requiring fullness.

Flat measure of treatment:	42	in.
Return to right:	+ 3	in.
Return to left:	+ 3	in.
Total width:	**48**	**in.**

Step 2: Determine widths.

Total width from Step 1:	48	in.
Multiply for fullness (× 2.5 or 3):	× 3	fullness
Total:	**144**	**in.**
Add 6 inches for side hems:	+ 6	in.
Total:	**150**	**in.**
Divide by width of fabric:	÷ 54	in.
Cuts/widths of fabric:	**2.78**	**widths**
Round up to whole number:	**3**	**full widths**

Step 3: Determine cut length.

Finished length	16	in.
Add for seam allowances:	+ 2	in.
Add bottom hem (double 2-in.):	+ 4	in.
Add for rod pocket and header:		
Add rod pocket size w/take-up allowance:	+ 4	in.
Add header height:	+ 1.5	in.
Total cut length:	**27.5**	**in.**
Calculate for repeat:		
Take cut length:	27.5	in.
Divide by length of repeat:	÷ 8	in.
Total:	**3.44**	**repeats**
Round up to whole number:	**4**	**full repeats**
Multiply by length of repeat:	× 8	in.
Adjusted cut length (ACL):	**32**	**in.**

Step 4: Determine yardage.

Take cut length or ACL from Step 3:	32	in.
Multiply by total widths from Step 2:	× 3	widths
Total:	**96**	**in.**
Divide by 36 to convert inches to yards:	÷ 36	in.
Total yards:	**2.67**	**yd.**
Round up to nearest ½ yard:	**3**	**yd. to be ordered**

Roman Shade

1. 27 inches × 83 inches = 2241 square inches ÷ 144 inches = 15.56 sq. ft.
2. 108 inches adjusted cut length
3. 3 yards face fabric. Some designers will add an additional repeat in order to control where the pattern falls. An additional 27 inches will add an additional yard to the 3 yards resulting in 4 yards ordered. Either answer is correct.
4. 93 inches ÷ 36 inches = 2.58 yards. Round up to 3 yards lining.

Step 1: Calculate cut width.

Finished width of shade:		27	in.
Add 6 inches for side hem:	+	6	in.
Total cut width:		**33**	**in.**

Step 2: Determine widths.

Cut width from Step 1:		33	in.
Divide by fabric width:	÷	54	in.
Total widths needed:		**.61**	**width**
Round up to whole number:		**1**	**full width**

Step 3: Determine cut length.

Finished length of shade:		83	in.
Add 10 inches for hem and board allowance:	+	10	in.
Total cut length:		**93**	**in.**

Calculate for repeat:

Total cut length from Step 3:		93	in.
Divide by length of repeat:	÷	27	in.
Number of repeats:		**3.44**	**repeats**
Round up to whole number:		**4**	**full repeats**
Multiply by length of repeat:	×	27	in.
Adjusted cut length (ACL):		**108**	**in.**

Step 4: Determine yardage.

Cut length or adjusted cut length:		108	in.
Multiply by number of widths:	×	1	in.
Total:		**108**	**in.**
Divide by 36 to convert inches to yards:	÷	36	in.
Total yards:		**3**	**yd.**
Round up to nearest ½ yard:		**3**	**yd. to be ordered**

INTERMEDIATE

Lambrequin

1. 88 inches + 96 inches + 96 inches = 280 inches ÷ 12 inches = 23.33-foot perimeter
2. 2 widths
3. 102 inches adjusted cut width
4. 6 yards for face fabric and 1½ yards for contrast cording

Step 1: Determine widths.

Finished width of treatment:		88	in.
Right return:	+	3	in.
Left return:	+	3	in.
Add 6 inches for upholstering:	+	6	in.
Total:		**100**	**in.**
Divide by fabric width:	÷	54	in.
Total widths needed:		**1.85**	**widths**
Round up to whole number:		**2**	**full widths**

Step 2: Determine cut length.

Finished length of treatment:		96	in.
Add 6 inches for upholstering:	+	6	in.
Total cut length:		**102**	**in.**

Step 3: Calculate for repeat.

There is no repeat, so we skip to Step 4.

Step 4: Determine yardage.

Cut length or adjusted cut length:		102	in.
Multiply by number of widths:	×	2	in.
Total:		**204**	**in.**
Divide by 36 to convert inches to yards:	÷	36	in.
Total yards:		**5.67**	**yd.**
Round up to nearest ½ yard:		**6**	**yd.**
For contrast welt:		**1.5**	**yd.**

Tabbed Valance

1. 21 tabs; 10 inches or .28 yard
2. 4 widths of fabric
3. 24 inches adjusted cut length
4. 3 yards face fabric and tabs
5. 2½ yards lining

Step 1: Determine widths for valance.

Flat measure of treatment:	120	in.
Multiply for fullness (× 1.5 or 2): ×	1.5	fullness
Total:	**180**	**in.**
Add return size × 2 for right and left returns: +	12	in.
Add 6 inches for side hems: +	6	in.
Total:	**198**	**in.**
Divide by width of fabric: ÷	54	in.
Cuts/widths of fabric:	**3.67**	**widths**
Round up to whole number:	**4**	**full widths**

Step 2: Determine widths for tabs.

Width of tab × 2:	1	in.
Add 1 inch for seam allowance: +	1	in.
Total cut tab width:	**2**	**in.**
Width of fabric:	54	in.
Divide by cut tab width: ÷	2	in.
Total tabs:	**27**	**tabs**
Round down to nearest whole number:	**27**	**tabs per width**
Number of tabs for treatment (120 in. ÷ 6 in. = 20 + 1 = 21 tabs):	21	tabs
Divide by tabs available per width: ÷	27	tabs
Total:	**.78**	**widths**
Round up to whole number:	**1**	**full widths**

Step 3: Determine cut length for valance.

Finished length of valance not including tabs:	16	in.
Add for seam allowances: +	2	in.
Add bottom hem (double 2-in. hem): +	4	in.
Total cut length:	**22**	**in.**

Calculate for repeat:

Take cut length:	22	in.
Divide by length of repeat: ÷	24	in.
Total:	**.92**	**repeats**
Round up to whole number:	**1**	**full repeats**
Multiply by length of repeat: ×	24	in.
Adjusted cut length (ACL):	**24**	**in.**

Step 4: Determine cut length for tabs.

Use Table 11.7 on page 194 to find tab length:	8	in.
Add 2 inches seam allowance: +	2	in.
Total cut tab length:	**10**	**in.**

Step 5: Calculate yardage.

Cut length or ACL from Step 3:	24	in.
Multiply by total widths from Step 1: ×	4	widths
Total A:	**96**	**in.**
Cut length or ACL from Step 4:	10	in.
Multiply by total widths from Step 2: ×	1	widths
Total B:	**10**	**in.**
Total A:	96	in.
Add Total B: +	10	in.
Total:	**106**	**in.**
Divide by 36: ÷	36	in.
Total yards:	**2.94**	**yd.**
Round up to nearest ½ yard:	**3**	**yd. to be ordered**

Step 6: Calculate lining for treatments.

Cut length from Step 3:	22	in.
Multiply by total widths from Step 3: ×	4	widths
Total:	**88**	**in.**
Divide by 36: ÷	36	in.
Total yards:	**2.44**	**yd.**
Round up to nearest ½ yard:	**2.5**	**yd. to be ordered for lining**

Mock Hobbled Shade

1. 48 adjusted cut length
2. 43 inches × 18 inches = 774 square inches ÷ 144 square inches = 5.38 square feet per valance
3. 11 yards face fabric for eight windows
4. 10½ yards lining for eight windows

Step 1: Calculate cut width. (Note: Unlike most other treatments, shades have a cut width.)

Finished width of shade:	43	in.
Add 6 inches for side hem: +	6	in.
Total cut width:	**49**	**in.**

Step 2: Determine widths.

Cut width from Step 1:	49	in.
Divide by fabric width:	÷ 54	in.
Total widths needed:	**.91**	**widths**
Round up to whole number:	**1**	**full widths**

Step 3: Determine cut length.

Finished length of shade:	18	in.
Multiply for fullness for mock bottom:	× 2	fullness
Total:	**36**	**in.**
Add 10 inches for hem and board allowance:	+ 10	in.
Total cut length:	**46**	**in.**

Calculate for repeat:

Total cut length:	46	in.
Divide by length of repeat:	÷ 6	in.
Number of repeats:	**7.67**	**repeats**
Round up to whole number:	**8**	**full repeats**
Multiply by length of repeat:	× 6	in.
Adjusted cut length (ACL) :	**48**	**in.**

Step 4: Determine yardage.

Cut length or adjusted cut length:	48	in.
Multiply by number of widths:	× 1	width
Total:	**48**	**in.**
Divide by 36:	÷ 36	in.
Total yards:	**1.33**	**yd.**
Multiply by number of windows:	× 8	windows
Total yards for all windows:	**10.64**	**yd.**
Round up to nearest ½ yard:	**11**	**yd.**

Calculate yardage for lining:

Cut length:	46	in.
Multiply by number of widths:	× 1	width
Total:	**46**	**in.**
Divide by 36 to convert inches to yards:	÷ 36	in.
Total yards:	1.28	yd.
Multiply by number of windows:	× 8	windows
Total yards for all windows:	**10.24**	**yd.**
Round up to nearest ½ yard:	**10.5**	**yd.**

Balloon Shade

1. 3 widths
2. 99 inches adjusted cut length
3. 34.5 inches × 56 inches = 1932 square inches per shade
4. 16.5 yards face fabric for 2 windows
5. 16 yards lining for 2 windows

Step 1: Calculate widths.

Finished width of shade:	34.5	in.
If outside mounted, add for returns (2 returns):	+ 7	in.
Total:	**41.5**	**in.**
Multiply for fullness (× 2.5 or 3):	× 3	fullness
Total:	**124.5**	**in.**
Add 6 inches for side hem:	+ 6	in.
Total:	**130.5**	**in.**
Divide by fabric width:	÷ 54	in.
Total widths needed:	**2.42**	**widths**
Round up to whole number:	**3**	**full widths**

Step 2: Determine cut length.

Finish length of shade:	56	in.
Add 20 inches to 30 inches for poufy bottom look:	+ 30	in.
Add 10 inches for hem and board allowance:	+ 10	in.
Total cut length:	**96**	**in.**

Calculate for repeat:

Total cut length from Step 3:	96	in.
Divide by length of repeat:	÷ 9	in.
Number of repeats:	**10.67**	**repeats**
Round up to whole number:	**11**	**full repeats**
Multiply by length of repeat:	× 9	in.
Adjusted cut length (ACL):	**99**	**in.**

Step 3: Determine yardage.

Cut length or adjusted cut length:	99	in.
Multiply by number of widths:	× 3	widths
Total:	**297**	**in.**
Divide by 36:	÷ 36	in.
Total yards:	**8.25**	**yd.**
Multiply by number of windows:	× 2	windows
Total yards for all windows:	**16.5**	**yd.**
Round up to nearest ½ yard:	**16.5**	**yd.**

Calculate yardage for lining:

Cut length:	96	in.
Multiply by number of widths:	× 3	widths
Total:	**288**	**in.**
Divide by 36:	÷ 36	in.
Total yards:	**8**	**yd.**
Multiply by number of windows:	× 2	windows
Total yards for all windows:	**16**	**yd.**
Round up to nearest ½ yard:	**16**	**yd.**

ADVANCED
Pulled-Up Valance
1. 4 widths
2. 27 inches adjusted cut length
3. 3 yards face fabric
4. 3 yards lining

Step 1: Determine total width dimension requiring fullness.

Flat measure of treatment:	78	in.
Multiply for fullness (× 1.5 or 2): ×	2	fullness
Total:	**156**	**in.**
Add return size × 2 for right and left returns: +	7	in.
Add 6 inches for side hems: +	6	in.
Total:	**169**	**in.**
Divide by width of fabric: ÷	54	in.
Cuts/widths of fabric:	**3.13**	**widths**
Round up to whole number:	**4**	**full widths**

Step 2: Determine cut length.

Finished length:	21	in.
Add for seam allowances: +	2	in.
Total cut length:	**23**	**in.**

Calculate for repeat:

Take cut length:	23	in.
Divide by length of repeat: ÷	27	in.
Total:	**.85**	**repeats**
Round up to whole number:	**1**	**full repeat**
Multiply by the length of repeat: ×	27	in.
Adjusted cut length (ACL):	**27**	**in.**

Step 3: Determine yardage.

Take cut length or ACL from Step 2:	27	in.
Multiply by total widths from Step 1: ×	4	widths
Total:	**108**	**in.**
Divide by 36 to convert inches to yards: ÷	36	in.
Total yards:	**3**	**yd.**
Round up to nearest ½ yard:	**3**	**yd. to be ordered**

Calculate yardage for lining:

Cut length:	23	in.
Multiply by number of widths: ×	4	widths
Total:	**92**	**in.**
Divide by 36: ÷	36	in.
Total yards:	**2.56**	**yd.**
Round up to nearest ½ yard:	**3**	**yd. to be ordered**

Swags and Cascades
1. 3 swags
2. 4½ yards for swags
3. 4 yards for cascade face
4. 8½ yards for swags and cascade face
5. 4½ yards lining for swags
6. 4 yards lining for cascades

Swags
Step 1:

Total width of treatment:	80	in.
Divide by 30 inches: ÷	30	in.
Number of swags:	**2.67**	**swags**
Round up or down to whole number:	**3**	**total number of swags**

80 in. ÷ 2 = 40 in.; 80 in. ÷ 3 = 26.67 in. Using Table 11.3, 40 inches is too wide and the pleats may fall out. If possible, the interior designer may suggest that the cascades overlap a little more or suggest a wider treatment.

Step 2:

Total number of swags:	3	swags
Multiply by 1½ to 2 yards: ×	1.5	yd.
Total yardage for swags: ×	**4.5**	**yd. to order**

This same amount will be needed for lining.

Cascades

Step 1: Determine widths.

Commonly, 1 width of fabric is needed per cascade:	1	width
Multiply by number of cascades (normally two per window):	× 2	cascade
Total number of widths necessary for treatment:	**2**	total widths

Step 2: Determine cut length.

Finished length of cascade:	60	in.
Add 4 inches for hems and placement:	+ 4	in.
Total cut length of cascade:	**64**	in.

Calculate for repeat:

Take cut length:	64	in.
Divide by length of repeat:	÷ 24	in.
Number of repeats:	**2.67**	repeats
Round up to whole number:	**3**	full repeats
Multiply by length of repeat:	× 24	in.
Adjusted cut length (ACL):	**72**	in.

Step 3: Determine yardage.

Cut length or adjusted cut length from Step 2:	72	in.
Multiply by widths from Step 1:	× 2	widths
Total:	**144**	in.
Divide by 36:	÷ 36	in.
Total yards:	**4**	yd.
Round up to nearest ½ yard:	**4**	yd. to be ordered

Calculate yardage for lining:

Cut length:	64	in.
Multiply by number of widths:	× 2	widths
Total:	**128**	in.
Divide by 36 to convert inches to yards:	÷ 36	in.
Total yards:	**3.56**	yd.
Round up to nearest ½ yard:	**4**	yd. to be ordered

Austrian Shade

1. 3 widths per window
2. 226 inches cut length
3. 42 inches × 72 inches = 3024 square inches
4. 75.5 yards

Step 1: Calculate widths.

Finished width of shade:	42	in.
If outside mounted, add for returns (2 returns):	+ n/a	in.
Multiply for fullness (× 2.5 or 3):	× 3	fullness
Total:	**126**	in.
Add 6 inches for side hem:	+ 6	in.
Total:	**132**	in.
Divide by fabric width:	÷ 48	in.
Total widths needed:	**2.75**	widths
Round up to whole number:	**3**	full widths

Step 2: Determine cut length.

Finished length of shade:	72	in.
Multiply for fullness (× 2.5 or 3):	× 3	fullness
Total:	**216**	in.
Add 10 inches for hem and board allowance:	+ 10	in.
Total cut length:	**226**	in.

Step 3: Determine yardage.

Cut length or adjusted cut length:	226	in.
Multiply by number of widths:	× 3	widths
Total:	**678**	in.
Divide by 36 to convert inches to yards:	÷ 36	in.
Total yards:	**18.83**	yd.
Multiply by number of windows:	× 4	windows
Total yards for all windows:	**75.32**	yd.
Round up to nearest ½ yard:	**75.5**	yd.

Pricing for Basic Gathered Valance

1. $204.00
2. $254.00
3. $458.00

	Materials										
	Mfr./ Vendor	Pattern	Color/ Finish	Width	Repeat	Qty.	Cost Per	Subtotal	Est. Ship.	Total	PO
Fabric						3 yd.	$48	$144	$12	$156	
Lining						2.5 yd.	$8	$20	n/a	$20	
Hdwr.						1	$18	$18	$10	$28	
Rod											
Brackets											
Supports											
Finials											
Batons											
							Subtotal for Materials			$204	

	Labor and Installation										
Labor						Qty.	Cost Per	Subtotal	Est. Ship.	Total	WO
						3/w	$58	$174	n/a	$174	
Install						1	$36	$36		$80*	
							Subtotal for Labor and Installation			$254	
							Overall Total			$458	

Diagram:

Advanced—Pricing for Basic Gathered Valance

*minimum charge is $80.00; $36.00 doesn't meet minimum so minimum is charged.

Pricing for Basic Roman Shade

1. $322.00
2. $329.20
3. $651.20

			Materials								
	Mfr./ Vendor	**Pattern**	**Color/ Finish**	**Width**	**Repeat**	**Qty.**	**Cost Per**	**Subtotal**	**Est. Ship.**	**Total**	**PO**
Fabric						3 yd.	$94	$282	$16	$298	
Lining						3 yd.	$8	$24	n/a	$24	
Hdwr.											
Rod											
Brackets											
Supports											
Finials											
Batons											
								Subtotal for Materials		$322	

			Labor and Installation								
Labor						**Qty.**	**Cost Per**	**Subtotal**	**Est. Ship.**	**Total**	**WO**
						15.56 sq. ft.	$20	$311.20	n/a	$311.20	
Install						1	$18	$18		$18	
							Subtotal for Labor and Installation			$329.20	
								Overall Total		$651.20	

Diagram:

Advanced—Pricing for Basic Roman Shade

Pricing for Advanced Swags and Cascades

1. $930.00
2. $490.00
3. $1420.00

	Mfr./Vendor	Pattern	Color/ Finish	Width	Repeat	Qty.	Cost Per	Subtotal	Est. Ship.	Total	PO
Materials											
Fabric			Face fabric for swags and cascades			8.5 yd.	$82	$697	$24	$721	
			Lining fabric for cascades			4.5 yd.	$36	$162	$15	$177	
Lining			Regular lining for swags			4 yd.	$8	$32	n/a	$32	
Hdwr.											
Rod											
Brackets											
Supports											
Finials											
Batons											
							Subtotal for Materials			$930	

						Qty.	Cost Per	Subtotal	Est. Ship.	Total	WO
Labor and Installation											
Labor											
					Swags	3	$75	$225	n/a	$225	
					Cascades	2	$60	$120	n/a	$120	
Install						1	$145	$145		$145	
						Subtotal for Labor and Installation				$490	
								Overall Total		$1420.00	

Diagram:

Advanced—Pricing for Advanced Swags and Cascades

Chapter 13: Pillows and Accent Table Coverings

BASIC

Throw Pillows

1. 2 pillow faces
2. 20-inch cut length
3. 1½ yards fabric
4. 4½ yards decorative cording

Step 1: Determine cut width of pillow.

Width of pillow:	18	in.
Add 2 inches for hems:	+ 2	in.
Total cut width:	**20**	**in.**

There is no horizontal repeat.

Step 2: Determine number of cuts from width of fabric.

Width of fabric:	54	in.
Divide by cut width or adjusted cut width from Step 1:	÷ 20	in.
Total pillow face cuts per width:	**2.7**	**cuts**
Round down to nearest whole number:	**2**	**total cuts per width**

Step 3: Determine cut length of pillow.

Length of pillow:	18	in.
Add 2 inches for hems:	+ 2	in.
Total:	**20**	**in.**

There is no vertical repeat.

Step 4: Determine number of widths/cuts.

Number of pillows:	2	pillows
Multiply by number of pillow faces:	× 2	faces
Total number of pillow faces:	**4**	**faces**
Divide by cuts per width from Step 2:	÷ 2	cuts
Total:	**2**	**widths**
Round up to whole number:	**2**	**full widths**

Step 5: Determine yardage to order.

Cut length or adjusted cut length from Step 3:	20	in.
Multiply by number of widths from Step 4:	× 2	widths
Total:	**40**	**in.**
Divide by 36 to convert inches to yards:	÷ 36	in.
Total yards:	**1.11**	**yd.**
Round up to nearest ½ yard:	**1.5**	**yd. to be ordered**

Cording:

Step 1: Determine perimeter.

Finished dimension side A:	18	in.
Add finished dimension side B:	+ 18	in.
Add finished dimension side C:	+ 18	in.
Add finished dimension side D:	+ 18	in.
Total finished perimeter:	**72**	**in.**

Step 2: Determine yardage.

Total from Step 1:	72	in.
Add 2 inches for start and stop of trim:	+ 2	in.
Total:	**74**	**in.**
Multiply by quantity of items:	× 2	quantity
Total inches:	**148**	**in.**
Divide by 36 to convert inches to yards:	÷ 36	in.
Total yards:	**4.11**	**yd.**
Round up to nearest ½ yard:	**4.5**	**yd. to be ordered**

Table Round

1. 76-inch finished diameter
2. 2 widths
3. 4½ yards fabric

Step 1: Determine finished width and length.

Diameter of table:	26	in.
Add drop to floor:	+ 25	in.
Add second drop to floor:	+ 25	in.
Total finished diameter of tablecloth:	**76**	**in. finished width and length**

Step 2: Determine cut width and cut length.

Finished diameter of tablecloth:	76	in.
Add for hems (2 in. each side):	+ 4	in.
Total cut width and cut length:	**80**	**in.**

There is no repeat.

Step 3: Determine widths.

Cut width from Step 2:	80	in.
Divide by fabric width:	÷ 54	in.
Total widths needed:	**1.48**	**widths**
Round up to whole number:	**2**	**full widths**

Step 4: Determine yardage.

Cut length or adjusted cut length from Step 2:	80	in.
Multiply by number of widths:	× 2	widths
Total inches:	**160**	**in.**
Divide by 36 to convert inches to yards:	÷ 36	in.
Total yards:	**4.44**	**yd.**
Round up to nearest ½ yard:	**4.5**	**yd. to be ordered**

Table Topper

1. 38 inches × 38 inches finished dimension
2. 1 width
3. 1½ yards fabric

Step 1: Determine side dimension.

Diameter of table:	26	in.
Add length of drop over edge:	+ 6	in.
Add drop again to account for both sides:	+ 6	in.
Total finished dimension per side of topper:	**38**	**in.**

Step 2: Determine cut length or adjusted cut length.

Finished dimension from Step 1:	38	in.
Add 1 inch each side for hems:	+ 2	in.
This is the cut width and cut length:	**40**	**in.**

Calculate for repeat.

Cut length from above:	40	in.
Divide by length of repeat:	÷ 18	in.
Number of repeats:	**4.11**	**repeats**
Round up to whole number:	**3**	**full repeats**
Multiply by length of repeat:	× 18	in.
Adjusted cut length (ACL):	**54**	**in.**

Step 3: Determine widths:

Cut width from Step 2:	40	in.
Divide by fabric width:	÷ 54	in.
Total widths needed:	**.74**	**widths**
Round up to whole number:	**1**	**full widths**

Step 4: Determine yardage.

Cut length or adjusted cut length from Step 2:	54	in.
Multiply by number of widths:	× 1	in.
Total inches:	**54**	**in.**
Divide by 36 to convert inches to yards:	÷ 36	in.
Total yards:	**1.5**	**yd.**
Round up to nearest ½ yard:	**1.5**	**yd. to be ordered**

INTERMEDIATE

Throw Pillows

1. 1 pillow face from a width
2. 30-inch adjusted cut length
3. 7 yards fabric
4. 9½ yards decorative tassel fringe

Step 1: Determine cut width of pillow.

Width of pillow:	20	in.
Add 2 inches for hems:	+ 2	in.
Total cut width:	**22**	**in.**

There is a horizontal repeat, so determine adjusted cut width.

Total cut width from above:	22	in.
Divide by horizontal repeat of fabric:	÷ 10.8	in.
Total:	**2.04**	**repeats**
Round up to whole number:	**3**	**full repeats**
Multiply by length of horizontal repeat:	× 10.8	in.
Total adjusted cut width:	**32.4**	**in.**

Step 2: Determine number of cuts from width of fabric.

Width of fabric:	54	in.
Divide by cut width or adjusted cut width from Step 1:	÷ 32.4	in.
Total pillow face cuts per width:	**1.67**	**cuts**
Round down to nearest whole number:	**1**	**total cuts per width**

Step 3: Determine cut length of pillow.

Length of pillow:	20	in.
Add 2 inches for hems:	+ 2	in.
Total cut length:	**22**	**in.**

There is a vertical repeat, so determine adjusted cut length.

Total cut length from above:	22	in.
Divide by vertical repeat:	÷ 10	in.
Total:	**2.2**	**repeats**
Round up to whole number:	**3**	**full repeats**
Multiply by length of vertical repeat:	× 10	in.
Adjusted cut length (ACL):	**30**	**in.**

Step 4: Determine number of widths/cuts:

Number of pillows:	4	pillows
Multiply by number of pillow faces:	× 2	faces
Total number of pillow faces:	**8**	**faces**
Divide by cuts per width from Step 2:	÷ 1	cut
Total:	**8**	**widths**
Round up to whole number:	**8**	**full widths**

Step 5: Yardage to order.

Cut length or adjusted cut length from Step 3:	30	in.
Multiply by number of widths from Step 4:	× 8	widths
Total inches:	**240**	**in.**
Divide by 36 to convert inches to yards:	÷ 36	in.
Total yards:	**6.67**	**yd.**
Round up to nearest ½ yard:	**7**	**yd. to be ordered**

Fringe:

Step 1:

Finished dimension side A:	20	in.
Add finished dimension side B	+ 20	in.
Add finished dimension side C	+ 20	in.
Add finished dimension side D:	+ 20	in.
Total finished perimeter:	**80**	**in.**

Step 2: Determine yardage.

Total from Step 1:	80	in.
Add 2 inches for start and stop of trim:	+ 2	in.
Total:	**82**	**in.**
Multiply by quantity of items/products:	× 4	quantity
Total:	**328**	**in.**
Divide by 36 to convert inches to yards:	÷ 36	in.
Total yards:	**9.11**	**yd.**
Round up to nearest ½ yard:	**9.5**	**yd. to be ordered**

Table Round

1. 88 inch finished diameter
2. 96-inch Adjusted cut length
3. 276.32-inch finished circumference
4. 5.33 yards × 4 table rounds = 21.32 yards. Round up to 21.5 yards *or* 5.5 yards × 4 table rounds = 22 yards.

Note: It is advisable to calculate the per table yardage and multiply by quantity such as 5.5 yards × 4 = 22 yards; however, total yardage can be calculated either way.

5. 7.73 yards × 4 table rounds = 30.92 yards. Round up to 31 yards *or* 8 yards × 4 table rounds = 32 yards.

Step 1: Determine finished width and length.

Diameter of table:	28	in.
Add drop to floor:	+ 30	in.
Add 2nd drop to floor (2 sides):	+ 30	in.
Total finished diameter of tablecloth:	**88**	**in. finished width and length**

Step 2: Determine cut width and cut length.

Finished diameter of tablecloth:	88	in.
Add for hems (2 in. each side):	+ 4	in.
Total cut width and length:	**92**	**in.**

Calculate for the repeat.

Total cut length from above:	92	in.
Divide by length of repeat:	÷ 24	in.
Number of repeats:	**3.83**	**repeats**
Round up to whole number:	**4**	**full repeats**
Multiply by length of repeat:	× 24	in.
Adjusted cut length (ACL):	**96**	**in.**

Step 3: Determine widths.

Cut width from Step 2:	92	in.
Divide by fabric width:	÷ 54	in.
Total widths needed:	**1.7**	**widths**
Round up to whole number:	**2**	**full widths**

Step 4: Determine yardage.

Cut length or adjusted cut length from Step 2:	96	in.
Multiply by number of widths:	× 2	widths
Total:	**192**	**in.**
Divide by 36 to convert inches to yards:	÷ 54	in.
Total yards:	**5.33**	**yd.**
Round up to nearest ½ yard:	**5.5**	**yd. to be ordered**

Step 5: Determine circumference for cording or fringe, if applicable.

Total from Step 1:	88	in.
Multiply by π (3.14):	× 3.14	π
Total circumference of hem:	**276.32**	**in.**
Add 2 inches for start and stop of trim:	+ 2	in.
Total:	**278.32**	**in.**
Divide by 36 to convert inches to yards:	÷ 36	in.
Total yards:	**7.73**	**yd.**
Round up to nearest ½ yard:	**8**	**yd. to be ordered**

Table Topper

1. 44 inches × 44 inches finished dimension
2. 46 inches ACL
3. 1.28 yards × 4 table toppers = 5.12 yards. Round up to 5.5 yards *or* 1.5 yards × 4 table toppers = 6 yards

Step 1: Determine side dimension.

Diameter of table:	28	in.
Add length of drop over edge:	+ 8	in.
Add drop again to account for both sides:	+ 8	in.
Total finished dimension of topper:	**44**	**in.**

Step 2: Determine cut length or adjusted cut length.

Finished dimension from Step 1:	44	in.
Add 1 inch each side for hems:	+ 2	in.
This is the cut width and cut length:	**46**	**in.**

Calculate for the repeat.

Cut length from above:	46	in.
Divide by length of repeat:	÷ 2	in.
Number of repeats:	**23**	**repeats**
Round up to whole number:	**23**	**full repeats**
Multiply by length of repeat:	× 2	in.
Adjusted cut length:	**46**	**in.**

Step 3: Determine widths.

Cut width from Step 2:	46	in.
Divide by fabric width:	÷ 54	in.
Total widths needed:	**.85**	**widths**
Round up to whole number:	**1**	**full widths**

Step 4: Determine yardage.

Cut length or adjusted cut length from Step 2:	46	in.
Multiply by number of widths:	× 1	in.
Total:	**46**	**in.**
Divide by 36 to convert inches to yards:	÷ 36	in.
Total yards:	**1.28**	**yd**
Round up to nearest ½ yard:	**1.5**	**yd. to be ordered**

ADVANCED

Throw Pillows

1. Pillows A: 2 pillow faces; Pillows B: 2 pillow faces
2. 27 inches ACL
3. Pillows A: 2 yards; Pillows B: 4 yards
4. Pillows A: 7½ yards; Pillows B: 11½ yards

Pillows A:

Step 1: Determine cut width of pillow.

Width of pillow:	22	in.
Add 2 inches for hems:	+ 2	in.
Total cut width:	**24**	**in.**

There is no horizontal repeat.

Step 2: Determine number of cuts from width of fabric.

Width of fabric:	54	in.
Divide by cut width from Step 1:	÷ 24	in.
Total pillow face cuts per width:	2.25	cuts
Round down to nearest whole number:	**2**	**total cuts per width**

Step 3: Determine cut length of pillow.

Length of pillow	22	in.
Add 2 inches for hems	+ 2	in.
Total cut length:	**24**	**in.**

There is no vertical repeat.

Step 4: Determine number of widths.

Number of pillows:	3	pillows
Multiply by number of pillow faces:	× 2	faces
Total number of pillow faces:	**6**	**faces**
Divide by cuts per width from Step 2:	÷ 2	cuts
Total:	**3**	**widths**
Round up to whole number:	**3**	**full widths**

Step 5: Yardage to order.

Cut length or adjusted cut length from Step 3:	24	in.
Multiply by number of widths from Step 4:	× 3	widths
Total inches:	**72**	**in.**
Divide by 36 to convert inches to yards:	÷ 36	in.
Total yards:	**2**	**yd.**
Round up to nearest ½ yard:	**2**	**yd. to be ordered**

Cording for Pillows A:

Step 1:

Finished dimension side A:	22	in.
Add Finished dimension side B: +	22	in.
Add Finished dimension side C: +	22	in.
Add Finished dimension side D: +	22	in.
Total finished perimeter:	**88**	**in.**

Step 2: Determine yardage.

Total from Step 1:	88	in.
Add 2 inches for start and stop of trim:	+ 2	in.
Total:	**90**	**in.**
Multiply by quantity of items/products:	× 3	
Total inches:	**270**	**in.**
Divide by 36 to convert inches to yards:	÷ 36	in.
Total yards:	**7.5**	**yd.**
Round up to nearest ½ yard:	**7.5**	**yd. to be ordered**

Pillows B

Step 1: Determine cut width of pillow.

Width of pillow:	20	in.
Add 2 inches for hems:	+ 2	in.
Total cut width:	**22**	**in.**

There is a horizontal repeat, so determine adjusted cut width:

Total cut width from above:	22	in.
Divide by horizontal repeat of fabric:	÷ 27	in.
Total:	**.81**	**repeats**
Round up to whole number:	**1**	**full repeats**
Multiply by horizontal repeat:	× 27	in.
Total adjusted cut width:	**27**	**in.**

Step 2: Determine number of cuts from width of fabric.

Width of fabric:	54	in.
Divide by cut width or adjusted cut width from Step 1:	÷ 27	in.
Total:	**2**	**cuts**
Round down to nearest whole number:	**2**	**total cuts per width**

Step 3: Determine cut length of pillow.

Length of pillow:	20	in.
Add 2 inches for hems:	+ 2	in.
Total cut length:	**22**	**in.**

There is a vertical repeat, so determine adjusted cut length:

Total cut length from above:	22	in.
Divide by vertical repeat:	÷ 27	in.
Number of repeats:	**.81**	**repeats**
Round up to whole number:	**1**	**full repeats**
Multiply by length of vertical repeat:	× 27	in.
Adjusted cut length (ACL):	**27**	**in.**

Step 4: Determine number of widths/cuts.

Number of pillows:	5	pillows
Multiply by number of pillow faces:	× 2	faces
Total number of pillow faces:	**10**	**faces**
Divide by cuts per width from Step 2:	÷ 2	cuts
Total:	**5**	**widths**
Round up to whole number:	**5**	**full widths**

Step 5: Determine yardage to order.

Cut length or adjusted cut length from Step 3:	27	in.
Multiply by number of widths from Step 4:	× 5	widths
Total inches:	**135**	**in.**
Divide by 36 to convert inches to yards:	÷ 36	in.
Total yards:	**3.75**	**yd.**
Round up to nearest ½ yard:	**4**	**yd. to be ordered**

Fringe for Pillows B:

Step 1:

Finished dimension side A:	20	in.
Add finished dimension side B:	+ 20	in.
Add finished dimension side C:	+ 20	in.
Add finished dimension side D:	+ 20	in.
Total finished perimeter:	**80**	**in.**

Step 2: Determine yardage.

Total from Step 1:	80	in.
Add 2 inches for start and stop of trim:	+ 2	in.
Total:	**82**	**in.**
Multiply by quantity of items/products:	× 5	quantity
Total inches:	**410**	**in.**
Divide by 36 to convert inches to yards:	÷ 36	in.
Total yards:	**11.38**	**yd.**
Round up to nearest ½ yard:	**11.5**	**yd. to be ordered**

Table Round

1. 120 inches finished diameter
2. 3 widths per table
3. 10.5 yards × 8 table rounds = 84 yards

Step 1: Determine finished width and length.

Diameter of table:	60	in.
Add drop to floor:	+ 30	in.
Add 2nd drop to floor (2 sides):	+ 30	in.
Total finished diameter of tablecloth:	**120**	**in. finished width and length**

Step 2: Determine cut width and cut length.

Finished diameter of tablecloth:	120	in.
Add for hems (2 in. each side):	+ 4	in.
Total cut width and length:	**124**	**in.**

Calculate for the repeat.

Total cut length from above:	124	in.
Divide by length of repeat:	÷ 21	in.
Number of repeats:	**5.9**	**repeats**
Round up to whole number:	**6**	**full repeats**
Multiply by length of repeat:	× 21	in.
Adjusted cut length (ACL):	**126**	**in.**

Step 3: Determine widths.

Cut width from Step 2:	124	in.
Divide by fabric width:	÷ 54	width
Total widths needed:	**2.3**	**widths**
Round up to whole number:	**3**	**full widths**

Step 4: Determine yardage.

Cut length or adjusted cut length from Step 2:	126	in.
Multiply by number of widths:	× 3	width
Total inches:	**378**	**in.**
Divide by 36 to convert inches to yards:	÷ 36	in.
Total yards:	**10.5**	**yd.**
Round up to nearest ½ yard:	**10.5**	**yd. to be ordered**

Table Topper

1. 80 inches × 80 inches finished dimension
2. 84 inches Adjusted cut length
3. 2 widths per table
4. 113.14 inches diagonal dimension; It won't touch the floor. The table cloth is 120 inches, which is to the floor.
5. 4.67 yards × 8 toppers = 37.36 yards, round up to 37.5 yards OR 5 yards × 8 toppers = 40 yards
6. 72 yards

Step 1: Determine side dimension.

Diameter of table:	60	in.
Add length of drop over edge:	+ 10	in.
Add drop again to account for both sides:	+ 10	in.
Total finished dimension per side of topper:	**80**	**in.**

Step 2: Determine cut length or adjusted cut length.

Finished dimension from Step 1:	80	in.
Add 1 inch each side for hems:	+ 2	in.
Cut width and cut length:	**82**	**in.**

Calculate for the repeat.

Cut length from above:	**82**	**in.**
Divide by length of repeat:	÷ 4	in.
Number of repeats:	**20.5**	**repeats**
Round up to whole number:	**21**	**full repeats**
Multiply by length of repeat:	× 4	in.
Adjusted cut length (ACL):	**84**	**in.**

Step 3: Determine widths.

Cut width from Step 2:	82	in.
Divide by fabric width:	÷ 54	width
Total widths needed:	**1.52**	**widths**
Round up to whole number:	**2**	**full widths**

Step 4: Determine yardage.

Cut length or adjusted cut length from Step 2:	84	in.
Multiply by number of widths:	× 2	widths
Total inches:	**168**	in.
Divide by 36 to convert inches to yards:	÷ 36	in.
Total yards:	**4.67**	yd.
Round up to nearest ½ yard:	**5**	yd. to be ordered

Find the diagonal dimension.

Step A: Determine Side A^2.

Side A:	80	in.
Multiply by Side A:	× 80	in.
Total Side A^2:	**6400**	in.

Step B: Determine Side B^2.

Side B:	80	in.
Multiply by Side B:	× 80	in.
Total Side B^2:	**6400**	in.

Step C: Determine the diagonal distance (C).

Total from Step A:	6400	in.
Add total from Step B:	+ 6400	in.
Equals C^2:	**12800**	in.
Use the square root (√) function on the calculator to find the root of C^2:	**113.14**	in.

This is the diagonal length of the topper in inches.

Cording:

Step 1:

Finished dimension side A:	80	in.
Add finished dimension side B:	+ 80	in.
Add finished dimension side C:	+ 80	in.
Add finished dimension side D:	+ 80	in.
Total finished perimeter:	**320**	in.

Step 2: Determine yardage.

Total from Step 1:	320	in.
Add 2 inches for start and stop of trim:	+ 2	in.
Total:	**322**	in.
Multiply by quantity of items/products:	× 8	quantity
Total inches:	**2576**	in.
Divide by 36 to convert inches to yards:	÷ 36	in.
Total yards:	**71.56**	yd.
Round up to nearest ½ yard:	**72**	yd. to be ordered

Pricing for Advanced Throw Pillows

1. Total price for Pillows A: $568.50
2. Total price for Pillows B: $1325.00
3. Total for all pillows: $1893.50

Throw Pillows			
Fabric A	**Quantity**	**Price**	**Total**
Fabric	2 yd.	$48.00/yd.	$96.00
Fabric shipping			$12.00
Labor	3 pillows	$76.00 each	$228.00
Trim	7.5 yd.	$30.00/yd.	$225.00
Trim shipping			$7.50
		Subtotal A	$568.50
Pillow B			
Fabric	4 yd.	$108.00/yd.	$432.00
Fabric shipping			$18.00
Labor	5 pillows	$70.00 each	$350.00
Trim	11.5 yd.	$45.00/yd.	$517.50
Trim shipping			$7.50
		Subtotal B	$1325.00
	Total for all Throw Pillows		$1893.50

Advanced—Pricing for Advanced Throw Pillows

Pricing for Advanced Table Round

1. Total price for all eight table rounds: $2997.00

Table Rounds			
Pillow A	**Quantity**	**Price**	**Total**
Fabric	84 yd.	$18.00/yd	$1512.00
Fabric shipping			$85.00
Labor	8	$175.00 each	$1400.00
	Total for all Table Rounds		$2997.00

Advanced—Pricing for Advanced Table Round

Pricing for Advanced Table Topper

1. Total price for all eight table toppers: $2714.00

Table Toppers			
	Quantity	**Price**	**Total**
Fabric	40 yd.	$26.00/yd.	$1040.00
Fabric shipping			$55.00
Trim	72 yd.	$12.00/yd.	$864.00
Trim shipping			$35.00
Labor	8	$90.00 each	$720.00
	Total for all Table Toppers		$2714.00

Advanced—Pricing for Advanced Table Topper

Chapter 14: Bedding

BASIC

Bedspread

1. See figure for seaming diagram.
2. 128.8 inches cut width
3. 3 widths
4. 162 inches adjusted cut length
5. 13½ yards

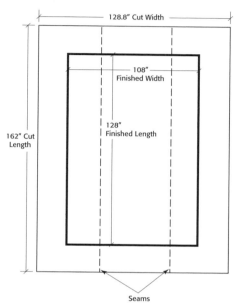

Practice Answer Basic—Bedspread seaming diagram; while not part of the seaming diagram, the bold line shows the finished size of the bedspread.

Step 1: Determine finished width and cut width.

Width of bed:	60	in.
Add drop:	+ 24	in.
Add second drop:	+ 24	in.
Total finished width:	**108**	**in.**
Add hems (2 in. each side):	+ 4	in. (2 sides)
Total:	**112**	**in.**
Add quilting allowance (10 to 15 percent):	× 1.15	(1.10 to 1.15)
Total cut width:	**128.8**	**in.**

Step 2: Determine number of widths to use.

Cut width from Step 1:	128.8	in.
Divide by width of fabric:	÷ 54	in.
Total widths:	**2.39**	**widths**
Round up to whole number:	**3**	**full widths**

Step 3: Determine finished length and cut length.

Length of bed:	80	in.
Add drop:	+ 24	in.
Add pillow tuck:	+ 24	in.
Total finished length:	**128**	**in.**
Add hems (2 in. each end):	+ 4	in.
Total:	**132**	**in.**
Add quilting allowance (10 to 15 percent):	× 1.15	(1.10 to 1.15)
Total cut length before repeat:	**151.8**	**in.**

The fabric has a repeat:

Take cut length from above:	151.8	in.
Divide by length of repeat:	÷ 27	in.
Total:	**5.62**	**repeats**
Round up to whole number:	**6**	**full repeats**
Multiply by length of repeat:	× 27	in.
Adjusted cut length (ACL):	**162**	**in.**

Step 4: Determine yardage to order.

Cut length or ACL from Step 3:	162	in.
Multiply by total number of widths from Step 2:	× 3	widths
Total inches:	**486**	**in.**
Divide by 36 to convert inches to yards:	÷ 36	in.
Total yards:	**13.5**	**yd. needed to order**

Bedscarf

1. 84 inches
2. 26 inches cut length
3. 3 yards

Step 1: Determine finished width and cut width.

Width of bed:	60	in.
Add drop:	+ 12	in.
Add second drop:	+ 12	in.
Total finished width:	**84**	**in.**
Add hems/seam allowance:	+ 2	in.
Total cut width:	**86**	**in.**

Step 2: Determine number of widths to use.

Cut width from Step 1:	86	in.
Divide by width of fabric:	÷ 54	in.
Total widths:	**1.59**	**widths**
Round up to whole number:	**2**	**full widths**
Multiply by number of scarf sides:	× 2	in.
Total number of widths:	**4**	**widths**

Step 3: Determine finished length and cut length.

Finished length of bedscarf:	24	in.
Add hems/seam allowance	+ 2	in.
Total cut length:	**26**	**in.**

There is no repeat.

Step 4: Determine yardage to order.

Cut length or ACL from Step 3:	26	in.
Multiply by total number of widths from Step 3:	× 4	widths
Total inches:	**104**	**in.**
Divide by 36 to convert inches to yards:	÷ 36	in.
Total yards:	**2.89**	**yd.**
Round up to nearest ½ yard:	**3**	**yd. needed to order**

INTERMEDIATE

Coverlet

1. 3 widths of fabric
2. See figure for seaming diagram.
3. 126 inches adjusted cut length
4. 10½ yards ordered

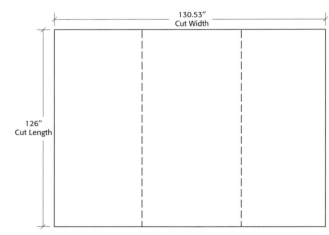

Practice Answer Intermediate—Coverlet seaming diagram.

Step 1: Determine finished width and cut width.

Width of bed:	75.5	in.
Add drop:	+ 17	in.
Add second drop:	+ 17	in.
Total finished width:	**109.5**	**in.**
Add hems (2 inches each side):	+ 4	in. (2 sides)
Total:	**113.5**	**in.**
Add quilting allowance (10–15 percent)	× 1.15	(1.10 to 1.15)
Total cut width:	**130.53**	**in.**

Step 2: Determine number of widths to use.

Cut width from Step 1:	130.53	in.
Divide by width of fabric:	÷ 54	in.
Total widths:	**2.42**	**widths**
Round up to whole number:	**3**	**full widths**

Step 3: Determine length.

Length of bed:	79.5	in.
Add drop:	+ 17	in.

No pillow tuck.

Total finished length:	**96.5**	**in.**
Add hems (2 in. each end):	+ 4	in. (2 sides)
Total:	**100.5**	**in.**
Add quilting allowance (10–15 percent):	× 1.15	(1.10 to 1.15)
Total cut length before repeat:	**115.58**	**in.**

The fabric has a repeat:

Take cut length from above:	115.58	in.
Divide by length of repeat:	÷ 21	in.
Total:	**5.5**	**repeats**
Round up to whole number:	**6**	**full repeats**
Multiply by length of repeat:	× 21	in.
Adjusted cut length (ACL):	**126**	**in.**

Step 4: Determine yardage to order.

Cut length or ACL from Step 3:	126	in.
Multiply by total number of widths from Step 2:	× 3	widths
Total inches:	**378**	**in.**
Divide by 36 to convert inches to yards:	÷ 36	in.
Total yards:	**10.5**	**yd. needed to order**

Gathered Bedskirt

1. 11 widths will be used
2. 30 inches adjusted cut length
3. 9½ yards to be ordered
4. 4½ yards for the decking (from Table 14.4)

Step 1: Find perimeter of bedskirt.

Width of box spring:	75	in.
Add length of box spring:	+ 79.25	in.
Second length of box spring:	+ 79.25	in.
Total perimeter of skirt:	**233.5**	**in.**

Step 2: Determine number of cuts/widths needed.

For gathered and box pleated bedskirt:

Total perimeter from Step 1:	233.5	in.
Multiply for fullness:	× 2.5	fullness
Total:	**583.75**	**in.**
Divide by width of fabric:	÷ 54	in.
Total widths of fabric:	**10.81**	**widths**
Round up to whole number:	**11**	**full widths**

Step 3: Determine cut length.

Drop from box spring to floor:	15	in.
Add top hem:	+ 2	in.
Top banding:	+ 6	in.
Add bottom hem (double 2-in.):	+ 4	in.
Total cut length:	**27**	**in.**

The fabric has a repeat:

Take cut length from above:	27	in.
Divide by length of repeat:	÷ 15	in.
Total number of repeats:	**1.8**	**repeats**
Round up to whole number:	**2**	**full repeats**
Multiply by length of repeat:	× 15	in.
Adjusted cut length (ACL):	**30**	**in.**

Step 4: Determine yardage to order.

Cut length or ACL from Step 3:	30	in.
Multiply by widths from Step 2:	× 11	widths
Total:	**330**	**in.**
Divide by 36 to convert inches to yards:	÷ 36	in.
Total yards:	**9.17**	**yd.**
Round up to nearest ½ yard:	**9.5**	**yd. needed to order**

ADVANCED

Duvet Cover

1. The comforter extends past the seam by 3 inches, so no flange or ruffle is necessary.

   Drop to seam 12 in. + 3 in. to go past = 15 in. needed as drop

   Mattress width 60 in. + 15 in. + 15 in. = 90 in. wide

   Mattress length 80 in. + 15 in. = 95 in. wide
   Minimum dimension need is 90 in. × 95 in.;
   comforter dimension 92 in. × 98 in..

2. 4 widths needed
3. 120 inches adjusted cut length
4. 13½ yards to be ordered

Step 1: Determine cut width.

Width of duvet/comforter:	92	in.
Add seam allowance:	+ 2	in.
Total cut width:	**94**	**in.**

Step 2: Determine total widths.

Cut width from Step 1:	94	in.
Divide by width of fabric:	÷ 54	in.
Widths:	1.74	widths
For same fabric both sides, multiply by 2:	× 2	sides
Total widths:	**3.48**	**widths**
Round up to whole number:	**4**	**full widths**

Step 3: Determine total widths.

Length of duvet/comforter:	98	in.
Add for closure:	+ 6	in.
Add seam allowance:	+ 2	in.
Total cut length before repeat:	**106**	**in.**

The fabric has a repeat:

Take cut length from above:	106	in.
Divide by length of repeat:	÷ 30	in.
Total number of repeats:	**3.53**	**repeats**
Round up to whole number:	**4**	**full repeats**
Multiply by length of repeat:	× 30	in.
Adjusted cut length (ACL):	**120**	**in.**

Step 4: Determine yardage to order.

Cut length or ACL from Step 3:	120	in.
Multiply by total number of widths from Step 2:	× 4	widths
Total inches:	**480**	**in.**
Divide by 36 to convert inches to yards:	÷ 36	in.
Total yards:	**13.33**	**yd.**
Round up to nearest ½ yard:	**13.5**	**yd. needed to order**

Bedskirt with Relaxed Pleat

1. 12 inches required per pleat
2. 6 widths of fabric required
3. 28 inches adjusted cut length
4. 5 yards to be ordered
5. From Table 14.4: Either 3½ yards or 4½ yards are needed for the decking, depending on where the workroom chooses to put the seam.

Step 1: Find perimeter of bedskirt.

Width of box spring:	59.5	in.
Add length of box spring:	+ 79.5	in.
Second length of box spring:	+ 79.5	in.
Total perimeter of skirt:	**218.5**	**in.**

Step 2: Determine number of cuts/widths needed.

For relaxed pleat bedskirt:

Depth of pleat:	3	in.
Multiply by 4:	× 4	in.
Total needed for pleat:	**12**	**in.**
Multiply by number of pleats:	× 5	pleats
Total:	**60**	**in.**
Add total perimeter from Step 1:	+ 218.5	in.
Total:	**278.5**	**in.**
Divide by width of fabric:	÷ 54	in.
Total widths of fabric:	**5.15**	**widths**
Round up to whole number:	**6**	**full widths**

Step 3: Determine cut length.

Drop from box spring to floor:	14	in.
Add top hem:	+ 2	in.
Add top banding:	6	in.
Add bottom hem (double 2-inch):	+ 4	in.
Total cut length:	**26**	**in.**

The fabric has a repeat:

Take cut length from above:	26	in.
Divide by length of repeat:	÷ 4	in.
Total number of repeats:	**6.5**	**repeats**
Round up to whole number:	**7**	**full repeats**
Multiply by the length of repeat:	× 4	in.
Adjusted cut length (ACL):	**28**	**in.**

Step 4: Determine yardage to order.

Cut length or ACL from Step 3:	28	in.
Multiply by widths from Step 2:	× 6	widths
Total:	**168**	**in.**
Divide by 36 to convert inches to yards:	÷ 36	in.
Total yards:	**4.67**	**yd.**
Round up to nearest ½ yard:	**5**	**yd. needed to order**

Sham with Ruffles

1. One pillow face per width
2. 22 inches cut length
3. 10 widths of fabric are needed for the ruffle for the two shams.
4. 8 inches adjusted cut length. It is the same as the cut length, since the repeat goes into the cut length equally.
5. Fabric A: 2½ yards to be ordered for the pillow body; Fabric B: 2½ yards to be ordered for the ruffle

Pillow Body

Step 1: Determine cut width of pillow.

Width of pillow:	30	in.
Add 2 inches for seam allowance:	+ 2	in.
Total cut width:	**32**	**in.**

There is no pattern repeat.

Step 2: Determine number of cuts from width of fabric.

Width of fabric:	54	in.
Divide by cut width or adjusted cut width from Step 1:	÷ 32	in.
Total number of cuts or sides:	**1.69**	**cuts or sides**
Round down to nearest whole number:	**1**	**total cuts/sides per width**

Step 3: Determine cut length of pillow.

Length of pillow:	20	in.
Add 2 inches for seam allowance:	+ 2	in.
Total cut length:	**22**	**in.**

There is no repeat.

Step 4: Determine number of widths/cuts.

Number of pillows:	2	pillows
Multiply by number of pillow faces:	× 2	pillow faces
Total number of pillow faces:	**4**	**faces**
Divide by cuts per width:	÷ 1	cuts per width
Total widths needed:	**4**	**widths**

Step 5: Determine yardage to order.

Cut length or ACL from Step 3:	22	in.
Multiply by number of widths from Step 4:	× 4	widths
Total inches:	**88**	**in.**
Divide by 36 to convert inches to yards:	÷ 36	in.
Total yards:	**2.44**	**yd.**
Round up to nearest ½ yard:	**2.5**	**yd. needed to order**

Pillow Ruffle:

Step 1: Determine perimeter.

Finished dimension side A:	30	in.
Add finished dimension side B:	+ 30	in.
Add finished dimension side C:	+ 20	in.
Add finished dimension side D:	+ 20	in.
Total finished perimeter:	**100**	**in.**

Step 2: Determine widths.

Total from Step 1:	100	in.
Multiply for fullness (× 2 to 3):	× 2.5	fullness
Total:	**250**	**in.**
Multiply by quantity of items/products:	× 2	quantity
Total:	**500**	**in.**
Divide by fabric width:	÷ 54	in.
Total widths:	**9.26**	**widths**
Round up to whole number:	**10**	**full widths**

Step 3: Determine length.

Length of flange or ruffle × 2 (3 × 2):	6	in.
Add 2 inches for seam allowance:	+ 2	in.
Total cut length:	**8**	**in.**

There is a vertical repeat, so determine adjusted cut length:

Total cut length from above:	8	in.
Divide by vertical repeat:	÷ 4	in.
Total number of repeats:	**2**	**repeats**
Multiply by vertical repeat:	× 4	in.
Adjusted cut length (ACL):	**8**	**in.**

Step 4: Determine yardage to order.

Cut length or ACL from Step 3:	8	in.
Multiply by number of widths from Step 2:	× 10	widths
Total inches:	**80**	**in.**
Divide by 36 to convert inches to yards:	÷ 36	in.
Total yards:	**2.22**	**yd.**
Round up to nearest ½ yard:	**2.5**	**yd. needed to order**

Pricing for Intermediate Coverlet
1. $1111.00

King-Size Coverlet			
	Quantity	**Price**	**Total**
Fabric	10.5 yd.	$62.00/yd.	$651.00
Fabric shipping	1	$22.00	$22.00
King labor	1	$400.00	$400.00
Shipping	1	$38.00	$38.00
Total price for finished coverlet			$1111.00

Advanced—Pricing for Intermediate Coverlet

Pricing for Intermediate Gathered Bedskirt
1. $539.00

King-size Gathered Bedskirt			
	Quantity	**Price**	**Total**
Fabric	9.5 yd.	$36.00/yd.	$342.00
Fabric shipping	1	$22.00	$22.00
King labor	1	$175.00	$175.00
Total price for finished bedskirt			$539.00

Advanced—Pricing for Intermediate Gathered Bedskirt

Chapter 15: New Upholstery

BASIC

1. From Figure 15.2, $7,390
2. The F-2 cushion adds $150
3. The brass nails add $240
4. The total retail price of the sofa:

	$7,390	base price
+	$150	cushion upgrade
+	$240	brass nail add-on
Total retail price	**$7,780**	

INTERMEDIATE

1. Base retail for:
   A. Chairs $2862 × 2 = $5,724
   B. Ottoman   + $1,268
   C. Total base   **$6,992**

2. Seat cushion upgrade:
   Per chair: $75 × 2 = $150
   Plus ottoman: + $60
   Total cushion upgrade: **$210**
   Plus swivel base: 180 × 2 = + $360
   Total upgrade and add-ons: **$570**

3. Fabric required per chair from Figure 15.6: 11.75 yards
   Fabric required for ottoman from Figure 15.6: 4.75 yards
   From chart on Figure 15.7:

Chairs: 14.5 yards × 2	29	yards
Ottoman: 6 yards	+ 6	yards
	35	yards

   a. 35 yards must be ordered for these three pieces.
   b. Total retail for fabric: 35 yards × 118.00/yard = $4130

4. Base price: + $6,992
   Upgrade and add-ons: + $570
   Fabric: + $4,130
   Total for 3 pieces: **$11,692**

ADVANCED

1. The base price of the sofa is $5070.
2. 11 yards of fabric and 150 square feet of leather are required by Stanford.
3. 150 square feet of leather divided by 55 square feet per hide = 2.72 hides. Round up to 3 hides. 3 hides × 55 square feet per hide = 165 square feet of leather to order.
4. Fabric: 11 yards × $76/yard = $836
   Leather: 165 square feet × $26 = + $4,290
   Total for fabric and leather: **$5,126**
5. Sofa: $5,070
   Fabric and leather: + $5,126
   Total sofa retail: **$10,196**

Chapter 16: Reupholstered and Slipcovered Furniture

BASIC

Reupholstered Chair
1. 8 yards
2. 9.5 yards

Step 1: Determine yardage.
Yardage required from
Upholstery Yardage Chart: 8   yd.

Step 2: Calculate for fabric narrower than 54 inches.
Fabric is 54 inches wide, so this step is skipped.

Fabric has a repeat, so continue to Step 3.

Step 3: Calculate for fabric with repeat.
Total from Step 1 or Step 2:   8   yd.
Multiply by percentage
from Allowance Chart: ×   1.15
Total: 9.2   yd.
Round up to nearest ½ yard: 9.5   yd. to be ordered

Slipcovered Chair
1. 15 percent
2. 10.5 yards

Step 1: Determine yardage.
Yardage required from
Upholstery Yardage Chart: 8   yd.

Step 2: Calculate for fabric narrower than 54 inches.
Multiply by percentage
from Allowance Chart: ×   1.15
Total: 9.2   yd.
Round up to nearest ½ yard: 9.5   yd. to be ordered

Step 3: Calculate for fabric with repeat.
There is no vertical repeat, so this step is skipped.

For Slipcover:

Total yards to be ordered
from Step 2:   9.5   yd.
Add 1 yard per seat: +   1   yd.
Total yards: 10.5   yd. to be ordered

INTERMEDIATE

Reupholstered Sofa
1. 16 yards
2. 10 percent
3. 35 percent
4. 24.5 yards

Step 1: Determine yardage.
Yardage required from
Upholstery Yardage Chart: 16   yd.

Step 2: Calculate for fabric narrower than 54 inches.
Multiply by percentage
from Allowance Chart: ×   1.1
Total: 17.6   yd.
Round up to nearest ½ yard: 18   yd. to be ordered

Fabric has a repeat, so continue to Step 3.

Step 3: Calculate for fabric with repeat.
Total from Step 1 or Step 2:   18   yd.
Multiply by percentage
from Allowance Chart: ×   1.35
Total: 24.3   yd.
Round up to nearest ½ yard: 24.5   yd. to be ordered

Slipcovered Loveseat
1. 10 percent
2. 21 yards

Step 1: Determine yardage.
Yardage required from
Upholstery Yardage Chart: 17   yd.

Step 2: Calculate for fabric narrower than 54 inches.
Fabric is 54 inches wide, so this step is skipped.

Fabric has a repeat, so continue to Step 3.

Step 3: Calculate for fabric with repeat.
Total from Step 1 or Step 2:   17   yd.
Multiply by percentage
from Allowance Chart: ×   1.1   repeat allowance
Total: 18.7   yd.
Round up to nearest ½ yard: 19   yd. to be ordered

For Slipcover:

Total yards to be ordered: 19   yd.
Add 1 yard per seat: +   2   yd.
Total yards: 21   yd. to be ordered

ADVANCED
Reupholstered Sofa
1. Base yardage according to Table 16.2: 20 yards
2. 360 square feet
3. 7 hides
4. 385 square feet

Step 1: Determine base square feet.

Yardage required from Upholstery Yardage Chart:	20	yd.
Multiply by leather allowance: ×	18	sq. ft.
Total:	**360**	**sq. ft.**

Step 2: Calculate number of hides.

Total from Step 1:	360	sq. ft.
Divide by square feet per hide: ÷	55	sq. ft.
Total:	**6.55**	**hides**
Round up to whole number:	**7**	**hides to be ordered**

Step 3: Calculate square feet to charge.

Total from Step 2:	7	total hides
Multiply by square feet per hide: ×	55	sq. ft.
Total:	**385**	**sq. ft. to be charged**

Slipcovered Sofa and Loveseat
1. (A) 19 yards; (B) 17 yards
2. 20 percent
3. (A) 26 yards; (B) 22.5 yards
4. A total of 48.5 yards must be ordered.

For Sofa #16

Step 1: Determine yardage.

Yardage required from Upholstery Yardage Chart:	19	yd.

Step 2: Calculate for fabric narrower than 54 inches.
Fabric is 54 inches wide, so this step is skipped.

Fabric has a repeat, so continue to Step 3.

Step 3: Calculate for fabric with repeat.

Total from Step 1 or Step 2	19	yd.
Multiply by percentage from Allowance Chart	1.2	repeat allowance
Total:	**22.8**	**yd.**
Round up to nearest ½ yard:	**23**	**yd. to be ordered**

For Slipcover:

Total yards to be ordered:	23	yd.
Add 1 yard per seat: +	3	yd.
Total yards:	**26**	**yd. to be ordered**

For Loveseat #17:

Step 1: Determine yardage.

Yardage required from Upholstery Yardage Chart:	17	yd.

Step 2: Calculate for fabric narrower than 54 inches
Fabric is 54 inches wide, so this step is skipped.

Fabric has a repeat, so continue to Step 3.

Step 3: Calculate for fabric with repeat.

Total from Step 1 or Step 2:	17	yd.
Multiply by percentage from Allowance Chart: ×	1.2	repeat allowance
Total:	**20.4**	**yd.**
Round up to nearest ½ yard:	**20.5**	**yd. to be ordered**

For Slipcover:

Total yards to be ordered:	20.5	yd.
Add 1 yard per seat: +	2	yd.
Total yards:	**22.5**	**yd. to be ordered**

Pricing for Intermediate Reupholstered Sofa

1. $1945.00
2. $1670.00
3. $3615.00

Reupholstery					
Labor Costs			**Material Costs**		
	Total			**Quantity**	**Price**	**Total**
Base labor	$1050.00	Fabric	24.5 yd.	$78.00/yd.	$1911.00
New cushions and wrap	$250.00	Shipping	1	$34.00	$34.00
Retying of coils	$300.00				
Pickup and delivery	$70.00				
Labor Total	**$1670.00**			**Material Total**	**$1945.00**
TOTAL	**$3615.00**				

Advanced—Pricing for Intermediate Reupholstered Sofa

Appendix B: Blank Worksheets

Paint Worksheet

Step 1: Find perimeter of room in feet (e.g., 65.3 ft.).

Wall A:	_____	ft.
Wall B:	+_____	ft.
Wall C:	+_____	ft.
Wall D:	+_____	ft.
Wall E (if applicable):	+_____	ft.
Total perimeter:	_____	**ft.**

Step 2: Find square footage of area to be covered.

Total from Step 1:	_____	ft.
Multiply by height:	×_____	ft.

Note: This may not be full height of wall.

Total square feet:	_____	**sq. ft.**

Step 3: Determine deductions.

Width of opening or cabinets w/same height:	_____	ft.
Width of opening or cabinets w/same height:	+_____	ft.
Total width of openings:	_____	**ft.**
Multiply by height of opening/cabinets:	×_____	ft.
Total square feet:	_____	**sq. ft.**

Repeat the deduction process for total openings in room and add all deductions together.

Note: Do not use entire height of door, window, or cabinet when only a portion of the wall is being painted (as in above or below a chair rail). Add together the widths of all openings that have the same height and then multiply by the height. Repeat as needed until total square footage is found.

Step 4: Determine square footage of paint needed.

Take total square feet from Step 2:	_____	sq. ft.
Subtract total from Step 3:	−_____	sq. ft.
Total square feet needed for 1 coat of paint:	_____	**sq. ft.**
Multiply by anticipated coats of paint	×_____	coats
Total square feet of paint needed:	_____	**sq. ft.**

Step 5: Determine gallons of paint needed.

Take total from Step 4:	_____	sq. ft.
Divide by square feet of coverage/gallon:	÷_____	sq. ft.
Total gallons of paint needed:	_____	**gallons**
Round up to whole number:	_____	**gallons of paint needed to purchase**

Wallcovering—Square Footage Method Worksheet

Step 1: Find perimeter of room in feet (e.g., 65.3 ft.).

Wall A: _____ ft.

Wall B: +_____ ft.

Wall C: +_____ ft.

Wall D: +_____ ft.

Wall E: +_____ ft. *Continue adding walls as necessary.*

Total perimeter: _____ **ft.**

Step 2: Find height of area.

Height of the area to be wallpapered: _____ **ft.**

If the wallpaper has a repeat:

Take the height of the area to be wallpapered: _____ ft.

Divide by the length of the repeat in feet: ÷_____ ft. (**Important:** convert inches to feet)

Total number of repeats: _____ **repeats**

Round up to whole number: _____ **full repeats**

Multiply by length of the repeat: ×_____ ft.

This is the new adjusted height: _____ **ft.**

For a drop match repeat:

Take the new adjusted height and add ½ the repeat back to it. For example, if the repeat is 18 inches, after finding the new adjusted height, add 9 inches to the total.

If drop match, add ½ the length of the repeat: +_____ ft.

New total height for paper with drop match: +_____ **ft.**

Step 3: Determine base square feet of area.

Height, adjusted or otherwise, from Step 2: _____ ft.

Multiply by total perimeter from Step 1: ×_____ ft.

Total square feet: _____ **sq. ft.**

Step 4: Determine deductions.

Only deduct openings or cabinets 41 inches wide or wider.

Width of deduction in feet (e.g., 4 ft. for 48 in.): _____ ft.

Multiply by height of deduction in feet: ×_____ ft.

Total square feet of deduction: _____ **sq. ft.**

Repeat this process for however many openings or cabinets are 41 inches or wider.

Note: Multiple areas that are the same height may be added together before multiplying by the height. Do not use entire height of door, window, or cabinet when only a portion of the wall is being papered (as in above or below a chair rail).

Step 5: Calculate total adjusted square feet.

Take total square feet from Step 3: _____ sq. ft.

Subtract total square feet of openings from Step 4: −_____ sq. ft.

Total adjusted square feet of wallpaper: _____ **sq. ft.**

Step 6: Calculate number of rolls to be ordered.

Adjusted square feet of wallpaper from Step 5: _____ sq. ft.

Divide by square feet of single roll of wallpaper: ÷_____ sq. ft.

- 27–28 in. wide—American-sized roll is 30 square feet per single roll.
- 20–22 in. wide—European/metric-sized roll is 26.5 square feet per single roll.
- 54 in. wide—Commercial roll has approximately 13.5 square feet per yard.

Total number of single rolls (or yards): _____ **s/r (or yds.)**

Note: Most wallpaper sold today is packaged in double-roll bolts, so quantity must be an even number.

Round up to nearest even whole number: _____ **total single rolls (or yards)**

Wall Tile Worksheet

Step 1: Calculate base square footage of space.

Take width of area in feet:	_____	ft.
Multiply by height of area in feet:	× _____	ft.
Total base square footage:	_____	**sq. ft.**

Step 2: Calculate additional materials for waste allowance.

For wall tile laid straight:

Take square footage from Step 1:	_____	sq. ft.
Multiply by 10 percent to allow for waste:	× _____1.10_____	waste allowance
Total square footage needed:	_____	**sq. ft.**

For wall tile laid diagonally and staggered:

Take square footage from Step 1:	_____	sq. ft.
Multiply by 15 percent to allow for waste:	× _____1.15_____	waste allowance
Total square footage needed:	_____	**sq. ft.**

If tile material is sold by the full box/carton, proceed to Step 3 to determine amount needed.

Step 3: Calculate number of full boxes/cartons to be ordered.

Take square footage needed from Step 2:	_____	sq. ft.
Divide by square footage per box/carton:	÷ _____	sq. ft.
Total boxes/cartons needed:	_____	**boxes/cartons**
Round up to whole number:	_____	**full boxes/cartons to be ordered**

Step 4: Calculate square feet in boxes/cartons ordered to calculate pricing to client for material.

Take number of boxes/cartons from Step 3:	_____	boxes/cartons
Multiply by square feet per box/carton:	× _____	sq. ft.
Total square footage ordered:	_____	**sq. ft.**

Paneling Worksheet

Step 1: Find perimeter of room in feet (e.g., 65.3 ft.).

Wall A:	_____	ft.
Wall B: +	_____	ft.
Wall C: +	_____	ft.
Wall D: +	_____	ft.
Wall E: +	_____	ft. *Continue adding walls as necessary.*
Total perimeter:	_____	**ft.**

Step 2: Calculate additional materials for waste allowance.

Total from Step 1:	_____	ft.
Multiply by 10 percent to allow for waste: ×	1.10	waste allowance
Total perimeter needed:	_____	**ft.**

Step 3: Calculate total number of panels to be ordered.

Take total from Step 2:	_____	ft.
Divide by width of panel: ÷	_____	ft.
Total panels needed:	_____	**panels**
Round up to whole number:	_____	**full panels to be ordered**

If items are sold by the piece, stop here. If items are sold by the square foot, continue to Step 4.

Step 4: Calculate square feet in panels ordered to calculate pricing to client for material.

Take number of panels from Step 3:	_____	panels
Multiply by square feet per panel: ×	_____	sq. ft.
Total square footage ordered:	_____	**sq. ft.**

Accent and Trim Worksheet

Step 1: Calculate total length of accent or trim needed.

Add length of trim needed:	_____	ft.
Add additional lengths:	+ _____	ft.
Add additional lengths:	+ _____	ft.
Add additional lengths:	+ _____	ft.
Add additional lengths:	+ _____	ft.
Total length needed for trim:	_____	**ft.**

If there are more lengths to add, continue to do so to achieve the total length needed.

Step 2: Deduct for openings. If this step is not needed, skip to Step 3.

Total length from Step 1:	_____	ft.
Subtract opening:	– _____	ft.
Continue to subtract as needed:	– _____	ft.
Continue to subtract as needed:	– _____	ft.
Total adjusted length:	_____	**ft.**

Step 3: Calculate total number of pieces of trim to be ordered.

Take total from Step 1 or Step 2:	_____	ft.
Divide by length of accent/trim piece:	÷ _____	ft.
Total pieces of trim needed:	_____	**pieces**
Round up to whole number:	_____	**full pieces to be ordered**

If items are sold by the piece, stop here. If items are sold by the foot, continue to Step 4.

Step 4: Calculate total length to be ordered.

Take total from Step 3:	_____	number of pieces
Multiply by actual length of pieces:	× _____	ft.
Total feet actually ordered:	_____	**ft.**

Note: Some trim pieces, such as out corners, can be manually counted and calculated.

Ceiling Panel/Tile Worksheet

Step 1: Calculate base square footage of space.

For odd-shaped rooms, divide room into geometric shapes and calculate for each space.

Space #1—Take width of room in feet:	_____	ft.
Multiply by length of room in feet:	× _____	ft.
Total base square footage of space:	_____	**sq. ft. #1**
Space #2—Take width of room in feet:	_____	ft.
Multiply by length of room in feet:	× _____	ft.
Total base square footage of space:	_____	**sq. ft. #2**
Space #3—Take width of room in feet:	_____	ft.
Multiply by length of room in feet:	× _____	ft.
Total base square footage of space:	_____	**sq. ft. #3**
Add all spaces together—Space #1:	_____	sq. ft.
Space #2:	+ _____	sq. ft.
Space #3:	+ _____	sq. ft.
Total Step 1:	_____	**sq. ft.**

Step 2: Calculate additional materials for waste allowance.

Take square footage from Step 1:	_____	sq. ft.
Multiply by 10 percent to allow for waste:	× 1.10	waste allowance
Total square footage needed:	_____	**sq. ft.**

Step 3. Calculate number of ceiling tiles to be ordered.

Take square footage needed from Step 2:	_____	sq. ft.
Divide by square footage of individual tiles:	÷ _____	sq. ft. per tile
Total tiles needed:	_____	**tiles**
Round up to whole number:	_____	**tiles to order**

Hard Flooring Material Worksheet

Step 1: Calculate base square footage of space.

For odd-shaped rooms, divide room into geometric shapes and calculate for each space.

Take width of room in feet:	_____	ft.
Multiply by length of room in feet:	× _____	ft.
Base square footage of space:	_____	**sq. ft.**

Step 2: Calculate for additional materials for waste allowance.

For tile or plank flooring laid "straight":

Take square footage from Step 1:	_____	sq. ft.
Multiply by 10% to allow for waste:	× 1.10	waste allowance
Total square footage needed:	_____	**sq. ft.**

For tile and plank flooring laid diagonally and tile flooring staggered:

Take square footage from Step 1:	_____	sq. ft.
Multiply by 15% to allow for waste:	× 1.15	waste allowance
Total square footage needed:	_____	**sq. ft.**

For hard flooring laid in a herringbone pattern:

Take square footage from Step 1:	_____	sq. ft.
Multiply by 25% to allow for waste:	× 1.25	waste allowance
Total square footage needed:	_____	**sq. ft.**

If hard flooring material is sold by the full box/carton, proceed to Step 3 to determine amount needed.

Step 3: Calculate number of full boxes/cartons to be ordered.

Take square footage needed from Step 2:	_____	sq. ft.
Divide by square footage per box/carton:	÷ _____	sq. ft.
Boxes/cartons needed:	_____	**boxes/cartons**
Round up to whole number:	_____	**boxes/cartons to order**

Step 4: Calculate square feet in boxes/cartons ordered to calculate pricing to client for material.

Take number of boxes from Step 3:	_____	boxes/cartons
Multiply by square feet per box/carton:	× _____	sq. ft.
Total square footage ordered:	_____	**sq. ft.**

Flooring Transition Worksheet

Step 1: Calculate total length of transition needed.

Add widths of flooring change: _____ ft.

Continue to add additional widths: + _____ ft.

Total length needed for transition: _____ **ft.**

Step 2: Calculate total number of pieces of transition to be ordered.

Take total from Step 1: _____ ft.

Divide by length of transition piece: ÷ _____ ft.

Pieces of transition needed: _____ **pieces**

Round up to whole number: _____ **full pieces needed**

Step 3: Calculate total length of transition to be ordered.

Take total from Step 2: _____ pieces

Multiply by actual length of pieces: × _____ ft. per piece

Total feet actually ordered: _____ **ft. ordered**

Carpet Tile and Resilient Tile Worksheet

Step 1: Draw diagram of room and take room dimensions.

Do not use inches. Convert everything to feet. A room 13 feet 8 inches converted to feet will be 13.67 feet.

Step 2: Calculate base square footage of space.

Take width of room in feet: _____ ft.
Multiply by length of room in feet: × _____ ft.
Base square footage of space: _____ **sq. ft.**

Step 3: Calculate additional material for waste allowance.

Take square footage from Step 2: _____ sq. ft.
Multiply by 10 percent to allow for waste: × ___1.10___ waste allowance
Total square footage needed: _____ **sq. ft.**

If material being calculated will not need additional replacement tiles ordered, skip to Step 5.

Step 4: Calculate additional materials for replacement allowance.

Take square footage from Step 2: _____ sq. ft.
Multiply by 20 percent to allow for replacement: × ___1.20___ replacement allowance
Total square footage needed: _____ **sq. ft.**

Step 5. Calculate number of full boxes/cartons to be ordered.

Take square footage needed from Step 3 or 4: _____ sq. ft.
Divide by square feet per box/carton: ÷ _____ sq. ft.
Total boxes/cartons needed: _____ **boxes/cartons**
Round up to whole number: _____ **full boxes/cartons to order**

Step 6. Calculate actual square feet in boxes/cartons ordered.

Take number of boxes/cartons from Step 5: _____ boxes/cartons
Multiply by square feet per box/carton: × _____ sq. ft.
Total square footage ordered: _____ **sq. ft.**

Sheet Goods Worksheet

Step 1: Draw diagram of room and take room dimensions.

Do not use inches. Convert everything to feet. A room 13 feet 8 inches, converted to feet, will be 13.67 feet.

Step 2: Determine width with allowance.

Take width of room in feet (e.g., 15.5 ft.): _____ ft.

Add 6 inches (.5 ft.): +_____.5_____ ft.

Total: _____ **ft.**

Step 3: Determine number of cuts based on material width.

Take total from Step 2: _____ ft.

Divide by width of material: ÷_____ ft.

Note: *4 ft. rubber, 6 ft. vinyl, 6.58 ft. linoleum/Marmoleum, or 12 ft. vinyl width.*

Total: _____ **cuts**

Round up to whole number: _____ **cuts**

Note: With vinyl it is desirable to have only one lengthwise seam, if any at all.

Step 4: Determine cut length.

Take length of room in feet (e.g., 9.25 ft.): _____ ft.

Add 6 inches (.5 ft.): +_____.5_____ ft.

Total length of cuts: _____ **ft.**

Note: *If more than one cut is necessary and the material has a repeat, divide this length by the length of the repeat to find full repeats necessary. Round up to a full number, and multiply by the length of the repeat. This will be the adjusted cut length.*

Step 5: Determine length to order.

Take total from Step 3: _____ cuts

Multiply by the total from Step 4: ×_____ ft.

Total length of material to be ordered: _____ **ft.**

Step 6: Determine square feet and square yards.

Take length of material from Step 5: _____ ft.

Multiply by width of material: ×_____ ft. (4 ft., 6 ft., 6.58 ft., or 12 ft. width)

Total square feet: _____ **sq. ft.**

Divide by 9 to convert to square yards: ÷_____9_____ sq. ft.

Total square yards needed: _____ **sq. yd.**

Round to two numbers to right of decimal point: _____ **sq. yd. needed to order**

Determine underlayment if necessary:

Step 1: Determine base square footage of room.

Take exact width of room: _____ ft.

Multiply by exact length of room: _____ ft.

Base square feet of room: _____ **sq. ft.**

Step 2: Determine square footage of underlayment needed.

Take total from Step 1: _____ sq. ft.

Multiply by 1.10 to allow for waste: ×_____ waste allowance

Total for underlayment: _____ **sq. ft.**

Round to two numbers to right of decimal point: _____ **sq. ft.**

Broadloom Carpet Worksheet

Step 1: Draw diagram of room and take room dimensions.

Do not use inches. Convert everything to feet. A room 13 feet 8 inches, converted to feet will be 13.67 feet.

Step 2: Determine carpet direction in room.

Decide which way the carpet will run. The length dimension of the room is determined by the direction the carpet will come off the roll. The width dimension of the room is the other dimension.

Step 3: Determine overall width with allowance.

Take width of room in feet (e.g., 15.5 ft.):	_____	ft.
Add 6 inches (.5 ft.): +	_____.5_____	ft.
Total cut width:	_____	**ft.**

Step 4: Determine whether fill is necessary.

Take cut width from Step 3: −	_____	ft.
Subtract width of carpet in feet: −	_____	ft.

Note: This will probably be 12-foot, 13.17-foot, or 15-foot-wide carpet.

Total:	_____	**ft.**

If this is a positive number (greater than 0), you have to determine seam placement and possible fill.

Step 5: Determine fill width.

Take width of carpet in feet:	_____	ft.
Divide by total from Step 4: ÷	_____	ft.
Total:	_____	**cuts**
Round down to nearest whole number:	_____	**full pieces from carpet width**

This tells you how many full strips will come out of a 12-foot-wide piece of carpet.

Step 6: Determine length of first cut.

Take length of room in feet (e.g., 9.25 ft.):	_____	ft.
Add 6 inches (.5 ft.): +	_____.5_____	ft.
Total length of the first cut.	_____	**ft.**

If carpet has a repeat, divide this length by the length of the repeat to find full repeats necessary. Round up to a whole number and multiply by the length of the repeat. This will be the adjusted cut length.

Step 7: Determine fill length.

Take length of room in feet + 6 inches (.5 ft.):	_____	ft.
Divide by total from Step 5: ÷	_____	full pieces from carpet width
Total length of second cut:	_____	**ft.**

Step 8: Determine total length to be ordered.

Take length of first cut from Step 6:	_____	ft.
Add length of second cut from Step 7: +	_____	ft.

If more rooms with same carpet, continue to add as many lengths as needed.

Total length of carpet to be ordered:	_____	**ft.**

Step 9: Determine square feet and square yards.

Take length of carpet from Step 8:	_____	ft.
Multiply by width of carpet: ×	_____	ft.
Total square feet:	_____	**sq. ft.**
Divide by 9 to convert to square yards: ÷	_____9_____	sq. ft.
Total square yards of carpet:	_____	**sq. yd.**

Note: When ordering carpet, you not only need to have square yards, but also the exact width and length of the cut. Convert any decimal total in Step 8 to inches. For example, to find how many inches are represented in the decimal, multiply the decimal by 12. For carpet that is 9.25 feet long, multiply .25 × 12 = 3 inches. The carpet length is 9 feet 3 inches. This would be ordered as 12 × 9 ft. 3 in., a total of 12.33 square yards.

See Carpeted Stairs Worksheet to determine amount of carpet needed for stairs.

Carpeted Stairs Worksheet

Step 1: Determine cut width.

Measure width of stair in inches: _____ in.

Note: If any side is upholstered, add 3 inches for each side to the width measurement.

Add 3 inches cut allowance: +_____3_____ in.

Total cut width: _____ **in.**

Convert to feet: ÷_____12_____ in.

Total cut width in feet: _____ **ft.**

Note: Sometimes stair widths will change from the top of the run to the bottom. In this case, write down the width measurements and how many treads this affects.

Step 2: Determine number of cuts from carpet width.

Take width of carpet in feet: _____ ft. (12 ft., 13.17 ft., or 15 ft.)

Divide by total from Step 1: ÷_____ ft.

Total: _____ **cuts**

Round down to nearest whole number: _____ **vertical cuts from carpet width**

This tells you how many full strips will come out of a 12-foot-wide piece of carpet.

Step 3: Determine total number of cuts for carpet length.

Take total number of treads: _____ treads

Divide by total from Step 2: ÷_____ cuts

Total: _____ **cuts**

Round up to whole number: _____ **total carpet cuts needed**

Step 4: Determine length of cuts.

Take length of stair cut (riser + tread + around nose) _____ in.

Add 3 inches cut allowance: +_____3_____ in.

Total: _____ **in.**

Convert to feet: ÷_____12_____ in.

Total: _____ **ft.**

Note: If carpet has a repeat, divide this length by the length of the repeat to find full repeats necessary. Round up to a full number and multiply by the length of the repeat. This will be the adjusted cut length.

Step 5: Determine total length of carpet.

Take total from Step 3: _____ cuts

Multiply by total from Step 4: ×_____ ft.

Total length of carpet needed: _____ **ft.**

Note: Landing space might be able to be found in carpet waste, if there is any, or will be added at the end of this step.

Step 6: Determine square feet and square yards.

Take length of carpet from Step 5: _____ ft.

Multiply by width of carpet ×_____ ft. (12 ft., 13.17 ft., or 15 ft.)

Total square feet: _____ **sq. ft.**

Divide by 9 to convert to square yards: ÷_____9_____ sq. ft.

Total square yards of carpet to order: _____ **sq. yd.**

Carpeted Stairs Worksheet—Quick Estimate

This can be used as long as the tread and riser measurements are equal to or less than 18 inches and the stair width is not more than 45 inches.

Step 1: Determine cuts of carpet.

Take number of treads:	_____	treads
Divide by 3: ÷	_____3_____	widths from 12-ft. carpet
Total:	_____	ft.
Round up to whole number:	_____	**cuts of carpet**

This tells you how many *cuts* will be needed in the length of a piece of carpet. (Hint: 13 to 15 treads will need 5 cuts of carpet.)

Step 2: Determine total length of carpet.

Take total from Step 1:	_____	cuts of carpet
Multiply by 2 ft.: ×	_____2_____	ft.
Total:	_____	**ft.**

Step 3: Determine square feet and square yards.

Take length of carpet from Step 2:	_____	ft.
Multiply by width of carpet: ×	_____	ft. (12 ft., 13.17 ft., or 15 ft.)
Total square feet:	_____	**sq. ft.**
Divide by 9 to convert to square yards: ÷	_____9_____	sq. ft.
Total square yards of carpet to order:	_____	**sq. yd.**

Note: If there is a pattern, the 2 ft. cut will need to be adjusted according to the pattern.

Area Rug Worksheet—Part One: Labor

Step 1: Draw the diagram.

Draw diagram of area rug and determine finished size of total rug (including size of borders, if applicable).

Step 2: Find the perimeter of the area rug for binding.

Add length of all sides together:

Side 1 in feet: _____	ft.
Side 2 in feet: +_____	ft.
Side 3 in feet: +_____	ft.
Side 4 in feet: +_____	ft.
Total perimeter of area rug for binding: _____	**ft.**

If there are more than 4 sides, continuing adding sides.

Step 3: Find perimeter of first seam, if applicable.

Total width of area rug in feet: _____	ft.
Subtract exact size of top border in feet: −_____	ft.
Subtract exact size of bottom border in feet: −_____	ft.
Subtotal A—width of inner border or field: _____	**ft.**
Total length of area rug in feet: _____	ft.
Subtract exact size of right side border in feet: −_____	ft.
Subtract exact size of left side border in feet: −_____	ft.
Subtotal B—length of inner border or field: _____	**ft.**
Take Subtotal A: _____	ft.
Add to Subtotal B: +_____	ft.
Total: _____	**ft.**

Note: Total represents one-half of the perimeter of the rectangle. Multiply by 2 to get the entire perimeter of the 4 sides.

× _____2_____	
Total perimeter for seaming first seam: _____	**ft.**

Step 4: Find perimeter of second seam, if applicable.

Take Subtotal A—width of inner border or field: _____	ft.
Subtract exact size of top border in feet: −_____	ft.
Subtract exact size of bottom border in feet: −_____	ft.
Subtotal C—width of next border or field: _____	**ft.**
Take Subtotal B—length of inner border or field: _____	ft.
Subtract exact size of top border in feet: −_____	ft.
Subtract exact size of bottom border in feet: −_____	ft.
Subtotal D—length of next border or field: _____	**ft.**
Take Subtotal C: _____	ft.
Add to Subtotal D: +_____	ft.
Total: _____	**ft.**
× _____2_____	
Total perimeter for seaming second seam: _____	**ft.**

Step 5: Calculate for backing.

Not all area rugs will be backed.

Take overall width of area rug in feet: _____	ft.
Multiply by overall length of area rug in feet: ×_____	ft.
Total square feet of area rug for backing: _____	**sq. ft.**

Area Rug Worksheet—Part Two: Materials

Use diagram from Part One.

If area rug is one piece, not bordered, skip to Step 3.

Step 1: Determine yardage needed for outer border.

Add length of border in feet + .25 ft. (3 in.):　　Top: ＿＿＿＿＿＿ ft.

Note: If any side of the area rug is less than 6 feet, 2 sides can be obtained from 1 cut. Adjust as needed:

　　　　　　　　　　　　　　Bottom: +＿＿＿＿＿＿ ft.
　　　　　　　　　　　　　　Side: +＿＿＿＿＿＿ ft.
　　　　　　　　　　　　　　Side: +＿＿＿＿＿＿ ft.

Note: If any side of the area rug is wider than 12 feet, take total width – 12 feet = fill width. Take width of carpet, subtract fill to determine if more than 1 fill can come from a cut of carpet:

　　　　　　　　　　　　　　Fill: +＿＿＿＿＿＿ ft.
　　　　　　　　　　　　　　Fill: +＿＿＿＿＿＿ ft.
Total length of carpet needed for outer border:　＿＿＿＿＿＿ **ft.**
Multiply by width of carpet in feet (normally 12 ft.):　×＿＿＿12＿＿＿ ft.
　　　　　　　Total square feet:　＿＿＿＿＿＿ **sq. ft.**
Divide by 9 to convert to square yards:　÷＿＿＿9＿＿＿ sq. ft.
Total square yards to be ordered for outer border:　＿＿＿＿＿＿ **sq. yd.**

Step 2. Determine yardage needed for inner border.

Note: If area rug does not have an inner border, skip to Step 3.

Add length of inner border in feet: + .25 ft. (3 in.):　　Top: ＿＿＿＿＿＿ ft.

Note: If any side of the area rug is less than 6 feet, 2 sides can be obtained from 1 cut. Adjust as needed.

　　　　　　　　　　　　　　Bottom: +＿＿＿＿＿＿ ft.
　　　　　　　　　　　　　　Side: +＿＿＿＿＿＿ ft.
　　　　　　　　　　　　　　Side: +＿＿＿＿＿＿ ft.

Note: If any side of the area rug is wider than 12 ft., take total width – 12 ft. = fill width. Take width of carpet, subtract fill to determine if more than 1 fill can come from a cut of carpet.

　　　　　　　　　　　　　　Fill: +＿＿＿＿＿＿ ft.
　　　　　　　　　　　　　　Fill: +＿＿＿＿＿＿ ft.
Total length of carpet needed for inner border:　＿＿＿＿＿＿ **ft.**
Multiply by width of carpet in feet (normally 12 ft.):　×＿＿＿12＿＿＿ ft.
　　　　　　　Total square feet:　＿＿＿＿＿＿ **sq. ft.**
Divide by 9 to convert to square yards:　÷＿＿＿9＿＿＿ sq. ft.
Total square yards to be ordered for inner border:　＿＿＿＿＿＿ **sq. yd.**

If more inner borders are used, continue this same process.

Step 3: Determine yardage needed for field (length and width can be found under labor calculations).

Take shortest side of field + .25 ft. (3 in.) for total length:　＿＿＿＿＿＿ ft.
Multiply by width of carpet in feet (normally 12 ft.):　×＿＿＿12＿＿＿ ft.
　　　　　　　Total square feet:　＿＿＿＿＿＿ **sq. ft.**
Divide by 9 to convert to square yards:　÷＿＿＿9＿＿＿ sq. ft.
Total of square yards to be ordered for field:　＿＿＿＿＿＿ **sq. yd.**

Step 4: Calculate for area rug pad.

Take dimension that is 12 feet wide or less. Round up to 12 feet:　＿＿＿12＿＿＿ ft.

Note: If pad is 6 feet wide, substitute 6 feet here.

Multiply by other dimension of area rug in feet:　×＿＿＿＿＿＿ ft.
　　　　　　Total square feet of pad:　＿＿＿＿＿＿ **sq. ft.**
Divide by 9 to convert to square yards:　÷＿＿＿9＿＿＿ sq. ft.
　　　　　　Total square yards of pad:　＿＿＿＿＿＿ **sq. yd.**

Note: Ideally there is no seam in the pad. Since the pad has no nap or direction, it can be laid in the most ideal direction to prevent a seam. However, if both sides are more than 6 feet or 12 feet (depending on type of area rug and type of pad), two or more pieces of pad will be used.

Slab/Sheet Countertop Worksheet

Step 1: Determine width of slabs or sheets to be used.

Width of slab or sheet being used in feet: _____ ft.

Divide by depth of counter in feet: ÷ _____ ft.

Note: The counter depth must include cabinet depth, overhangs (normally 1 inch each overhang from base cabinet but can be more for counter and bar overhangs), and any integrated, seamless backsplash (normally 4 inches to 6 inches tall and 1 inch deep).

Total number of counter cuts possible from slab/sheet: _____ cuts

Round down to nearest whole number: _____ cuts per slab/sheet

Step 2: Determine number of slabs/sheets to be used.

Length A of counter to counter/wall in feet: _____ ft.

Note: Counter length must include cabinet length plus overhangs.

Divide by length of slab/sheet being used in feet: ÷ _____ ft.

Total: _____ **slabs/sheets**

Round up to whole number—Total A: _____ **full slabs/sheets**

Note: If this number is greater than 1, seam placement must be considered.

This step may need to be repeated for additional counters; continue adding as needed.

Length B of counter to counter/wall in feet: _____ ft.

Note: Counter length must include cabinet length plus overhangs.

Divide by length of slab/sheet being used in feet: ÷ _____ ft.

Total: _____ **slabs/sheets**

Round up to whole number—Total B: _____ **full slabs/sheets**

Note: If this number is greater than 1, seam placement must be considered.

Step 3: Determine total number of slabs/sheets needed.

Take Total A from Step 2: _____ slabs/sheets

Add Total B from Step 2: + _____ slabs/sheets

Continue adding lengths as necessary.

Total: _____ **slabs/sheets**

Divide by total from Step 1: ÷ _____ cuts per slab/sheet

Total: _____ **slabs/sheets**

Step 4. Find square feet of material.

Width of slab or sheet being used in feet: _____ ft.

Multiply by slab/sheet length: × _____ ft.

Total square footage of slab or sheet: _____ **sq. ft.**

Multiply by total from Step 3: × _____ slabs/sheets

Total square footage priced: _____ **sq. ft.**

Tile Countertop Worksheet

Step 1: Calculate base square footage of space.

Take depth of counter in feet: _____ ft.

Note: The counter depth must include cabinet depth, overhangs (normally 1 inch each overhang from base cabinet but can be more for counter and bar overhangs).

Multiply by length of counter in feet: × _____ ft.
Base square footage of space: _____ **sq. ft.**

Step 2: Calculate additional materials for waste allowance.

For tile laid straight:

Take square footage from Step 1: _____ sq. ft.
Multiply by 10 percent to allow for waste: × _____1.10_____ waste allowance
Total square footage needed: _____ **sq. ft.**

For tile laid diagonally or staggered:

Take square footage from Step 1: _____ sq. ft.
Multiply by 15 percent to allow for waste: × _____1.15_____ waste allowance
Total square footage needed: _____ **sq. ft.**

For tile laid in a herringbone pattern:

Take square footage from Step 1: _____ sq. ft.
Multiply by 25 percent to allow for waste: × _____1.25_____ waste allowance
Total square footage needed: _____ **sq. ft.**

Step 3: Calculate square feet to be ordered.

Total from Step 2: _____ sq. ft.
Divide by tile unit (width × length): ÷ _____ sq. ft.
Total tiles: _____ **tiles**
Round up to whole number: _____ **full tiles**
Multiply by the tile unit: × _____ sq. ft.
Total square feet ordered: _____ **sq. ft.**

If tile material is sold by the full box/carton, proceed to Step 4 to determine amount needed.

Step 4. Calculate number of full boxes/cartons to be ordered.

Take square footage needed from Step 3: _____ sq. ft.
Divide by carton square footage: ÷ _____ sq. ft. per box/carton
Boxes/cartons needed: _____ **boxes/cartons**
Round up to whole number: _____ **full boxes/cartons to order**

Step 5. Calculate square feet in boxes/cartons ordered to calculate pricing to client for material.

Take number of boxes/cartons from Step 4: _____ boxes/cartons
Multiply by square feet per box/carton: × _____ sq. ft. per box/carton
Total square footage ordered: _____ **sq. ft.**

Tile Countertop—Trim Worksheet

Step 1: Calculate total length of counter edge, accent, or trim needed.

Depending on the different trims (including edge and accent) needed, this process may need to be done several times.

Add length of trim needed:	_____	ft.
Add additional lengths: +	_____	ft.
Add additional lengths: +	_____	ft.
Add additional lengths: +	_____	ft.
Add additional lengths: +	_____	ft.
Total length needed for accent or trim:	_____	**ft.**

If there are more lengths to add, continue to do so to achieve the total length needed.

Step 2: Calculate total number of pieces of trim to be ordered.

Take total from Step 1:	_____	ft.
Divide by length of trim piece: ÷	_____	ft.
Equals pieces of trim needed:	_____	**pieces**
Round up to whole number:	_____	**full pieces**
Add 2 to allow for breakage: +	2	breakage allowance
Total:	_____	**pieces to be ordered**

If items are sold by the piece, stop here. If items are sold by the foot, continue to Step 3.

Step 3: Calculate total length to be ordered.

Take total from Step 2:	_____	pieces
Multiply by actual length of pieces: ×	_____	ft.
Total feet actually ordered:	_____	**ft.**

Note: Some trim pieces, such as out corners, can be counted and should just be manually calculated.

Poured Countertop Worksheet

Step 1: Determine running length of counter in feet (do not add in counter depth or island depth).

Length A of counter to counter/wall: _____ ft.

Length B of counter to counter/wall: + _____ ft.

Continue adding lengths as necessary.

Length C of counter to counter/wall: + _____ ft.

Length D of counter to counter/wall: + _____ ft.

Length E of counter to counter/wall: + _____ ft.

Total length: _____ **ft.**

Note: Don't forget to include 1-inch overhang in the length. Counter to counter will have a 2-inch overhang. Counter to wall will have a 1-inch overhang.

Step 2: Determine depth of countertop.

Take depth of cabinet in feet: _____ ft.

Add overhang (normally 1 in. = .08 ft.): + _____ ft.

If applicable, add height of backsplash: + _____ ft.

Note: Normally, backsplash is approximately 4 inches to 6 inches tall + 1 inch deep.

Total depth of counter material: _____ **ft.**

Note: This backsplash is one that is a seamless continuation of the counter material. A separate backsplash does not need to be calculated here. Use the Wall Tile Worksheet on page 43 in Chapter 4 for a tiled backsplash.

Step 3: Find cubic feet to order.

Take total from Step 1: _____ ft.

Multiply by total from Step 2: _____ ft.

Total: _____ **sq. ft.**

Multiply by thickness of counter: × _____ ft.

Note: Remember to divide inches by 12 to get feet.

Total: _____ **cu. ft.**

Gathered Curtains Worksheet

Step 1: Calculate finished width of treatment.

Take flat measure of treatment:	_____	in.
Add right return: +	_____	in.
Add left return: +	_____	in.
Total finished width to be gathered:	_____	**in.**

Step 2: Calculate the number of widths of fabric.

Take total finished width from Step 1:	_____	in.
Multiply for fullness: ×	_____	fullness

Note: If this is a heavy-weight fabric, × 2; standard is × 2.5 or × 3; very lightweight is × 3 or × 4.

Total fullness:	_____	**in.**
Add 6 inches for side hems: +	6	in.
Total:	_____	**in.**
Divide by width of fabric: ÷	_____	in.
Total widths:	_____	**widths**
Round up to whole number:	_____	**full widths**

Step 3: Calculate length of each width.

Finished length:	_____	in.
Add for seam allowances (this number may vary): +	2	in.
Add bottom hem: +	_____	in.

- For double 2-inch hem, add 4 inches.
- For double 4-inch hem, add 8 inches.

Add additional amount for rod pocket and/or header (if rod and header are applicable):

Add rod pocket size w/take-up allowance: +	_____	in.
Add header height: +	_____	in.
Total cut length (CL):	_____	**in.**

If there is a repeat involved, continue with the following step. If not, skip to Step 4.

Take cut length:	_____	in.
Divide by length of repeat: ÷	_____	in.
Resulting number is the number of repeats:	_____	**repeats**
Round up to whole number:	_____	**full repeats**
Multiply by the length of repeat: ×	_____	in.
Adjusted cut length (ACL):	_____	**in.**

Step 4: Combine Steps 2 and 3.

Take cut length or ACL from Step 3:	_____	in.
Multiply by total widths from Step 2: ×	_____	widths
Total fabric required:	_____	**in.**
Divide by 36 to convert inches to yards: ÷	36	in.
Total yards:	_____	**yd.**

Note: Fabric yardage must be ordered in ½-yard increments.

Round up to nearest ½ yard:	_____	**yd. to be ordered**

To find yardage for lining: Multiply CL × W = total inches, divide by 36 inches to find yards, round up or stay at the nearest yard or ½ yard.

Note: Should the center draw traversing drapery consist of panels that use a portion of a width, the workroom will charge as if it is a whole width. For example: Center draw traversing draperies require 3 widths of fabric. There are 2 panels in a center draw. 3 widths ÷ 2 panels = 1½ widths per panel. Fabric will be ordered for 3 widths. Labor will be calculated as 4 widths, since there is the same amount of labor for a 1½-width panel as a 2-width panel.

Stationary Side Panel Worksheet

Step 1: Calculate flat measure of stationary side panels.

Take trim-to-trim measure of window:	_____	in.
Multiply by 25 percent: ×	.25	
Total:	_____	in.
Divide by 2 to determine width per side: ÷	2	sides
Total flat measure each side of window:	_____	in.

Note: Minimum flat measures for most windows needs to be 12 inches.

If less than 12 inches, round up to 12 inches:	_____	in.

Step 2: Calculate the number of widths of fabric.

Desired flat measure of side panel:	_____	in.
Multiply for fullness (× 2.5 or 3): ×	3	fullness

Note: If this is a heavy-weight fabric, × 2; standard is × 2.5 or × 3; very lightweight is × 3 or × 4.

Total fullness:	_____	in.
Add 6 inches for side hems: +	6	in.
Add depth of return: +	_____	in.
Total:	_____	in.
Multiply by number of side panels desired: ×	_____	side panels
Total:	_____	in.
Divide by width of fabric (normally 48 or 54 in.): ÷	_____	in.
Number of widths of fabric:	_____	widths
Round up to whole number:	_____	full widths

Step 3: Calculate length of each width.

Take the finished length (FL) of drapery:	_____	in.
Add 18 in. for hems and heading: +	18	in.

Note: 18 inches allows for double 6-inch hem; if narrower or wider hem, this number will change.

Total cut length (CL):	_____	in.

If there is a repeat involved, continue with the following step. If not, skip to Step 4.

Take cut length:	_____	in.
Divide by length of repeat: ÷	_____	in.
Resulting number is the number of repeats:	_____	repeats
Round up to whole number:	_____	full repeats
Multiply this number by the length of the repeat: ×	_____	in.
Adjusted cut length (ACL):	_____	in.

Step 4: Combine Steps 2 and 3.

Take cut length or ACL from Step 3:	_____	in.
Multiply by number of widths from Step 2: ×	_____	widths
Total fabric required:	_____	in.
Divide by 36 to convert inches to yards: ÷	36	in.
Total yards:	_____	yd.

Note: Fabric yardage must be ordered in ½-yard increments.

Round up to nearest ½ yard:	_____	yd. to be ordered

To find yardage for lining: Multiply CL × W = total inches, divide by 36 inches to find yards, and round up or stay at the nearest yard or ½ yard.

Note: Should side panels consist of 1½ or 1¾ widths, workroom will charge for 2 widths per panel since they involve the same amount of labor as 2 widths.

Traversing, Pleated Draperies Worksheet

Step 1: Calculate flat measure of treatment.

Take trim-to-trim measure of window: _____ in.

Multiply to allow for stack (15 to 33 percent): × _____ (1.15 to 1.33)

Note: This explains why we are multiplying × 1.15 to 1.33.

Total flat measure (FM) of treatment: _____ **in.**

Step 2: Calculate the number of widths of fabric.

Total flat measure from Step 1: _____ in.

Multiply for fullness: × ___3___ fullness

Note: If this is a heavy-weight fabric, × 2; standard is × 2.5 or × 3; very lightweight is × 3 or × 4.

Total fullness: _____ **in.**

Add 20 in. for overlaps and returns for center draw (10 in. if a 1-way draw): + ___20___ in.

Note: This allows for 3-inch to 4-inch returns.

If returns are deeper, add additional beyond amount allowed: + _____ in.

Total: _____ **in.**

Divide by width of fabric (normally 48 or 54 in.): ÷ _____ in.

Widths of fabric: _____ **widths**

Round up to whole number: _____ **full widths**

Step 3: Calculate length of each width.

Take the finished length (FL) of drapery: _____ in.

Add 18 in. for hems and heading: + ___18___ in.

Note: 18 inches allows for double 6-inch hem; if narrower or wider hem, this number will change.

Total cut length (CL): _____ **in.**

If there is a repeat involved, continue with the following step. If not, skip to Step 4.

Take cut length: _____ in.

Divide by length of repeat: ÷ _____ in.

Resulting number is the number of repeats: _____ **repeats**

Round up to whole number: _____ **full repeats**

Multiply this number by the length of the repeat: × _____ in.

Adjusted cut length (ACL): _____ **in.**

Note: If it is important to control where the pattern starts at the top, add another full repeat to ACL.

Step 4: Combine Steps 2 and 3.

Take cut length or ACL from Step 3: _____ in.

Multiply by number of widths from Step 2: × _____ widths

Total length of fabric required: _____ **in.**

Divide by 36 to convert inches to yards: ÷ ___36___ in.

Total yards: _____ **yd.**

Note: Fabric yardage must be ordered in ½-yard increments.

Round up to nearest ½ yard: _____ **yd. to be ordered**

To find yardage for lining: Multiply CL × W = total inches, divide by 36 inches to find yards, and round up or stay at the nearest yard or ½ yard.

Note: Should the center draw traversing drapery consist of panels that use a portion of a width, the workroom will charge as if it is a whole width. For example: Center draw traversing draperies require 3 widths of fabric. There are 2 panels in a center draw. 3 widths ÷ 2 panels = 1½ widths per panel. Fabric will be ordered for 3 widths. Labor will be calculated as 4 widths since there is the same amount of labor for a 1½-width panel as for a 2-width panel.

Seamless, Traversing Draperies (118+ inches wide) Worksheet

Step 1: Calculate length of each width.

Take the finished length (FL) of drapery:	_____	in.
Add 18 inches for hems and heading: +	18	in.

Note: 18 inches allows for double 6-inch hem; if narrower or wider hem, this number will change.

Total cut length (CL):	_____	**in.**

If there is a repeat involved, continue with the following step. If not, skip to Step 2.

Take cut length:	_____	in.
Divide by length of repeat: ÷	_____	in.
Resulting number is the number of repeats:	_____	**repeats**
Round up to nearest whole number:	_____	**full repeats**
Multiply this number by the length of the repeat: ×	_____	in.
Adjusted cut length (ACL):	_____	**in.**

Note: If it is important to control where the pattern starts at the top, add another full repeat to ACL.

Step 2: Determine if selected fabric will railroad.

If the cut length is the same or less than the fabric width, it can be used as intended. If the cut length is more than the fabric width, it can't be used as seamless.

If the fabric width is more than the cut length, proceed to the next step.

Step 3: Calculate flat measure of treatment.

Take trim-to-trim measure of window:	_____	in.
Multiply to allow for stack (15–33 percent): ×	_____	(1.15 to 1.33)
Total flat measure (FM) of treatment:	_____	**in.**

Step 4: Calculate yardage.

Total from Step 3:	_____	in.
Multiply for fullness: ×	3	fullness

Note: If this is a heavy-weight fabric, × 2; standard is × 2.5 or × 3; very lightweight is × 3 or × 4.

Total fullness:	_____	**in.**
Add 20 in. for overlaps and returns for center draw (10 in. if a 1-way draw): +	20	in.

Note: This allows for 3-inch to 4-inch returns.

If returns are deeper, add additional beyond amount allowed: +	_____	in.
Total fabric required:	_____	**in.**
Divide by 36 to convert inches to yards: ÷	36	in.
Total yards:	_____	**yd.**

Note: Fabric yardage must be ordered in ½-yard increments.

Round up to nearest ½ yard:	_____	**yd.**

Step 5. Calculate number of labor widths of fabric the workroom will charge

Total of fabric in inches:	_____	in.
Divide by 48 inches to find labor widths: ÷	48	in.
Widths of fabric:	_____	**widths**
Round up to the nearest even whole number:	_____	**labor widths**

Note: Should the center draw traversing drapery consist of panels that use a portion of a width, the workroom will charge as if it is a whole width. For example: Center draw traversing draperies require 3 widths of fabric. There are 2 panels in a center draw. 3 widths ÷ 2 panels = 1½ widths per panel. Fabric will be ordered for 3 widths. Labor will be calculated as 4 widths since there is the same amount of labor for a 1½-width panel as for a 2-width panel.

Cornice and Lambrequin Worksheet

Step 1: Determine widths.

Finished width of treatment:	_____ in.
Add right return: +	_____ in.
Add left return: +	_____ in.
Add 6 inches for upholstering: +	6 in.
Total:	_____ **in.**
Divide by fabric width: ÷	_____ in.
Total widths needed:	_____ **widths**
Round up to whole number:	_____ **full widths**

Step 2: Determine cut length.

Finished length of treatment:	_____ in.
Add 6 inches for upholstering: +	6 in.
Total cut length:	_____ **in.**

Note: For a shaped bottom edge or lambrequin, take the longest point of the length. Usually 2 widths are needed for the length of the lambrequin legs. Calculate any widths beyond what is needed for the legs at the shorter length.

If necessary:

Finished length of treatment:	_____ in.
Add 6 inches for upholstering: +	6 in.
Total cut length:	_____ **in.**

Step 3: Calculate for repeat.

If there is no repeat, proceed to Step 4. Normally a repeat doesn't affect the width.

Total cut length from Step 2:	_____ in.
Divide by length of repeat: ÷	_____ in.
Number of repeats:	_____ **repeats**
Round up to whole number:	_____ **full repeats**
Multiply repeats by the length of the repeat: ×	_____ in.
Adjusted cut length (ACL):	_____ **in.**

For lambrequins with more than 2 widths, repeat Step 3 for the different lengths involved.

Step 4: Determine yardage.

Cut length or adjusted cut length:	_____ in.
Multiply by number of widths: ×	_____ widths
Total:	_____ **in.**
Divide by 36 to convert inches to yards: ÷	36 in.
Total yards:	_____ **yd.**
Round up to nearest ½ yard:	_____ **yd.**

This step may have to be repeated for a lambrequin with more than 2 widths.

For self-welt, add 1 to 1.5 yards: +	_____ yd.
Total:	_____ **yd. to be ordered**

Gathered Valance Worksheet

Step 1: Determine total width dimension requiring fullness.

Flat measure of treatment:	_____	in.
Add right return : +	_____	in.
Add left return : +	_____	in.
Total width:	_____	**in.**

Note: If this is the first window treatment layer, the return is 3 inches; if it is the second, it is 6 to 6.5 inches; if it is the third, it is 9 to 10 inches.

Step 2: Determine widths.

Total width from Step 1:	_____	in.
Multiply for fullness (× 2.5 or 3): ×	_____	fullness
Total:	_____	**in.**
Add 6 inches for side hems: +	6	in.
Total:	_____	**in.**
Divide by width of fabric: ÷	_____	in.
Total widths of fabric:	_____	**widths**
Round up to whole number:	_____	**full widths**

Step 3: Determine cut length.

Finished length:	_____	in.
Add for seam allowances (this number may vary): +	2	in.
Add bottom hem (1.5 in. for shirt-tail hem; 4 in. for double 2-in. hem): +	_____	in.

Add for rod pocket and/or header (if applicable):

Add rod pocket size with take-up allowance: +	_____	in.
Add header height: +	_____	in.
Total cut length:	_____	**in.**

If the fabric has a repeat:

Take cut length:	_____	in.
Divide by length of repeat: ÷	_____	in.
Total:	_____	**repeats**
Round up to whole number:	_____	**full repeats**
Multiply by the length of repeat: ×	_____	in.
Adjusted cut length (ACL):	_____	**in.**

Step 4: Determine yardage.

Take cut length or ACL from Step 3:	_____	in.
Multiply by total widths from Step 2: ×	_____	widths
Total:	_____	**in.**
Divide by 36 to convert inches to yards: ÷	36	in.
Total yards:	_____	**yd.**
Round up to nearest ½ yard:	_____	**yd. to be ordered**

To find yardage for lining: Multiply CL × W = total inches, divide by 36 inches to find yards, round up or stay at the nearest yard or ½ yard.

Tabbed Valance Worksheet   part 1 of 2

Step 1: Determine widths for valance.

Flat measure of treatment: _____ in.

Multiply for fullness (× 1.5 or 2): × _____ fullness

Total: _____ **in.**

Add return size × 2 for right and left returns: + _____ in.

Note: If this is the first window treatment layer, the return is 3 inches; if it is the second, it is 6 to 6.5 inches; if it is the third, it is 9 to 10 inches.

Add 6 inches for side hems: + _____6_____ in.

Total: _____ **in.**

Divide by width of fabric: ÷ _____ in.

Total widths of fabric: _____ **widths**

Round up to whole number: _____ **full widths**

Step 2: Determine widths for tabs.

Width of tab × 2: _____ in.

Add 1 inch for seam allowance: + _____1_____ in.

Total cut tab width: _____ **in.**

Width of fabric: _____ in.

Divide by cut tab width: ÷ _____ in.

Total tabs per width: _____ **tabs**

Round down to nearest whole number: _____ **tabs per width**

Number of tabs desired for treatment: _____ tabs

Divide by tabs available per width: ÷ _____ tabs

Total widths: _____ **widths**

Round up to whole number: _____ **full widths**

Step 3: Determine cut length for valance.

Finished length of valance not including tabs: _____ in.

Add for seam allowances (this number may vary): + _____2_____ in.

Add bottom hem (1.5 in. for shirt-tail hem; 4 in. for double 2-in. hem): + _____ in.

Total cut length: _____ **in.**

If the fabric has a repeat:

Take cut length: _____ in.

Divide by length of repeat: ÷ _____ in.

Total: _____ **repeats**

Round up to whole number: _____ **full repeats**

Multiply by the length of repeat: × _____ in.

Adjusted cut length (ACL): _____ **in.**

Step 4: Determine cut length for tabs.

Use Table 11.7 on page 194 to find tab length: _____ in.

Add 2 inches seam allowance: + _____2_____ in.

Total: _____ **in.**

Usually the repeat is ignored for tabs; however, if it is important, calculate for repeat as shown above.

Step 5: Calculate yardage.

Cut length or ACL from Step 3: _____ in.
Multiply by total widths from Step 1: × _____ widths
Total A: _____ **in.**

Cut length or ACL from Step 4: _____ in.
Multiply by Total widths from Step 2: × _____ widths
Total B: _____ **in.**

Total A: _____ in.
Add Total B: + _____ in.
Total: _____ **in.**
Divide by 36 to convert inches to yards: ÷ _____36_____ in.
Total yards: _____ **yd.**
Round up to nearest ½ yard: _____ **yd. to be ordered**

Step 6: Calculate lining for treatments.

Cut length from Step 3: _____ in.
Multiply by total widths from Step 3: × _____ widths
Total: _____ **in.**
Divide by 36 to convert inches to yards: ÷ _____36_____ in.
Total yards: _____ **yd.**
Round up to nearest ½ yard: _____ **yd. to be ordered for lining**

Step 1: Determine total width dimension requiring fullness.

Flat measure of treatment:	_____	in.
Multiply for fullness (× 1.5 or 2): ×	_____2_____	fullness
Total:	_____	**in.**
Add return size × 2 for right and left returns: +	_____	in.

Note: If this is the first window treatment layer, the return is 3 inches; if it is the second, it is 6 to 6.5 inches; if it is the third, it is 9 to 10 inches.

Add 6 inches for side hems: +	_____6_____	in.
Total:	_____	**in.**
Divide by width of fabric: ÷	_____	in.
Widths of fabric:	_____	**widths**
Round up to whole number:	_____	**full widths**

Step 2: Determine cut length.

Finished length:	_____	in.
Add for seam allowances (this number may vary): +	_____2_____	in.
Total cut length:	_____	**in.**

If the fabric has a repeat:

Take cut length:	_____	in.
Divide by length of repeat:	_____	in.
Total:	_____	**repeats**
Round up to whole number:	_____	**full repeats**
Multiply by the length of repeat: ×	_____	in.
Adjusted cut length (ACL):	_____	**in.**

Step 3: Determine yardage.

Take cut length or ACL from Step 2:	_____	in.
Multiply by total widths from Step 1: ×	_____	widths
Total:	_____	**in.**
Divide by 36 to convert inches to yards: ÷	_____36_____	in.
Total yards:	_____	**yd.**
Round up to nearest ½ yard:	_____	**yd. to be ordered**

Step 4: Determine yardage for lining.

The lining of pulled-up valances will show. Recommend using contrast lining for lining.

Finished length:	_____	in.
Add for seam allowances (this number may vary): +	_____2_____	in.
Total cut length:	_____	**in.**
Multiply by total widths from Step 1: ×	_____	widths
Total:	_____	**in.**
Divide by 36 to convert inches to yards: ÷	_____36_____	in.
Total yards:	_____	**yd.**
Round up to nearest ½ yard:	_____	**yd. to be ordered for lining**

Yardage for Tabs:

If tabs will be used to pull up the valance over a rod, calculate yardage for tabs.

Step A: Determine widths for tabs.

Width of tab × 2:		in.
Add 1 inch for seam allowance: +	1	in.
Total cut tab width:		**in.**
Width of fabric:		in.
Divide cut tab width: ÷		in.
Total tabs:		**tabs**
Round down to nearest whole number:		**tabs per width**
Number of tabs desired for treatment:		tabs
Divide by tabs available per width: ÷		tabs
Total widths:		**widths**
Round up to whole number:		**full widths**

Step B: Determine cut length for tabs.

Use Table 11.7 on page 194 to find tab length:		in.
Add 2 inches seam allowance: +	2	in.
Total cut tab length:		**in.**

Step C: Calculate yardage for tabs.

Cut length from Step B:		in.
Multiply by total widths from Step A: ×		widths
Total:		**in.**
Divide by 36 to convert inches to yards: ÷	36	in.
Total yards:		**yd.**
Round up to nearest ½ yard:		**yd. to be ordered**

Swags, Cascades, and Jabots Worksheet

Swags

Step 1: Determine number of swags,

Total width of treatment:		in.
Divide by 30 inches: ÷	30	in.
Number of swags:		swags
Round up or down to whole number:		**total number of swags**

Step 2: Determine yardage for swags.

Total number of swags:		swags
Multiply by 1.5 to 2 yards: ×	1.5	yd.
Total yardage for swags:		**yd. to order**

Note: This same amount will be needed for lining.

Cascades

Step 1: Determine widths.

Commonly, 1 width of fabric is needed per cascade:		width
Multiply by number of cascades (normally 2 per window) : ×		cascade
Total number of widths necessary for treatment:		**widths**

Step 2: Determine cut length.

Finished length of cascade:		in.
Add 4 inches for hems and placement: +	4	in.
Total cut length of cascade:		**in.**

If there is a repeat, factor for the repeat. If lining is solid, calculate from the cut length.

Take cut length:		in.
Divide by length of repeat: ÷		in.
Number of repeats:		**repeats**
Round up to whole number:		**full repeats**
Multiply by the length of the repeat: ×		in.
Adjusted cut length (ACL):		**in.**

Step 3: Determine yardage.

Cut length or adjusted cut length from Step 2:		in.
Multiply by widths from Step 1: ×		widths
Total:		**in.**
Divide by 36 to convert inches to yards: ÷	36	in.
Total yards:		**yd.**
Round up to nearest ½ yard:		**yd. to order**

Jabots

Step 1: Determine widths.

Determine total area per jabot to be covered:		in.
Multiply for fullness (× 2.5 or 3): ×	3	fullness
Total:		**in.**
Divide by width of fabric: ÷		in.
Total widths:		**widths**
Round up to whole number:		**full widths**
Multiply by total number of jabots used: ×		jabots
Total widths:		**widths**

Step 2: Determine cut length in exactly the same manner as for cascades.

Step 3: Combine Steps 1 and 2 in exactly the same manner as for cascades.

This same amount needs to be ordered for the back of the jabot, since the back of the jabot shows to the front.

Roman/Hobbled Shade Worksheet

Basic Flat Roman Shade

Step 1: Calculate cut width.

Note: Unlike most other treatments, shades have a cut width.

Finished width of shade:	_____	in.
Add 6 inches for side hem: +	6	in.
Total cut width:	_____	**in.**

Step 2: Determine widths.

Cut width from Step 1:	_____	in.
Divide by fabric width: ÷	_____	in.
Total widths needed:	_____	**widths**
Round up to whole number:	_____	**full widths**

Step 3: Determine cut length.

Finish length of shade:	_____	in.
Add 10 inches for hem and board allowance: +	10	in.
Total cut length:	_____	**in.**

If necessary, calculate for repeat in the length at this point. Normally a repeat doesn't affect the width. If there is no repeat, skip to Step 4.

Total cut length from Step 3:	_____	in.
Divide by length of repeat: ÷	_____	in.
Number of repeats:	_____	**repeats**
Round up to whole number:	_____	**full repeats**
Multiply repeats by the length of the repeat: ×	_____	in.
Adjusted cut length:	_____	**in.**

Step 4: Determine yardage.

Cut length or adjusted cut length:	_____	in.
Multiply by number of widths: ×	_____	widths
Total:	_____	**in.**
Divide by 36 to convert inches to yards: ÷	36	in.
Total yards:	_____	**yd.**
Round up to nearest ½ yard:	_____	**yd. to be ordered**

Hobbled Roman (has fullness to the length)

Modified Step 3 for Hobbled Roman

Finish length of shade:	_____	in.
Multiply for fullness (× 2): ×	2	fullness
Total:	_____	**in.**
Add 10 inches for hem and board allowance: +	10	in.
Total cut length:	_____	**in.**

If necessary, calculate for repeat in the length. Continue regular calculations from this point.

Balloon and Austrian Shades Worksheet

Basic Balloon Shade

Step 1: Calculate widths.

Finished width of shade:		_____	in.
If outside mounted, add return size × 2 for right and left returns:	+	_____	in.
Total:		_____	**in.**
Multiply for fullness (× 2.5 or 3):	×	3	fullness
Total:		_____	**in.**
Add 6 inches for side hem:	+	6	in.
Total:		_____	**in.**
Divide by fabric width:	÷	_____	in.
Total widths needed:		_____	**widths**
Round up to whole number:		_____	**full widths**

Step 2: Determine cut length.

Finish length of shade:		_____	in.
Add 20 to 30 inches for poufy bottom look:	+	30	in.
Add 10 inches for hem and board allowance:	+	10	in.
Total cut length:		_____	**in.**

If necessary, calculate for repeat in the length at this point. Normally a repeat doesn't affect the width. If there is no repeat, skip to Step 3.

Total cut length from above:		_____	in.
Divide by length of repeat:	÷	_____	in.
Number of repeats:		_____	**repeats**
Round up to whole number:		_____	**full repeats**
Multiply repeats by the length of the repeat:	×	_____	in.
Adjusted cut length (ACL) in inches:		_____	**in.**

Step 3: Determine yardage.

Cut length or adjusted cut length:		_____	in.
Multiply by number of widths:	×	_____	widths
Total:		_____	**in.**
Divide by 36 to convert inches to yards:	÷	36	in.
Total yards:		_____	**yd.**
Round up to nearest ½ yard:		_____	**yd. to be ordered**

Austrian Shade (has fullness to width and length)

Modified Step 2 for Austrian Shade

Finished length of shade:		_____	in.
Multiply for fullness (× 2.5 or 3):	×	3	fullness
Total:		_____	**in.**
Add 10 inches for hem and board allowance:	+	10	in.
Total cut length:		_____	**in.**

If necessary, calculate for repeat in the length and continue regular calculations in Step 3. Note that the amount of fabric in an Austrian can make it heavy to operate.

Mock Roman/Hobbled Shade Worksheet

Step 1: Calculate cut width

Note: Unlike most other treatments, shades have a cut width.

Finished width of shade:		in.
Add 6 inches for side hem: +	6	in.
Total cut width:		**in.**

Step 2: Determine widths.

Cut width from Step 1:		in.
Divide by fabric width: ÷		in.
Total widths needed:		**widths**
Round up to whole number:		**full widths**

Step 3: Determine cut length.

Finished length of mock shade:		in.
Multiply for fullness for mock bottom: ×	2	fullness
Total:		**in.**
Add 10 inches for hem and board allowance: +	10	in.
Total cut length:		**in.**

If necessary, calculate for repeat in the length at this point. Normally a repeat doesn't affect the width. If there is no repeat, skip to Step 4.

Total cut length:		in.
Divide by length of repeat: ÷		in.
Number of repeats:		**repeats**
Round up to whole number:		**full repeats**
Multiply repeats by the length of the repeat: ×		in.
Adjusted cut length (ACL):		**in.**

Step 4: Determine yardage.

Cut length or adjusted cut length:		in.
Multiply by number of widths: ×		widths
Total:		**in.**
Divide by 36 to convert inches to yards: ÷	36	in.
Total yards:		**yd.**
Round up to nearest ½ yard:		**yd. to be ordered**

Throw Pillow Worksheet

Step 1: Determine cut width of pillow.

Width of pillow:	_____	in.
Add 2 inches for hems: +	2	in.
Total cut width:	_____	**in.**

If there is a horizontal repeat, determine adjusted cut width.

Total cut width from above:	_____	in.
Divide by horizontal repeat of fabric: ÷	_____	in.
Total:	_____	**repeats**
Round up to whole number:	_____	**full repeats**
Multiply by horizontal repeat: ×	_____	in.
Total adjusted cut width:	_____	**in.**

Step 2: Determine number of cuts from width of fabric.

Width of fabric:	_____	in.
Divide by cut width or adjusted cut width from Step 1: ÷	_____	in.
Total pillow face cuts per width:	_____	**cuts**
Round down to nearest whole number:	_____	**total cuts per width**

Step 3: Determine cut length of pillow.

Length of pillow:	_____	in.
Add 2 inches for hems: +	2	in.
Total cut length:	_____	**in.**

If there is a vertical repeat, determine adjusted cut length.

Total cut length from above:	_____	in.
Divide by vertical repeat: ÷	_____	in.
Number of repeats:	_____	**repeats**
Round up to whole number:	_____	**full repeats**
Multiply by the length of the vertical repeat: ×	_____	in.
Adjusted cut length (ACL):	_____	**in.**

Step 4: Determine number of widths.

Number of pillows:	_____	pillows
Multiply by number of pillow faces: ×	_____	pillow faces
Total number of pillow faces:	_____	**total** pillow faces

Note: If the front and back of the pillow are the same, this requires 2 faces per pillow.

Divide by cuts per width from Step 2: ÷	_____	cuts
Total:	_____	widths
Round up to whole number:	_____	**full widths**

Step 5: Determine yardage to order.

Cut length or adjusted cut length from Step 3:	_____	in.
Multiply by number of widths from Step 4: ×	_____	widths
Total inches:	_____	**in.**
Divide by 36 to convert inches to yards: ÷	36	in.
Total yards:	_____	**yd.**
Round up to nearest ½ yard:	_____	**yd. to be ordered**

Table Round Worksheet

Step 1: Determine finished width and length.

Diameter of table:	_____	in.
Add drop to floor: +	_____	in.
Add second drop to floor (2 sides): +	_____	in.
Total finished diameter to tablecloth:	_____	**in. finished width and length**

Step 2: Determine cut width and length.

Finished diameter of tablecloth:	_____	in.
Add for hems (2 inches each side): +	4	in.
Total cut width and length:	_____	**in.**

Note: When calculating an oval cloth, you must calculate the width and length separately.

If there is a repeat in the length, calculate for the repeat; if not, proceed to Step 3. Normally a repeat doesn't affect the width.

Total cut length from above:	_____	in.
Divide by length of repeat: ÷	_____	in.
Number of repeats:	_____	**repeats**
Round up to whole number:	_____	**full repeats**
Multiply this number by the length of the repeat: ×	_____	in.
Adjusted cut length (ACL):	_____	**in.**

Step 3: Determine widths.

Cut width from Step 2:	_____	in.
Divide by fabric width: ÷	_____	in.
Total widths needed:	_____	**widths**
Round up to whole number:	_____	**full widths**

Step 4: Determine yardage.

Cut length or adjusted cut length from Step 2:	_____	in.
Multiply by number of widths: ×	_____	widths
Total inches:	_____	**in.**
Divide by 36 to convert inches to yards: ÷	36	in.
Total yards:	_____	**yd.**
Round up to nearest ½ yard:	_____	**yd. to be ordered**

Step 5: Determine circumference for cording or fringe, if applicable.

Total finished diameter from Step 1:	_____	in.
Multiply by π (3.14): ×	3.14	π
Total circumference of hem:	_____	**in.**
Add 2 inches for start and stop of trim: +	2	in.
Total inches:	_____	**in.**
Divide by 36 to convert inches to yards: ÷	36	in.
Total yards:	_____	**yd.**
Round up to nearest ½ yard:	_____	**yd. to be ordered**

Table Topper Worksheet

Step 1: Determine side dimension.

Diameter or length of one side of table:		in.
Add length of drop over edge (at least 4 in.): +		in.
Add drop again to account for both sides: +		in.
Total finished length per side of topper:		**in. finished width and length**

Step 2: Determine cut width and cut or adjusted cut length.

Finished dimension from Step 1:		in.
Add 1 inch each side for hems: +	2	in.
This is the cut width and cut length:		**in.**

If there is a repeat in the length, calculate for the repeat; if not, proceed to Step 3.

Cut length from above: ÷		in.
Divide by length of repeat: ÷		in.
Resulting number is the number of repeats:		**repeats**
Round up to whole number:		**full repeats**
Multiply by the length of the repeat: ×		in.
Adjusted cut length (ACL):		**in.**

Step 3: Determine widths.

Cut width from Step 2:		in.
Divide by fabric width: ÷		in.
Total widths needed:		**widths**
Round up to whole number:		**full widths**

Step 4: Determine yardage.

Cut length or adjusted cut length from Step 2:		in.
Multiply by number of widths: ×		widths
Total inches:		**in.**
Divide by 36 to convert inches to yards: ÷	36	in.
Total yards:		**yd.**
Round up to nearest ½ yard:		**yd. to be ordered**

Note: To determine the diagonal distance across a square topper to see how long the points fall over the side, use $a^2 + b^2 = c^2$. This is important to know when you are adding tassels on the ends of square toppers, to ensure the tassels don't drag on the floor.

Step A: Determine Side A².

Side A:		in.
Multiply by Side A: ×		in.
Total Side A²:		**in.**

Step B: Determine Side B².

Side B:		in.
Multiply by Side B: ×		in.
Total Side B²:		**in.**

Step C: Determine the diagonal distance (C).

Total from Step A:		in.
Add total from Step B: +		in.
Equals C²:		**in.**
Use the square root ($\sqrt{\ }$) function on the calculator to find the root of C²:		in.

This is the diagonal distance of the topper in inches.

Fringe and Cording Worksheet

Step 1: Determine finished perimeter.

Finished dimension side A:	_____	in.
Add finished dimension side B:	+ _____	in.
Add finished dimension side C:	+ _____	in.
Add finished dimension side D:	+ _____	in.
Total finished perimeter:	_____	**in.**

Step 2: Determine yardage.

Total from Step 1:	_____	in.
Add 2 inches for start and stop of trim:	+ _____ 2 _____	in.
Total:	_____	**in.**
Multiply by quantity of items/products:	× _____	quantity
Total inches:	_____	**in.**
Divide by 36 to convert inches to yards:	÷ _____ 36 _____	in.
Total yards:	_____	**yd.**
Round up to nearest ½ yard:	_____	**yd. to be ordered**

For round shapes: determine circumference:

Step 1: Determine diameter.

Diameter of table:	_____	in.
Add drop to floor:	+ _____	in.
Add second drop to floor (2 sides):	+ _____	in.
Total finished diameter to tablecloth:	_____	**in.**

Step 2: Determine yardage.

Total finished diameter from Step 1:	_____	in.
Multiply by π (3.14):	× _____ 3.14 _____	π
Total circumference of hem:	_____	**in.**
Add 2 inches for start and stop of trim:	+ _____ 2 _____	in.
Total inches:	_____	**in.**
Divide by 36 to convert inches to yards:	÷ _____ 36 _____	in.
Total yards:	_____	**yd.**
Round up to nearest ½ yard:	_____	**yd. to be ordered**

Bedspread and Coverlet Worksheet

Step 1: Determine finished width and cut width.

Width of bed: _____ in.

Add drop: + _____ in.

Note: The drop used in the calculation must already have ¼ inch to ½ inch deducted from the actual drop if the bedspread/coverlet is not to drag on the ground.

Add second drop: + _____ in.

Total finished width: _____ **in.**

Add hems (2 in. each side): + ____4____ in. (2 sides)

Total: _____ **in.**

Add quilting allowance (10 to 15 percent): × _____ (multiply by 1.10 to 1.15)

Total cut width: _____ in.

Step 2: Determine number of widths to use.

Cut width from Step 1: _____ in.

Divide by width of fabric: ÷ _____ in.

Total widths: _____ **widths**

Round up to whole number: _____ **full widths**

Step 3: Determine finished length and cut length.

Length of bed: _____ in.

Add drop: + _____ in.

Add pillow tuck if applicable (24 in. is plenty): + ____24____ in.

Total finished length: _____ **in.**

Add hems (2 in. each end): + ____4____ in.

Total: _____ **in.**

Add quilting allowance (10 to 15 percent): × _____ (multiply by 1.10 to 1.15)

Total cut length before repeat: _____ **in.**

If the fabric has a repeat:

Take cut length from above: _____ in.

Divide by length of repeat: ÷ _____ in.

Total: _____ **repeats**

Round up to whole number: _____ **full repeats**

Multiply by length of repeat: × _____ in.

Adjusted cut length (ACL): _____ **in.**

Step 4: Determine yardage to order.

Cut length or adjusted cut length (ACL) from Step 3: _____ in.

Multiply by total number of widths from Step 2: × _____ widths

Total inches: _____ **in.**

Divide by 36 to convert inches to yards: ÷ ____36____ in.

Total yards: _____ **yd.**

Round up to nearest ½ yard: _____ **yd. needed to order**

Duvet Cover Worksheet

Step 1: Determine cut width.

Width of duvet/comforter:	_____	in.
Add seam allowance: +	_____2_____	in.
Total cut width:	_____	**in.**

Step 2: Determine total widths.

Cut width from Step 1:	_____	in.
Divide by width of fabric: ÷	_____	in.
Widths:	_____	**widths**
For same fabric both sides, multiply by 2: ×	_____2_____	sides
Total widths:	_____	**widths**
Round up to whole number:	_____	**full widths**

Step 3: Determine length.

Length of duvet/comforter:	_____	in.
Add for closure: +	_____6_____	in.
Add seam allowance: +	_____2_____	in.
Total cut length before repeat:	_____	**in.**

If the fabric has a repeat:

Take cut length from above:	_____	in.
Divide by length of repeat: ÷	_____	in.
Total number of repeats:	_____	**repeats**
Round up to whole number:	_____	**full repeats**
Multiply by length of repeat: ×	_____	in.
Adjusted cut length (ACL):	_____	**in.**

Step 4: Determine yardage to order.

Cut length or adjusted cut length (ACL) from Step 3:	_____	in.
Multiply by total number of widths from Step 2: ×	_____	widths
Total inches:	_____	**in.**
Divide by 36 to convert inches to yards: ÷	_____36_____	in.
Total yards:	_____	**yd.**
Round up to nearest ½ yard:	_____	**yd. needed to order**

Note: Sometimes the duvet must cover more area than the comforter allows. In these instances, flanges (possibly padded) and ruffles can be added to the sides.

Bedskirt Worksheet

Step 1: Find perimeter of bedskirt.

Width of box spring:	_____	in.
Add length of box spring: +	_____	in.
Second length of box spring: +	_____	in.
Total perimeter of skirt:	_____	**in.**

Step 2: Determine total widths.

For gathered and box-pleated bedskirt:

Total perimeter from Step 1:	_____	in.
Multiply for fullness: ×	2.5	fullness

Note: Depending on the fabric and style, this could be more or less fullness.

Total:	_____	**in.**
Divide by width of fabric: ÷	_____	in.
Total widths of fabric:	_____	**widths**
Round up to whole number:	_____	**full widths**

For relaxed pleat bedskirt:

Depth of pleat:	_____	in.
Multiply by 4: ×	4	in.
Total needed for pleat:	_____	**in.**
Multiply by number of pleats: ×	_____	pleats
Total:	_____	**in.**
Add total perimeter from Step 1: +	_____	in.
Total:	_____	**in.**
Divide by width of fabric: ÷	_____	in.
Total widths of fabric:	_____	**widths**
Round up to whole number:	_____	**full widths**

Step 3: Determine cut length.

Drop from box spring to floor:	_____	in.
Add top hem: +	2	in.
Optional top banding (6 in.): +	_____	in.
Add bottom hem: +	_____	in.

- For shirt-tail hem, add 1.5 inches.
- For double 2-inch hem, add 4 inches.

Total cut length:	_____	**in.**

If the fabric has a repeat:

Take cut length from above:	_____	in.
Divide by length of repeat: ÷	_____	in.
Total number of repeats:	_____	**repeats**
Round up to whole number:	_____	**full repeats**
Multiply by the length of repeat: ×	_____	in.
Adjusted cut length (ACL):	_____	**in.**

Step 4: Determine yardage to order.

Cut length or adjusted cut length (ACL) from Step 3:	_____	in.
Multiply by widths from Step 2: ×	_____	widths
Total inches:	_____	**in.**
Divide by 36 to convert inches to yards: ÷	36	in.
Total yards:	_____	**yd.**
Round up to nearest ½ yard:	_____	**yd. needed to order**

Bedscarf Worksheet

Step 1: Determine finished width and cut width of bedscarf.

Width of bed:	_____	in.
Add drop: +	_____	in.
Add second drop: +	_____	in.
Total finished width:	_____	**in.**
Add hems/seam allowance: +	2	in.
Total cut width:	_____	**in.**

Step 2: Determine number of widths to use.

Cut width from Step 1:	_____	in.
Divide by width of fabric: ÷	_____	in.
Total widths:	_____	**widths**
Round up to whole number:	_____	**full widths**
Multiply by number of scarf sides: ×	_____	scarves/scarf sides
Total number of widths:	_____	**widths**

Step 3: Determine finished length and cut length.

Finished length of bedscarf (commonly 21 to 26 in.):	_____	in.
Add hems/seam allowance: +	2	in.
Total cut length:	_____	**in.**

If the fabric has a vertical repeat:

Take cut length from above:	_____	in.
Divide by length of repeat: ÷	_____	in.
Total number of repeats:	_____	**repeats**
Round up to whole number:	_____	**full repeats**
Multiply by length of repeat: ×	_____	in.
Adjusted cut length (ACL):	_____	**in.**

Step 4: Determine yardage to order.

Cut length or adjusted cut length (ACL) from Step 3:	_____	in.
Multiply by total number of widths from Step 2: ×	_____	widths
Total inches:	_____	**in.**
Divide by 36 to convert inches to yards: ÷	36	in.
Total yards:	_____	**yd.**
Round up to nearest ½ yard:	_____	**yd. needed to order**

Sham Worksheet

Step 1: Determine cut width of pillow.

Width of pillow:	_____	in.
Add 2 inches for seam allowance:	+ _____2_____	in.
Total cut width:	_____	**in.**

If there is a horizontal repeat, determine adjusted cut width:

Total cut width from Step 1:	_____	in.
Divide by horizontal repeat of fabric:	÷ _____	in.
Total number of repeats:	_____	**repeats**
Round up to whole number:	_____	**full repeats**
Multiply by horizontal repeat	× _____	in.
Total adjusted cut width:	_____	**in.**

Step 2: Determine number of cuts from width of fabric.

Width of fabric:	_____	in.
Divide by total cut width or adjusted cut width from Step 1:	÷ _____	in.
Total number of cuts or sides:	_____	**cuts or sides**
Round down to nearest whole number:	_____	**total cuts/sides per width**

Step 3: Determine cut length of pillow.

Length of pillow	_____	in.
Add 2 inches for seam allowance	+ _____2_____	in.
Total cut length:	_____	**in.**

If there is a vertical repeat, determine adjusted cut length:

Total cut length from above:	_____	in.
Divide by vertical repeat:	÷ _____	in.
Total number of repeats:	_____	**repeats**
Round up to whole number:	_____	**full repeats**
Multiply by vertical repeat:	× _____	in.
Total adjusted cut length (ACL):	_____	**in.**

Step 4: Determine number of widths.

Number of pillows:	_____	pillows
Multiply by number of pillow faces:	× _____	pillow faces
Total:	_____	**pillow faces**

Note: If the front and back of the pillow are the same, this requires 2 faces per pillow.

Divide by cuts per width:	÷ _____	cuts per width
Total widths needed:	_____	**widths**
Round up to nearest whole number:	_____	**full widths**

Step 5: Determine yardage to order.

Cut length or ACL from Step 3:	_____	in.
Multiply by number of widths from Step 4:	× _____	widths
Total:	_____	**in.**
Divide by 36 to convert inches to yards:	÷ _____36_____	in.
Total yards:	_____	**yd.**
Round up to nearest ½ yard:	_____	**yd. needed to order**

Flange and Ruffle Worksheet

Step 1: Determine perimeter

Finished dimension side A:	_____	in.
Add finished dimension side B: +	_____	in.
Add finished dimension side C: +	_____	in.
Add finished dimension side D: +	_____	in. (if applicable)
Total finished perimeter:	_____	**in.**

Step 2: Determine number of widths.

Flange:

Total finished perimeter from Step 1:	_____	in.
Add 4 inches for each corner: +	_____	in.
Total:	_____	**in.**
Multiply by quantity of items/products: ×	_____	quantity
Total:	_____	**in.**
Divide by fabric width: ÷	_____	in.
Total widths:	_____	**widths**
Round up to whole number:	_____	**full widths**

Ruffle:

Total finished perimeter from Step 1:	_____	in.
Multiply for fullness (× 2 to 3): ×	_____	fullness
Total:	_____	**in.**
Multiply by quantity of items/products: ×	_____	quantity
Total:	_____	**in.**
Divide by fabric width: ÷	_____	in.
Total widths:	_____	**widths**
Round up to whole number:	_____	**full widths**

Step 3: Determine length.

Length of flange or ruffle: ×	2	in.
Add 2 inches for seam allowance: +	2	in.
Total cut length:	_____	**in.**

If there is a vertical repeat, determine adjusted cut length:

Total cut length from above:	_____	in.
Divide by vertical repeat: ÷	_____	in.
Total number of repeats:	_____	**repeats**
Round up to whole number:	_____	**full repeats**
Multiply by vertical repeat: ×	_____	in.
Total adjusted cut length (ACL):	_____	**in.**

Step 4: Determine yardage to order.

Cut length or ACL from Step 3:	_____	in.
Multiply by number of widths from Step 2: ×	_____	widths
Total inches:	_____	**in.**
Divide by 36 to convert inches to yards: ÷	36	in.
Total yards:	_____	**yd.**
Round up to nearest ½ yard:	_____	**yd. needed to order**

Reupholstery and Slipcover Worksheet

Step 1: Determine yardage.

Yardage required from Upholstery Yardage Chart: _____ yd.

If fabric is 54 inches wide or wider and has no repeat, use yardage as shown on Upholstery Yardage Chart. Otherwise, follow steps as necessary below.

Step 2: Calculate for fabric narrower than 54 inches.

Multiply by percentage from Allowance Chart: × _____ narrowness allowance

Total: _____ yd.

Round up to nearest ½ yard: _____ **yd. to be ordered**

If fabric has a repeat, continue to Step 3.

Step 3: Calculate for fabric with repeat.

Total from Step 1 or Step 2: _____ yd.

Multiply by percentage from Allowance Chart: × _____ repeat allowance

Total: _____ yd.

Round up to nearest ½ yard: _____ **yd. to be ordered**

For slipcover:

Total yards to be ordered: _____ yd.

Add 1 yard per seat: + _____ yd.

Total yards: _____ **yd. to be ordered**

Fabric Yardage Conversion to Leather Hides Worksheet

Step 1: Determine base square feet.

Yardage required from Upholstery Yardage Chart: _____ yd.

Multiply by leather allowance: × _____18_____ sq. ft.

Total: _____ **sq. ft.**

Step 2: Calculate number of hides.

Total from Step 1: _____ sq. ft.

Divide by square feet per hide: ÷ _____ sq. ft.

Total: _____ hides

Round up to whole number: _____ **hides to be ordered**

Step 3: Calculate square feet to charge.

Total from Step 2: _____ total hides

Multiply by square feet per hide: × _____ sq. ft.

Total: _____ **sq. ft.to be charged**

Appendix C: Metric Conversion Table

Imperial to Metric Conversion				
Inches (in.)	Feet (ft.)	Millimeter (mm)	Centimeter (cm)	Meter (m)
1 in.	0.08 ft.	25.4 mm	2.54 cm	0.0254 m
2 in.	0.16 ft.	50.8 mm	5.08 cm	0.0508 m
3 in.	0.33 ft.	76.2 mm	7.62 cm	0.0762 m
4 in.	0.25 ft.	101.6 mm	10.16 cm	0.1016 m
5 in.	0.42 ft.	127 mm	12.7 cm	0.127 m
6 in.	0.5 ft.	152.4 mm	15.24 cm	0.1524 m
7 in.	0.58 ft.	177.8 mm	17.78 cm	0.1778 m
8 in.	0.67 ft.	203.2 mm	20.32 cm	0.2032 m
9 in.	0.75 ft.	228.6 mm	22.86 cm	0.2286 m
10 in.	0.83 ft.	254 mm	25.4 cm	0.254 m
11 in.	0.92 ft.	279.4 mm	27.94 cm	0.2794 m
12 in.	1 ft.	304.8 mm	30.48 cm	0.3048 m
24 in.	2 ft.	609.6 mm	60.96 cm	0.6096 m
36 in.	3 ft.	914.4 mm	91.44 cm	0.9144 m
48 in.	4 ft.	1219.2 mm	121.92 cm	1.2192 m
60 in.	5 ft.	1524 mm	152.4 cm	1.524 m
72 in.	6 ft.	1828.8 mm	182.88 cm	1.8288 m
84 in.	7 ft.	2133.6 mm	213.36 cm	2.1336 m
96 in.	8 ft.	2438.4 mm	243.84 cm	2.4384 m
108 in.	9 ft.	2743.2 mm	274.32 cm	2.7432 m
126 in.	10 ft.	3048 mm	304.8 cm	3.048 m

Common Dimensions of Materials				
Inches (in.)	Feet (ft.)	Millimeter (mm)	Centimeter (cm)	Meter (m)
Wallpaper				
20.5 in.	1.71 ft.	521.208 mm	52.1208 cm	0.521208 m
27 in.	2.25 ft.	685.8 mm	68.58 cm	0.6858 m
36 in.	3 ft.	914.4 mm	91.44 cm	0.9144 m
54 in.	4.5 ft.	1371.6 mm	137.16 cm	1.3716 m
1 sq. ft. = .0929 sq. m; 1 yd. = 3 ft.; 26.5 sq. ft. = 2.4619 sq. m; 30 sq. ft. = 2.787 sq. m; 40.5 sq. ft. = 3.762 sq. m				
Tile and Rolled Goods				
48 in.	4 ft.	1219.2 mm	121.92 cm	1.2192 m
72 in.	6 ft.	1828.8 mm	182.88 cm	1.8288 m
78 in.	6.5 ft.	1981.2 mm	198.12 cm	1.9812 m
79 in.	6.58 ft.	2005.584 mm	200.5584 cm	2.005584 m
144 in.	12 ft.	3657.6 mm	365.76 cm	3.6576 m
158 in.	13.16 ft.	4011.17 mm	401.117 cm	4.01117 m
180 in.	15 ft.	4572 mm	457.2 cm	4.572 m
1 ft. = .3048 m; 1 sq. ft. = .0929 sq. m; 9 sq. ft. = .83612 sq. m				
Fabric				
36 in.	3 ft.	914.4 mm	91.44 cm	0.9144 m
48 in.	4 ft.	1219.2 mm	121.92 cm	1.2192 m
54 in.	4.5 ft.	1371.6 mm	137.16 cm	1.3716 m
118 in.	9.83 ft.	2997.2 mm	299.72 cm	2.9972 m

Bibliography

Al's Home Improvement Center Suspended Ceiling Components. Accessed September 13, 2012. http://alsnetbiz.com/homeimprovement/htseries/susceil.html.

American Olean. Accessed September 1, 2012. http://americanolean.com/series.cfm?series=13&c=49.

Armstrong Ceiling Product. Accessed September 13, 2012. http://www.armstrong.com/resclgam/na/ceilings/en/us/select-a-product.html.

Artistic Frame. Artistic Frame Price List.

Benjamin Moore, 2006. Accessed June 26, 2012. http://www.benjaminmoore.com.

The Company Store. Accessed December 10, 2012. http://www.thecompanystore.com

Designer's Express. *Custom Bedding and Upholstery Catalog,* 1995.

Eagle Group Stainless Steel Countertops Catalog Specification Sheet No. EG004.12. Accessed December 26, 2012. http://www.eaglegrp.com/LitLib/eg04.12.pdf.

Elements of Green Countertops. Accessed December 26, 2012. http://www.elements-of-green.com.

Formica Laminate by Formica Group Technical Data. Accessed December 26, 2012. http://www.formica.com/trade/Documents.aspx.

Godsey, L. *Interior Design Materials and Specifications.* New York: Fairchild Publishing, 2008.

Hunter Douglas. Designing Windows, 2 (*1*), 2007.

Kasmir Fabric. *Kasmir Fabric Custom Expressions Book,* 2012.

International Cast Polymer Alliance. Accessed December 27, 2012.
  http://www.icpa-hq.org/consumers/culturedmarble.cfm.

Kenneth A. Larson Design. Accessed September 13, 2012.
  http://www.kesigndesign.com/code/en_grot1.htm.

Merida Sisal Rugs. Accessed September 26, 2012.
  http://www.meridameridian.com/area-rugs/seagrass.cfm.

National Decorating Products Association. *The New Guide to Soft Window Treatments.* St. Louis, MO: National
  Decorating Products Association, 1993.

National Kitchen and Bath Association. *The Essential Kitchen Design Guide.* New York: Wiley, 1996.

Neal, M. *Custom Draperies in Interior Design.* Norwalk, CT: Appleton & Lange, 1982.

Piotrowski, C. *Professional Practice for Interior Designers,* 4th ed. New York: Wiley, 2008.

Paint & Decorating Retailers Association. *Seabrook: How to Hang Wallcoverings*, 1997.

Pearson Furniture. Pearson Furniture 2012 Price List.

Ramsay, L. *Secrets of Success for Today's Interior Designers and Decorators: Easily Sell the Job, Plan It Correctly,
  and Keep the Customer Coming Back for Repeat Sales.* Oceanside, CA: Touch of Design, 1992.

Ramsay, L. *Start Your Own Interior Design Business and Keep It Growing! Your Guide to Business Success.*
  Oceanside, CA: Touch of Design, 1994.

Robert Allen Design Hardware. Accessed June 29, 2012.

http://www.robertallendesign.com/hardware/collection_ra.aspx.

Sampson, C. *Techniques for Estimating Materials Costs and Time for Interior Designers.* New York: Watson-Guptill
  Publications, 2001.

Sherwin-Williams. Accessed June 20, 2012,
  http://www.sherwin-williams.com.

Silestone by Cosentino Countertops, Floors, Walls, Partitions. Accessed December 27, 2012.
  http://www.silestoneusa.com.

Stanford Furniture. Stanford Furniture 2012 Price List.

WF Norman Corporation Decorative Tin Ceilings. Accessed September 13, 2012.
  http://wfnorman.com/about/designs#2.

Window Fashions. February 1990.

Index